The Liberals' Moment

The Liberals' Moment

The McGovern Insurgency and the Identity Crisis of the Democratic Party

Bruce Miroff

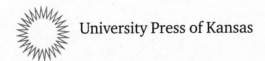 University Press of Kansas

Published by the University Press of Kansas (Lawrence,
Kansas 66045), which was organized by the Kansas
Board of Regents and is operated and funded by
Emporia State University, Fort Hays State University,
Kansas State University, Pittsburg State University, the
University of Kansas, and Wichita State University
Library of Congress Cataloging-in-Publication Data
British Library Cataloguing-in-Publication Data is
available.

Library of Congress Cataloging-in-Publication Data

Miroff, Bruce.
   The liberals' moment : the McGovern insurgency and
the identity crisis of the Democratic Party / Bruce Miroff.
      p.   cm.
   Includes bibliographical references and index.
   ISBN 978-0-7006-1546-9 (cloth : alk. paper)
      1. Democratic Party (U.S.)   2. Liberalism—United States.
3. Presidents—United States—Election—1972.
4. McGovern, George S. (George Stanley), 1922–   I. Title.
   JK2316.M45 2007
   324.973'0924—dc22   2007021521

Printed in the United States of America
10 9 8 7 6 5 4 3 2 1

Contents

Preface

When I contacted former McGovern campaign workers to arrange interviews for this book, the initial reaction from many was surprise. They knew that they had taken part in a remarkable political insurgency three decades earlier. Yet apart from periodic derision by conservatives, few people paid attention any more to the campaign that the McGovernites had waged to end the war in Vietnam and achieve liberal ideals. Not a single book had been written about the McGovern campaign since the 1970s.

I became interested in examining the McGovern insurgency during the final years of Bill Clinton's presidency. It was apparent by that point that the hopes for change with which Clinton had first entered office had devolved into a mixed bag of progressive and conservative policies amid pervasive ideological confusion. Knowing that Clinton and many of his aides got their start in the McGovern campaign, I became curious about their political odyssey. How had they—in fact, how had American liberalism itself—reached this uncertain state? What had happened to the liberal idealism of 1972? Questions like these sent me back to the McGovern campaign. What I found there was more complex—and more intriguing—than I anticipated.

The book took me six years to research and write. The reader may observe an unresolved tension in it: I present the McGovern campaign sympathetically yet fully acknowledge that it produced an electoral disaster. The tension might have been readily resolved in either of two ways: (1) embrace the conventional wisdom that the McGovern campaign was a mistaken lunge to the left—and a thoroughly negative object lesson for Democrats, who must never repeat the blunder; or (2) defend the campaign as a principled and valiant one that might have run a respectable race against a powerful incumbent save for the fratricidal hostility of Old Guard Democrats, the ruthless machinations of Richard Nixon, and the string of unfortunate events that culminated in the disastrous Eagleton affair. But I have resisted both of these alternatives. Each, in my estimation, contains a mix of truth and error. More important, both close off analysis with simplistic judgments and prevent us from learning anything new about a watershed in modern American political history. Rather than seeking escape from the tension, then, I highlight the ambiguities of the McGovern insurgency and its paradoxical implications for our own times.

Because I aim not only to tell a largely forgotten tale but also to explore its deeper meanings, I have adopted an unconventional approach for this book. The first part of the book is the story of 1972. The opening two chapters provide historical background in the politics of the 1960s and biographical background in the life and character of George McGovern. The next three narrate the events of the campaign, from the stunning upsets at the start by a long-shot insurgency to the demoralizing breakdowns at the end by a campaign on the rocks.

The second part of the book examines the meaning of the McGovern campaign through explorations of liberal ideology, grassroots organizing, struggles within the Democratic Party, new social movements, and Republican attack politics. Trying to stuff these extended explorations into the narrative of the campaign would have bogged it down. By bringing together the material thematically, without the constraint of chronology, the format of Part II allows for a more in-depth treatment of the campaign. Since the themes here are the ones most relevant to American politics not only in 1972 but in our own day as well, this approach highlights why the McGovern insurgency is of more than mere historical interest.

The third part of the book considers the legacy of the McGovern campaign. It looks at this legacy in two ways: through the history of the Democratic Party since 1972 and through the later political careers of the young McGovernites. Many analysts prefer to move on quickly after discussing the losers in landslide defeats, figuring that they have little of value to teach us. It is the burden of my argument that the repercussions of the losing McGovern campaign have continued to shape—and to haunt—the Democratic Party. The enduring identity crisis of the party, so often bemoaned by Democratic activists, cannot be fully understood until the legacy of the McGovern campaign is unraveled.

Although almost all of the events depicted in the book took place more than three decades ago, most of the principal actors in them are still around. My interviews with participants in the 1972 campaign—including a few of the McGovern insurgency's sharpest critics as well as a far larger number of its key players—were the most enjoyable part of the research. They were also the most fruitful: from comic or poignant anecdotes to profound political insights, my interview subjects brought a denser and more vivid texture to the account of 1972 than contemporary records and archival materials alone would have supplied. This book contains many voices beyond my own, all of them well worth attending.

Among the debts that I have incurred in the course of researching and writing the book, none is as important as the one I owe to the forty-seven individuals who gave me their time and allowed me to tape their recollections of the McGovern insurgency. A complete list of the interviews can be found at the end of the text. Most of the subjects I approached for interviews were pleased to cooperate; only nine either declined my request or did not reply to repeated phone calls and e-mails. It is perhaps unfair to single out any of my interview subjects for their unusual graciousness, since most were very helpful and sympathetic to a stranger, but George McGovern deserves special mention in this regard.

Help on the project came from many quarters. I am grateful to the graduate research assistants who tracked down data for me: Paul Alexander, Sesan Badejo, Yong-Hoo Sohn, and Fred Wood. Andor Skotnes and Susan McCormick tutored me in conducting and taping interviews. Debbie Neuls transcribed the tapes of some of my longer interviews. Research travel was made possible by a Faculty Research Award from the State University of New York, Albany, and from the unstinting support of a wonderful dean, Frank Thompson. I also thank the archivists who facilitated my research in the McGovern Papers at Princeton, the Mankiewicz Papers at the Kennedy Library in Boston, and the Meany Archives in Maryland.

Earlier versions of several chapters were presented to the Politics and History group at Albany, the Workshop on Rhetoric and Identity in American Political Development at Harvard, and a panel at the 2006 annual meeting of the American Political Science Association. I am grateful to the participants in these events for their ample and penetrating commentary.

For testing my story and its themes I have relied most heavily on feedback from friends and colleagues, many of long standing. Thanks to Jim Burns, Susan Dunn, Steve Robbins, Ray Seidelman, Steve Skowronek, and Todd Swanstrom. Their insights often led me to clarify or rethink what I wanted to say, although the flaws remaining in the book show that I did not always accept their sage counsels.

As always, it has been a distinct pleasure to work with Fred Woodward at the University Press of Kansas. To a deep appreciation of both history and political science, Fred adds a discerning eye and a judicious tone. As many of his authors will attest, it means a lot when Fred likes your work. I also value the experience of working with Susan Schott and Susan McRory at Kansas, who, like so many people I encounter, well remember the idealistic spirit of 1972.

I am especially blessed by family members that bring not only love and support to my work but also intellectual skills of their own. My teenaged daughter, Anna, brings a precocious wit along with her sweetness to my family. My son, Nick, a journalist and a better storyteller than I, has been on the lookout from the start for sharpening my narrative approach. My wife, Melinda Lawson, a historian, has both encouraged and challenged me, never letting me get by with a sloppy or confusing formulation of an issue. Her love is my rock.

Introduction

For American liberals, the past few decades have been bleak. Conservative leaders and conservative programs have been ascendant, and when the opponents of conservatism have occasionally wrested back power, their words have been guarded and their policies cautious. It has been a long time since liberals have had their moment in presidential politics, their chance to speak of their goals with enthusiasm and their dreams with fire. The last true liberal moment of this kind came in 1972, with the political insurgency led by Senator George McGovern.

The McGovern presidential campaign was one of the most remarkable—and strangest—in American political history. What was initially a small band of antiwar liberals stunned the political establishment and the pundits and captured the presidential nomination of the Democratic Party through a grassroots uprising. Yet almost at the instant that the insurgents successfully stormed the heights of American politics, they found themselves on the brink of one of the worst free falls on record. Briefly hailed for their brilliance, they came to be disparaged as blunderers, and the liberal idealism that fueled their rise was assailed as a foolish radicalism that guaranteed their collapse. The liberals' moment in 1972 was short, but its fate cast a lengthened shadow over their party and their political philosophy.

In the modern history of the Democratic Party, the McGovern insurgency was a watershed. It marked a generational and class upheaval as well as an ideological crusade, and the party would never again look like the urban-labor coalition of the New Deal era. The roots of Bill Clinton's political network—and of many other politicians, issue advocates, and campaign specialists who continue to shape Democratic and liberal politics in the first decade of the twenty-first century—can be found in the insurgency of 1972. Liberal politics since 1972 cannot be understood apart from the repercussions of the McGovern campaign. It is a key to the enduring identity crisis of Democratic leaders and activists.

Yet the McGovern campaign seldom receives serious attention. When the campaign is recalled at all, it is usually with derision. The one event that most people associate with it is the Eagleton affair, the greatest campaign fiasco of modern times. If it has a persistent symbolic value in American politics, it is as a handy rhetorical device—"McGovernism"—by which conservative Republicans (and sometimes conservative Democrats) mock liberals as weak on foreign policy and defense. When Congressman Jack Murtha, a decorated Marine veteran and hawkish Democrat, proclaimed the war in Iraq a failure and called for U.S. troop withdrawal in November 2005, conservative columnist David Brooks of the *New York Times* reached quickly for the McGovern specter. What Murtha was proposing, Brooks claimed, would inevitably lead to an Iraqi civil war. "If the Democrats become the party of withdrawal," Brooks wrote, "this is what they will have to live with. Are they really going to become the Come Home America party of George McGovern once again?"[1]

Apart from the right's rhetorical jabs, the McGovern campaign has been slighted by both scholars and popular historians. This is the first book written about it since the campaign memoirs of the 1970s. The most obvious explanation for the neglect of its significance is the scale of its defeat and the notoriety of its errors. Why should we want to read a story about such monumental losers?

Beyond our preference for reading about winners and our assumption that losers don't have much to teach us, there is a more subtle reason for the obscurity of the McGovern insurgency in contemporary American memory: the shadow of 1968. To most historians and political pundits, it is 1968 that was the political earthquake, while 1972 was a mere aftershock. The presidential election of 1968 was undeniably epochal. Captured in indelible images of the riotous Chicago convention, 1968 marked the fatal rupture that divided the dominant Democratic coalition. That year brought to power, in the person of Richard Nixon, the harbinger of the conservative ascendance that, interrupted by the Watergate scandal, would take full hold with the Reagan Revolution. The tale of 1968 also holds special emotional resonance for what, in the eyes of many Democrats, might have been: the doomed crusade of the last romantic liberal hero, Robert F. Kennedy.

But the explosive events of 1968 should not blind us to the comparable significance of 1972. The election of 1968 looked back to the signature controversies of the 1960s and rendered a negative verdict on the party whose policies had shattered the calm of the previous decade. Thus, as challenger, Richard Nixon could excoriate the Democratic establishment's candidate, Vice President Hubert Humphrey, on the issue of "law and order," evoking ghetto riots and minority crime rates. The election of 1972, while equally preoccupied with the war in Vietnam that had been the sixties' cataclysmic event, looked forward to the culture wars that would increasingly polarize the parties. This time, Nixon as incumbent could blast insurgent George McGovern for (allegedly) advocating "the three A's—acid, amnesty, and abortion." Nineteen sixty-eight ended an era; 1972 introduced the era to come. Consider the transformative events of the latter year:

1. It was the McGovern campaign that shifted power among Democrats from the urban, blue-collar party created during the New Deal to a party dominated by suburban, issue-oriented, and college-educated activists.

2. It was the McGovern campaign that introduced new cultural forces, especially the women's movement and the gay-rights movement, as constitutive elements in the Democratic Party.

3. It was in the McGovern campaign that the Democratic Party shed its Cold War past and embraced an antiwar orientation and skepticism toward American military buildups and overseas interventions.

4. It was the McGovern campaign that demonstrated how to win in the brand-new electoral game of presidential primaries—even though its grassroots style of mass organizing and populist fundraising would be taken up more by Republicans than Democrats after 1972.

5. It was the McGovern campaign that brought the New Politics version of sixties liberalism to its zenith; McGovern's massive defeat stigmatized the left wing of the Democratic Party for the next generation and became a rationale for the party's drift to the center.

Despite the landslide defeat, the McGovern campaign bequeathed to the Democrats a talented, youthful cadre of strategists, organizers, and wordsmiths who as they aged would largely shape the evolution of the party over the following decades. Every presidential campaign brings new activists into electoral politics, and some stay for the long haul. But for Democrats, the McGovern campaign produced a more distinctive and influential generation of political operatives than any campaign since. We can identify McGovernites—a term I use descriptively, hoping to detach it from the pejorative implications it is often given by right-wing commentators. But we do not speak of Mondaleites, Dukakisites, or Goreites, and even the senior Clintonites were McGovernites further down the political road. The McGovern insurgency was an initiation in presidential campaigning not only for later Democratic leaders like Gary Hart and Bill Clinton but also for future Democratic strategists like Bob Shrum and John Podesta. It marked the political coming of age for a new breed of Democratic activists, beneficiaries of the postwar explosion in higher education and alumni of the great causes of the 1960s, civil rights and the antiwar struggle. The 1972 campaign was the last time Democratic activists could wear their hearts on their sleeves all the way up to Election Day; the hopes they entertained, and the devastating disappointment they found in the end, were formative experiences whose reverberations are still felt in the politics of the Democratic Party.

It was the McGovern campaign, in its passions and in its tribulations, that gave birth to the continuing identity crisis of Democratic Party activists, torn between their hearts and their heads, between idealistic convictions about equality and peace originally forged in the struggles over civil rights and the war in Vietnam, and practical calculations of how to win elections in a country whose majority evidently does not share such convictions. Liberals in the Democratic Party cannot give up the insurgent impulse altogether, and in later elections many initially turned their hopes to such heirs of 1972 as Ted Kennedy, Jesse Jackson, Tom Harkin, Paul Wellstone, and Howard Dean. Since 1972, however, the majority in the party has always thought twice, always opted for the safer, more moderate, and more "electable" candidate in the end. Yet in muffling the liberal message, the Democrats have produced a muddle. Afraid of what will happen if they wear their hearts on their sleeves again, they go into presidential campaigns armed with anger at their fervent conservative opponents but only tepid feelings for their own pallid centrist champions.

Fixated on its ultimate collapse, we have missed the McGovern insurgency's importance in modern American history. Reading back into 1972 the easy triumph of Richard Nixon, we have also largely forgotten what an extraordinary political year 1972 promised to be before the crumbling of the McGovern campaign in the fall. In the first half of that year, the presidential campaign was a whirlwind of alienation and anger, of soaring hopes and apocalyptic fears. Some of the alienation and anger was expressed by George Wallace rather than George McGovern, and after Wallace's shooting and subsequent withdrawal from the race, it was turned against McGovern. But much of it came from the left, and at its heart it was about "the War." By 1972 the war in Vietnam had raged on a large scale for seven years—a political lifetime for the young activists who made up the core McGovern constituency. Election surveys would later indicate that for a majority of Americans, President Nixon was satisfactorily winding down the conflict. But to antiwar activists, the Nixon years offered only fresh horrors— the invasion of Cambodia, the incursion into Laos, the revelation of the My Lai massacre—and the war remained an unrelieved heartache. Ending the war was George McGovern's "magnificent obsession" and the rationale for his presidential bid.[2] It was equally the obsession for nearly every McGovernite whom I interviewed, the overriding reason why they signed up to work for a dark horse who, pundits proclaimed, had no chance of winning.

Once McGovern rose, seemingly out of nowhere, to home in on the Democratic presidential nomination in the spring of 1972, he became the carrier of the hopes as well as the fears of sixties liberals. Even beyond Vietnam, McGovern articulated the New Politics hope for a transformed U.S. foreign policy—a peaceful internationalism that broke with decades of Cold War militarism and interventionism. McGovern was the champion of political and social equality for minorities, women, youth—all of the insurgent forces eager to battle the powerful and complacent white males who made the old liberalism appear so hypocritical. He was the reincarnation of an economic populism that had been buried beneath the consensus liberalism of the Kennedy-Johnson years, proposing to do more for the have-nots while making the rich pay for it. Not since the New Deal and Fair Deal era had a successful candidate for the Democratic presidential nomination voiced such a full-throated liberal creed.

During its hope-filled springtime, the McGovern campaign attracted not only the sixties generation but also their left-liberal forebears. The intellectual lions of liberalism, such as John Kenneth Galbraith and Arthur Schlesinger Jr., rallied behind McGovern and wrote impassioned articles on his behalf. Among an even older generation on the left, the McGovern campaign appeared as an unexpected opening for progressive possibilities. In June 1972, Schlesinger wrote to McGovern about attending the funeral of the great literary critic Edmund Wilson at Wellfleet on Cape Cod: "Elena Wilson, Edmund's widow, told me that you were the only major-party candidate for whom Edmund had shown any enthusiasm in his entire life . . . In his last weeks, though quite sick, he insisted on watching the California debate [between McGovern and Hubert Humphrey] and showed constant concern about how the campaign was going."[3]

The McGovern springtime was international. For overseas opponents of U.S. foreign policy, who viewed Vietnam as part of a long-standing pattern of American support for repressive dictatorships, McGovern's candidacy represented the promise of a new American stance toward the world. The Greek actress Melina Mercouri, best known in the United States for her role in *Never on Sunday,* had been exiled by the military junta that had seized power in Athens in 1967 and later became cozy with the Nixon administration. Permitted by the dictatorship to come home briefly for the funeral of her mother, upon her return to Paris, Mercouri penned a short note to McGovern: "You must know that whoever talked to me [in Athens] kept repeating your name—McGovern, McGovern—whispered, but with such hope and admiration."[4]

In the months when McGovern's presidential chances seemed credible, the dreams of the left were countered by nightmares on the right. Conservative writers had not grown so apoplectic about a Democratic candidate since Franklin Roosevelt. In fact, their attacks on McGovern closely resembled Republican diatribes about William Jennings Bryan in 1896, purporting to unmask a liberal politician as a stalking horse for Jacobin revolution. As the now-defunct *First Monday* put it, "While South Dakota Sen. George McGovern may give the impression of being a mild-mannered milquetoast, a sort of benign political Liberace, he is in reality a dedicated radical extremist who as President would unilaterally disarm the United States of America and open the White House to riotous street mobs."[5] The flagship magazine of the right, William Buckley's *National Review,* was at first more sophisticated, observing that most of McGovern's campaign contributors came not from the unwashed urban masses but from "the posher suburbs and exurbs."[6] Yet once McGovern began to score startling victories in the primaries, the *National Review's* analysis grew as agitated as the scenario in *First Monday*: "The electorate tends toward dissolution into an anonymous mass. The mass, the mob—unstable, fickle, swaying with the changing winds of political fashion and feeling—is the correlate of the demagogue . . . McGovern, with his quiet manner, flat dull voice, and square clothes, is not like the standard caricature of the demagogue, but when we look more closely we see that he is in a classic American demagogic tradition."[7]

Soaring hopes on the left and dark fears on the right both vanished swiftly in the wake of the Democratic convention and the Eagleton fiasco. During its final stage, the McGovern campaign evoked pathos for some and scorn from even more. The endgame of the 1972 presidential campaign was so one-sided and devoid of suspense that it tended to obliterate the excitement that had come before. It was like a riveting work of fiction whose closing pages stumble into confusion. But there was still an important theme there, waiting to be recovered.

The Liberals' Moment tells the story of this largely forgotten campaign, with its contradictory phases of triumph and disaster. The book is not a standard campaign narrative. It is not a comprehensive portrait of the 1972 campaign, much less an insider account in the genre originated by Theodore White. The story of the McGovern campaign, with its victories limited to its pursuit of the Democratic nomination and its failures multiplying the rest of the way, does not lend itself to the suspenseful plot development that makes elections like 1948, 1960, or 2000 so entertaining. The significance of the McGovern campaign ultimately lies elsewhere, in its remaking of, and repercussions for, American liberalism. Picking beneath the rubble of McGovern's electoral collapse, we find many important political artifacts that illuminate the development of liberal politics and the Democratic Party from the 1960s to today.

The story of the McGovern campaign is a story of political insurgency. George McGovern's campaign on the left, much like Barry Goldwater's campaign on the right, has been one of the few insurgencies that succeeded in capturing a major-party nomination. Through an examination of the McGovern campaign, there is much to be learned about how insurgencies develop and flourish, as well as about the formidable obstacles they confront. Insurgent politics is a wellspring of political creativity, but it is eventually shadowed by powerful political contradictions. What the McGovern campaign suggests is that while the long-term implications of partisan insurgency may be profound, in the short term the politics of insurgency is likely to flounder amid seemingly insurmountable dilemmas.

My ultimate aim is to explore, through the phenomenon of the McGovern campaign and its aftermath, the transformation of American liberalism from the 1960s to the present. Insightful analyses have been written about the rise of the right that began with the Goldwater campaign. There has been much fascination with the fate of the New Left, with the political evolution of the young radicals of SDS and the Weathermen. What still lacks close examination is the trajectory from the passionate New Politics of the late 1960s and early 1970s to the defensive and drifting stances of the most recent Democratic campaigns for the presidency. I argue that the McGovern campaign is both a window on this development and a critical chapter in it. The transformation of the Democratic

Party and its persisting identity crisis can be measured by what has happened to the kind of ideas George McGovern articulated and the kind of rhetoric that he employed. It can likewise be measured through the careers of the McGovernites, in the political journeys that took the young New Politics liberals of the 1960s generation, as they matured, to frequent defeats at the hands of the right and occasional triumphs that brought surprisingly little satisfaction in the end.

The Liberals' Moment is divided into three parts. Part I is a narrative account of the McGovern campaign. Part II probes underneath the narrative, analyzing in depth those features of the McGovern campaign that are most illuminating for the politics of contemporary liberalism. Part III takes the McGovern insurgency from Election Day 1972 to the present and reveals its paradoxical legacy.

This organization is unconventional by its departure, in Part II, from a strictly chronological framework. There is a dramatic tale to tell in the McGovern insurgency. But I am after more than just an absorbing narrative; I look as well for the meanings that the McGovern campaign yields, both in its own political moment and for our own. In its liberal ideology and rhetoric, its grassroots style, its battle to transform the Democratic Party, its alliance with new social movements, and its vulnerability to Republican attack politics, the McGovern campaign confronted issues that have hardly been superseded for Democrats today. This book is poised between history and the present, between the events of thirty-five years ago and the political dilemmas that we have inherited from them.

A final word of introduction: I approach my subject with sympathy and admiration for George McGovern and the McGovernites, who dedicated themselves, above all, to ending the war in Vietnam. Yet I do not want to counter the prevailing, derisive view of the McGovern campaign by bathing it in a sentimental and nostalgic glow. If the historical significance of the McGovern campaign is to be recognized, it must be through an account attuned to its illusions and failures as well as to its insights and achievements. If the meaning of the McGovern campaign is to be made available to the contemporary political community, it must be through an account that is faithful to its paradoxical features and fate.

Most of all, it is Democrats, especially liberal Democrats, who need to understand their own history. In the story of the McGovern campaign, political history can serve as political therapy—a way to recover and examine the origins of Democrats' continuing identity crisis. There is no denying that full-throated liberalism, as voiced by McGovern, was rejected by the electorate, and liberal Democrats must come to grips with the persisting unpopularity of some of their goals. But there is also a cost when centrist Democrats conceal or deny the party's bedrock convictions about equality at home and cooperation abroad. Democrats must find ways to make these convictions more politically appealing or else continue to plod along with the depressing feeling that their party does not stand for anything. However daunting it may appear, Democrats need to resolve their identity crisis before they can regain their historic role as agents of progressive change.

PART I

The Rise and Fall of the McGovern Insurgency

1

"A Sixties Campaign in the Seventies"

For George McGovern, 1972 may not have been the ideal year to run for the presidency. He had been invited to be the standard-bearer for the "Dump Johnson" Democrats in 1968, but facing a tough reelection contest in South Dakota and fearing to be merely a sacrificial offering for antiwar frustrations, he passed the mantle on to Eugene McCarthy. By 1972, McGovern was unencumbered by a Senate race and better prepared for a presidential run, but the currents of national politics had turned more treacherous for his brand of liberalism. In a postelection interview, Hunter Thompson suggested to McGovern that he had run "a sixties campaign in the seventies." His response was a forlorn "yeah."[1]

McGovern's 1972 insurgency carried the liberal idealism of the 1960s to its electoral peak in the competition for the Democratic presidential nomination, but his landslide defeat at the hands of Republican Richard Nixon suggested that a majority of Americans had had enough of that idealism. As McGovern put it to Thompson,

> I think there was a lot of apathy . . . and a lot of weariness over the
> activism of the sixties—the civil rights movement, the peace movement,
> the crusades, the marches, the demonstrations. Nixon kind of put all that
> behind us. Things quieted down . . . I think that people were afraid of
> anything that kind of looked like fundamental change—that maybe we'd
> be right back into that same kind of energetic protest . . . that they'd grown
> weary of in the sixties.[2]

If McGovern, as a representative of the political causes of the 1960s, was rejected by the majority, he was embraced enthusiastically by the minority who wanted to complete the unfinished business of the previous decade, especially the imperative of ending the war in Vietnam. What made the McGovern campaign so unusual—so authentic and meaningful to its supporters, so disquieting and offensive to its opponents—had its roots in the politics of the 1960s. In that still-controversial decade lie the bitter conflicts, the political upheavals, and the democratic dreams without which the McGovern campaign would literally have been unthinkable.

Among all the events and features of the tumultuous 1960s, three were particularly critical for the later emergence of the McGovern insurgency. The growth of an antiwar movement, and the allied formation of an antiwar band in the U.S.

Senate, provided the McGovern insurgency with its hallmark passion. The turn of antiwar forces to presidential politics, in the insurgencies of Eugene McCarthy and Robert Kennedy in 1968, drew the activist spirit of a "New Politics" into fierce competition with the Old Guard of the Democratic Party and introduced a new cadre of grassroots organizers who would reshape the dynamics of campaigning. And the reform of the rules of delegate selection for the presidential nomination after 1968 made "participatory democracy," the watchword of 1960s activism, into an unpredictable new force that rocked the Democratic Party to its foundations. McGovern was an actor in all three of these political struggles, yet it was a large and diverse cast of 1960s activists that made possible his presidential bid. The liberals' moment in 1972 was fired by the personal passion and ambition of George McGovern. It was, in equal part, the collective accomplishment of a political generation.

Stop the War

It did not take an antiwar movement to make McGovern a critic of America's brewing disaster in Vietnam. He had expressed opposition to the U.S. policy in Vietnam long before the Americanization of the war in the early months of 1965. But the eruption of a peace movement in the wake of this Americanization began a process wherein millions of citizens came to share McGovern's views and to become the core constituency for his presidential run.

Like other major mass movements in American history, the antiwar movement of the 1960s was anything but monolithic. As a Central Intelligence Agency report observed in 1967, "Diversity is the most striking characteristic of the peace movement . . . Indeed it is this very diversity which makes it impossible to attach specific political or ideological labels to any significant section of the movement. Diversity means that there is no single focus in the movement."[3] From the start, the antiwar movement was a loose collection of often discordant groups, from Marxist factions on the left (who feuded even more with their sectarian rivals than with liberals) to moderate peace groups within the political mainstream. For a cause that brought together pacifists with advocates of militant confrontations with authority, and that combined free-thinking skeptics with priests, ministers, and rabbis, agreement on philosophy, strategy, or tactics was never really possible.

The antiwar movement grew as the war in Vietnam grew. Deepening involvement in Vietnam sent a shock through American society, as the mounting carnage of the conflict sowed both moral revulsion and pragmatic doubt among many Americans who had heretofore believed in the conventions of the Cold War. Division over Vietnam was evident in both political parties, with a number of moderate Republicans, especially in the Senate, eventually joining liberal

Democrats in dissent. Communities, even families, were split over the war. The fracture line over Vietnam could be found even in the homes of the war's architects, at least during the Johnson administration. Paul Nitze was in charge of defending the Pentagon against a massive antiwar march in 1967; three of his four children were among the marchers. Even in the home of Defense Secretary Robert McNamara, associated more closely with the war's planning than any other official, there was fervent dissent: McNamara's teenage son Craig hung a Viet Cong flag on one wall of his bedroom; on the opposite wall, placed upside down, was a U.S. flag.[4]

There were two different dynamics at work as the antiwar movement mushroomed after 1965. Increasing militancy and radicalism were the hallmarks of the first dynamic. In the first flush of large-scale opposition to the escalation of the war early in 1965, the signature event was the "teach-in," an intellectual and moral forum for dissent at major universities. As frustration and despair mounted over the expansion of the conflict, however, an important segment of the peace movement became impatient with the seeming imperviousness of the war machine and looked to move from words to actions in order to stop the war. Each year the actions, even when undertaken by only a small number of participants, became more confrontational: blocking draft centers in 1967, flooding the streets of Chicago to protest the Democratic convention of 1968, smashing property and fighting police in "Days of Rage" in Chicago in 1969, bombing government and military-related buildings in 1970 and thereafter.[5] Militant and sometimes violent tactics vented the rage of the most radical antiwar activists, but they saddled the movement as a whole, as public opinion surveys indicated, with a destructive image.[6] Some of that image was bound to rub off onto a presidential candidate linked to the movement and thus became part of the depiction of McGovern as a "radical."

Central to the development of a mass base for McGovern's presidential bid was the second dynamic, the spread of antiwar sentiments to a large, heterogeneous, and nonradical segment of the American people. A handy marker of this broader movement is the response to the two national protest events that took place in the fall of 1969. On October 15, a Vietnam moratorium called across the nation drew more than two million participants. Huge crowds assembled in a number of cities. A rally for antiwar businesspeople on Wall Street brought out a throng of twenty thousand. Thousands of federal workers in the nation's capital took part in antiwar meetings. A month later, the more militant Mobilization against the War mounted enormous marches in Washington, D.C., and San Francisco. The gathering in Washington, wrote historian Charles DeBenedetti, "was the largest protest demonstration in American history, with a size and diversity that not even the participants could comprehend."[7]

As President Nixon proceeded to reduce the number of American troops deployed to the combat zone and to "Vietnamize" the war, however, the antiwar movement began to lose steam. It is often assumed that what undercut the movement was the approaching disappearance of the draft, but this explanation is too simple. A lottery system was proposed by the president in 1969 to replace the hated classifications of the Selective Service System, yet when Nixon ordered U.S. forces to invade Cambodia in the spring of 1970, college campuses still erupted in outrage, with over five hundred shutting down at least temporarily.[8] By the following year, however, mass demonstrations had noticeably begun to wane. Some who opposed the war were encouraged that it appeared to be winding down; others retained their distrust of Nixon's plans but increasingly felt the weight of exhaustion from the seemingly endless marches.[9] Besides, an electoral option was now available again, especially in the insurgent candidacy of McGovern.

The antiwar movement could not stop the war that it loathed so passionately, but its impact on U.S. policy should not be measured narrowly. Beyond constraining both the Johnson and Nixon administrations at critical junctures in the war, it presented a moral challenge and fostered a climate for dissent extending beyond its own activist forces. The Cold War consensus that had prevailed in America with minimal challenge since the Truman years was cracked by the antiwar protests. The shibboleths of authority were attacked on a wide scale, and ingrained respect for presidential pronouncements was supplanted by a "credibility gap." Of all the Americans who came by their own path to share the questioning spirit of the movement, none were more important to the antiwar cause than a small but growing cohort of U.S. senators.

Congress was largely acquiescent to the executive in foreign policy matters during the first two decades of the Cold War, and if presidents had anything to fear in this arena it was thunder from the anti-Communist right. So it took considerable time—and the genesis of audacious new arguments contrary to the Cold War consensus—for congressional skepticism about the war in Vietnam to develop. During the Kennedy presidency, when U.S. involvement in South Vietnam significantly expanded, only two Democratic senators, Wayne Morse of Oregon and George McGovern of South Dakota, expressed strong reservations. When President Lyndon B. Johnson seized upon ambiguous events in the Gulf of Tonkin in 1964 to extract a resolution from Congress that his administration regarded as a "blank check" to escalate hostilities, the House supported him unanimously, and there were only two dissenting votes—from Morse and from Ernest Gruening of Alaska—in the Senate. However, once LBJ commenced the massive bombing and troop deployments that "Americanized" the war early in 1965, the Senate became the governmental hub of dissent to his policies. At first, the vocal senators, McGovern among them, who opposed what they suspected would prove a futile pursuit of military victory in Vietnam and advocated a negotiated settlement to the conflict instead were few in numbers. As the war grew much bloodier in Southeast Asia and much more controversial at home, the ranks of the Senate dissenters swelled, though they never reached a majority of the chamber. By 1966 more than twenty Democratic senators were on record as critical of the administration's policy, and they were gradually joined by moderate Republicans as well, including John Sherman Cooper of Kentucky and Jacob Javits of New York.[10]

A watershed in the Senate dissenters' emergence as a counterpoising voice to the administration was the public hearings held by the Senate Foreign Relations Committee during the winter of 1966. Chaired by J. William Fulbright of Arkansas, the most respected figure in the Senate in the field of foreign policy, the televised hearings were the first occasion on which the American public was exposed to extensive criticism of the war that came not from movement protestors but from establishment luminaries. When retired general James Gavin, former U.S. ambassador to France, and ex-diplomat George Kennan, famous for authoring the "containment" doctrine that set the strategy for the United States during the Cold War, spoke out against the military track in Vietnam and called for a negotiated settlement, opposition to LBJ's war took on a changed character. As Robert Mann writes, "Johnson and his aides had feared that the hearings might undermine public confidence in the president's handling of the war, and they were right to a degree that may have even surprised them. For the first time, well-known, respected political, diplomatic, and military leaders had openly questioned the wisdom and direction of America's military role in Vietnam."[11]

Over the next six years, the band of antiwar senators, like the antiwar movement beyond the Capitol, could constrain but not halt the conduct of the war. Yet these senators became important models for respectable dissent—and for political bravery. Presidents Lyndon Johnson and Richard Nixon were vindictive men who took criticism personally; they and their aides were not reluctant to malign antiwar senators as appeasers who were only encouraging the enemy. Rather than backing down, though, antiwar senators only became bolder, eventually coming close to ending the war by cutting off appropriations for it. It was this boldness that made the Senate of the 1960s a breeding ground for insurgent presidential candidates: Eugene McCarthy and Robert F. Kennedy in 1968, and George McGovern in 1972. The campaigns of the first two men reshaped American politics—and set the stage for the third.

Gene and Bobby

The presidential campaigns of McCarthy and Kennedy in 1968 created a new model of political insurgency on which McGovern would capitalize four years later. McGovern himself played a small but significant part in the surprising events of 1968, both at the beginning and at the end of the insurgent challenge to the Democratic establishment. In fall 1967, Allard Lowenstein, the sparkplug of the "Dump Johnson" movement within the Democratic Party, unable to convince his first choice for challenger to the president, Robert Kennedy, to enter the race, approached McGovern. McGovern was tempted, but he passed on the opportunity because he was up for reelection in 1968 and knew that a seemingly hopeless crusade to topple LBJ would lose him the voters of South Dakota. Like several others, McGovern suggested to Lowenstein an alternative candidate who was not up for reelection the next year: Eugene McCarthy.[12]

McCarthy had not been one of the more prominent doves in the Senate, but he had strong backing from the Adlai Stevenson liberal camp within the Democratic Party. At the time he announced his candidacy, the prospects of an insurgent challenge to a sitting president looked as bleak as McGovern had imagined. In a later interview, McCarthy admitted that when he entered the race, "we didn't think we could win. We wanted to debate the issue of the war."[13] But though McCarthy's campaigning was desultory, two developments gave his insurgency an enormous boost. At home, McCarthy's challenge to Johnson inspired a largely spontaneous grassroots uprising, as volunteer workers, many of them new to politics, seized the unexpected opportunity to express their fervent opposition to the war through the electoral process.[14] In Vietnam, the Viet Cong's Tet Offensive in the winter of 1968 mocked the optimistic pronouncements of the Johnson administration about the progress of the American effort, and the president's standing with the public, already damaged by the duration of the war, plummeted by a further 25 percent.[15]

In March 1968, insurgency produced an explosion in American politics. On March 12, the nation's first presidential primary was a shocker, as New Hampshire Democrats gave McCarthy 42 percent of their votes compared to 49 percent for the president. Although exit surveys showed that some McCarthy voters were unhappy that LBJ was not even more hawkish on the war, the ballot was an unmistakable sign of his unpopularity.[16] Four days later, Robert Kennedy ended months of wavering and joined the race, further intensifying the political turmoil. To admiring biographers, Kennedy's entry was the product of agonized reflection; to critical biographers, it was the fruit of cold-blooded calculation.[17] Regardless, the competing insurgencies of McCarthy and Kennedy made Johnson's political situation untenable. Facing almost certain humiliation at the hands of McCarthy in the upcoming Wisconsin primary on April 2, the president took to the airwaves on March 31 to announce that he would not be a candidate in the fall.[18]

With the president out of the Democratic race, so was the issue of Vietnam for the most part, and McCarthy and Kennedy, who never liked each other and became bitterly hostile as the contest progressed, battled it out across a string of primaries. In what became a highly personal competition, McCarthy had most of the students and the antiwar segment of the educated middle class, both of whom tended to view Kennedy as a latecomer and an opportunist. Kennedy was the favorite of minorities, some blue-collar Catholics (though not as many as later legend had it), and Kennedy loyalists nostalgic for his slain brother. Hubert Humphrey, who inherited the president's mantle and who stayed out of the primaries, had something better than either insurgent under the rules that governed the Democratic nomination contest in 1968: the support of party regulars and organized labor, which together controlled the process of delegate selection in the majority of states.

The climactic Democratic primary in 1968, as it would be in 1972, came in early June in California, where Kennedy defeated McCarthy by 4½ percent—approximately the margin of McGovern's victory over Humphrey in the later contest.[19] Kennedy was assassinated while exiting his Los Angeles victory celebration, and with his violent death the air went out of insurgent politics. With no real hope left of preventing a Humphrey nomination by the Old Guard, antiwar forces shifted their focus over the summer to the Democratic platform, seeking to commit the party to a peace plank. It was in the midst of this downhearted mood that Kennedy delegates and supporters prevailed on McGovern, Kennedy's friend and a much-admired Senate dove, to hold their forces together for the critical votes at the Chicago convention. McGovern announced his presidential candidacy on August 10, only sixteen days before the convention opened.[20]

Although McGovern's short-lived 1968 candidacy was not launched with the thought of capturing the Democratic nomination, it had two important consequences for his run in 1972. The lesser of these was the lasting resentment of Gene McCarthy. Transferring some of his hostility from Bobby Kennedy to Kennedy's substitute, McCarthy was particularly irritated when McGovern supporters, disillusioned by the gulf between McCarthy's heroic-martyr image and his maddeningly self-centered campaign style, adopted a slogan first coined by Gloria Steinem: "George McGovern is the real Eugene McCarthy."[21] More important for the future was the impact on McGovern of his hurried taste of presidential politics. Although the event was a small, quiet one amid the incredible chaos at Chicago, a televised debate before the California delegation was a personal turning point for McGovern. Facing off against a truculent McCarthy and a defensive Humphrey, McGovern was the undisputed winner in the eyes of the antiwar Californians.[22] "It was," McGovern later wrote, "a unique experience for a junior Senator from South Dakota to know that he had bested two highly talented colleagues before the television viewers of the nation. I confess that thoughts of a future bid for the presidency entered my mind . . . that day."[23]

The McGovern insurgency of 1972 grew out of the rival Democratic insurgencies of 1968. To be sure, there were substantial differences between McGovern's character and campaign and those of McCarthy and Kennedy—differences worth examining for their relevance to 1972 and beyond. As Steinem's ironic slogan suggested, George was not much like Gene—and the comparison worked mostly to his advantage among activists. McGovern may not have been witty and poetic like the senator from Minnesota, but he was hardworking, steady, unpretentious, and compassionate—a sharp contrast to McCarthy, who developed the reputation in 1968, especially among his closest aides, of being self-indulgent, vain, condescending, and erratic.[24] (McCarthy was even more erratic in 1972: first he promised Humphrey his backing for the California primary; then he endorsed McGovern instead; and still later, he turned against McGovern at the Miami Beach convention.[25]) Furthermore, McGovern, despite his much-vaunted niceness, possessed a tough-minded will to win that McCarthy never manifested.[26]

There were also numerous differences between Kennedy's hastily improvised campaign in 1968 and McGovern's long-planned presidential run in 1972. Bobby Kennedy's personality was intense and magnetic; he evoked fierce loyalty from some and deep mistrust from others. He could fire up crowds with emotions that made troubled reporters toy with the word *demagogue* to describe him.[27] His campaign's organization had little in common with either the McCarthy campaign of 1968 or the McGovern campaign of 1972: it was top-down rather than grassroots, with a high command composed of several generations of Kennedy men. Indeed, it was less an insurgent-style campaign at all than a classic Kennedy operation, with little to distinguish it from John F. Kennedy's 1960 organization save for the absence of a commanding campaign manager like brother Bobby.[28] Robert Kennedy's constituency in 1968 was also unlike McGovern's four years later: he had overwhelming support from racial minorities, but he was weak among antiwar students, who held against him his belated entry into the race.

Despite these dissimilarities between McGovern and his predecessors in insurgent politics, the McGovern campaign in 1972 was still a synthesis of the McCarthy and Kennedy campaigns four years earlier. It was the McCarthy campaign that established a novel form of grassroots activism within the Democratic Party. McCarthy had scant support from professional politicians, but once he announced his challenge to LBJ, thousands of volunteers, mostly middle-class liberals and college students fiercely opposed to the war in Vietnam, sprang into motion across the country. Regardless of their candidate's quirks, these volunteers were dedicated to a cause that he symbolized more than he led.[29] McCarthy's grassroots following was a spontaneous force, largely organizing itself; after 1968, its remnants were available to be remobilized in a more systematic fashion. And many of those who had gained invaluable experience in organizing at the grassroots during the McCarthy campaign were also available to another insurgent candidate who could give voice to their antiwar convictions.

Although McGovern's grassroots style owed most to the McCarthy campaign, his campaign's leadership was primarily Kennedy people. Frustrated by the experience of working for the erratic McCarthy, many of his top staff looked for a 1972 candidate who was against the war but could win the presidency—and they signed up with Democratic frontrunner Edmund Muskie.[30] The long-shot

McGovern did not look like a good bet to pragmatic political operatives, but the talent he managed to attract in the early going came to him largely because of his association with Bobby Kennedy, who had called him "'the most decent man in the Senate.'"[31] McGovern's top campaign managers, Gary Hart and Frank Mankiewicz, were Kennedy men, as was his shrewd adviser Fred Dutton, among others. Hart told me why McGovern was able to persuade him to leave his Denver law practice for an improbable insurgent effort:

> I think three things made him appeal to me personally . . . One was his representation of the Kennedy forces at Chicago in '68, [Hart] having worked as a volunteer for both John Kennedy and Robert Kennedy. Second was his lifelong fight against hunger—and that as a metaphor for concern for the poor. And third, his opposition to the Vietnam War . . . It was the combination of those three things and . . . the elimination of Ted Kennedy from the race [after Chappaquiddick] that led me to his doorstep.[32]

McGovern was the inheritor of the insurgencies of 1968. He had McCarthy's middle-class and youthful antiwar activists, and the grassroots organizers who had first learned their art in his campaign. He had the Kennedy people and the Kennedy image of compassion for the poor (though not the Kennedy "charisma" or appeal to minorities). With this combination, McGovern was in a position by 1972 to defeat the establishment candidate who had prevailed over insurgent politics in 1968, Hubert Humphrey. But one more ingredient was necessary for insurgency to take the Democratic Party by storm the second time around: a thoroughgoing reform of the rules by which it picked its presidential nominees.

An Open Party

To the insurgents of 1968 it seemed manifestly unjust that while Gene McCarthy and Bobby Kennedy were openly competing before the Democratic electorate in the primaries, Hubert Humphrey and his backers were corralling a much larger number of Democratic delegates in the semiprivate settings of party caucuses and conventions. The reform wing of the Democratic Party was particularly in-flamed by the numerous anomalies and abuses in delegate selection that came to light in 1968 and afterward. More than one-third of Democratic delegates for 1968 were selected before the year—and the insurgent campaigns—began. The majority of delegates were not chosen in primary elections, and these delegates were often the tools of state party leaders. In the words of the party's reform commission, "'secret caucuses, closed slate-making, widespread proxy vot-ing—and a host of other procedural irregularities—were all too common.'"[33] By means fair or—too often—foul, it appeared, as McGovern later put it, "that the

Democratic presidential nominating process was dominated by party wheel horses, entrenched office holders, and local bosses."[34]

It was a group of McCarthy supporters, disgruntled by their underrepresentation at the 1968 convention, that brought the issue of reform in delegate selection before the gathering in Chicago. By a very narrow margin, the McCarthy group succeeded with a motion to establish a party reform commission—the only victory that insurgents won at all in Chicago. One reason that the convention accepted a reform commission was that the victorious Humphrey forces saw it as a sop that might placate angry insurgents; another was that few party regulars grasped the implications of the motion for 1972.[35] Ironically in light of what would develop during the 1972 nomination season, after the 1968 election McGovern was asked to chair the reform commission as a compromise candidate. The regulars did not want a McCarthy backer to lead the reform effort, so McGovern, an insurgent who had nonetheless endorsed and campaigned for Humphrey in 1968, was the acceptable alternative. McGovern took the post "because I believed that I could bridge the gap between the Humphrey and the McCarthy-Kennedy elements of the party and ensure effective reforms and a more unified Democratic Party."[36]

McGovern chaired the reform commission until January 1971, when he officially launched his campaign for the presidency. His successor was Congressman Donald Fraser of Minnesota, and the commission has since come to be known as the McGovern-Fraser Commission. Although McGovern was chosen as a compromise figure between the regular and the reform forces, both the internal dynamics and the political logic of the commission's work pushed it toward the reform side. It was less McGovern as chair than the committee's staff and consultants, especially former McCarthy activists Eli Segal and Anne Wexler (both of whom later served in the McGovern campaign), that were the driving forces for fundamental reform. The reformers dominated the commission not only because they had the initiative and the expertise but also because the regulars put up a pathetic fight. Contemptuous of the very idea that the Democratic Party, within which they had long been powerful, needed reform, representatives of organized labor dropped off the commission early on; and the remaining party officials continued to underestimate the significance of changes in the rules of the game. Thus, in what political scientist Byron Shafer dubbed the "quiet revolution," the McGovern-Fraser Commission proceeded with "the most extensive planned change in the process of delegate selection—and hence presidential nomination—in all of American history."[37]

The New Politics reformers on the commission were, they claimed, not deliberately trying to reverse the results of 1968 and ensure an insurgent victory in 1972. Neither were they scheming, as some critics charged, to dislodge the regulars and assure their own ascendance. Their objective was more neutral: an open and participatory Democratic Party, fully in tune with the new democratic spirit of the times. Eli Segal argued that the guidelines the commission generated "were based on the notion of making the party open. The old system was not going to work any more." According to Segal, the new system of widespread primaries that emerged, beginning in 1972 and accelerating thereafter, was not what the reformers envisioned: their chief interest was in making selection processes in the nonprimary states more transparent, timely, and fair to ordinary citizens.[38]

Democratic idealism was not the only basis for the reformers' case. They also insisted that the party had to reform itself or else face repeats of the disastrous split of 1968—or worse. The commission's report, *Mandate for Reform*, made the danger of inertia plain:

> We believe that popular participation is more than a proud heritage of our Party, more than a first principle. We believe that popular control of the Democratic Party is necessary for its survival . . . If we are not an open party, if we do not represent the demands of change, then the danger is not that people will go to the Republican Party; it is that there will no longer be a way for people committed to orderly change to fulfill their needs and desire within our traditional political system. It is that they will turn to third and fourth party politics or the anti-politics of the street.[39]

Many of the McGovern-Fraser Commission guidelines that were adopted by the party for 1972 worked in the direction of an open party. They urged the elimination of fees to make it possible for low-income Democrats to serve as delegates. They banned proxy voting and the unit rule to prevent party leaders from controlling caucuses and conventions. They required that delegates be chosen in the calendar year of the national convention, that there be "adequate public notice" of meetings that picked delegates, that slate-making be done in public view, and that state parties "extend to the process of nominating delegates all guarantees of full and meaningful opportunity to participate."[40] Taken together, these guidelines undercut the traditional control of party elites over presidential selection and opened the contest for the party's nomination to whichever forces could win in a dramatically transformed electoral environment.

The most disputed McGovern-Fraser reforms were not these guidelines about participation, one of the chief themes of 1960s liberalism, but additional ones about another of its trademark concerns: equality for groups previously excluded from political power. African Americans were the initial target for affirmative action, but the commission quickly broadened its focus to include women and young people as well. Compared to their proportions in the population, all three of these groups were underrepresented at the Democrats' 1968 convention: only 6 percent of delegates that year were black, 14 percent were female, and 2 percent were under age thirty.[41] Commission guidelines crafted in 1969 sought to remedy this situation, requiring that racial minorities, women, and young people be included in each state's delegation to the national convention "in reasonable relationship to their presence in the state as a whole." Some commissioners were alarmed that this language smacked of quotas, and the commission as a body put in the record that it was not envisioning the imposition of any such mandate.[42] In 1971, after McGovern left the commission, pressure on the party from feminists produced a reinterpretation of the "reasonable relationship" language to require numerical targets—quotas in all but the nomenclature.[43]

The McGovern-Fraser reforms, even though periodically amended in later years, permanently transformed the way in which the Democratic Party selects its presidential nominees. Although they attracted surprisingly little notice while they were in the process of development, once put into practice they became immensely controversial. Critics charged, with some validity, that the reforms hurt the Democrats in 1972. The expanded number of primaries and the provisions for openness at caucuses and conventions drastically reduced the number of party office holders who served as delegates, while the de facto quotas for minorities, women, and youth diminished representation of blue-collar and white-ethnic constituencies. Rather than repairing the rift of 1968 as intended, the reforms largely perpetuated it, only with a different side in 1972 carrying away a tainted prize.[44] However, there was no validity to a second and more explosive charge, based on the fact that McGovern chaired the reform commission and then captured the presidential nomination: that he and his allies stacked the deck of reform, rewriting the rules with the ulterior motive of bringing him victory.[45]

There is little question that the McGovern-Fraser reforms were essential to McGovern's success in 1972. An insurgent like McGovern could not have won under the old rules of nomination politics in the Democratic Party. An increase in primaries and in open caucuses and conventions substantially expanded the number of rank-and-file participants for 1972. Still, these remained relatively low turnout events, offering an advantage to a campaign that could count on large numbers of committed activists. Finally, McGovern had on his staff Rick Stearns, who had interned with the commission and written an Oxford thesis on its work, and Eli Segal, the commission's counsel; these strategists provided his campaign greater expertise about how to play by the new rules than any of his rivals possessed.

However, there is no evidence that the reforms were rigged to favor a particular candidate. McGovern did not have that kind of power as commission chair, and the staff and consultants for the commission were not, for the most part, his partisans; Segal only joined the McGovern campaign after his preferred candidate, Senator Harold Hughes of Iowa, abandoned his presidential bid, while Wexler went to work for McGovern even later after her original choice, Muskie, flopped as a candidate.[46] Even with a more favorable playing field in the nomination contest, McGovern could not have won without his own tireless efforts, an exceptional grassroots organization, and a shrewd strategy for the primaries. Had there been a formidable regular Democrat in the race—if Muskie, for instance, had been as impressive a figure in the flesh as the pundits dubbed him before the primaries commenced—the reformed rules would have made little difference to the outcome. The McGovern-Fraser reforms were critical in 1972 because they made victory for McGovern's liberal insurgency *possible*. But they hardly made it *probable*.

Conclusion

Orderly opposition to the war in Vietnam, the McCarthy and Kennedy insurgencies of 1968, the McGovern-Fraser reforms—all three were expressions of a New Politics inside the Democratic Party. The New Politics should not be confused with the New Left of the same era. Adherents of the New Left considered themselves radicals, convinced that fundamental change in American life could not be achieved through the existing "system." Adherents of the New Politics considered themselves liberals, hopeful that the abuses and injustices of the 1960s against which they mobilized could be stopped by using the official channels of American electoral democracy.[47] Yet there remained, in values and aspirations, much in common between the two. For its advocates, challenging the old politics of the despised political "Establishment," the New Politics would be a moral politics, infused with the spirit of social justice and peace gestating in the civil rights and antiwar movements. It would be an open politics, seeking transparency and truth in contrast to the closed-door manipulations of political bosses and the secrecy and deception of the presidency. And it would be a participatory politics, displacing entrenched elites by putting into practice the ancestral American ideal of an engaged citizenry.

In the eyes of its critics, the idealistic rhetoric of the New Politics liberals served as a facade hiding an old-fashioned grab for power. They alleged that the New Politics group was just another elite—in this case, middle-class, highly educated, and with superior knowledge of the language and arts of political activism—out to dislodge the dominant blue-collar coalition forged in the New Deal and downplay the historic mission of the Democratic Party to serve the underdogs in American society. In their attack on the McGovern-Fraser reforms, future neoconservatives Penn Kemble and Joshua Muravchik spelled out these suspicions about the liberal cadre of the New Politics:

> The purpose of the McGovern quotas was not to make the convention more representative of the Democratic electorate as a whole, but to favor the affluent liberals within the party and to diminish the influence of its lower-middle and working-class constituents . . . Participatory democracy, as

defined by the new politicians, meant in practice the opening of political institutions to greater influence for the militant, activist liberal . . . [The New Politics liberals] constitute an interest group which differs from the "old" interest groups chiefly in its refusal to acknowledge the degree to which it hungers for political power and patronage.[48]

For a political movement whose socioeconomic roots, as supporters and opponents agreed, lay in the middle class of an emerging postindustrial society, George McGovern appeared an unlikely leader. A minister's son raised on the prairie during the Great Depression sought to champion the causes of an affluent, suburban, and largely secular following. A senator from one of the most rural and conservative of the heartland states sought to represent the values flourishing in the most cosmopolitan regions of the country. Yet, as the next chapter shows, McGovern had, in his background, experience, and character, qualities that strongly resonated with the supporters of the New Politics. Under his leadership, the new liberalism achieved its signal success: capture of the 1972 Democratic presidential nomination. Yet McGovern was also the leader for the signature debacle of the New Politics, the general election of 1972, which permanently scarred its reputation.

2

Decent Ambition

George McGovern was an easy man to underestimate. Before the 1972 campaign season opened, the reasons why most pundits believed he had little chance to become the Democratic presidential nominee had less to do with ideology than with personality. McGovern, it was commonly said, was too mild-mannered, too soft-spoken, and—the most frequently used adjective—too decent to make a strong president. He could not, so the argument went, be a plausible candidate because in the post-Kennedy era of political television he was utterly lacking in glamour. McGovern had a sturdy physique and a pleasant countenance, but the lines on his face and his partially bald pate made him look older than his half-century. And then there was his voice, enunciating his sometimes-passionate words in the stolid cadence and dry tone of the Great Plains.[1]

Even after two decades as a professional politician, McGovern often came across to audiences like the earnest classroom teacher he had originally been. A few months before the first primary of 1972, Frank Mankiewicz, who had been Bobby Kennedy's press secretary and was now McGovern's political director, was still combating McGovern's professorial mannerisms. Mankiewicz had three "admonitions" for his boss's public speeches:

1. Remain at the podium and acknowledge the applause, standing etc. before you begin to speak.

2. Even more important, remain at the podium and acknowledge the applause after you finish. I know it is customary for us lecturers modestly to tuck our speech into our pocket and leave the podium quickly, but this is not a lecture series.

3. At the beginning and end of the speech, and particularly when you enter the hall, I think you should, painful as it might be, wave to the audience.[2]

But 1972 was not a year for the much-overrated "charisma." The one Democratic entry in the race with media glamour was New York Mayor John Lindsay—and he flopped almost instantly. McGovern's major rivals in 1972—Edmund Muskie and Hubert Humphrey in the Democratic contest, and later Richard Nixon—were as deficient in popular charms as he was. The election of 1972 was about serious matters—and beneath the obvious and mostly superficial drawbacks, in the depths of character and intellect, McGovern was an impressively serious man.

McGovern was not just a teacher; he was a professional historian, only the second major-party presidential candidate in history—Woodrow Wilson was the first—to possess a Ph.D. (His dissertation adviser at Northwestern, Arthur Link, went on to become the foremost Wilson scholar in the nation, and Wilsonian internationalism would be an important influence on McGovern's own thinking.) McGovern's perspective on contemporary politics was framed by familiarity with the entire American political tradition. His outspoken attacks on the Vietnam War were rooted in a more knowledgeable historical critique of the Cold War than any of his Democratic competitors could offer. By 1972 even Hubert Humphrey was calling on the United States to end its involvement in Vietnam, but the antiwar constituency that played so large a role in the Democratic primaries could tell that McGovern understood the terrible meaning of the war in a deeper way than other Democrats did.

Even less apparent to the pundits who dismissed McGovern's chances was the force of his ego. Accustomed to the raging ambitions of a Lyndon Johnson or a Richard Nixon, the press had a hard time detecting the quiet throb of McGovern's desire for high office. McGovern once told me, with the trace of a smile playing in his eyes, "You have to be an egomaniac to think you should be president of the United States."[3] He applied this wisdom to himself and was prepared to do what it took to become president, so long as he could run a race consistent with his principles. His candidacy would express a proud independence; he never kowtowed to someone in a superior position, as Hubert Humphrey had done to Lyndon Johnson, first in the Senate and again as vice president.[4] But it would also express a fierce will to win: comparing McGovern to Edmund Muskie, McGovern's campaign manager, Gary Hart, remarked that the senator from Maine was handicapped in the primaries because "he didn't have McGovern's instinct for the jugular."[5]

This chapter presents a biographical sketch of George McGovern, taking him up to his campaign for the presidency in 1972. My approach is thematic and selective, and it sometimes departs from the chronological unfolding of his life. I emphasize those aspects of McGovern's background, experiences, and personality that are essential for understanding his role as the leader of a liberal insurgency. At the core of this biographical sketch is a combination of qualities that are usually regarded as opposites: McGovern as a man of decent ambition.

Minister's Son

George Stanley McGovern was a child of the Great Plains—of vast prairies, a harsh economy, and a steadfast religiosity. He was born in the tiny town of Avon, South Dakota, on July 19, 1922, and he grew up in the somewhat larger environs of Mitchell, South Dakota. Until World War II called him away, he was very much the American provincial, staying in his small hometown even for college at Dakota Wesleyan University.[6]

McGovern's father, Joseph, was a minister, a Wesleyan—fundamentalist—Methodist. The minister's household was governed by his religious precepts. His children were called to daily Bible readings and to a Sunday consumed by church activity, and they were repeatedly instructed that they lived in full view of the community and must uphold the highest standards of a Christian life. George and his siblings were admonished not to yield to the sensual pleasures that would subvert spiritual duties. As he recalled in his autobiography, "Movies were off-limits to good Wesleyan Methodists, as were dancing, card-playing, smoking or drinking."[7]

The impact of Joseph McGovern on his sensitive son appears to have been profound. In his early fifties when George was born, Joseph was an honorable and supportive father, but he was a stern and distant parent. During the 1972 campaign McGovern told an interviewer for *Life*, "I was always a little in awe of him, though he could joke and kid us too. But there was never an easy conversational relationship. He was so much older."[8] Lacking a father to whom he could open up, George as a boy was emotionally closed down. As Robert Sam Anson, author of a campaign biography of McGovern, observed, "He was a shy boy, almost withdrawn. He had very nearly failed the first grade because his teacher interpreted his reluctance to read aloud in class as lack of intelligence."[9]

Nurturing teachers began to bring George out of his shell, and he made great strides against his shyness when he took up debating in high school. Soon, he was a champion debater in high school and college—a talent that would be important at several junctures in his future career. But the emotional pallor of his childhood never fully went away. Its remnant was a deep sense of emotional reserve. To his close associates in his political life McGovern was unfailingly kind and generous, and many came to view him as loveable. But few felt that they understood what was inside of him or could approach him as an intimate friend. Several have remarked that only the unknowing called him "George" to his face; the standard address, even to longtime associates, was "Senator."[10]

Joseph McGovern also influenced his son's religious faith—although not in the manner that he intended. Rejecting his father's prohibition on worldly allurements, George began at an early age to sneak off to the movies. It was a benign form of youthful rebellion, but also a precursor to a more thoroughgoing rejection of his father's fundamentalist beliefs. Yet even though George fell away from the religious strictures of his childhood, he carried away from his father's house a strong moral streak. As a student he read widely in the texts of the Social Gospel and was drawn to its "ethical imperative for a just social order."[11] Shortly after returning from World War II, he enrolled at the Garrett Seminary, located on the campus of Northwestern University, and became a student pastor at a Methodist church. However, his father's occupation, he soon realized, was not for him. Revealingly, in a pattern that would be reproduced in his Senate career and presidential candidacy, he liked writing and delivering sermons but was little interested in day-to-day ministerial duties. Moreover, "baptizing babies, officiating at weddings, administering the communion rituals, and presiding at funerals—these tasks left me feeling excessively pious and ill at ease."[12]

Leaving the seminary, McGovern chose history over the ministry—but his take on American history, and later his stance in American politics, were inflected with his moral commitments. He would often be assailed as a radical, but far from being a Marxist, he was a philosophical and practical Christian. His later public speeches were laced with scriptural passages and replete with scriptural themes. The values at the core of his liberal political ideology are the values of the Sermon on the Mount; the bedrock concerns of his political life to this day are to feed the hungry and to be a peacemaker.

George McGovern was not a scion of the comfortable middle class. In his youth, Joseph McGovern had been a "breaker boy" in the coal mines of Pennsylvania. A gifted athlete, he became a minor-league ballplayer in the St. Louis Cardinals organization, but the hustlers and whores who frequented the world of professional baseball drove him away from sports and toward the ministry. Joseph McGovern found a living from his faith—but in the small agricultural towns of South Dakota it would never be a prosperous one.[13]

As the Great Depression settled over the plains states, the McGovern family shared the straits of most of its neighbors. As Anson relates, "Never well off to start with, the family teetered on the poverty line all through the 1920s and 1930s and nearly fell off when Reverend McGovern's modest real estate holdings were sucked under. It was not, however, the kind of penury that kept food out of their mouths."[14] Writing about his own youth in his autobiography, George McGovern focused less on his family's struggles than on the greater distress of the farmers in his community. He remembered vividly the tough men reduced to tears by economic and environmental disasters beyond their control.[15] In the hardscrabble Dakota economy of his youth, McGovern found little to sustain the traditional American shibboleths of self-reliance and laissez-faire.

McGovern's parents were Republicans in an overwhelmingly Republican state, but they were not politically active or doctrinaire. In contrast, the formative political experience of George's adolescence was the New Deal of Franklin D. Roosevelt. The young McGovern watched appreciatively as a bold new version of active liberal government brought relief and progress to his home state. Later, he became a personal beneficiary of New Deal policy, as FDR's GI Bill of Rights provided him with the funds to finish college and to attend graduate school.[16] The New Deal always remained a touchstone for McGovern's liberalism, its resonance for him as personal as it was political. Asked by a reporter about his political philosophy, FDR replied: "Philosophy? I am a Christian and a Democrat—that's all."[17] The same words can serve as a simple summation for McGovern as well.

Bomber Pilot and Peacemaker

It was world war that first transformed the young provincial. A few months after Pearl Harbor, McGovern, then a nineteen-year-old student at Dakota Wesleyan, signed up with the Army Air Force. Earlier, at the urging of a friend, he had taken flying lessons at a local airport and earned a pilot's license. But flying made him fearful, and after he won his license he had stayed away from airplanes. Suppressing this fear once the war broke out, McGovern became a bomber pilot. Called to service early in 1943, he was trained to fly a B-24 and shipped out with his crew to the European theater a year later. Based in Italy, he flew the required thirty-five combat missions, the last only two weeks before the conflict in Europe ended. For his bravery he was awarded the Distinguished Flying Cross with three oak leaf clusters.[18]

Thirty-five bombing missions over German targets were commonplace for fliers like McGovern—and utterly harrowing. Repeatedly, he piloted his B-24 through intense enemy flak, which blasted many of his comrades out of the sky, and on several occasions he made extremely hazardous emergency landings of his damaged plane. McGovern's heroism as a bomber pilot, vividly recreated by Stephen Ambrose in *The Wild Blue* as exemplary of American airmen in World War II, is a great story.[19] Perhaps more remarkable, though, is that this twenty-two-year-old, with a pregnant wife back home and an inner dread of flying, appeared to his crew as calm, steady, and self-possessed no matter how near death came. Although McGovern still felt a powerful fear, he did not show it to the men who looked to him for leadership.

McGovern's war record was not widely known to the voters in 1972. Besides his distaste for boasting, he belonged to an old American tradition that distrusted militarism, reflected in Abraham Lincoln's view, expressed during the Mexican War, of "military glory—that attractive rainbow, that rises in showers of blood—that serpent's eye, that charms to destroy."[20] The handling of his wartime experiences by his presidential campaign was different than the dramatization of John Kerry's bravery during the 2004 Democratic convention. The tale of the young bomber pilot was sometimes used by the McGovern campaign to good effect, as in Charles Guggenheim's biographical film for the primaries and in the fall's stump speech, demonstrating that the antiwar critic was a deep-dyed American patriot who had risked his life for his country. Yet in the most important speech of the campaign, the acceptance address at the Democratic convention, there was no mention of wartime bravery. Speechwriter Robert Shrum prepared a passage on the young bomber pilot, but antiwar activists on the staff succeeded in striking it from the acceptance address, he says, because McGovern was the "peace candidate."[21] In his pungent fashion, campaign aide Jeff Smith recalls their argument as to why McGovern's military career should not be played up in 1972: "It was almost a campaign against the military establishment, and . . . it seemed hypocritical to turn around and embrace it by saying, 'you know what, I killed more people than any of you guys.'"[22]

Firsthand experience turned the quiet warrior into a vocal peacemaker. Like a number of young veterans of World War II, McGovern returned home imbued with the idealistic conviction that the terrible sacrifices of his generation must not be repeated in the future. He later wrote that "I wanted to be a part of that postwar effort to build a structure of peace on the smoldering ruins of war."[23] McGovern entertained the idea of a world government and later belonged to the United World Federalists organization. Although that visionary postwar goal of superseding nationalism was soon dissipated by the onset of the Cold War, McGovern, loyal to the tradition of Wilson and Roosevelt, continued to hold onto hope for the unrealized potential of the United Nations.[24]

McGovern's opposition to the recourse to war as a standard instrument of a "realistic" foreign policy was even more visceral than it was intellectual. The young bomber pilot had watched in anguish as fellow American airmen were blown out of the air by German gunners. He was especially hard hit when his navigator, Sam Adams, was missing in action after being shot down while flying with another crew. "For the rest of the war," McGovern wrote, he and the two other officers in his tent "lived with Sam's empty bunk, his treasured photographs, and his neatly hung clothing, waiting for further word that never came."[25] During the long years in which he challenged first Johnson's and then Nixon's war, McGovern often bottomed his opposition on the maimed and mangled bodies, American and Vietnamese, that inevitably resulted from the illusion of "containing communism" in Southeast Asia. He was not a pacifist: he never regretted going into battle against Fascism, and many years later he comfortably supported President Clinton's use of military force to halt genocide in Bosnia and Kosovo.[26] But World War II left McGovern with a lifelong horror of war—and a lifelong anger at the aged armchair warriors who sent the young to die in it.[27]

Historian

The Northwestern University campus that housed McGovern's seminary also contained one of the finest history departments in the country, and it did not take much for him to be drawn away from the ministry and into scholarship. In high school, Bob Pearson, the debate coach who had been the most important single force in helping him find his voice and his self-confidence, was a history teacher, and from that point on Pearson's occupation held an enormous appeal to his protégé. Moving across the Northwestern campus, McGovern eagerly turned to graduate work in history, which suited him far better than the ministry. Before completing his doctoral dissertation he took a teaching position at his alma mater, Dakota Wesleyan University, in 1951. The dissertation was completed there, and a Northwestern Ph.D. was awarded to him in 1953.[28]

McGovern's doctoral thesis, under the supervision of Professor Arthur Link, was on the Colorado coal strike of 1913–1914, which climaxed in the notorious "Ludlow Massacre" of wives and children of miners. In the late 1940s the majority of U.S. historians, Link among them, were starting to gravitate toward a "consensus" view of the nation's past, a perspective that emphasized the exceptional moderation of Americans' political, economic, and intellectual disagreements compared to the profound and often violent divisions elsewhere in the world. Nicely adapted for leaving the class-conscious 1930s behind and reflecting postwar prosperity and conformity, the consensus school prevailed through the 1950s but was shattered by the upheavals of the 1960s. McGovern's choice of a dissertation topic signaled that he was unreceptive to the emerging consensus. Attracted instead to the older "conflict" approach to American history, usually associated with the Progressive historians, he wrote a lengthy study marked by sympathy for the struggles of working people and criticism of repression and violence by the powerful.[29]

Even more consequential for McGovern's future career than his populist interpretation of the American past was his extensive reading about the emerging Cold War. A favorite professor of his at Northwestern was Lefton ("Lefty") Stavrianos, a specialist on the Balkans and Eastern Europe. Stavrianos, McGovern later wrote, "was no apologist for the Soviet Union, but his lectures gave one a more balanced view of the Cold War that was then beginning to develop."[30] Inspired by Stavrianos, McGovern plunged into the provocative literature of the time about communism and the West, much of which dealt with the revolutionary upsurge in China. Among the authors who shaped his view of Asian developments was Owen Lattimore, soon to be attacked by Joseph McCarthy as, allegedly, a top Soviet agent. (To this day, the dispute continues about Lattimore's innocence or guilt.)[31]

From this reading McGovern took away a perspective on his times at odds with the ascendant Cold War liberalism of the Truman administration. The United States, he believed, was misconstruing a genuine revolutionary nationalism in Asia as a front for a global communist conspiracy and, in response, cementing alliances with reactionary dictators like Chiang Kai-shek that placed a once-progressive nation on the wrong side of history. With a number of his fellow graduate students, he also pursued this dissenting view into political activism, supporting the left-leaning presidential candidacy of Henry Wallace in 1948.[32]

This historical understanding of world—and especially Asian—politics, first formed in graduate school, was to make McGovern somewhat unique among the political leaders who came to oppose the war in Vietnam. The presidential candidate of 1972 was, in an important sense, still the history teacher trained at Northwestern a quarter-century earlier. His principal lesson in 1972, he told me,

> was the blindness in our opposition to communism, the feeling that somehow we were ordained by history, if not by God, to stop communism everywhere that it raised its head, whether it was in Cuba or Korea or Vietnam. We had a special preoccupation with little countries, little communist countries; the smaller they were, the more exercised we were . . . My mission was to try to show the American people that we didn't have any mission to police the world. Nobody appointed us to that, and as a matter of fact, where we had made an initiative to try to get along with people whose ideology we disagreed with, it worked out pretty well . . . Nixon became a hero opening up relations with China. And I felt the same options were open to us with Vietnam, Korea, Cuba, and elsewhere.[33]

Despite his unconventional left-liberal views, McGovern returned to conservative South Dakota to become a faculty member in his hometown college. It was not a very prestigious academic position for a doctoral candidate at Northwestern. But it was a valuable home base if McGovern had larger ambitions that would take him away from a life of scholarship and teaching. He was apparently unsure at this point about which career—history or politics—held the greater promise for his idealistic desire for service and his ego's drive for prominence. In the fall of 1952 he actively pursued a faculty appointment at the University of Iowa. There were eighty-some applicants for a vacant position in its history department, and McGovern, with stellar recommendations from his Northwestern professors, was one of three finalists. But he did not land the job. Had he become a professor at a highly ranked university like Iowa, his life might have taken a different course.[34]

Politician

Fittingly enough for someone with a strong moral streak, McGovern's impulse to plunge into a career in politics was aroused in a losing campaign. Attracted by the high-minded speeches of Adlai Stevenson in 1952, McGovern wrote articles for the local press and delivered a statewide radio address in support of the Democratic presidential nominee. Through these efforts he caught the eye of Ward Clark, chairman of the South Dakota Democratic Party, who made McGovern a startling offer: a position as executive secretary—essentially, field organizer—for the party.[35]

What made the offer startling was even less the requirement that McGovern abandon an academic post than the apparent hopelessness of the mission presented to him. The Democratic Party in South Dakota, never strong to begin with, was then at a nadir: in the 1952 elections Democrats won only 2 out of 110 seats in the state legislature (and Stevenson, of course, was trounced). For months, McGovern pondered Clark's offer—all of his friends and associates advised him to turn it down—but in the spring of 1953, with a gambler's wager foreshadowing his course in 1972, he accepted it. The position appealed to his principles; he was eager to battle the McCarthyite cold warriors in the Republican Party of South Dakota. And it appealed to his ambition for a larger platform: as Anson writes, "He was taking the job, he made clear to Clark, only with the understanding that one day in the not too distant future he would use the organization he meant to build to further his own political career."[36]

For the next two and a half years the history professor transformed himself into a one-man grassroots operation. Crisscrossing South Dakota, alone or with a companion, in a succession of used cars, he doggedly descended to the grittiest of political tasks. Initially there was little response by dispirited local Democrats to his urgent appeals. Gradually, however, by personally contacting and conversing with South Dakotans from all walks of life, McGovern brought a moribund party back to life. One by one, on "a 3 x 5 card, carefully annotated and filed," he compiled a list of prospective Democratic recruits.[37] Over time, he added 35,000 of these cards to his filing system—a shoebox—and built a strong grassroots network for his party. The fruits of his tireless efforts were visible in the 1954 state elections, which increased Democratic representation in the legislature from two to twenty-four.[38]

It was on his trips through the small towns of South Dakota that McGovern learned the arts of the professional politician. Indeed, his political education was more many-sided than for most of his peers; with scant resources and small help from his party, he had to be an organizer, fundraiser, publicist, speechwriter, and strategist all in one.[39] Some of these arts did not come easily to the reserved young man. Writing about McGovern's first South Dakota campaign, Anson observed his initial awkwardness—but determined application—in gladhanding:

At first it wasn't easy. He was uncomfortable accosting a stranger on the street, thrusting his hand at him, and in the next breath asking him to buy one of his campaign buttons. The whole thing seemed so contrived, so needlessly ritualistic. "But it seemed to matter to people," he says, "and so I learned to do it. And after a while I got to be quite good at it."[40]

By 1956 McGovern was ready to use the revivified party he had forged as a platform for his own quest for office. Challenging Harold Lovre, a three-term

Republican congressman, McGovern defeated him handily; he was reelected by an even larger vote margin in 1958. South Dakota Republicans, McGovern recognized, were increasingly vulnerable because of the unpopularity of the Eisenhower administration's farm policy, associated with the secretary of agriculture, Ezra Taft Benson. Pounding on Benson, McGovern tapped into his state's populist legacy. His low-cost campaign was populist in style as well. "At times," he recalled, "I or someone traveling with me . . . would go up and down the streets selling large campaign buttons for a dollar apiece so that we could get enough money for a tank of gas or a hotel room at the next town."[41] As McGovern caught up with and passed Lovre, Republicans resorted to red-baiting him. His support for Henry Wallace in 1948 was highlighted, as was as his advocacy of admitting "Red China" to the United Nations. But with low crop prices a more pressing issue than distant foreign-policy ones, the charge of radicalism did not stick to McGovern in 1956 as it would sixteen years later.[42]

McGovern's campaign experience was confirmed during his years in the House of Representatives: South Dakotans were largely indifferent to his unconventional stance on foreign policy so long as he provided solid services to constituents and fought for the interests of farmers. His first roll call as a congressman came on a resolution to grant President Eisenhower broad authority for American intervention in the Middle East (a forerunner of the Gulf of Tonkin resolution seven years later). McGovern was part of a small minority that opposed the resolution, yet this vote did not hurt him back home. His constituents were more interested in his vigorous support for higher agricultural support payments and in his collaboration with Senator Hubert Humphrey to expand existing policy on the disposal of crop surpluses into a bold "Food for Peace" program. After two successful terms in the House, McGovern cast his eye on a Senate race in 1960. Again, principle and ambition coincided: he was out to knock off incumbent Republican Karl Mundt, his state's most prominent exemplar of the politics McGovern most detested. Like his onetime collaborator Richard Nixon, Mundt had built his career in national politics on the politics of the "red scare."[43]

Senator

McGovern's future opponent Richard Nixon lost by the narrowest of margins to John Kennedy in 1960—and so did McGovern to Mundt. Mundt was a well-connected senior senator and an effective campaigner, but the decisive element in the race was the Kennedy factor. Kennedy's Catholicism did not play well in mostly Protestant South Dakota, which went for Nixon by a landslide. McGovern had not hesitated to associate himself with the Kennedy-Johnson ticket and paid the price when Mundt defeated him by a single percentage point.[44]

The president-elect and his brother Robert appreciated McGovern's sacrifice; besides, both liked the South Dakotan. Hence they created a position for him in the new administration: special assistant to the president in charge of an upgraded Food for Peace program. It was a marvelous opportunity for McGovern to take the lead on an issue close to his heart and to enhance his national stature at the same time. Aggressively seizing his opening, in short order he made Food for Peace one of the notable successes of the Kennedy administration's foreign policy. The "Food for Wages" component of the program, directed toward speeding up Third World development, was expanded nearly sixfold compared to the Eisenhower record. Still more heartening for McGovern was the humanitarian school lunch program, which was feeding about 35 million children around the globe by the middle of 1962.[45]

Still wanting to be a senator, McGovern resigned as director of Food for Peace midway through 1962 to challenge South Dakota's other Republican incumbent, Francis Case. Shortly after McGovern announced his candidacy, Case died of a heart attack, and McGovern's opponent became Case's appointed successor, former state attorney general Joseph Bottum. This time McGovern won, but only after a recount put him ahead by a mere 597 votes out of a quarter-million cast.[46] Victory by such a squeaker reminded him that his political career in South Dakota would always be tenuous, and it affected the kind of senator he would become. McGovern would never be a member of the Senate's "inner club," the informal elite who exercised disproportionate influence inside the chamber. He was too personally reserved and ideologically committed to be one of these gregarious and accommodating types. But he was also mindful of his precarious South Dakota base, wary of becoming too exposed on issues that might hurt him in his state.[47]

Continuing with the practices that had fortified his standing with South Dakota voters while in the House, McGovern constructed a crack constituency service operation in his Senate office and devoted considerable attention to the promotion of agricultural interests. Joining the Agriculture Committee, he was instrumental in establishing controls on beef importation and in making the wheat certificate program more appealing to farmers, both of which impressed the home folks, for whom beef and wheat were the leading commodities. On agricultural issues like these, which did not tap into his personal passions, McGovern was a consummate pragmatist.[48] Indeed, almost all of the deviations from his generally liberal Senate voting record came on matters where South Dakota interests clashed with the interests of the urban liberal-labor coalition. McGovern first aroused the ire of AFL-CIO president George Meany by denouncing the labor federation for attempting to scuttle grain sales to the Soviet Union because the deal did not provide the customary work for the maritime unions.[49]

McGovern was a patron of farm interests in the Senate, but he was not an expert—or even particularly interested—in the details of agricultural economics.

The one issue concerning food about which he cared deeply was hunger. His vision at Food for Peace of using agricultural surpluses in the United States to feed the hungry worldwide was an inspiration for the most constructive work he accomplished while in the Senate. Touched and troubled by a CBS documentary on hunger in America, McGovern in 1968 persuaded his fellow senators to establish a Select Committee on Nutrition and Human Needs, and he served as its chair for nearly a decade. The select committee functioned with an unusual degree of bipartisanship; Republican Senator Robert Dole of Kansas, one of McGovern's nastiest critics during the 1972 campaign, was his highly valued coadjutor on the issue of hunger. The humane accomplishments of McGovern's committee are evident in the dramatic improvements in existing nutrition policies: the food-stamp program expanded nearly sixfold, the school breakfast program expanded over sevenfold, and the school lunch program was made completely free for students from the lowest income brackets.[50]

Apart from the issue of hunger, the promotion of peace was McGovern's preoccupation during his Senate years. In 1963, in one of his first Senate speeches, he made the bold proposal for a 10 percent reduction in the defense budget. Adopting the argument of the only postwar president to question the opportunity costs of the arms race, Dwight Eisenhower, McGovern spoke of what a $5 billion savings on arms would represent for the American people: freeing up these funds, earmarked mostly to buy redundant nuclear weapons, would allow the federal government to "'build a $1 million school in every one of the nation's 3,000 counties, plus 500 hospitals costing $1 million apiece, plus college scholarships worth $5,000 each to 100,000 students—and still permit a tax reduction of a billion dollars.'"[51] Throughout his Senate career McGovern kept coming back to the illogical wastefulness of the arms race and proposing that the nation begin planning a conversion of defense industries for civilian uses, maintaining jobs while enhancing the quality of American life.[52] His controversial proposal as a presidential candidate of a sizably reduced defense budget for the post-Vietnam era was the culmination of a decade's effort to chip away at the military-industrial complex.

Overshadowing all else in McGovern's Senate career (though not of course to constituents back home) was his role as a critic of the Cold War. Although he had recently been a member of the administration, he was not hesitant as a freshman senator to raise doubts about Kennedy's more conventional Cold War policies. As he related in his autobiography, "The topic of my maiden Senate speech, on March 15, 1963, was 'Our Castro Fixation versus the Alliance for Progress.' The thesis of the speech was that the Administration and the Congress were so absorbed in their fears of Fidel Castro that they were overlooking the real challenge to the United States in Latin America—'the economic, political, and social ills' of the nations to the south of us."[53] Starting with this speech, McGovern would speak out for the next four decades about the irrationality of U.S. policy toward

Cuba.[54] Even more striking as a critique of Kennedy were some remarks that Mc-Govern included in his speech on behalf of reductions in defense spending. To illustrate U.S. overdependence on military means in international relations, he chose the case of Vietnam—and he did not mince words: "The current dilemma in Vietnam is a clear demonstration of the limitations of military power. This is scarcely a policy of victory. It is a policy of moral debacle and political defeat."[55]

McGovern was not one of the lonely dissenters who resisted Johnson's Gulf of Tonkin Resolution in 1964. Persuaded by Senate Foreign Relations chair J. William Fulbright that LBJ was merely seeking political cover on Vietnam for the 1964 election, he voted for the resolution despite his continuing concern that the United States was heading for deep trouble in Southeast Asia.[56] Once Johnson began to escalate the war in Vietnam early in 1965, however, McGovern resumed his stance as one of its fiercest critics. During a televised CBS panel discussion in March 1965, in which McGovern was the only dove in the room, he issued a haunting prophecy about the war's future: "I think there will be a staggering loss of human life out of all proportion to the stakes involved and I see no guarantee that once we go through that kind of a murderous and destructive kind of a military effort that the situation out there will be any better. In fact, I think it will be a lot worse."[57] Utterances like this soon made McGovern *persona non grata* at the White House.

U.S. intervention in Vietnam summed up for McGovern everything that was wrong with the twisted logic of the Cold War. But his obsession with Vietnam deepened—and became more emotional—after he made his first trip to the war-torn country late in 1965. As he later wrote:

A visit to an American military hospital made me sick at heart as I met young Americans without legs, or arms, or faces, or genitals—all of them victims of land mines, booby traps, or sniper fire . . . While in Da Nang, on a tip from an American reporter, I requested permission to visit a hospital for civilian casualties. The scene will stay in my memory as long as I live.

A decrepit, unbelievably overcrowded building staffed by several young Danish doctors and Vietnamese nurses was filled with savagely wounded men, women, and children of all ages . . . One large open ward was jammed with two hundred patients who had been mangled by shrapnel from American bombs and artillery . . . I left that hospital determined to redouble my efforts against the war . . . to do whatever might persuade the Congress and the American people to stop the horror.[58]

Between 1965 and 1972 McGovern was among the most active and outspoken of the flock of Senate doves. First Johnson and then Nixon considered him a major pain in their sides. Johnson was particularly scornful of McGovern's call for negotiations with the Communists, incredulously telling one group of advisers that the South Dakota senator "wants to talk to the Viet Cong."[59] McGovern was heartened as more and more senators, some of them Republicans, joined his cause, but he was profoundly frustrated by the war's duration and destructiveness. His most serious bid to tie the hands of war-making presidents came in April 1970 with the McGovern-Hatfield Amendment to End the War. Introduced as a rider to a military procurement bill, the amendment prohibited the expenditure of funds for military operations in Southeast Asia after the year's end and established a timetable for the withdrawal of all U.S. combat forces by mid-1971. The amendment was greeted enthusiastically by the antiwar movement and attracted majority support in at least one public-opinion poll, but it failed in the Senate by a vote of 55–39. Almost two-fifths of senators were on record in favor of ending the Vietnam disaster swiftly, yet the White House could still make war unchecked by Congress.[60]

It was during floor debate on the McGovern-Hatfield Amendment that the senator from South Dakota made one of the most remarkable speeches of the entire era. On September 1, 1970, with nearly every senator present, McGovern, aware that his amendment would fall short of majority support, called his colleagues to account for the moral catastrophe of Vietnam:

Every senator in this chamber is partly responsible for sending 50,000 young Americans to an early grave. This chamber reeks of blood. Every senator here is partly responsible for that human wreckage at Walter Reed and Bethesda Naval [hospitals] and all across our land—young men without legs, or arms, or genitals, or faces, or hopes. There are not very many of these blasted and broken boys who think this war is a glorious adventure. Do not talk to them about bugging out, or national honor, or courage. It does not take any courage at all for a congressman, or a senator, or a president to wrap himself in the flag and say we are staying in Vietnam, because it is not our blood that is being shed. But we are responsible for those young men and their lives and their hopes. And if we do not end this damnable war, those young men will some day curse us for our pitiful willingness to let the Executive carry the burden that the Constitution places on us.[61]

Fellow senators were shocked, and some were personally offended, by McGovern's brief speech. His words were all the more surprising because he was all but officially running for president at this point. Such tough, accusatory language from him would be echoed in his 1972 presidential campaign—only then his impolitic insistence on moral responsibility for the disaster in Vietnam would not be aimed only at members of the Senate. McGovern certainly wanted to become president. His hatred for the war in Vietnam, however, was even stronger than his ambition.

Conclusion

George McGovern could lash out at the moral delinquency of the war's architects and advocates, but those who worked with and for him were never subjected to such treatment. The moral combatant was a mild boss, and his personal decency was one of his most winning qualities. Joseph Grandmaison was a regular Democrat who had been a Johnson delegate in 1968; the antiwar cause was remote from his consciousness. But he was the top young Democratic organizer in New Hampshire, and both the Muskie and McGovern campaigns sought his services as campaign manager for the state's critical primary in 1972. Grandmaison decided to give the rival candidates a tryout by advancing a public appearance in New Hampshire by each man. Most of his friends were backing Muskie, but after observing him and McGovern close up, he had no hesitation in picking the latter. Grandmaison "listened carefully to what McGovern said, and he very easily and quickly won me over. [It was] just the decency of the man." After a long career in politics, including a post in the Clinton administration, Grandmaison, a savvy political operative, still enthuses that "I love George McGovern. I think he's unquestionably, outside of family, the finest, most generous person I've ever met."[62]

Grandmaison's sentiments are shared by almost all of the McGovernites that I interviewed, who still speak about their former leader with affection. For someone in a profession known for self-absorption and brusqueness toward subordinates, McGovern was unusually considerate toward the people on his staff or in his campaign. Longtime aide John Holum observes that McGovern "could express disappointment, but he was never harsh, never cruel—fundamentally [he was] a decent person, very sensitive to the feelings of people around him."[63]

Qualities like these fed the skeptics' charge that McGovern was simply too "nice" to be a credible president. The claim was, in fact, not altogether without substance. McGovern's most humane characteristics sometimes hindered him as a political operator. He was reluctant to wound aides' feelings by firing them, which sometimes left him with less than the most effective help. He had an unfortunate tendency to make advisers feel comfortable by seeming to concur with their counsel, concealing his disagreements and thus generating confusion about where he stood. McGovern might have been even stronger as a politician if he had not been as kind a person.[64]

At a deeper level, though, decency was not inconsistent with toughness. One meaning of toughness, presumably, is a refusal to play it safe or yield to fear and a readiness to defy the odds. McGovern's life and career repeatedly displayed this form of toughness—as a bomber pilot, a rebuilder of a hugely outnumbered party in South Dakota, a challenger to vindictive chief executives, a long-shot candidate for the presidency. He was not only the most liberal candidate on the Democratic side in 1972; he was also the toughest.

Ironically, the toughness that McGovern's critics failed to appreciate may have been responsible for some of the errors that were ascribed to softness instead. Beating the odds so often, McGovern possessed a flinty vein of self-confidence. The source of his extraordinary drive, it was also at the root of his more imprudent actions. At critical moments in his quest for the presidency, he behaved impulsively, as in his vice-presidential selection process, or stubbornly, as when he rejected pleas to alter his managerial style in the face of organizational disarray.

If McGovern was tougher, more ambitious, and more strong-willed than most observers recognized at the start of the 1972 campaign season, those same observers were right, in a way, about his decency. Although almost all American voters in 1972 were sick of the war in Vietnam, the majority believed that McGovern the dove lacked the strong hand that impressed them in the hawkish Nixon. To the minority who rallied behind McGovern, however, his decency was a more potent emblem. For these Americans, the horrors of a brutal war in Southeast Asia and the deceitfulness and repressiveness of the powerful at home made it an indecent moment in American history. McGovern's personal decency represented for them a promise that a different America was possible—not a new one still to be forged, but an older one remembered, and desperately needing to be restored.

3

The Left-Center Strategy

Seven people were assembled at Cedar Point, a farmhouse on the eastern shore of Maryland, on July 25, 1970. The farmhouse belonged to Senator George McGovern, and besides the senator and his wife, the group included Richard Wade, an urban historian; George Cunningham, the senator's administrative assistant; Pat Donovan, his secretary; and Gary Hart and Rick Stearns, two recently hired campaign aides. They had gathered not for a holiday weekend in the country but to plot a dark-horse run for the presidency.[1]

A few months later, Jimmy "the Greek" Snyder, the famous odds-maker, calculated that McGovern's chances of capturing the Democratic presidential nomination were 200–1.[2] Had Jimmy the Greek been able to look in on the Cedar Point meeting, he would not have found anything on the surface to challenge the long odds he had set. The candidate was the junior senator from one of the least-populated states in the nation, and political pundits agreed that he was too mild-mannered and uncharismatic to excite the electorate as a prospective president. His Senate aides, Cunningham and Donovan, were cool to a presidential bid, fearing that it would prove fatal to McGovern's—and their—career in Washington. The young aides who had signed up for the presidential race, Hart and Stearns, had limited experience in a national campaign and were hardly the kind of respected strategists that other candidates, with stronger prospects, would have recruited.

Yet if the plans of this small group seemed quixotic in the summer of 1970, they were more solidly rooted than at first appearance. McGovern's unprepossessing exterior concealed the spirit of an ambitious and savvy politician, and along with a genuine moral streak, the minister's son had the instincts of a political gambler. His assets for a presidential run were more substantial than the odds-makers recognized. As the most outspoken dove in the U.S. Senate, he was positioned to be the leader of the antiwar forces in the Democratic race. As the chair of the Democrats' commission to rewrite the rules for delegate selection, his name was more closely associated with party reform than any other. And once Ted Kennedy was forced out of contention for the 1972 nomination after the incident at Chappaquiddick in 1969, McGovern held a special appeal to the liberals who still mourned for Robert F. Kennedy. As John Douglas, an aide to Kennedy and a friend of McGovern's, recalls, "With Bobby's death, there was a distinct feeling that people who thought of him as the repository of their hopes looked favorably upon a McGovern effort" for the presidency.[3] The helpers Mc-Govern had drawn into his quest were also much stronger than their thin campaign resumes would suggest. Although untried in national political combat, Hart and Stearns proved remarkably talented in different, and complementary, tasks of campaign leadership.

The Cedar Point meeting sized up McGovern's likely rivals for the Democratic nomination and debated how early he should announce his candidacy and move to the front of the pack. But the most consequential subject discussed at Cedar Point was the strategy that McGovern would follow to the nomination. Gary Hart credited Professor Wade with giving it a name: "the left-centrist strategy."[4] At Cedar Point, Hart wrote, there was agreement that McGovern should "co-opt the left, precluding the possibility of other liberal candidates, and, at the same time, make the campaign open and acceptable to party regulars. The issues, together with early organizational activity, would help nail down the left, but the most convincing argument for the party regulars, the center, would be organizational strength—victories in the middle and later primaries and superior numbers of people in the caucuses in the non-primary states."[5]

The left-centrist strategy was one of the most important keys to the fate of the McGovern insurgency. Because we know the outcome—and particularly because so much went amiss from the Democratic convention to the day of the election in 1972—McGovern and his top aides have gained a reputation as maladroit rookies in the big leagues of presidential politics. Recollecting that the same group took a 200–1 long shot to the Democratic Party nomination in 1972, however, should prompt us to doubt the validity of this judgment. A testimonial to the adroitness of the McGovern campaign in capturing the Democratic prize came from an unexpected source: the enemy camp. After the election, Nixon campaign manager Jeb Magruder commented, "One of the characteristics of the McGovern activity was its fantastically effective planning—at least from what we [in the Committee for Re-Election] could see. On the other hand, there was a fantastic lack of planning on the part of almost every other Democratic candidate."[6]

Just as the McGovern campaign's failings in the fall can be overestimated, its skills in the spring can be exaggerated. As Frank Mankiewicz, McGovern's political director, comments, "We were not as smart as we seemed in the primaries and we were not as dumb as we seemed in the general election."[7] Still, if we examine McGovern's campaign for the nomination in light of the strategy established at Cedar Point, what is striking is how much it unfolded according to the original plan. Up to the Democratic convention, it might be said that the left-center strategy was the foundation for a brilliant success, carrying the apparently amateur McGovernites to victory over their more experienced and highly touted rivals.

Considering the entire sweep of the campaign, however, the Cedar Point strategy contained a hidden flaw. What it gained for McGovern in taking the nomination, it cost him in his hopes for taking the presidency. The "left" part of the strategy did the trick in the spring, but it haunted him in the fall. And there was no winning over the regulars in the center or shifting back there himself in his ideological positioning. Indeed, even in moments of strategic triumph for the McGovern campaign during the primary season, there were foreshadows of troubles that came to pass in the general election. The story of McGovern's bid for the Democratic nomination, which this chapter narrates, is a story about both the potential and the pitfalls in liberal insurgent politics.

Before New Hampshire

The McGovern presidential campaign really began in 1968, at least in the mind of the candidate. Although his last-minute entry into the 1968 race came at the urging of Bobby Kennedy's supporters after the assassination, the brief taste of presidential politics, especially the heady experience of besting both Humphrey and McCarthy in a debate before the California delegation in Chicago, left him with the conviction that he could be the Democratic nominee in 1972.[8] McGovern's moves after the 1968 election were made with an eye to his presidential prospects. When he was offered the chairmanship of the party's new reform commission, campaign biographer Robert Sam Anson wrote in 1972, McGovern was reluctant to accept the position, assuming that it would generate more enemies than friends.[9] But McGovern's aide Jeff Smith, whom he had hired for his Senate staff in 1968 in preparation for a presidential run, remembers it differently: "We sat and discussed [the position], and we figured that not only would this get him meeting a better class of people but a lot of richer people and a lot of democratic power people, and it would also give him an excuse to travel and meet as many Democrats as possible."[10]

Along with his travels on behalf of the McGovern-Fraser Commission, McGovern hit the road often to speak against the war in Vietnam, particularly on college campuses. "Throughout 1969 and 1970," he wrote, "I made more university appearances than any senator in recent history."[11] Well before McGovern began to assemble a campaign staff, he was starting to build his base on the left wing of the Democratic Party. He collected the names of supporters on the same index cards that he had used in his South Dakota campaigns. Student antiwar activists were especially valuable to him as prospective campaign volunteers. McGovern knew that he would be short on endorsements from party heavyweights and donations from party fat cats, and that any hope he had for the nomination rested with a grassroots campaign sparked by insurgent enthusiasm.

It was on one of his trips, a visit to Denver to speak at a Jefferson-Jackson Day dinner in March 1970 (his address was titled "Come Home, America"), that McGovern made the first, and most critical, hire for his presidential campaign staff.

He invited the young man who had made the arrangements for his Denver visit, thirty-three-year-old lawyer Gary Hart, to become his coordinator for the western states and, soon afterward, he requested that Hart come East and run his national campaign.[12] The campaign manager that McGovern recruited, in a choice that reflected the senator's impulsiveness and self-confidence, had an unusual background for an insurgent on the Democratic left. Born in small-town Kansas in 1936, the son of parents who belonged to the strict, conservative Nazarene denomination of Christianity, Hart attended Bethany Nazarene College in Oklahoma and, taking his faith seriously, went on to divinity school at Yale. It was the appeal of John F. Kennedy in 1960 that turned Hart's thoughts from religion to politics and redirected him to Yale Law School. After a stint in the Department of the Interior under Stewart Udall, Hart returned to Denver and, apart from working in Bobby Kennedy's campaign, was, at the time McGovern met him, a politically active local lawyer with little to distinguish him from numerous others who fit that description.[13]

McGovern's choice of an untested young attorney—Hart describes himself as a "greenhorn" in 1970—to be his campaign manager can be viewed as a mark of his own lack of political standing at the time.[14] No one with seniority and experience would sign up for such an improbable candidate as McGovern. Yet in plucking Hart out of obscurity, McGovern's sharpest instincts as a political gambler were also in evidence. In Hart, McGovern discovered a smart, talented, and energetic political organizer with a powerful conviction about grassroots politics similar to the candidate's and a formidable ability to inspire loyalty from a growing cadre of field operatives. Hart's willingness to work for McGovern reflected an equally keen instinct. The McGovern presidential campaign was the making of Hart's career; he became a national political figure as McGovern's campaign manager, embarking on a path that nearly led him to the White House.

It was also at this very early stage that McGovern made a second hire that was as consequential as the choice of Hart. Rick Stearns, a Rhodes Scholar, had served as a summer intern at the Democratic reform commission in 1969 and developed a personal and academic interest in the new politics of delegate selection. On a winter break from Oxford at the end of 1969 and at the urging of John Douglas, Stearns offered his services to McGovern. He came aboard the McGovern campaign full-time at the same moment as Gary Hart, a few weeks before the meeting at Cedar Point.[15]

Rick Stearns was only twenty-six at the time, but he understood the nature of the emerging electoral game in the Democratic Party better than anyone else in the country. Whereas the Democratic favorites, first Edmund Muskie and later Hubert Humphrey, would follow the old prereform playbook for the most part, Stearns gave the McGovern campaign a vital edge by his mastery of the new rules. "Endorsements had mattered previously," he says, "because large numbers of delegates were simply being hand-selected by the very people whose endorsement political leaders sought." But 1972 would be different: "What you were looking at now was a selection system that was actually open and fluid." The advantage, he recognized, rested with the candidate who could turn out activists for the primaries and caucuses, neither of which would elicit high rates of participation. Looking past the early polls, Stearns's insight was that what motivated most activists in the Democratic Party was "hostility to the war in Vietnam," and that if McGovern was their preferred candidate, "this constituency . . . could very well be a vehicle to give McGovern the early victories that he needed to eventually consolidate a leading position and become the party's nominee."[16]

With a skeletal staff in place, McGovern publicly announced his intention to run for the presidency in January 1971—the earliest such announcement since Andrew Jackson. Getting out of the gate first would establish his reputation for boldness and hopefully persuade possible competitors for the left-activist constituency to stay off the track. His declaration of candidacy established the fundamental themes upon which he would run. Beginning with his signature stance, his early and fervent opposition to the war in Vietnam, McGovern set a lofty tone and pledged to move the nation beyond the dishonest politics of the Johnson and Nixon years:

> Thoughtful Americans understand that the highest patriotism is not to
> blindly accept official policy, but to love one's country deeply enough to call
> her to a higher standard. I seek the presidency because I believe deeply in
> the American promise, and I can no longer accept the diminishing of that
> promise . . . The kind of campaign I intend to run will rest on candor and
> reason; it will be rooted not in the manipulation of our fears and divisions,
> but in a national dialogue based on mutual respect and common hope . . .
> For my part, I make one pledge above all others—to seek and speak the
> truth with all the resources of mind and spirit I command.[17]

Gradually, the McGovern insurgency began to come together in 1970 and 1971. Young organizers, whose enormous energy was less surprising than their exceptional savvy at grassroots politics, were recruited for what the McGovern staff had identified as the critical early primaries in New Hampshire and Wisconsin. Laboring largely in obscurity throughout 1971, Joe Grandmaison in New Hampshire and Gene Pokorny in Wisconsin would become legendary figures among McGovernites in the early months of 1972. A similarly committed and skilled cadre of young staffers came together at McGovern's Washington headquarters during the year before the first primary to take on the multiple tasks of a national campaign. Even if McGovern surprised the odds-makers in the early primaries, he would not be able to capitalize on these victories in other states' contests unless the young staffers established a foundation for a full-blown national effort.[18]

Becoming a McGovern field organizer or headquarters staffer scarcely seemed a smart career move in 1970–1971. The individuals who signed up full-time to work for this long-shot campaign were motivated by their ideals and not by their hopes for future employment. Mostly under age thirty-five, the first McGovernites were emblematic of the 1960s protest generation (excepting a minority on the hard left), driven by a love for the country and a revulsion at what was being done in its name around the globe. They were drawn to McGovern because, far more than any other Democrat, he was articulating a renunciation of prevailing U.S. foreign policy that they shared.

Marcia Johnston, the first director of McGovern volunteers, was typical. Teaching in South Korea while her army husband was stationed there, she had become "radicalized" by the antipathy to the war in Vietnam that she saw all around her and was eager to work for McGovern because "he was so far ahead of everybody else" in principled opposition to the war.[19] Vietnam was the most important but not the only 1960s foreign-policy fiasco that shaped the insurgent sentiments of young McGovernites. Kirby Jones was serving as a Peace Corps volunteer in the Dominican Republic in the spring of 1965 when President Johnson sent in U.S. troops to put down an alleged communist insurrection. Like many of his Peace Corps colleagues, Jones protested the American invasion. The locals among whom he had been living, including his baseball teammates, were rebels, but nothing that the U.S. government was saying about them was true. "I saw the U.S. government lying," Jones remembers. "They would lie at two o'clock about something that I saw at ten o'clock."[20]

Not all of the early volunteers for McGovern were 1960s activists of a familiar stripe. The "uncharismatic" McGovern attracted some of the most glamorous stars in Hollywood for his antiwar insurgency. Shirley MacLaine took a year off from her movie career to join the McGovern campaign and, after the Democratic convention, became its chief spokesperson on women's issues. Her brother, Warren Beatty, also threw his energies into the McGovern insurgency long before the first primary. Beatty charged up crowds at McGovern rallies and later organized celebrity concerts to raise funds for the campaign. A frequent presence on the campaign trail, he became a buddy of Hart, and other McGovernites amusedly observed that as their clothes and hair styles became increasingly similar, the two men began to look alike. As Amanda Smith notes, "One of the things that was really fun to watch was the relationship between Gary Hart and Warren Beatty because each one wanted to be the other one."[21]

In the summer of 1971 the McGovern campaign took on a somewhat altered organizational cast with the addition of two older and more experienced hands: Frank Mankiewicz and Ted Van Dyk. Attracting these two was something of a coup for McGovern, since at this stage there were few signs that his insurgency was poised to take off. Mankiewicz and Van Dyk brought seasoning and stature to what was looking to most observers like a hopeless youth crusade. But they also brought a Washington-based, top-down conception of presidential campaigning that clashed with the grassroots guerrilla style of Hart and Stearns.

Over the next year and a half, Mankiewicz and Hart periodically wrestled over the management and direction of the campaign. Even apart from their disparity in age, the two men had little in common. Born in 1924, Frank Mankiewicz was a child of liberal and Jewish Hollywood; his father, Herman Mankiewicz, won an Oscar for the script of *Citizen Kane*. A World War II infantryman, he graduated from UCLA in 1947 and obtained a master's degree in journalism from Columbia the following year. He did share with Hart the possession of a law degree—Mankiewicz's was from Berkeley—and a political identity as a Kennedy loyalist. During the 1960s Mankiewicz had been the Peace Corps's director for Latin America and the press secretary for Bobby Kennedy in his 1968 campaign. In this latter role he became a prominent figure on the public stage, with national contacts far superior to those of the novice Hart.[22]

The two top McGovern managers were a contrast in style as well as in background. Whereas Hart was vigorous and dashing, Mankiewicz was wry and rumpled. Celebrated for his wisecracking, behind the affable persona was a masterful handler of the media and a canny political operator. Beyond these qualities, Mankiewicz provided McGovern, surrounded by so much youth, a companion from his own generation, and while in appearance there was a gulf between an earnest South Dakotan and a jaded Californian, the two men were, in important respects, kindred spirits.

Although Ted Van Dyk was only two years older than Hart, his roots were in the previous generation of Democratic politics. Born in the state of Washington in 1934, the son of a sawmill worker and union militant, Van Dyk, like Mankiewicz, had a master's degree from the Columbia School of Journalism. But his political career prior to working for McGovern had been tied to one of Bobby Kennedy's rivals in 1968, Hubert Humphrey. Joining the Minnesotan's Senate staff in 1963, during the vice-presidential years he was Humphrey's chief speechwriter and all-purpose adviser. In the 1968 campaign, Van Dyk was part of the camp that pushed Humphrey to move away from identification with LBJ's Vietnam policy, and he took a lead role in drafting the Salt Lake City, Utah, speech that finally put some distance between the candidate and the president. Feeling afterward that Humphrey was too tarred by Vietnam to run again, Van Dyk turned to McGovern in 1971 as offering "the best hope of bridging the gap between the peace movement and the party regulars." He brought to the McGovern campaign some valuable leavening from a mainstream perspective, but for that same reason he was, among the top staff, most often at odds with the strategy and passions of the grassroots insurgency.[23]

As the start of the campaign season loomed, the prospects of this insurgency did not look particularly bright. Van Dyk sent McGovern a "State of the Campaign" memo at the end of November 1971, and from his traditional political standpoint the situation was scarcely encouraging. "We are still weak," he wrote, "weaker than we should be after this many months' campaigning. If the elections were being held today (as of course they aren't), I believe we'd be badly beaten in New Hampshire, destroyed in Florida, and would run more weakly than we suspect in Wisconsin. In other words, we'd be out of the race."[24]

Although Hart had greater faith in the potential of the insurgency, he too had some anxious moments during the winter before New Hampshire. It was discouraging enough that although McGovern had been campaigning longer and harder than any of the growing list of competitors for the Democratic nomination, the national press largely ignored him and his weak numbers in the polls barely budged. Two factors feeding the poll numbers worried Hart even more. First, the campaign was desperately short of money. Requiring large sums for paid media and small amounts for the prosaic functions of grassroots organizing, the McGovern campaign seemed perpetually on the verge of going broke. Second, the Democratic frontrunner, Edmund Muskie, corralled so many endorsements from leading party figures that his campaign began to look like a bandwagon leaving the McGovernites in the dust. Particularly disheartening to Hart was the endorsement of Muskie by Iowa's senator Harold Hughes. Hughes was committed to the same positions as McGovern, so when even this champion of the Democratic left threw in with Muskie, it looked like McGovern had hardly any allies left.[25]

From all appearances, the least worried person in the McGovern camp was the candidate. Maybe it was his formidable self-confidence, which served him well in this daunting period. But McGovern also understood that he was in better shape than most of his top staff realized. If his campaign scored poorly by conventional criteria, its strengths as an insurgency, largely outside the ken of most observers, were on the rise at the end of 1971. Dedicated and talented organizers were in place and putting together the best grassroots operations of any candidate in the key primary and caucus states. The Cedar Point strategy of "coopting" the left wing of the party was well advanced, with McGovern increasingly the favorite of peace and women's rights groups, and when late arrivals, like John Lindsay and Eugene McCarthy, attempted to move onto this terrain, they discovered that McGovern already occupied it.[26]

McGovern also perceived some of the weaknesses in his opponents positioned in the center and on the right. An impressive election eve television broadcast in 1970 had catapulted Ed Muskie, Humphrey's running-mate in 1968, to the head of the Democratic pack for 1972. Media commentators were wowed that night by the Maine senator's "Lincolnesque" calm in contrast to President Nixon's strident rhetoric. But McGovern saw what would become increasingly evident once the primaries began: apart from their similar height, Muskie was a bland and unexciting campaigner who had few of Lincoln's deeper strengths. Hubert Humphrey would likely pick up centrist support once Muskie faded, but his was a tired political face, and among Democratic liberals he was cursed by his association with the war. On the right, Scoop Jackson was an unreconstructed Cold Warrior in a party rapidly abandoning its Cold War legacy, and George Wallace was unacceptable to any Democrat who had thrilled to the moral summons of the civil rights movement.

So if McGovern seemed to most election analysts to be just as unlikely a contender a year after his announcement for the presidency as he had at that earlier moment, the field of play was in fact favorable for him as the primary and caucus season opened. McGovern would be the insurgent in a time of continuing party turmoil. His would be the fresh face and the voice of a more truthful politics. His grassroots campaign would ride the intense passions stirred up by the 1960s, even though they were beginning to ebb. On the eve of the New Hampshire primary, this dark horse was poised to shock party regulars and pundits alike.

Six Assumptions

Looking back, with the advantages of hindsight, McGovern's capture of the 1972 Democratic presidential nomination does not seem so surprising. The same hindsight, however, makes his hopes of capturing the presidency itself seem quixotic. Knowing the size of the landslide that buried McGovern in November 1972, it has been easy to argue, as some analysts since 1972 have done, that he was doomed from the outset to be defeated handily by Nixon. The implication can even be drawn that in pursuing so dubious a quest for the presidency, the McGovernites tarnished the reputation of liberalism for a generation to come.

From the vantage point of early 1972, though, McGovern's presidential chances did not appear so slim. His campaign's scenario for winning the presidency incorporated at least six assumptions about the political landscape of the 1972 election. All six assumptions were eminently plausible as the campaign season commenced. It was the McGovernites' misfortune that all six proved to be erroneous by Election Day. A consideration of these assumptions will clarify how McGovernites thought they could carry the election—and why they got it wrong:

Assumption 1: *Nixon is an unpopular incumbent.* When McGovern announced for the presidency in January 1971, the Republican Party, on the upswing in the 1966 and 1968 elections, had achieved mediocre results in the 1970 congressional race. The president's approval rating had mostly been falling over the course of 1970, and in the first Gallup Poll taken after the date upon which McGovern officially became a candidate, it stood at only 51 percent. At the beginning of 1972, before Nixon's trip to China, his approval level was still at 49 percent.[27] Even better evidence for how vulnerable Nixon was considered at the time was the long list of Democrats who declared their intention to challenge him. Omitting several prospective Democratic candidates, such as senators Birch Bayh of Indiana and

Harold Hughes of Iowa, who terminated active presidential bids before the end of 1971, the lineup of Democratic aspirants during the spring of 1972 included, in addition to McGovern, all of the following: Senator Edmund Muskie of Maine, Senator Hubert Humphrey of Minnesota, Senator Henry Jackson of Washington, Senator Vance Hartke of Indiana, Congresswoman Shirley Chisholm of New York, Congresswoman Patsy Mink of Hawaii, Congressman Wilbur Mills of Arkansas, Governor George Wallace of Alabama, Mayor John Lindsay of New York, Mayor Samuel Yorty of Los Angeles, former senator Eugene McCarthy of Minnesota, and former governor Terry Sanford of North Carolina. Amid this swarm of candidates, few Democrats focused on how Nixon's popularity was rising in the spring of 1972.

Assumption 2: *George Wallace will eventually become a third-party candidate, as in 1968, and split the conservative vote with Nixon.* McGovern and his strategists thought there was a significant possibility that once George Wallace failed to gain the Democratic nomination for 1972, he would launch another third-party run and lure many right-wing voters away from the president. In later reflections, McGovern has generally cited Wallace's shooting as one of the handful of events that played the largest role in dashing his presidential prospects.[28] McGovern's hopes about Wallace matched Nixon's fears. In 1968 Wallace's independent campaign had nearly cost Nixon the election, and the president was concerned lest the same threat materialize in 1972. As Nixon aide H. R. Haldeman wrote in his diary, "[The] main key for us is to keep this a two-way race."[29] Nixon and his aides made several moves to contain the threat from Wallace. By dropping a threatened federal investigation of Wallace's brother for tax fraud, they induced the Alabama governor to run as a Democrat in the first place. Even after Wallace was shot and could no longer pursue the Democratic nomination, they made sure that there would not be another third-party venture. The Nixon campaign arranged to pay Wallace staffers so that they would discourage the governor from another run, while presidential emissary John Connally made a secret visit to Wallace's hospital room and stoked his dislike of McGovern.[30]

Assumption 3: *A mood of alienation is rampant among the electorate, and McGovern is the candidate who can best speak to it.* In the first rounds of the Democratic nominating game, as the establishment candidate, Muskie, stumbled, and the voices of discontent, McGovern and Wallace, surprised observers with their surge, there was much talk of an alienated electorate. Columnist David Broder wrote on the day of the Wisconsin primary that "the voters are more fed up with unending war and inflation, unfair taxes and unresponsive officials, bureaucracy and official bunkum, than anyone in the Democratic presidential derby had calculated."[31] McGovern came in first and Wallace second in Wisconsin, and a Yankelovich poll found many Wallace voters claiming that McGovern was their second choice.[32] Columnists Rowland Evans and Robert Novak reported from Wisconsin that "as McGovern passed down factory aisles the last two weeks, worker after worker told him his choice was between Wallace and McGovern."[33] So it seemed plausible to McGovernites that once the Alabama governor was beaten, they would inherit the support of a good number of Wallace Democrats. Before long, however, conservative critics, Evans and Novak prominent among them, were pounding on McGovern's supposed radicalism, and Wallace voters were turning against him en masse. Alienation was not, in fact, all of a piece, and if Wallace primary voters might agree with McGovern on inflation or tax reform, they were at the opposite pole on an issue like busing. In the end, most chose stability with Nixon over McGovern's brand of change.

Assumption 4: *Despising Nixon, and fearing a reprise of the divisions of 1968, Democrats will unite behind whoever wins the party's presidential nomination.* McGovern's left-center strategy relied upon a limit to internal party bloodletting and a common front for the fall campaign. Even if he was staking out a campaign strategy on the left of the party, he was indisputably a loyal Democrat. McGovern had built the Democratic Party of South Dakota from the ground up. His record in the Senate was very liberal, but so was the record of many party stalwarts. In 1968, while Eugene McCarthy had angrily spurned the Humphrey-Muskie ticket at Chicago, McGovern was, in his own words, "the first person up on the platform holding up [Humphrey's] hand and saying I was going to back him all the way."[34] McGovern could even argue persuasively that unless he offered a vehicle for the antiwar wing of the party, it might stand aside again, as in 1968, or form a new party, wrecking the Democratic nominee's hopes. He could not imagine at the start of the primary season the anger among party regulars that would intensify through the increasingly bitter conflict for the nomination and shatter Democratic unity for the fall.

Assumption 5: *In the present political era, Democrats are the natural majority party.* Of the six optimistic assumptions McGovernites made at the start of 1972, the belief that Democrats had the advantage in a presidential election—unless they were badly split or else the Republicans nominated a charismatic candidate—was the most plausible of all. Indeed, it was an assumption shared by Richard Nixon, one of the chief reasons his reelection campaign downplayed his Republican identity. In 1972 Democrats dominated a majority of the state governments, had controlled Congress for eighteen years running, and enjoyed a considerable lead among voters in partisan identification. Since the Great Depression, they had won seven of the past ten presidential contests. No matter if both sides agreed that Democrats were the majority party and started presidential contests with a built-in advantage; the assumption was nonetheless flawed, the result of focusing on the wrong data. Unlike in state or congressional elections, and regardless of their party identification, voters in Cold War presidential contests placed a high premium on strength in foreign policy, and in surveys dating as far back as the Korean War, Republicans were perceived as superior in the area of national security.[35] Removing Franklin D. Roosevelt and restricting the scorecard for recent presidential elections to the Cold War era, Democrats had won exactly half. In the six presidential elections from 1948 through 1968, only once—in 1964—had a Democratic candidate taken a majority of the popular vote.[36] The most relevant data, in other words, suggest that there simply was no natural Democratic majority for the presidential election of 1972.

Assumption 6: *Thanks to the adoption of the Twenty-sixth Amendment and the demographic bulge of the baby boom, a huge influx of young voters since 1968 will tilt the presidential playing field for 1972 in McGovern's favor.* In the minds of the McGovernites, young first-time voters were a key to their hopes for victory over Nixon. At the forefront of social change in the 1960s, young people composed the original political base that McGovern established—and there were going to be a lot more of them in the electorate in 1972 than there had been in 1968. The Twenty-sixth Amendment, adopted in 1971, gave the ballot to eighteen-year-olds, and in 1972 young people born between 1948 and 1954, a huge cohort because of the postwar baby boom, were now eligible to vote. But McGovernites overestimated the progressivism of the young. The conservatively clad Youth for Nixon, with their monotonous chant of "four more years," became an irritant to reporters and a joke to liberals, but they represented a rightward trend among college students that would increasingly counter the leftist bent of campus protesters. And among the majority of youth who did not attend college, McGovern was no more popular than Nixon or even Wallace. McGovern would do better among young than among older voters, but not by enough to make a difference in the election results.

Beginnings of an Upset

Frontrunner Edmund Muskie planned to run everywhere during the 1972 primaries and prove that he was the Democrats' most electable candidate against Nixon. McGovern's campaign, by contrast, picked its spots, concentrating its scarce resources on the spring contests that offered it the most promising openings. McGovern's was the shrewder strategy, and although events did not always unfold as anticipated, the prescience of McGovern strategists about the dynamics of the nomination contest remains impressive to behold. Theirs was a classic insurgent approach, an American politics version of the guerrilla war maxim to avoid frontal attacks against the enemy's big guns and instead conduct raids at its exposed flanks.

Even before the New Hampshire primary, the McGovernites caught the Muskie forces off guard in the Iowa caucuses, held on January 24. The Iowa caucuses were not the marquee event in 1972 that they would become in 1976, when they proved to be the launching pad for Jimmy Carter's surprising success. Still, they presented the first opportunity for McGovern to slow Muskie's momentum and sharpen his own faint profile in the media.[37] Iowa's Senator Hughes had been expected to dominate the home state caucuses, but he had recently dropped out of the race. (The real reason, according to McGovern organizer Carl Wagner, was that Hughes had revealed to reporters that he spoke regularly with his brother, who was, unfortunately, deceased.[38]) After his departure, Muskie obtained Hughes's endorsement, and the rest of the party establishment in Iowa fell in line behind the senator from Maine. Everything seemed in place for a comfortable caucus win that would confirm Muskie's elevated stature as the Democrats' surefire nominee.

Beneath the press's radar, however, the McGovern campaign, spearheaded by Carl Wagner, cultivated an alternative constituency in Iowa. Developing a network that united antiwar activists, dissident union workers, and Bobby Kennedy loyalists from 1968, Wagner brought an unexpected contingent of highly motivated McGovern supporters to the caucuses on a brutally cold and stormy evening.[39] Muskie still defeated McGovern in the final caucus tally, 39 percent to 27 percent. However, since McGovern support had registered only at 3 percent in the most recent Gallup Poll while Muskie's figure was ten times as large, Muskie's literal victory was interpreted by the media as McGovern's triumph instead. McGovernites were particularly delighted by a metaphor in the *ABC Evening News* story: "The Muskie bandwagon slid off an icy road in Iowa last night."[40]

It was not obvious at the beginning of 1972 that the McGovern campaign should stake its hopes so heavily on the March 7 primary in New Hampshire. According to Gary Hart's chronicle, Mankiewicz and Van Dyk, anticipating a strong run by Muskie in New Hampshire, wanted to direct more of the campaign's resources to other early contests in Florida and Illinois.[41] New Hampshire was, after all, nearly home turf for Muskie. Moreover, it was a relatively conservative state that hardly seemed fertile ground for a candidate positioned on the left wing of the Democratic Party.

But Hart and the grassroots organizers struggled successfully to preserve the intensive focus on New Hampshire that had been central to their original plan. And they had cogent reasons for believing that the McGovern campaign could pull off an upset in the state. Writing off the New Hampshire primary, certain to draw enormous media attention, was dangerous because a Muskie cakewalk would make him look all the stronger and McGovern all the weaker. Because New Hampshire was a small state, it was tailor-made for a grassroots campaign featuring one-on-one contacts with voters. Abundant volunteers would be available, not only from the state's colleges but from the large pool of campus activists in the Boston area. And McGovern himself, not running in nearly as many states as Muskie, could devote more of his own campaign schedule to New Hampshire. Precisely because the prognosticators were saying that Muskie was expected to dominate the New Hampshire primary, running a strong second in the state would sidetrack his bandwagon and establish McGovern as a serious contender.[42]

As it turned out, New Hampshire helped McGovern enormously and hurt Muskie even more. A comparison between their respective campaigns shows that on almost every critical score, McGovernites had the better hand to play. Their campaign's advantages began with superior organizing. In Joe Grandmaison, his chief New Hampshire organizer, McGovern had lined up the best young political operative in the state. Grandmaison had extensive contacts throughout the Granite State and a deep knowledge of the local political terrain. By contrast, Muskie brought in outside organizers to run his New Hampshire campaign. Some—like Tony Podesta, who later joined the McGovern campaign—were talented, but many of them, in Grandmaison's estimation, were "jerks."[43]

Grandmaison set to work organizing the state well in advance of the Muskie operatives. Painstakingly, he built McGovern's support with small-scale events that relied on activists rather than money from the national campaign: Hart described these as "house parties and local receptions for the candidate, local leadership, emphasis on New Hampshire issues—taxes, jobs, etc., reliance on local media exposure."[44] McGovern's own extensive travels through the state—in the two months before the primary he devoted twenty-four days to New Hampshire compared to Muskie's thirteen—provided Grandmaison with a vital asset. As Hart related, McGovern was a tireless trooper in New Hampshire:

> Stopping in four, or as many as six, towns in a day, he mixed local radio appearances with handshaking tours of main streets and shopping centers, house parties, speeches at schools and on campuses, receptions and press conferences. Most important were his visits to plants and factories. Many of the state's voting Democrats work in factories—shoes, textiles, electronics. So it was out early—5:30, 6, 6:30 A.M.—to the plant gate to shake hands with the morning shift. Cold, freezing, dark. "Hello, I'm George McGovern. I'm running for President and I'd like your help."[45]

In McGovern, Grandmaison had not only a more active candidate but a more freewheeling one as well. The cautious frontrunner, Muskie tried to minimize his risks in the New Hampshire contest. As the underdog, McGovern was much the bolder of the two candidates. He challenged Muskie to debate—but Muskie demurred. Trumpeting a new politics of openness and honesty, he made public his personal and campaign finances—but Muskie hesitated to follow suit. To the antiwar constituency McGovern was the more courageous voice. Exhibiting his integrity and decency, he made headway even among conservative Democrats, who appeared, *Newsweek* reported, "impressed with his straightforwardness."[46]

McGovern also had two advantages that were largely invisible at the time. Not all of his campaign in New Hampshire was a picturesque grassroots insurgency. Miles Rubin, a wealthy California entrepreneur who came to New Hampshire to evaluate the campaign, looked askance at the McGovernites' indifference to standard marketing techniques. Using his own money and funds from affluent associates, Rubin hired professional telephone operators and provided them with a script for an extensive phone-banking campaign on McGovern's behalf.[47] McGovern also received unwitting help. Convinced that Muskie was the strongest potential challenger to President Nixon, covert agents from the president's reelection campaign harassed him with a string of dirty tricks. One of these led to the most notorious episode of the New Hampshire primary: standing on a flatbed truck in front of the Manchester *Union-Leader* as snow swirled around him and denouncing its right-wing publisher, William Loeb, for defaming his wife, Muskie began to cry.[48] Political legend has often magnified this event and made it the overwhelming, or even sole, cause of Muskie's poor showing in the New Hampshire primary. In reality, it was only one factor among many in affecting the contest. Still, the same conventions about presidential toughness that disparaged McGovern later in the campaign condemned Muskie at this moment for daring to show a touch of human frailty.

Presidential primaries are usually evaluated not as elections, where what matters is who gets the most votes, but through the lens of expectations of how the rival candidates should perform. The final advantage that McGovern held over Muskie in New Hampshire was that his staff was cannier at the expectations game. An unnamed Muskie staffer was quoted in the press before Election Day as saying, "If Muskie doesn't get 50 percent, I'll shoot myself."[49] Meanwhile, Mankiewicz, an experienced media handler, carefully worked campaign reporters, insinuating the premise that a closer-than-expected second-place finish for McGovern would represent a stunning victory.[50]

Mankiewicz's spin set the tone when McGovern pulled 37 percent in New Hampshire to Muskie's 46 percent (other candidates drew the remainder of the votes). *Time* magazine was typical in depicting a "haggard and weary" Muskie whose disappointing showing "raised doubts as to whether he could sew up the Democratic nomination before the convention" while noting McGovern's unexpected drawing power in blue-collar as well as collegiate precincts.[51] Muskie was starting to be framed in the media's narrative as a fading star, while McGovern enjoyed a boost to both campaign morale and attention from the press. Had Muskie met expectations in New Hampshire, the conventional wisdom about his inevitability and McGovern's fecklessness would have been validated, and the insurgency likely would have withered. Instead, the McGovernites' strategy racked up its first landmark success.

On to Wisconsin

As crucial to an insurgency as the battles it enters are the battles it evades. In the early going, the McGovernites' most astute tactical evasion was the Florida primary, which took place a week after the New Hampshire primary. Among the high command of the McGovern campaign, there had been considerable debate over the previous winter about devoting resources to Florida. If Muskie scored as well as the pundits predicted in New Hampshire, McGovern would need to score well in an early primary like Florida's if he hoped to survive until Wisconsin. Hart and the grassroots organizers wanted to stick with the original strategy, which gave priority to running the risk in New Hampshire and would not divert resources from Wisconsin. On the other side, Mankiewicz believed that "Florida can be had."[52] Perhaps the most telling voice in the debate ultimately belonged to Van Dyk, who was dispatched on a scouting trip to Florida. Even before his departure, he warned that "we're headed for disaster in Florida." Not only was McGovern weak in the polls for what would be a multicandidate race in Florida; more important, Van Dyk observed, the state did not offer him any natural political base.[53]

The McGovern campaign thus made only a modest effort in the Florida primary. As Van Dyk had anticipated, McGovern did poorly, attracting only 6 percent of the vote. Hardly anyone noticed, however, because attention was fixed on the candidates who had concentrated their resources on Florida. Centering his campaign on fierce opposition to busing, George Wallace won by a landslide, taking 42 percent of the votes. Whereas Wallace dominated among white voters, Hubert Humphrey capitalized on his appeal in the black community to launch yet another of his campaigns for the presidency with a respectable 18 percent. Wallace as the big winner in Florida shared press attention with the big losers, Edmund Muskie and John Lindsay. Muskie's weak 9 percent, coming a week after his disappointing showing in New Hampshire, made clear that his frontrunner strategy had collapsed. Lindsay, relying on a massive media campaign and telegenic looks, limped in at 7 percent, removing the threat to McGovern of a serious rival for the support of the Democratic left. Apart from Humphrey's limited success, the Florida primary, by undermining two of his competitors, made its own contribution to the left-center strategy of the McGovern campaign.[54]

There was one more primary left before Wisconsin. The contest in Illinois was merely a fruitless side trip for McGovern, but it proved to be fatal for the holdover fantasies of a predecessor. The McGovern campaign filed some delegate slates in the downstate region, but it avoided the separate preferential primary contest, which did not bind any Illinois delegate. Its efforts were ineffectual, but once more the press was focused elsewhere.[55] A wounded Muskie faced off in the Illinois preferential contest against a lonely Eugene McCarthy, who had chosen the state for his bid to revisit the glories of 1968. The erratic and aloof McCarthy had lost almost all of his former strategists and organizers by 1972 to either McGovern or Muskie. Despite his heavy spending in the state, he polled only 37 percent to Muskie's 63 percent, and the antiwar constituency was now even more McGovern's possession. Trouncing yesterday's insurgent, although Muskie's biggest victory of the primary season, could not revive his drooping prospects either.[56]

Wisconsin had always been at the heart of the McGovern insurgency's primary strategy, and there was no debate within the staff about concentrating the campaign's limited resources on its April 4 contest. The state had a proud tradition as a bastion of progressivism, making it a more hospitable political milieu for McGovern's message than New Hampshire had been. In the University of Wisconsin it had a campus population rich in votes and volunteers for McGovern. And his strategists knew that in the eyes of the press the Wisconsin primary possessed a historic importance nearly equal to that of the New Hampshire primary: in 1960, Wisconsin had established John F. Kennedy's drawing power over Hubert Humphrey, while in 1968 the possibility of an embarrassing loss to Eugene McCarthy in the state had prompted Lyndon Johnson to abandon his quest for reelection. A win in Wisconsin—or even a close second—would erase the question mark after McGovern's name and establish him in the front ranks of aspirants for the Democratic nomination.

As with New Hampshire, the McGovernites dispatched one of their finest organizers to the state far ahead of any rival campaign. Eugene Pokorny, a Nebraskan who had been a field operative for McCarthy in 1968, arrived in Wisconsin in November 1970 armed only with a list of fifty names culled from the ranks of progressive activists. Paid just $200 a month, and taking up free residence in the home of a McGovern enthusiast (Milwaukee attorney Bill Dixon), Pokorny provided the McGovern insurgency with services that the other campaigns, spending large sums at the campaign's endgame, could not come close to matching. Crisscrossing the state for nearly a year and a half, Pokorny planted McGovern committees everywhere, opening thirty-nine local campaign headquarters and compiling a list that eventually reached 10,000 prospective volunteers. He was as imaginative as he was indefatigable. Realizing that primary day was scheduled during the University of Wisconsin's spring break, he placed forms in the campus newspaper that made it easy for students to obtain absentee ballots. McGovern received an estimated 70 percent of the student vote.[57]

Perhaps Pokorny's most important tactical move—one characteristic of McGovern field operatives—was to turn unpaid volunteers into small-scale organizers. Gary Hart described a mailing sent out by Pokorny to the massive list of McGovern supporters a month before the primary date:

Each was asked to donate to the campaign two hours a week for the last four primary weeks. The first week, raise one dollar from each of ten friends and send the ten dollars to the state headquarters; the second, put McGovern bumper strips on the cars of ten friends; the third, find ten new McGovern voters in their neighborhood; the final, primary week, get those ten new

McGovern voters to the polls. Thus, every McGovern supporter in the state was given meaningful assignments for the crucial last four weeks.[58]

McGovern's support in Wisconsin was not limited to liberal activists or college students. Targeting Wisconsin, as he had New Hampshire, in his campaign schedule, he made frequent trips to the state throughout 1971 and the early months of 1972. McGovern tapped into a rich vein of economic discontent that his rivals would also seek to mine, sharply attacking the high property taxes and rate of inflation that were feeding a mood of alienation and anger among Wisconsin voters. Not neglecting the hotbed of antiwar sentiment, the campuses, he was as often to be found stopping in at bowling alleys and greeting their blue-collar clientele.[59] Wisconsin was a high point for the populist McGovern, and his economic message resonated even among a constituency assumed to belong to Muskie: Polish-American voters in the blue-collar neighborhoods of Milwaukee. Carl Wagner recalls a Polish housewife in Milwaukee who organized two hundred women for him. These women, who had never been active in politics before, wrote personal letters praising McGovern and mailed them "to all of their Christmas card lists."[60]

As the date of the primary approached, the twelve-candidate race turned frenetic. McGovern was now no longer the only one spending exhaustingly long days on the campaign trail in Wisconsin. George Wallace had originally planned only a brief foray into Wisconsin, but he evoked such a wild response from a speech in Milwaukee's civic auditorium that he stayed on, thundering his right-wing brand of populism to eleven rallies over the next eight days.[61] Hubert Humphrey, planning to seize the centrist mantle from the faltering Ed Muskie in a state next door to Minnesota, was his usual blur of campaign activity even as he submitted to a makeover of his fusty pre-sixties persona. As *Time* magazine recounted, "With mod glasses and carefully darkened hair, 61-year-old Humphrey bounced through 19-hour days."[62] While McGovern, Wallace, and Humphrey surged forward, Muskie continued to insist that he was the most electable candidate for the ultimate conflict against Nixon.[63] But few Wisconsin Democratic voters were listening, and he was reduced at the end to the look of a sad also-ran. In the words of the same *Time* article, "Muskie failed to come across clearly on any topic. His organization, top-heavy with endorsements and contributors, never took root at the local levels where primaries are won. He failed to define a constituency."[64]

Election Day brought a clear-cut victory for McGovern. He captured 30 percent of the primary vote in Wisconsin, beating out Wallace with an unexpected 22 percent, Humphrey with a mildly disappointing 21 percent, Muskie with a disastrous 10 percent, Jackson with a hopeless 8 percent, and Lindsay with a 7 percent total that he wisely took to be the coup de grace to his campaign. McGovern's win was all the more impressive for its breadth: he took seven of the state's nine congressional districts and ran well among suburbanites, urban workers, farmers, and youth alike. Only among black voters was McGovern's showing weak and Humphrey's strong.[65] On election night, McGovern told his celebrating troops that Wisconsin represented "the first giant step toward victory in Miami Beach in July . . . and, we hope, toward the inauguration of a people's president in January."[66] As his strategists examined the redrawn contours of the race for the nomination, it was apparent that Muskie was finished and that Wallace would take primary votes away from other candidates on the right. Humphrey had emerged in Florida and Wisconsin as the main stumbling block to a McGovern triumph, but it was hard for McGovernites to imagine, in the flush of victory in Wisconsin, that Democrats would select a representative of their tarnished past over the idealistic New Politics of their man.

In retrospect, the Wisconsin primary was an early zenith for McGovernite hopes. "These may have been the happiest days of the campaign," Gordon Weil remembered, "because we were still the fighting underdog, but the smell of victory was in the air."[67] But with McGovern's first victory came the first round of skepticism about his candidacy as less solid than the vote totals implied. The critique of his Wisconsin success focused chiefly on the crossover vote that the state's election laws allowed. McGovern had drawn a sizeable number of Republican voters, second only to Wallace, in a primary election where there was no significant contest on the GOP side. Rather than suggesting some scrambling of ideological categories, the skeptics used McGovern's crossover vote to argue that he was less popular among Democrats than he appeared.[68]

These were only small rumblings of the onslaught to come. They were amplified in a widely cited column by Rowland Evans and Robert Novak sounding the warning that McGovern would prove to be the "Barry Goldwater of the left."[69] In a staff memo, "Thoughts after Wisconsin," Weil indicated that his feeling of unalloyed joy from McGovern's victory had been fleeting: "The Evans and Novak column . . . is a source of real concern because it is supposed to represent the line that the Humphrey forces are pushing . . . The allegations of the Evans and Novak piece are the kinds of charges that truly are divisive and give potentially effective ammunition to the Republicans."[70] After Wisconsin, McGovern's support continued to build—but so did the hostility of opponents within his own party.

Signs of War

There was a three-week gap in April between the Wisconsin primary and the next two primaries: Massachusetts and Pennsylvania. Muskie was still in the race, but his electoral standing was in free fall. Wallace continued to draw votes in the North as well as the South, but no one viewed him as a potential nominee of the Democratic Party. Pundits continued to speculate about Ted Kennedy's availability, especially in the event of a deadlocked convention, but his refusal to run remained unshakeable. The real war for the nomination, it was increasingly apparent, was going to be waged between two old friends: George McGovern and Hubert Humphrey.

Massachusetts demonstrated in April why it would be McGovern's best state—indeed his only state—in November. Like New Hampshire, the pundits and early polls foresaw a runaway victory for Muskie in Massachusetts. After Wisconsin, however, the relative standing of Muskie and McGovern was reversed, and McGovern cruised to a crushing victory in the Bay State. Through numerous television appearances on Boston stations beamed at the primary electorate in New Hampshire and through the mobilization of Boston-area students to travel north, McGovern had previously established a strong liberal base in Massachusetts. Campaigning after the Wisconsin primary, he was free to concentrate on blue-collar and ethnic communities in the eastern part of the state, where the warm reception he received resembled his successes with these constituencies in earlier contests. An added attraction for the Massachusetts primary was Kennedy support. Although Senator Edward Kennedy maintained a scrupulous silence (but was known to be sympathetic to McGovern), Robert Kennedy's eldest children, Joe and Kathleen, accompanied McGovern in his Boston campaigning. On April 25, McGovern scored perhaps his most impressive primary win, beating Muskie 52 percent to 22 percent.[71]

Muskie was not the only establishment politician that McGovern clobbered in Massachusetts. The senator from Maine had lined up most of the Bay State's Democratic elite not only for endorsements but as his delegates in primary contests. In his corner were such local notables as the State Senate president, Kevin Harrington; the House Democratic whip, Tip O'Neill; and the mayor of Boston, Kevin White. All were handily beaten by little-known McGovernites; White could not even carry his home precinct. A few days before the primary, with the scale of his victory already showing up in late polling, McGovern met secretly with the mayor in his office to mend fences. White was friendly—so much so that he nearly became McGovern's choice for a running mate at the convention. As McGovern nailed down the left, he was beginning to turn toward the center and to find a place for party regulars in his insurgency. The Cedar Point strategy was effectively implemented in Massachusetts. It would prove much harder to pull off after later primaries.[72]

April 25, 1972, was a banner day for Hubert Humphrey as well. Skipping Massachusetts, Humphrey concentrated on defeating Muskie in Pennsylvania. Muskie had the backing of the party leadership in the state, but Humphrey had the muscle of his old allies in the AFL-CIO leadership behind him. The McGovern campaign made a limited effort in Pennsylvania, seeking some convention delegates in bastions of liberalism, and the Wallace campaign also gave the state token attention. Both nonetheless ran slightly ahead of the vanishing Muskie, while Humphrey easily garnered his first primary victory in a career of presidential campaigning dating back to 1960. Twin blowouts in Massachusetts and Pennsylvania hastened Muskie's exit from the race. Instead of withdrawing altogether, however, he announced that he was "suspending" his campaign, thereby holding on to his delegates and keeping alive the slim possibility that a stalemated convention would bow to the same centrist logic that had governed his misshaped campaign from the outset.[73]

The race turned uglier in Ohio, whose primary was held on May 2. Originally the McGovern strategy had been to make a modest effort in Ohio; the state had less of a liberal base than Wisconsin, and its Democratic politicians and labor chieftains would mobilize for either Muskie or Humphrey. But the Wisconsin win gave McGovern momentum and Patrick Caddell's polls for him showed an opening in Ohio, so three and a half weeks before its primary, Hart and Mankiewicz committed to a blitz of the state. Neither liberal nor conservative luminaries in Ohio gave McGovern their blessing, and the best endorsements McGovern could obtain were from local leaders like Cincinnati's Jerry Springer. Nor was there a McGovern operation in place on the ground comparable to New Hampshire, Wisconsin, or Massachusetts. But the McGovern insurgency was by now battle-tested, and it hurriedly poured experienced field operatives into the state, led by such crack organizers as Harold Himmelman, Dick Sklar, and Carl Wagner. Money, carefully hoarded for critical contests, was also made available for Ohio, financing radio and television spots devised by McGovern's media expert, Charles Guggenheim.[74]

What had looked like an easy Humphrey victory in Ohio now turned into a dogfight, with the momentum clearly favoring McGovern. The Ohio primary produced an impressive demonstration of McGovern's broad support in his party at this stage. As Haynes Johnson wrote in the *Washington Post* on the day after the election, McGovern "cut into the blue-collar vote, the labor union vote, the potential George Wallace vote, and the small town and rural vote. And perhaps most important of all, McGovern captured half of all voters who said they were planning to vote for Muskie earlier this year."[75] Yet a show of strength was not really what the McGovernites wanted for Ohio. They wanted an upset victory—but in the final tally Humphrey won the state, 41 percent to McGovern's 39 percent.

On election night—and to this day—McGovernites believed that *they* had won Ohio. In a primary marked by ballot place irregularities throughout the state, the election hinged on the vote in the Twenty-first Congressional District in Cleveland, the stronghold of black Congressman Louis Stokes. Results from the Twenty-first came in more slowly than elsewhere, and when they did appear they left the McGovern staff astonished and incensed. Precinct after precinct, as Gary Hart wrote, showed Humphrey leading McGovern by unbelievable margins like "110 to 2, 98 to 1, 116 to 4."[76] Ohio, recalls Harold Himmelman, the head McGovern organizer for the state, was "a fabulous success—except for Cleveland and

Mr. Stokes and Mr. Humphrey, who without a question robbed us of our vote."[77] The tainted results in Ohio produced the first major "what if" of the McGovern insurgency. As Hunter Thompson, who spent primary night with the McGovern campaign leadership, put it in his caustic style, "If McGovern had been able to win Ohio with his last-minute, half-organized blitz it would have snapped the psychic spine of the Humphrey campaign . . . because Hubert had been formidably strong in Ohio, squatting tall in the pocket behind his now-familiar screen of Organized Labor and Old Blacks."[78] A McGovern upset in Ohio might have turned his battle with Humphrey into a rout, inducing many Democratic regulars to make their peace with him rather than continuing to fight him, with mounting resentment, all the way to Miami Beach.

The apparent election fraud in Cleveland was only one sign that the contest with Humphrey was growing nastier. The Ohio primary was also the birthplace of attacks on McGovern by his Democratic rivals as a dangerous radical. Humphrey began to call attention to the questionable company that McGovern kept, informing audiences that the sober senator from South Dakota was attracting support from anarchistic Yippie pranksters Abbie Hoffman and Jerry Rubin.[79] Even more disturbed by the insurgent's rise than was Humphrey, Scoop Jackson, in his swan song for the primary season, lashed into McGovern as a left-wing "extremist" who was indifferent to America's defense and its traditional moral values alike. Jackson echoed the Evans and Novak line that McGovern was the Democrats' Goldwater.[80] Ohio raised the stakes and heightened the emotions on both sides, making future confrontations between McGovern and Humphrey, particularly in California, all the more destructive.

Press coverage focused on winners and losers in the big primaries like Ohio's, but the nomination in Miami would come down to a count of delegates. In the nonprimary states, twenty-eight in all, which picked delegates in caucuses or conventions, the McGovern grassroots operation, attracting notice from only a handful of reporters, outstripped that of Humphrey or any other candidate. Rick Stearns, the strategic genius behind the McGovern nomination campaign, was in charge of the delegate hunt for the nonprimary states, and he understood that with superior organization, enthusiasm, and knowledge of the new reform rules, the McGovern campaign could seize an advantage in most of these states. Stearns and his regional coordinators, working with local McGovern activists, masterfully mobilized their people for the caucuses. Their activities were unconcealed, but they went about the work quietly so as not to disturb the torpor of established party elites. In these sparsely attended arenas for selecting delegates, McGovernites were generally more numerous and prepared than any rivals.[81]

Stearns points out that McGovern's well-publicized primary victories greatly facilitated his field operation in the nonprimary contests. Nonetheless, states such as Kansas, Montana, and Oklahoma—hardly McGovern country—produced many more delegates for him than could be explained by his popular appeal among their electorates.[82] One of the few journalistic accounts of a local caucus captured the ability of Stearns and his grassroots troops to steal a march on their opponents:

> There were no network television cameras watching, no pack of national reporters scribbling their notes, when chairwoman Gay Davis called to order the Democratic Party caucus of Idaho's Fourteenth Legislative District one evening in the ballroom of the Boise Hotel. "As your name is called," Mrs. Davis asked the crowd of a little more than 100, "will you please stand and announce your Presidential preference." Idaho's popular Gov. Cecil Andrus, who had endorsed Edmund Muskie early and once seemed to have carried the state solidly into his camp, smiled wanly from a back-row seat. The first three votes were for Muskie, the next three for George McGovern—and the rest was a walkaway. The final tally: McGovern 64, Muskie 33, Hubert Humphrey 6, George Wallace 2.[83]

Considering how narrow was the majority McGovern brought to Miami Beach, Stearns's little-publicized success in the nonprimary states was as indispensable to the insurgency as the dramatic outcomes in New Hampshire, Wisconsin, Massachusetts, and California.

High Noon in California

After Ohio, it was clear to all that the California primary, scheduled for June 6, would be the decisive showdown between McGovern and Humphrey. But the two tangled in Nebraska a week after the disputed Ohio primary in an ominous preview of the coming confrontation. In Nebraska the erstwhile dark horse, accustomed to the freewheeling stance of the insurgent, was thrown onto the defensive for the first time. McGovern was now under ferocious fire, and it would not let up until November.

Nebraska had always been part of the McGovernites' strategy for the primaries. Gene Pokorny had returned to his home state after the Wisconsin contest and established another first-class grassroots organization. Now it was the Humphrey campaign that decided on a last-minute blitz and rushed resources into the state. Humphrey did not have grassroots organizers to match McGovern's, but he did have his own fevered campaigning, his labor union network, and, most important, a plan for a campaign of attacks. Borrowing from the disparaging caricatures of McGovern advanced by Scoop Jackson and by hostile columnists, the Humphrey campaign sought to paint McGovern as far too radical for conservative Nebraskans. The most damaging piece of campaign literature was an ad placed in the Catholic newspaper of Omaha, where 30 percent of the state's

Democrats resided. Quoting from attacks on McGovern by Evans and Novak and by Joseph Kraft, it alleged that McGovern advocated legalization of abortion and marijuana, pledged immediate amnesty for draft evaders, and opposed any federal aid to parochial schools.[84]

Expected to win in Nebraska before Humphrey's late entry into the race, McGovern had to switch to a defensive posture to counter such allegations and pull out a victory. He and his aides played defense effectively in Nebraska—better, it turned out, than they would in California. Filmmaker Charles Guggenheim hastily taped a thirty-minute discussion between McGovern and eight Nebraska citizens, one of them a Catholic nun, on the weekend before the voting. Broadcast in the campaign's final hours, the film allowed McGovern to state his actual positions—for example, that abortion was a matter for the states and not the federal government—and to condemn the slurs against him. McGovern also enlisted Nebraska's popular former governor, Frank Morrison, to vouch for the fact that the South Dakota senator was no radical.[85] In his autobiography, McGovern amusedly recalled that Morrison elicited applause from the insurgent's young supporters when he noted that McGovern was allegedly in favor of legalized abortion and pot—but silence when he refuted the false charges.[86]

McGovern held off the Humphrey offensive and won the Nebraska primary 41 percent to 35 percent. Gary Hart told the press that the victory "laid to rest the potential tactic and political future of misrepresentations by political opposition."[87] Drawing this lesson from the returns in Nebraska was, however, premature, as the McGovernites learned in California. The Omaha Catholic vote, the prime target of the attack ad, had broken sharply for Humphrey. With his vastly superior field organization, McGovern barely carried the state, rescued by the rural vote and the liberal vote from Lincoln, home of the state university.[88] Nebraska's outcome was ambiguous: it sent the McGovernites into California with continuing momentum, but it also demonstrated that there was a receptive audience for the construction of George McGovern the radical.

Following Nebraska, the McGovern campaign was fully focused on the winner-take-all contest in California, with 271 delegates at stake. It had begun its buildup in the state even earlier, prepositioning resources on the ground in early April for the huge battle to come.[89] Michigan and Maryland held primaries on May 16, the week after Nebraska, but McGovern made only a brief expedition into the first, where busing was the hot issue, and undertook almost no effort in the second, essentially conceding both states to George Wallace. It was the day before the Maryland primary that the deranged Arthur Bremer shot and crippled Wallace at his campaign rally in Laurel. Stunning all of the candidates, as a reminder of the assassinations of the 1960s, the Wallace shooting still produced only a brief pause in the spiraling hostilities on the Democratic side. Its most important effect in 1972 was to help the candidate who was watching—and pulling secret strings—in the White House.

As the battle for California shaped up, there was an ironic reversal of roles between the candidates. McGovern, the improbable insurgent of January, was the Democratic frontrunner by May and owned more valuable campaign assets. Humphrey, the pillar of the party establishment, appeared to be the outmatched underdog, a pathetic figure to his detractors and a poignant one to his admirers. McGovern's advantages began with money. Never really grasping how much the campaign game had been transformed from 1968 to 1972, the Humphrey high command spent almost all of its money in earlier primaries and had little left in its treasury for California.[90] Dependent on large contributors, who had already been tapped, Humphrey's forces had no capacity to mobilize the kind of legion of small donors that was sending money to McGovern in response to his brilliant direct-mail operation. In California, the McGovernites were also funded by a celebrity concert organized by Warren Beatty and by a network of wealthy antiwar liberals pieced together by Miles Rubin. Rubin estimates that the McGovern campaign had over $2 million to spend in the state, about four times as much as what the beleaguered Humphrey camp could raise.[91] In paying for expensive media advertising, traditionally the *sine qua non* for winning California, the McGovernites were far ahead.

Amply funded for the first time, the McGovernites brought a new dimension to their trademark grassroots operation. The McGovern army poured almost all of its forces into California to face an opponent who had no field operation to speak of. All of the best McGovern organizers headed west, along with hordes of volunteers, and there were plenty of indigenous activists to join with them. In a state so vast that it had always been assumed that a grassroots campaign was impossible, the McGovernites set out to establish personal contact with every California Democrat. They came close: with over 200 local headquarters in full operation, Eli Segal (the coordinator for California) and Sandy Berger (his deputy) reported after the election that 90 percent of Democratic households in the state had been canvassed and left with McGovern literature.[92]

What made the grassroots campaign different in California than in earlier primaries was not its scale, however, so much as its combination with sophisticated technology. If the index card was the primitive technology of low-income insurgents in New Hampshire or Wisconsin, the computer, a brand-new device for political uses, was the advanced technology of the well-heeled McGovern campaign in California. Miles Rubin was once again the key figure in injecting business techniques into a guerrilla uprising. Working with a number of associates, Rubin used computers to organize scattered county registration data and print out canvassing forms for the volunteers in the field. Canvassers had to ship filled-out forms back to a central headquarters, where they were run through the computers to generate letters to undecided voters and further canvassing sheets for turning out McGovern supporters on primary day.[93] Many McGovern organizers were unhappy about the centralized computer system, complaining that it undercut the autonomy and creativity that had been hallmarks of the field operation in the past.[94] But the central staff defended the computer program. As Segal and Berger put it, "Given the short period of time we had, we could not have achieved the degree of canvass ultimately undertaken without some data processing capabilities."[95]

The McGovern campaign also supplemented its canvassers in the field with an expensive professional calling system, communicating with notoriously mobile California voters by phone as well as by foot. According to Rubin, a paid staff of about 1,500 phone operators contacted Democrats on behalf of McGovern. Already concerned that the computer system would convey an image of professional slickness at odds with the prevailing picture of a gritty McGovernite populism, the campaign showed the press the much smaller volunteer phone-bank operation instead.[96] This bit of image management reflected one of many paradoxes besetting a successful insurgency.

In addition to money, technology, and the biggest grassroots army ever seen in California politics, McGovern had the advantage over Humphrey in key endorsements—albeit not the kind that had proven so useless to Muskie in the early races. Badly trailing Humphrey in minority support in previous primaries, McGovern scored endorsements and campaign help from Coretta Scott King and Cesar Chavez in the weeks before the California election.[97] Another valuable endorsement came from a galaxy of Hollywood stars that worked Beatty's Los Angeles fundraiser and later hit the campaign trail for McGovern. In a state whose residents liked to think of themselves as the nation's cultural vanguard, McGovern was now anointed with glamour by association, while Humphrey seemed the epitome of squareness.[98]

Humphrey might have been swamped by this McGovern tide. Yet he had some serious assets of his own. One was his own fierce drive to be president, which had hardly flagged since the 1940s. He was the oldest major candidate in the Democratic field, but no one could outrace HHH in personal campaigning. Another was his long-established base, which reeked of the old politics to McGovern's insurgents but was underestimated only at their risk. Organized labor, older blacks, Jews (especially of moderate income), and senior citizens were Humphrey's people, and he gravitated to their meetings rather than trying to emulate the mass rallies where McGovern fired up his largely youthful troops. Most of all, Humphrey, by all accounts a kindly person, had the recklessness of an aging politico fearing his last hurrah. His campaign in California would not partake of his famed—and much mocked—"politics of happiness": it would be a slashing attack all the way.[99]

Humphrey badmouthed McGovern up and down the state of California. To his supporters, he was simply pointing out the flaws in McGovern's ill-conceived and radical nostrums, which would be ventilated soon enough should McGovern survive to face President Nixon. But to McGovern supporters—and to many reporters—the Humphrey campaign in California used distorted arguments in a desperate attempt to sow fear. Humphrey warned aerospace workers in Southern California that McGovern's proposed cuts in the defense budget would jeopardize the nation's security and their jobs alike. He claimed before Jewish voters that those same defense cuts would leave Israel defenseless. To middle-income and working-class voters, he predicted that McGovern's demogrant proposal for income maintenance would raise their taxes while swelling the ranks of welfare recipients.[100] All of these criticisms of McGovern—and more—were slammed home by Humphrey in the first of their three California debates, televised nationally. (A full-blown treatment of the McGovern-Humphrey debate, one of the watershed events of the 1972 presidential campaign, appears in Chapter 8.)

As the frontrunner at last, with visions of unifying his party after California, McGovern tried to stay positive. His approach seemed to be succeeding, and Humphrey's failing, when the respected Field Poll of California announced four days before the election that McGovern had surged to a stunning 46 percent to 26 percent lead. This poll result was probably the single most consequential of all of the hundreds of poll findings reported during the election year. The Humphrey camp denounced it as a gross error, and even the McGovern camp found it misleading, since its own polls, run by Patrick Caddell, indicated a McGovern lead closer to 15 points.[101] Regardless, the Field Poll, taken as reputable by journalists and voters alike, created the expectation of a McGovern blowout on Election Day. Some McGovernites grew overconfident, while the Humphrey campaign lashed itself even more furiously toward the finish line. A modest margin of victory in California would have represented a solid success for McGovern only weeks before. Now—and especially to those angry Old Guard Democrats desperate to block his nomination—it became a sign that he could still be stopped.

In the remaining days between the release of the Field Poll and the primary itself, top national reporters offered premature salutes to the anticipated McGovern landslide and bittersweet political obituaries for Humphrey.[102] Covering the journey of the "McGovern Victory Special" train from the Bay Area through the Central Valley to Los Angeles, Haynes Johnson wrote,

> And they all climbed aboard that train today: movie stars, jocks, beautiful people, old politicians, new politicians, erstwhile Kennedy and McCarthy followers, big pooh-bahs of the press and other assorted people on the make. They are all attracted by the sweet smell of success and the aura of a winner. For George McGovern and his once-improbable campaign, today's whistle-stop journey on this spring day in California is a far cry from the earlier political stumping in the snows of New Hampshire and Wisconsin. Then, McGovern staff workers were living in $5 rooms at the "Y" and worrying about surviving until the next in the long series of primaries. Now,

they are traveling first class and talking about the November election and the inauguration.

While they have been cruising the state in a chartered 737 jet, their opponent has been limping around California heading for what now appears to be a humiliating defeat Tuesday. The contrast between the McGovern and Humphrey campaigns could not be greater. Hubert Humphrey is running out of time, money, and opportunity. His campaign is in disarray. His crowds are smaller, his press contingent half as large, and his travels marked by a series of misadventures. His very campaign is symbolized by the sputtering, smoking old DC-6 charter, with the third engine missing, that carries him from rally to rally.[103]

But as McGovernites took a victory lap in advance, their lead was slipping away. The Field Poll and subsequent media hoopla about a McGovern landslide appear to have depressed turnout among McGovern's strongest constituency, young voters. Meanwhile, the Humphrey campaign scraped together funds for a last-minute media barrage in Los Angeles, which, hitting on threatened job losses in California defense industries and military peril to Israel in the event of a McGovern presidency, moved some blue-collar and Jewish voters in its direction. McGovern was also hurt by an event outside California: meeting in Houston at the National Governors' Conference, Democratic state executives voiced their fears of a party debacle in November with McGovern atop the ticket. When he flew there on the day before the election to calm the storm, he lost valuable campaigning time in California, and its voters were reminded of his difficulties in reconciling regulars to his candidacy. Undecided Democrats broke toward Humphrey, the new underdog.[104]

Thus there was no McGovern blowout in California—just a five-point victory, 44 percent to 39 percent, with other candidates splitting the remaining votes. Northern California had remained securely in McGovern's corner. But Humphrey's barbs had stung in Southern California, where his 80,000 vote margin in Los Angeles County had pulled him closer statewide.[105]

Still, there was mostly good news for McGovern in analyses of the exit polls, which showed that in California he had put together his broadest coalition yet, an important prerequisite for a fall contest with Nixon. Holding on to his previous support from liberals, women, and young people, he had pulled even with Humphrey among black and working-class voters. In affluent suburbs, however, McGovern had lost his prior edge. And he still lagged behind Humphrey among seniors and Jews—although in a projected fight with Nixon he could be expected to do better with these constituencies by paying obeisance to the New Deal and pledging allegiance to the cause of Israel.[106]

At the same time, national polls began to contain some ominous signs for McGovern. While he was coming under fire for his alleged radicalism, starting in Ohio, intensifying in Nebraska, and reaching a peak in California, Nixon was playing the statesman's role to the hilt at the Moscow Summit and signing the SALT I treaty. Even as McGovern drew nearer to the chance to compete with Nixon, the president began to leap ahead in the poll match-ups. Ten points behind Nixon in the head-to-head Gallup Poll at the time of the Ohio primary, McGovern fell nineteen points behind according to Gallup by the time of his California debate with Humphrey.[107] In the Harris Poll for roughly the same period, McGovern dropped from seven points down to sixteen points behind Nixon.[108] As Jeb Magruder observed two months after the election, the Nixon campaign's private surveys suggested that the California primary was "probably the most critical point in the campaign." Once voters nationwide were exposed by Humphrey's attacks in California to the view of McGovern as "a candidate of a relatively extreme left position"—the correct view from the perspective of the Nixon campaign—McGovern's standing in the polls "went downhill from that day on and never recovered."[109]

June 6, 1972, might have been one of the most triumphant moments in the story of the McGovern insurgency. Not only did it capture California's winner-take-all primary, but it also scored victories in the other three primary contests held that day in New Jersey, New Mexico, and South Dakota. McGovern pulled away from the pack in the delegate count, and his original competitors, trailing far behind, were each tarnished by major primary defeats. Yet the California primary victory was not the decisive blow that guaranteed McGovern the Democratic presidential nomination. Warning McGovern's campaign leadership in mid-May that they needed a sizeable win in California to silence their critics, Fred Dutton predicted that "the satraps of the party will try to stall and finally put him off if he does not come to the convention with a very big head of steam."[110] As the illusory landslide that would have overwhelmed the Democratic regulars failed to form, they were spurred on by McGovern's most embittered foes to mount a last-ditch resistance. The diehards would battle him into the Democratic convention in Miami Beach, as party insurgency turned to partisan fratricide.

Conclusion

Once McGovern was defined as a dangerous radical by his foes, there were few bounds to the charges that were leveled against him. One of the strangest, coming ten days after the California primary, is worth mentioning not because the charge stuck but as a precursor to a far more potent defamation of character thirty-two years later. William Loeb's right-wing newspaper in Manchester, New Hampshire, ran a story alleging, on the basis of information from the John Birch Society and "intelligence sources," that McGovern had been a coward in World War II. The story claimed that as a bomber pilot in the European theater,

McGovern had refused to fly his mandatory final mission, been relieved of his command, and was issued an official letter of reprimand. The McGovern campaign quickly jumped all over the story. Three of McGovern's crew aboard the "Dakota Queen" informed the press that the story was an outrageous lie and described McGovern's perilous last flight in detail. McGovern swiftly obtained his records from the Defense Department, proving that he had flown all of his required missions and had never been reprimanded.[111]

Attacks on McGovern were to be expected, but their character and ferocity suggested a flaw in his campaign's original strategy. Gathering at Cedar Point, the small nucleus of what became an enormous McGovern insurgency crafted a left-center approach that took the long-shot candidate to the 1972 Democratic nomination for president. In the broadened coalition of his California primary showing, there were signs that he had made inroads in the center even as he retained the loyalty of the Democratic left. But California—and the national reaction to its exposure of McGovern's supposed radicalism—also suggested that something was happening that had not been envisioned at Cedar Point: having successfully "co-opted" the left wing of the Democratic Party for the primaries, McGovern was now identified with it—or worse, with caricatures that associated him with American radicalism's wildest and most threatening extremes.

The left-center strategy presumed that ideology and identity were fluid, that they could be readjusted for McGovern over the course of the campaign as the composition of the electorate changed. But positions taken and statements issued to attract constituencies on the Democratic left could not be relegated to the past once the nomination was secured. McGovern's foes culled out from his primary campaign—indeed from his entire political career—the material that best served their frame of leftist "extremism." When McGovern sought to moderate some of his stances to appeal to centrists, his opponents insisted that the new ideology and identity were dodges, concealing the essential, radical McGovern. Or else they ignored the modifications altogether: President Nixon instructed his surrogate campaigners to pound on McGovern for his early rhetoric while acting as if he had never revised it.

The left-center strategy also presumed that it would be possible to oust the Democratic Old Guard from power and then welcome it back in to the McGovern campaign as helpmate. What it underestimated were the antipathies building among both insurgents and regulars as a result of their primary battles. Some McGovernites—especially liberal activists with memories of 1968, when Vice President Humphrey used his grip over the party machinery to claim the presidential nomination without running in a single primary—regarded the regulars as amoral power-mongers. But resentments of their adversaries cut even deeper among the regulars. McGovern was not perceived as an upstart like JFK in 1960, using glamour and his father's money to push aside establishment veterans. He was seen as something much more dangerous: a reformer marching at the head of a column of New Politics insurgents, intent on an upheaval that would totally transform the Democratic Party, sweeping its old leaders and power blocs into the dustbin of history.

There was a third and more subtle drawback to the left-center strategy, as Lanny Davis, a New Politics activist who worked for Muskie in preference to what he saw as a "purist" McGovern campaign, astutely noted: it fostered negative impressions not only of the candidate's ideology but of his character as well. Even apart from the Eagleton affair, Davis suggested, McGovern was bound to lose his image as a different and more truthful type of political leader once he came under pressure to undertake an ideological shift toward the center. By distancing himself from his original spot on the purist left and moving into the pragmatic middle on several issues, he opened himself to the charge that he was indecisive, inconsistent, or opportunistic. The most hidden cost in the left-center strategy, according to Davis's analysis, was the loss to McGovern's credibility.[112]

Five weeks remained between the primary in California and the opening of the Democratic convention in Miami Beach. Had the left-center strategy worked as planned, with the centrists in the party acknowledging McGovern's huge lead in delegates and grudgingly adjusting to the prospect of his nomination, the McGovernites would have had a breathing space in which to mend fences and make preparations for the fall campaign. Instead, they were stuck in a fight for their political lives.

4

A Downward Arc

Long after their crushing defeat at the hands of Richard Nixon, a number of Mc-
Governites can still run over the arc of the 1972 campaign in their minds and pick
out several "what ifs" that could have drawn the race tighter. What if Congressman Stokes and his Humphrey allies had not manipulated vote tallies in Cleveland, denying McGovern a dramatic upset that could have left the Humphrey
campaign reeling and unable to recover? What if gunfire from Arthur Bremer
had not eliminated George Wallace from the 1972 campaign? What if, as an unnamed McGovern staffer quoted in *Newsweek* put it, "the Field Poll had never
come out [in California]? Everybody would be saying whoopee. Now everybody
is saying 'what happened?'"[1]

The most painfully tantalizing near misses came in the immediate aftermath
of the California primary. According to Gary Hart's account, several days before
California Democrats voted, the Humphrey camp, fearing the result predicted
by the Field Poll, opened secret negotiations with the McGovern camp. The proposed deal: Humphrey would endorse McGovern after his defeat in California,
and in exchange the McGovern campaign would assume $250,000 in Humphrey
campaign debts. But after the primary, Humphrey, encouraged by his late rally
and egged on by influential backers who detested McGovern, announced that
he was staying in the race. A few days later, the McGovernites thought that they
had arranged a similar bargain with Ed Muskie. However, Muskie surprised
them—and reporters assembled at the National Press Club—by announcing
that he, too, was not ending his campaign. The withdrawal of either man, as
Newsweek reported in the case of Muskie, would have "put the nomination effectively on ice and preserve[d] some semblance of peace and good order in the
party."[2]

Instead of collapsing, opposition coalesced into a stop-McGovern movement, encompassing all of his Democratic rivals, from George Wallace to Shirley
Chisholm. The awkwardly shaped coalition had a rationale: McGovern, it claimed,
was really not that popular among Democrats, having won so many primaries
only because the multiple candidates in the center and on the right had split
the votes of the party's majority, and he would prove even less appealing to the
national electorate, dragging down the Democratic ticket from Congress to the
lowest-level candidates. The coalition also found a vehicle for its objective: a
challenge to California's winner-take-all result, which, if successful, would fore-

close a first-ballot victory for McGovern and impel the convention to search for a more acceptable nominee.

In the memory of McGovernites, this desperate resistance by all of their adversaries was responsible for what might be called "the lost month." Scott Lilly, one of the early McGovern staffers, argues that "if there had been a recognition that McGovern had won, and I think he had won by any standard of fairness," the campaign could have more effectively shown the nation the appealing McGovern, especially the war hero, during this period, but because of the stop-McGovern movement's California challenge, "we had no ability to think about anything other than how to nail down delegates and get out of the convention."[3] Frank Mankiewicz laments that "we were thrown for a loss by the challenge . . . It sucked up an enormous amount of intellectual energy."[4] Not surprisingly, the memory of "the lost month" is most poignant for McGovern himself:

> That California challenge . . . sent all of us into the convention thoroughly fatigued. We should have had a month after winning the four big primaries the first Tuesday in June to concentrate ourselves on getting ready for the convention. I couldn't believe that the other candidates would do that to us . . . If we had had that month of leisurely time, and the positive press we should have had during that period, and the time to think about the vice-presidential selection, a lot of these later problems might have been avoided.[5]

Having to battle the stop-McGovern forces all the way to Miami Beach, McGovern and his supporters believe, cost his campaign heavily. In their view, it was not possible during "the lost month" to effect reconciliation with party regulars, since they were still trying to sink McGovern's candidacy. Time and energy were lacking to elaborate a comprehensive and detailed plan for the fall campaign against President Nixon. Key personnel, assigned to line up delegates or combat the challenge, could not be diverted to a careful consideration of potential running mates. And the sheer physical and mental toll could not be overestimated: after a marathon race for the nomination, going back for a core group to the Cedar Point gathering two years earlier, there could be no pause for rest and recuperation before the Democratic convention so long as the nomination still hung in the balance.

Some of the McGovernites' laments about "the lost month" smack of *post hoc* rationalizations for their mistakes at Miami Beach and afterward. Surely, one thinks, a number of high-level staffers could have been spared from the struggle with the anti-McGovern coalition for careful planning of the vice-presidential choice and the fall strategy. Nonetheless, the McGovernites have a point: many of the problems with their campaign after the California primary, attributed by critics to their amateurism and bungling, had their origins in "the lost month."

Warning of a McGovern disaster in November, the coalition that assembled to deny him the nomination helped to produce what it had predicted.

Bitter-Enders

The stop-McGovern cause was an amorphous movement, most of whose activities occurred behind the scenes and are difficult to trace decades later. Some press reports emphasized the role of southern Democrats, especially the influential Arkansas congressman Wilbur Mills, who, speculation had it, was angling for a vice-presidential slot on a ticket other than McGovern's.[6] In other versions of the story, the key organizers of the movement were the top political lieutenants of AFL-CIO president George Meany, Al Barkan and Robert Keefe.[7] Both southerners and organized labor appear to have been collaborating in constructing a network to prevent McGovern's nomination, although if one actor should be singled out as indispensable to the drive against McGovern, it was Al Barkan. The political principals kept their official distance from the movement, but the man who stood behind it—and could not hide his jubilation every time it achieved a success—was Hubert Humphrey.[8] Conventional wisdom at the time suggested that should McGovern fall short of a majority on the first two ballots at the convention, his support would slip and Humphrey would be the likely beneficiary.[9]

Denying that they were engaging in a power grab or carrying out a vendetta, leading figures associated with the stop-McGovern movement attempted to turn the moral tables on the McGovernite reformers. McGovern needed to be stopped, it was said, because his campaign was "elitist," disdainful of the views and values of rank-and-file Democrats. His young supporters were arrogant; as Ben Wattenberg, Scoop Jackson's top adviser, later put it, they "felt that they were smarter than the rest of America."[10] Even worse, the McGovernites were hypocrites. Arguing on the McGovern reform commission that party democracy required rejection of the old unit rule for convention delegations and its replacement with proportional representation based on vote percentages in each state, McGovern and his followers now were violating the spirit of reform and embracing winner-take-all for the California delegation because it worked to their advantage.[11]

But the moral high ground that the stop-McGovern forces claimed was shaky. McGovern had not supported winner-take-all for California while on the reform commission. Even so, the commission guidelines, while endorsing proportional representation, had not formally banned a winner-take-all system for 1972, and that system was enshrined in California law.[12] During the primary contest, no candidate had even hinted at the prospect of challenging winner-take-all once the results were in. Humphrey was on the record as accepting the existing rules in California: asked by Walter Cronkite in a televised interview two days before the California vote if he might challenge the outcome on the basis of reform commission principles, Humphrey answered, "I think that you might be able to if you wanted to be a spoilsport, but I'm not . . . I don't believe in that kind of politics."[13]

During the California contest, McGovern, hoping to unify a party that he expected to lead against President Nixon, refrained from sharp attacks against Humphrey. But as Humphrey continued to malign him as a radical and the California challenge gathered momentum, McGovern began to fire back in kind. Two weeks after the California vote, the final contest of the primary season gave McGovern a sweeping victory in New York, where the Humphrey campaign, starved for resources, had failed to file district delegate slates. McGovern used the occasion of this victory to decry Humphrey's tactics:

> It is sad to see a nationally-known figure like Hubert Humphrey
> undermining his reputation and jeopardizing his party by the kind of
> misleading statements he has been making about my positions. He knows
> that I am a reasonable man: yet he persists in twisting my positions to serve
> his own desperate purposes . . . I am afraid that my old friend has forgotten
> that there is such a thing as wanting too much to be elected.[14]

McGovern also lashed out during this period at the coalition of bitter-enders that had formed to block his nomination. In an interview with *Life* magazine conducted before, but published after, the Democratic Credentials Committee meeting in Washington that ruled on the California challenge, he issued a dark threat to the party's Old Guard:

> I think I have come to the point where I have earned the nomination. And
> if a bunch of old established politicians gang up to prevent me from getting
> the nomination because I didn't come to them for help—just a negative,
> spiteful movement that subverts the democratic process—if I feel that has
> happened, then I will not let them get away with it. There's been so much
> hard work and emotion poured into this campaign by so many thousands
> of people—it would be such an infuriating, disillusioning experience for
> them all—that I would repudiate the whole process. I would run as an
> independent or support somebody else on an independent ticket. So if I'm
> denied the nomination by an illegitimate power play, that nomination will
> not be worth anything to the person who gets it.[15]

Even some of his own aides believed that fiery warnings of a party bolt were an act of petulance on McGovern's part and would complicate even further the task of reconciling regulars to his candidacy.[16] Yet while his anger at the stop-McGovern movement was genuine, it was also a deliberate stance, designed to drive home to the regulars the price they would pay if they were to take the nomination away from him.[17] He was countering the stop-McGovern movement's prediction of a disaster in November with him atop the party ticket by warning of an even greater calamity for Democrats: should his two-year-long insurgency, having achieved its remarkable conquest, have its victory snatched away at the last moment by an underhanded trick, the resulting civil war at the convention would make Chicago in 1968 look like a mere rumble in the alley.

The McGovern staff thought that with their substantial lead in delegates they had built in comfortable majorities on the Credentials, Platform, and Rules committees meeting in Washington two weeks before the opening of the Miami Beach convention. However, when the Credentials Committee decided the California challenge on June 29, the vote was 72–66 to overturn winner-take-all and divide the state's representation proportionally, taking away 151 of McGovern's 271 California delegates and throwing his nomination into doubt. While the stop-McGovern forces had quietly been lining up every last vote for the California challenge, the McGovern forces had been uncharacteristically complacent, failing to notice that the ten McGovern members of the Credentials Committee from California would be barred from voting on a matter affecting their own legitimacy.[18] The McGovern camp was incensed, with their candidate calling the committee vote "an incredible, rotten, stinking political steal."[19]

By itself, the success of the California challenge on June 29 ratcheted up animosities between McGovernites and regulars to a whole new level. But its immediate impact was not yet complete. The next day, with the ten committee members from California voting and members from Illinois excluded, infuriated McGovernites retaliated. By a 71–61 margin, they voted to disqualify the delegation headed by Chicago mayor Richard Daley, which had won in the Illinois primary (and had supported the California challenge), on the grounds that it violated party guidelines prohibiting the slating of delegates in secret meetings and requiring full representation for minorities, women, and youth. In its place, the McGovernite majority on the Credentials Committee seated a rival delegation headed by Chicago alderman William Singer and black leader Jesse Jackson. McGovern and his top aides opposed the ejection of Daley and his forces, knowing that without the mayor's backing they would not have a prayer of carrying Illinois in November. But the McGovern army was not always disciplined, and the angry troops on the Credentials Committee were striking back on their own volition.[20]

Both the McGovern forces and the Daley forces raced to the courts. The U.S. Court of Appeals ruled for McGovern—but not for Daley—and restored the winner-take-all results for California. But the U.S. Supreme Court, taking the case on an emergency basis, stayed the circuit court order three days before the scheduled opening of the Democratic convention. A 6–3 majority ruled that it was inappropriate for the federal judiciary to intervene in the internal deliberations of a political party and that a decision on credentials challenges must be left to the final authority of the convention.[21] With no legal resolution, the bitter disputes over California and Illinois guaranteed that the party's gathering in Florida would begin with a bang.

The Credentials Committee was the cockpit of conflict in preconvention maneuvering, but a separate set of convention fights was brewing in the Platform Committee. The Platform Committee turned out to be the only place where the original left-center strategy of the McGovern campaign still survived. The McGovern high command put Ted Van Dyk, its most moderate member, in charge of McGovern's forces in drawing up the platform. Working comfortably with the director of the committee staff, Harvard professor Richard Neustadt, the nation's leading scholar on the presidency and a shrewd pragmatist, Van Dyk rode herd over the restless McGovern delegates to ensure, in his recollection, that "we didn't lose the campaign before we ever left Miami Beach." Taking control of the small group fashioning platform language, Van Dyk and his allies "resisted a lot of the wild impulses and got a fairly moderate draft out of the process." In the full Platform Committee, "one group after another just kept pouring into the breach, and we held them back as best we could."[22]

The centrist character of the Platform Committee product was evident in the fact that the only members it made unhappy were Wallace supporters and McGovern supporters. The Wallace camp was angry over the plank on busing. Rank-and-file McGovernites on the left, described in the press as "agitated" over the platform, had a more extensive list of complaints. They argued that many of McGovern's signature policies had been watered down by the vague language of the platform. And some were disappointed that the platform avoided taking positions on the most progressive cultural issues, abortion rights and gay rights.[23] Since only 10 percent of the full committee was required to bring a minority plank before the convention, disgruntled McGovern supporters, sympathetic to the feminist and gay causes, voted to take their issues to Miami Beach. So the McGovern leadership headed into the convention facing a credentials battle on its right and a platform battle on its left.

Credentials

On the eve of the Democratic convention, television viewers who tuned in to a special two-hour broadcast of *Meet the Press* were treated to a remarkable spectacle: four of the leading candidates for the presidential nomination warned that a fifth—the most likely nominee of the party—was going to lead Democrats straight into the ground. Senators Humphrey, Jackson, and Muskie, and Congresswoman Chisholm cast a potential McGovern nomination as a recipe for Democratic disaster in November. While McGovern sought to defend himself, his rivals assailed him with their four-sided fire. Scoop Jackson was the most ferocious in predicting a McGovern inferno: "Whenever three Democrats get to-gether . . . they are talking about losing the House and the Senate [with McGov-ern heading the ticket] . . . Wherever you get together with a group here at the convention, they're all scared to death."[24]

The rival camps girded for a life-or-death battle for the nomination in Miami Beach, but the outcome peculiarly hinged on arcane matters of rules and proce-dures. On July 9, the day before the opening session, representatives of the can-didates met with Democratic National Committee chair Lawrence O'Brien and convention parliamentarian James G. O'Hara, a congressman from Michigan, to argue about two critical questions. First was the definition of a majority: would a vote to overturn a prior ruling of the Credentials Committee require an absolute majority of convention delegates—1,509—or only a majority of those eligible to vote on a particular credentials challenge, with the challenged delegates ex-cluded? In the case of the California challenge, the latter definition would re-duce the number the McGovernites needed to get back the delegates stripped from them two weeks earlier from 1,509 to 1,433. Second was the eligibility of unchallenged members of a delegation to vote on credentials disputes involv-ing their own state. In the case of California, would McGovern's uncontested 120 delegates be allowed to vote to restore the convention seats of their 151 col-leagues?[25]

O'Brien and O'Hara sided with the McGovern camp on both questions. The arithmetic was stark—McGovernites would need only 1,433 votes to recapture their lost 151 California delegates, with their 120 uncontested delegates from Cal-ifornia contributing to their vote total—and meant the difference between a first-ballot victory or a likely loss on later ballots.[26] Representatives from the other camps were irate at the two decisions, with Humphrey's chief political adviser, Max Kampelman, charging that O'Brien and O'Hara had been "intimidated" by McGovern's threat to bolt the party.[27] In Kampelman's recollection, O'Brien took him aside and said, "Look, Max, if I rule for Humphrey, the McGovern people are going to walk out. If I rule for McGovern, the Humphrey people will not walk out."[28] Kampelman is probably correct that O'Brien was fearful of a fatal party split if adverse rulings blocked McGovern's nomination. Yet it is equally plausible that O'Brien and O'Hara were responding to the merits of the arguments, since the McGovern representatives had the more logical case.

Though frustrated by the parliamentary rulings, the stop-McGovern coalition was not about to surrender, and the field of battle now shifted to an even more arcane and confusing conflict. By the rules of the convention, credentials dis-putes were not taken up in alphabetical order, and a challenge to the makeup of the South Carolina delegation, on the grounds that it did not provide adequate representation for women as mandated in the new party rules, was to precede the vote on California. If the vote on the South Carolina challenge fell between the majority of eligible voters (1,497 in this instance) and the absolute majority of 1,509, the anti-McGovern forces could bring a point of order, challenging the O'Brien definition of a majority. What made their prospects promising for the South Carolina case was that their 151 California delegates would be voting on this question.[29]

So the South Carolina challenge on the opening Monday night became the decisive moment of the convention. As Gary Hart put it, "Two years of work would come down to one vote."[30] For this conclusive struggle, the McGovernites brought to bear all of their operational skills in what would be one of the last great triumphs of their organization. Never before had the McGovern army, proud of its decentralized and grassroots bent, been so hierarchically ordered and immaculately disciplined. From a trailer outside the convention hall, Rick Stearns, unparalleled as a vote counter, served as field general in close consultation with Gary Hart and Frank Mankiewicz. On the floor of the convention were 250 McGovern whips and McGovern leaders in every state delegation where he had support, all of them primed to respond swiftly to commands from the top.[31] The 1972 Democratic convention was an assemblage of novices—over 80 percent of the delegates were attending their first national convention.[32] But on the opening night of the conclave the masses of McGovern delegates were well schooled, ready to act like political pros and move in unison.

What made the vote on the South Carolina challenge even more bizarre was that McGovern had pledged to the women's caucus that he would support the feminist position on gender balance. But as the South Carolina vote began, Stearns and Hart could not be sure that their total would not fall in the dreaded window between 1,497 and 1,509, providing the stop-McGovern forces with an opportunity to overturn the ruling defining a majority. By the time that the eleventh state, Kansas, responded to the roll call, Stearns decided that the outcome was too close to call. Consequently, he and Hart decided that regardless of McGovern's promise to the women, the campaign would take a dive and lose the vote on South Carolina so as not to jeopardize the decisive vote on California. With masterful control and finesse, they communicated to their whips and state leaders subtly to pull a few votes here and there. The stop-McGovern forces were slow to realize what was happening—and were too poorly organized to act on the realization once the McGovern ploy dawned on them. The South Carolina challenge thus failed by a vote of 1,555.75 to 1,429.05, precluding a point of order and saving the day for the California vote about to come.[33]

The McGovern maneuver on South Carolina was so obscure that it took awhile for the feminists to comprehend what had been done—at which point they erupted in fury at the betrayal. The press was befuddled because of McGovern's previous pledge to win the challenge for the women. Mike Wallace of CBS approached Hart on the convention floor and asked him, "Isn't this a serious defeat for the McGovern forces?" Hart evaded the implication, saying that the ballot on South Carolina was not a test vote for the California challenge, but

Walter Cronkite told television viewers that McGovern's nomination was now in doubt.[34] The media's misperception put Theodore White, by now a famous chronicler of campaigns, on the spot. Researching his book on the 1972 campaign, none of whose details would be made public until after the election, White was allowed on the inside and was privy to the McGovern strategy. Questioned by Cronkite about what had just transpired on the South Carolina challenge, the veteran journalist upheld his pledge of confidentiality to the candidates and withheld what he knew from his colleagues.[35]

The showdown vote on the California delegation soon followed, but it was somewhat anticlimactic, since the McGovern camp had more than the 1,433 votes it needed in accordance with the O'Brien-O'Hara rulings. The debate on California did produce one of the dramatic highlights of the convention, as Willie Brown, cochair of the state's McGovern delegation and a rising star in black politics, made an emotional plea to the convention to restore the 151 votes that the stop-McGovern forces had taken away:

> [The McGovern] delegation is the most balanced delegation in this convention. It has 41 percent of the people under the age of thirty. It has fifty-one blacks; it has fifty-three Chicanos; it has 50 percent women. It's old people, young people, and 60 percent poor . . . And now I'm forced with 120 people to remove a net loss of twenty-nine blacks from my delegation, to remove twenty-three Chicanos from my delegation, to take half of my youth . . . and seventy-six of my women . . . Seat my delegation. I did it for you in Mississippi in '64, in Georgia in '68, and it's now California in '72. I desire no less. Give my back my delegation![36]

McGovern delegates, under tight control for the pivotal vote on South Carolina, released their pent-up emotions, screaming and chanting for Brown.[37] When the roll was finally called, his speech appears to have padded their margin, with the motion to restore winner-take-all for California receiving over 1,600 votes, an absolute majority of the convention.

This string of credentials battles was still not finished, for the question of the contested Illinois delegation remained. McGovern and his top aides worked desperately for weeks to find a compromise on Illinois. They could not dump the Singer-Jackson reform slate without sending shock waves through their political base and undercutting their whole claim to a New Politics. Yet if Mayor Daley and his forces were excluded from the convention in front of a national television audience, more than the hope of carrying Illinois in November was endangered; the message to regular Democrats, especially white ethnics, throughout the nation was that they were not welcome in the McGovern Democratic Party. Gary Hart carried a compromise offer to the Daley machine: the McGovernites would arrange to bend the rules of the convention and seat both of the Illinois slates, with each delegate having half of a vote. Daley turned the offer down flat.[38]

After a failed attempt to suspend convention rules and ram the compromise through, the McGovern camp had no option left but to support the full Singer-Jackson slate. When the reform delegation won a narrow victory, it exploded in excitement, as the Daley delegates, symbols to New Politics activists of the mayor's repressive tactics against antiwar protestors at the 1968 Democratic convention, looked on in dejection. The mayor himself was absent, sequestered at his summer retreat on Lake Michigan, but his followers were subjected to the celebratory antics of Jesse Jackson, their despised adversary in Chicago affairs.[39] For the more pragmatic McGovern staffers, it was an ominous scene. As Eli Segal later remarked, "Humiliating Daley with Jesse Jackson and all he was identified with was very bad."[40]

Credentials battles consumed the first session of the convention until 5:20 in the morning. It was to be the first of four long nights in Miami Beach, where nothing would come easily to the McGovern organization. On this opening night, they had won a decisive victory over the stop-McGovern coalition. But there were a number of other grueling struggles ahead—and fatigue itself was becoming a silent enemy stalking the McGovernites.

An Open Convention

After the first night of the convention, McGovern's nomination was assured, but many of the regular Democrats who composed the stop-McGovern movement were far from reconciled to his candidacy. Muskie, the least hostile to McGovern, formally withdrew from the race on Tuesday morning. So did Humphrey, who had done the most to broadcast the image of McGovern the radical, throwing his delegate support to Scoop Jackson.[41] The South was still unfriendly to McGovern: Wallace continued his candidacy, and an early stop-McGovern spokesman, Governor Jimmy Carter of Georgia, made the principal nomination speech for Jackson.[42] Behind the scenes, key figures in the stop-McGovern coalition talked quietly about staying in touch, concentrating on congressional races, and taking back the party after the November election.[43]

Tuesday, July 11, the second day of the convention, was devoted to the platform. The McGovernites' left-center strategy, which had held during the platform drafting sessions in Washington, was again tested in Miami Beach. It survived once more, with the McGovern campaign extracting from the convention a moderate platform that aimed to minimize problems for the fall campaign. Nonetheless, this was a remarkably open convention, with participatory democracy in all of its glorious messiness on public display, and the televised debates over minority planks linked the McGovern campaign to controversial groups even as it managed to suppress their proposals.

Not all of the minority planks came at the McGovernites from the left. George Wallace was brought onto the convention stage in his wheelchair to argue for capital punishment, a constitutional amendment to permit prayer in the schools, and a ban on busing. The McGovern leadership instructed its delegates to greet Wallace graciously, but once he had left the stage they shouted down every plank he had proposed.[44] It was another reminder of the flaw in the left-center strategy. As Gordon Weil ruefully commented, "We had repeatedly made efforts to gain Wallace's support and to appeal directly to his supporters and then we made a national display of our opposition to those positions he deemed the most important."[45]

Most of the seemingly endless platform session was taken up with the minority planks from the left. Passions spilled over as feminists made their case for abortion rights and homosexuals presented a militant gay rights plank. These were egalitarian causes close to the heart of the majority of McGovernites, but in the eyes of the McGovern strategists they spelled only trouble for their candidate in the fall. Thus, the McGovern organization pulled off its second operational feat of the convention, keeping its delegates in line to defeat the women's and gays' planks. Whereas the night before it had only had to violate its promise to the women's caucus, now it had to stifle most of its political base. Weil pointed out the irony: "The entire McGovern floor operation—regional desk people in the candidate's trailer behind Convention Hall, and regional whips spotted on the floor supplemented by Van Dyk's own whips—was devoted to defeating our supporters."[46]

On one plank, McGovernite discipline broke down. Senator Fred Harris of Oklahoma proposed a radical tax reform that eliminated all deductions and exemptions, even the mortgage deduction. This audacious populist stroke captured the fancy of rank-and-file McGovernites and Wallacites alike, and it was evident that a majority on the convention floor favored the plank.[47] Van Dyk rescued the McGovern campaign from a move that might have scared off both wealthy contributors and middle-class homeowners.

> I went under the podium and wrote a little note to Yvonne Braithwaite Burke, who was chairing the session, and in the note I said, "No matter what happens, this plank must lose." So, in the chaos and noise . . . , she called the vote on the plank. She said, "All those in favor of the plank?" And a lot of people said, "Aye." And then she said, "All those opposed?" A lesser number, clearly a lesser number, said, "Nay." She brought down the gavel and said, "The plank is defeated." And she moved on.[48]

The McGovern staff represented the New Politics, but they were certainly not political amateurs. If Mayor Daley was watching the proceedings on television, he could have taken notes.

The McGovern leadership could keep the left out of the platform, but it could not keep it off the television screen. Images from the platform session, some observers believed, had a more powerful impact than platform language that nobody read. Convention parliamentarian James O'Hara argued later that "we lost the election at Miami." It was not what McGovern did or said that was the problem. Rather, "the American people made an association between McGovern and gay lib, and welfare rights, and pot-smoking, and black militants, and women's lib, and wise college kids, and everything else that they saw as threatening their value systems."[49] Along with the unsettling images, there was the sheer sense of disorder in the Democrats' house. On this second night of the convention, adjournment was at 6:24 A.M.

Wednesday, July 12, should have been a more relaxing day for the McGovern leadership, a day to savor as it would conclude with McGovern's official nomination. But a new crisis erupted and further taxed the time and energy of McGovern and his staff. The day before, McGovern had issued a statement to a delegation of POW wives, pledging that until the American captives were released by the North Vietnamese, he would, as president, keep residual naval and air forces in Southeast Asia. Rumors began to fly around Miami Beach that McGovern was selling out and abandoning his stalwart antiwar position. A militant throng, estimated by police to number 300 protestors, occupied the lobby of the Doral Hotel, McGovern's campaign headquarters, on Wednesday afternoon, refusing to leave until the candidate appeared before it and reaffirmed his orthodoxy to the left. As police and Secret Service agents grew increasingly nervous, a standoff ensued. Finally, even as the third evening session was opening at the Convention Hall, McGovern came before the protestors and, without giving ground on any issue, calmed and dispersed them.[50]

At the time, the demonstration at the Doral seemed one more indication of the McGovern campaign's often vexing alliance with militant movements on the left. What happened at the Doral, however, took on a new dimension once the Watergate cover-up began to unravel. Gary Hart is convinced that the Doral incident was a Nixon dirty trick:

> We arrived in the lobby and here were hundreds of people I have never seen in my life. And they were visibly scruffy and they were not McGovern supporters . . . I knew virtually everyone, state by state, and so did Rick Stearns. We all knew who our supporters were. So these people, who were occupying the lobby and demanding that McGovern reconfirm his position on the war, even more extremely than he ever had before, were put there by somebody. No question in my mind.[51]

Not surprisingly, evidence on just who composed the crowd at the Doral is fragmentary. Some participants appear to have been Zippies, a group that split off from the Yippies because it decided that the notorious Yippie founders,

Abbie Hoffman and Jerry Rubin, had become too tame.[52] But others may well have been exactly what Hart alleged: Nixon plants. In a deposition taken by the Senate Watergate Committee in September 1973, E. Howard Hunt acknowledged that one of the Watergate burglars, Bernard Barker, had earlier been assigned "to recruit some persons who might be disreputable looking young men, hippies, to pose as McGovern supporters." The Nixon campaign's faux McGovernites "were supposed to demonstrate in front of the Doral Hotel some evening and behave outrageously to bring discredit on the bulk of the useful McGovern supporters."[53]

Wednesday evening was the only uncomplicated moment for the McGovernites in the entire convention. Ensconced in his suite at the Doral, McGovern watched the balloting for the presidential nomination on television with deep satisfaction. Despite abundant evidence of a badly divided Democratic Party, he still believed that unity was possible. He had defeated the party establishment with his grassroots army in a fair and open fight, and now he would place that army in the service of every Democrat, up and down the ticket, who supported him.[54] At the Convention Hall, the balloting was uneventful, with the McGovern camp serene in its strength, 200 votes safely above what it needed for a majority. It was the Illinois delegation, Daley-less, whose support put McGovern over the top—a subtle sign of the price paid for this victory. Just before midnight the nomination was his, and while there were more states in the roll call and late vote switches to record, the convention soon wrapped up for the evening with its earliest adjournment of the week.

A Day for Disasters

On Thursday, July 13, McGovernites, savoring their remarkable success in winning the Democratic presidential nomination, had no inkling of impending disasters. By now thoroughly exhausted, they made two fatal errors on this final day for convention sessions. In a frenetic and muddled decisionmaking process, McGovern was driven to make an ill-considered, last-minute choice of Senator Thomas Eagleton of Missouri as his running mate. And in the breakdown of McGovernite discipline on the convention floor, the Democratic nominee's acceptance speech, the most important of the entire campaign, was pushed back into the middle of the night.

Later, reflecting on the awful consequences of these twin fiascoes on July 13, McGovern regretted the decision he had *not* made that day. As the party's nominee, he might have insisted that the convention schedule be changed to accommodate his needs. With too little time for careful consideration and vetting of a running mate, and with numerous nominating speeches for vice-presidential candidates on tap to tie up the evening session for hours, a little foresight would at least have suggested some problems ahead. What if McGovern had decided to arrange for an extra convention session the next day on the vice-presidential nomination, clearing the way for his acceptance speech that night to be shown during prime time and buying extra hours for scrutinizing prospective running mates?[55]

Why was the choice of Eagleton—the number one disaster in the history of modern presidential campaigns—made in a slapdash fashion? During the "lost month" before the convention, the McGovern staff had been so preoccupied with the California challenge and the hunt for every last delegate that it had given minimal attention to vice-presidential possibilities.[56] McGovern stubbornly continued to assume that he could overcome the vocal resistance of Ted Kennedy, the first choice of almost all Democrats, and cajole him to join the ticket.[57] Moreover, while the process that produced Eagleton seems incredible today, it was actually close to the norm for its era. When party conventions still determined the identity of the nominee, running mates were usually selected only after the winner had been anointed. Humphrey's choice of Muskie and Nixon's choice of Agnew in 1968 were also made in a chaotic rush.[58] One legacy of the Eagleton disaster was that it transformed the way presidential candidates go about picking running mates. By 1976, Jimmy Carter, with the nomination wrapped up well ahead of the convention, employed a systematic process in determining his running mate, complete with questionnaires and personal interviews for the top contenders.[59]

When twenty or so sleep-deprived McGovern staffers and advisers gathered at 9 A.M. on July 13 to come up with recommendations for the vice-presidential nominee, the lack of forethought was evident in the enormous list—Hart puts it at three dozen names—with which the meeting began. Several rounds of elimination followed over the next two hours, reducing the total first to two dozen and then to seven or eight (participants' accounts vary). With the official convention deadline for filing a vice-presidential nomination only a few hours away—at 3 P.M.—the scramble began as McGovern personally pondered the list. Ted Kennedy at last had definitively taken himself out of consideration, and an early feeler to Senator Walter Mondale of Minnesota was, as anticipated, unsuccessful. McGovern next turned to Mayor Kevin White of Boston, an urban Catholic who would bring Old Guard credentials (he had opposed McGovern in the Massachusetts primary) and regional balance to the ticket. White was amenable to the offer.[60]

It was now past 2 P.M., with precious time ticking away but with a candidate at last in hand. Or so it seemed—until White came under attack from his home state. Ted Kennedy did not want the nomination himself, but he was cool to letting it go to a rival Bay State politician. McGovern's leaders in the state's convention delegation, John Kenneth Galbraith and Father Robert Drinan, were adamantly opposed to their opponent from the primary, of whom they held a low opinion, and threatened a walkout should White be the choice. A one-hour postponement in the filing deadline had been secured, and with White now effectively vetoed, McGovern had sixty minutes left to come up with a running mate.[61]

Senator Eagleton made the original list, but he was not well known to McGovern or his staff and had not been near the top. Like White, Eagleton appeared on paper as a good bet for conciliating the regulars, since he was an urban Catholic with strong labor ties who had backed Muskie in the primaries.[62] Gordon Weil had volunteered to check out both White and Eagleton, and he heard rumors that Eagleton had a drinking problem and had been hospitalized in Missouri under mysterious circumstances. But Weil, who was later scapegoated for a supposedly shoddy inquiry into Eagleton, had too little time to track down information and was left with the impression that the rumors were unfounded.[63] In the meantime, McGovern and his staff were hearing positive reports about the senator from Missouri. Uneasy about selecting a running mate with whom he was personally unfamiliar, McGovern sought in desperation to recruit a longstanding friend from the Senate, Gaylord Nelson of Wisconsin. Nelson said no and chimed in with another endorsement of Eagleton. With only minutes left before the filing deadline, the final offer, largely by default, went to Eagleton.[64]

McGovern already had word that Eagleton was sure to accept an offer, and when he phoned, the Missouri senator jumped at the opportunity. Frank Mankiewicz came on the line to speak to Eagleton, and with their conversation, a drama of deception and misperception began. Eagleton later told reporters that Mankiewicz asked him if he had "any old skeletons rattling around your closet," and interpreting the words to refer to something evil or corrupt, he said no.[65] Mankiewicz says he did not use this phrase—as an experienced wordsmith, the cliché was beneath him—but he certainly queried Eagleton about whether there was anything in his background that the McGovernites needed to know, and Eagleton did not even hint at the mental-health problems in his past.[66] Under the gun of a deadline McGovern possibly could have altered, he had a running mate who was about to blow up his campaign.

The McGovernites' day for disasters was only half over. The final session of the convention began that evening with a consideration of a party reform charter. The McGovern campaign prevailed in obtaining a postponement of a decision, but the discussion had eaten up time. Not nearly as much time, however, as the nominating speeches for vice-presidential candidates. After three late-night sessions, and with the tension of close votes and consequential choices seemingly relaxed, the McGovern majority of delegates acted like punchy party animals, more akin to Yippies than to political pros. The feminists brought the only serious challenge to Eagleton, putting forward Sissy Farenthold of Texas as a candidate to make a point about women's new power. But McGovernites and their foes alike were in a rebellious mood. Speeches were made and votes cast for a wide array of candidates, some of them fictional. Among those who attracted support were Archie Bunker, Martha Mitchell, Roger Mudd, and Jerry Rubin. One vote was even temporarily recorded for Mao Tse-tung when the roll call clerk misheard a voice from the chaotic floor. The upshot of all this uproarious behavior was that when McGovern strode out on the podium to deliver his nationally televised acceptance address, it was 2.45 A.M.[67]

McGovern and his speechwriters had labored extensively on the acceptance address, which would, if presented to the huge audience tuned in to the convention during prime time, be his single best opportunity of the campaign to define himself on his own terms. According to Bob Shrum, who played an important role in composing it, the convention speech was carefully designed to erase the threatening radical image and to project McGovern as a moderate figure.[68] The speech was a paean to the democratic process—especially the one that had just resulted in the nomination of George McGovern: "The destiny of America is safer in the hands of the people than in the conference rooms of any elite. Let us give our country the chance to elect a government that will seek and speak the truth, for this is a time for truth in the life of our nation." Yet whatever softening of the McGovern image was intended, the peroration of the speech—the rhetoric that became indelibly associated with the McGovern campaign—remained provocative and stirring:

> So join with me in this campaign. Lend me your strength and your support—and together, we will call America home to the ideals that nourished us in the beginning.
> From secrecy, and deception in high places, come home, America.
> From a conflict in Indochina which maims our ideals as well as our soldiers, come home, America.
> From military spending so wasteful that it weakens our nation, come home, America.
> From the entrenchment of special privilege and tax favoritism—
> From the waste of idle hands to the joy of useful labor—
> From the prejudice of race and sex—
> From the loneliness of the aging poor and the despair of the neglected sick, come home, America.
> Come home to the affirmation that we have a dream.
> Come home to the conviction that we can move our country forward.
> Come home to the belief that we can seek a newer world . . .
> This is the time.[69]

Instead of approximately 70 million viewers—the estimated audience tuned in earlier in the evening—hearing McGovern at his best, the late-night audience had dwindled to about 15 million viewers, most of them presumably Democratic diehards.[70] This lost opportunity for America to hear him as he wanted to be heard still haunts McGovern. Committed to a more participatory and open politics, nonetheless he regrets that his forces did not "take charge" that evening and "impose a little of the old discipline . . . I should have just said, look, I don't care what you do on that convention floor, but I'm going to speak at ten o'clock, no later than that, eastern time." But McGovern and his aides were asleep to the danger, and so when he finally delivered his great speech, "there was nobody awake other than the insomniacs."[71]

Departing Miami Beach, the McGovernites, unaware of the crises looming, felt pretty good. Grim predictions that "the blood will be ankle deep at the Democratic convention in Miami Beach" had not been vindicated.[72] On the contrary, the press was pleased that the reformed convention's tussles had, in light of the potential for acrimony, been surprisingly well-mannered.[73] "If you look at the '72 convention," Gary Hart observes, "and put it up against '68, when the regulars dominated, there's no comparison. This was a love-in compared to '68." Without the McGovern-Fraser reforms, however, or with a successful stop-McGovern movement, "you would have had '68 cubed in Miami."[74]

David Broder of the *Washington Post* was skeptical of the McGovern insurgency from the start, but in a column published a few days after the convention, he too paid tribute to the accomplishment of the reformers at Miami Beach. "The Democratic reforms," Broder pointed out, "succeeded, far better than it had seemed possible, in making this a delegates' convention." The amateurs had taken over from the professionals, and open deliberations on the floor had replaced secret deals in smoke-filled rooms, and to Broder the transformation was a healthy one. "Purposeful, decent, demonstrative, good-humored, indefatigable, and, above all, diverse," he wrote, the delegates "shaped the week's decisions." Refuting expectations of bitter explosions, "the Democrats did so much better—not only for themselves but for the credibility of our political system—than they might have that congratulations and even celebrations are in order."[75]

Though the Democratic convention of 1972 might be regarded as an advance for popular democracy, it was hardly a political plus for the winning candidate. Already well behind Nixon in the polls, McGovern received no bounce from the convention, no movement by disenchanted conservative and moderate Democrats back to the party fold.[76] Rather, negative images of him, previously broadcast by Humphrey and soon to be elaborated by the president's men, were reinforced and not rebutted at the convention. Marcia Johnston, Gary Hart's assistant, observes that the same Miami Beach scenes that warmed the hearts of McGovernites played very differently to television viewers who looked at them through a conventional lens:

> What people saw was frightening to them. We loved it on the floor: it was exciting and it was democracy at work, messy but wonderful. But to have Willie Brown screaming "Give me back my delegation!" and for people to see what we might now celebrate in America—black, brown, yellow, men,

women, this big explosion of people that didn't look like suburbanites—in terms of introducing [McGovern] to America, it couldn't have been worse.[77]

Coming on the heels of the arduous "lost month" after the California primary, the swirling conflicts in late-night sessions at the convention took a further toll on the McGovern campaign, generating a number of ill-starred decisions. The candidate and his top staff headed off for badly needed vacations, but they were to find little rest even there, for one of the decisions made in Miami Beach was about to throw them into turmoil even worse than what they had just surmounted. As much as anything else, fatigue sapped the McGovern insurgency at its moment of victory. When McGovern looked back on what had happened to his campaign at the convention, fittingly he chose a common metaphor of troubled sleep: "The convention, which was the culmination of a dream, was . . . producing its share of nightmarish moments."[78]

The Eagleton Affair: A Hidden History

The Eagleton affair, occupying three devastating weeks right after the Democratic convention, produced a disastrous new image for George McGovern—both cold-blooded opportunist and hapless bungler. As McGovern's reputation was sinking, Eagleton's was rising; he was the recipient of a bounty of sympathy as a man wronged. When McGovern told Dick Cavett in a televised interview a month after the election that the affair was the "saddest part of the campaign," viewers might easily have taken the reference to be to his own political humiliation.[79] But McGovern's expression of sadness hinted at a truly agonizing decision process, many of whose dimensions were concealed from the public. He never denied that he handled the affair poorly, but the nature of the decision he faced was not in his power to reveal at the time. What came across to the public in 1972 as a McGovern comedy of errors was instead a hidden political tragedy.

There were at least four critical dimensions to the Eagleton affair that only came to light after the election or much later. The first was that Eagleton's concealment from McGovern of his mental-health problems continued after the convention. Even as the final evening session of the convention made Eagleton the Democratic nominee for vice president, rumors began to circulate on the floor of alcohol or mental problems in the candidate's past. Shortly before the 4 A.M. victory party at the Doral, which followed McGovern's 2:45 A.M. acceptance speech, Gordon Weil asked Douglas Bennet, Eagleton's administrative assistant, about the rumors. Bennet, who may not have known the full story about Eagleton's health, replied that his boss had been hospitalized for exhaustion and depression after his 1960 campaign to be attorney general of Missouri, but that "the whole matter had seemed so minor that it had not occurred to [him or to

Eagleton] to mention it."[80] Weil passed this information on to Hart and Mankiewicz at the party, but both men, by then thoroughly beat, failed to catch the warning signals.

Hart and Mankiewicz soon headed out for a much-needed vacation at the Virgin Islands estate of campaign finance director Henry Kimelman. Careful to maintain his populist image, McGovern did not join them; instead, after a weekend in Washington, he flew to his home state for a working vacation in the Black Hills. The exhausted McGovern leadership planned this period for recuperation, but as a result they were slow to respond to the emerging Eagleton crisis and physically isolated when they finally did so.

From the Virgin Islands, Mankiewicz arranged for a phone conversation with Eagleton on Saturday night, July 15. Concerned that the McGovern campaign was short on facts and that reporters were beginning to snoop around Missouri for the story, Mankiewicz asked Eagleton about his health and how it should be explained to the press, and Eagleton answered: "I was just exhausted after campaigning, and that's all that needs to be said."[81] Mankiewicz was still uneasy, and in another conversation with Eagleton on Sunday, he elicited from the senator the fact that Eagleton had been hospitalized more than once and for something like depression or melancholy. But it was only the next day, when Hart talked to Marcia Johnston at McGovern headquarters in Washington, that he and Mankiewicz began to grasp the potential magnitude of the disaster ahead. An anonymous caller had left messages that Eagleton had been hospitalized three times for mental illness and that his treatment had involved electric-shock therapy. The caller also indicated that he had passed the same message to the Knight-Ridder newspapers.[82]

The identity of this anonymous caller has never been determined. He claimed to be a McGovern supporter who was alerting the campaign to damaging news before it broke in the press. Some McGovernites suspected, on the contrary, that the call came from a Nixon operative, aiming to stir up trouble in the McGovern camp. In any case, Hart and Mankiewicz could be confident that the White House, with the FBI's files available to it, knew more about Eagleton's medical history than they did.[83] Before flying back to Washington from the Virgin Islands, they arranged to meet with Eagleton and Bennet the next morning in the Senate dining room.

On Thursday, July 20, a full week after Eagleton's selection, Hart and Mankiewicz were finally able to question the vice-presidential candidate in person. They had to push and probe before they could confirm their worst fears. Eagleton admitted to three hospital stays—in 1960, 1964, and 1966 (the middle one having nothing to do with a campaign)—but said at first that his treatment had mainly consisted of rest and some medication. Asked about the diagnosis of his physicians, Eagleton, according to Mankiewicz's recollection, used the word "melancholia." Mankiewicz was incredulous: "Tom, there's no such disease. Maybe there was a hundred years ago."[84] Alerted by the anonymous caller, it was the McGovernites who broached the issue of shock treatments, and Eagleton, for the first time, acknowledged that he had undergone them during two of his three hospitalizations. Hart and Mankiewicz said that McGovern needed to examine Eagleton's medical records before he could decide what should be done, and Eagleton agreed to bring them to the Black Hills when he stopped to see McGovern there in five days.[85]

That same day, McGovern had interrupted his Black Hills vacation to return to Washington for an important vote in the Senate. With a busy schedule in the capital, and still not cognizant of the extent of the Eagleton problem, McGovern made his first mistake during this critical period. He put off hearing about the Hart and Mankiewicz meeting with Eagleton until they could brief him on the return flight to South Dakota the following day. "I should have insisted," he lamented in his autobiography, "on being fully briefed as quickly as possible, and the return to Custer [in the Black Hills] should have been delayed so Eagleton and I could have had a long discussion right there with the best-qualified advisers we could assemble in Washington."[86]

It was on the plane returning to South Dakota that McGovern finally learned from Hart and Mankiewicz of what deep trouble the campaign was now facing. Its problem was unprecedented: a presidential nominee had never dropped his running mate before in the midst of the campaign. Nonetheless, Mankiewicz was convinced by this point that Eagleton had to go. Hart wanted to wait to see what Eagleton's medical records contained, figuring that they would either offer reassurance that the mental illness was licked or suggest that the nation's welfare and security could not be risked by placing an unstable individual, in the common cliché, a heartbeat away from the presidency. McGovern agreed to hold off making a decision until he talked to Eagleton the following Tuesday and reviewed the medical records he would be bringing with him.[87] The presidential candidate returned to Sylvan Lake in the Black Hills, and to all outward appearances, his relaxed sojourn there resumed. As William Greider, one of the campaign journalists with the McGovern party, wrote at the time, the McGovernites seemed a cheerful bunch that weekend, gathering "after dinner one night in the pine-paneled lobby of their resort lodge [to sing] folk songs." There was no premonition of the approaching political storm that would turn their vacation into "an ordeal."[88]

Eagleton and his wife, Barbara, arrived at Sylvan Lake Monday night and breakfasted with the McGoverns the next day. Eagleton related his medical history, apologized for not informing McGovern about it at the convention, and insisted that he was now in excellent mental health. At a subsequent meeting, Eagleton repeated his story to two of McGovern's staff, Frank Mankiewicz and press secretary Dick Dougherty.[89] And then, to the astonishment of the reporters at Sylvan Lake, the story was unveiled to the nation at a news conference. Just as with McGovern's men earlier, Eagleton doled out his story to the press reluctantly, leaving the electric-shock therapy out of his statement and only mentioning it in response to a reporter's question. But if Eagleton was still guarded, McGovern was the opposite, presenting a forceful—and ill-considered—defense for his original choice of the senator from Missouri that would come back to bite him: "As far as I am concerned, there is no member of the Senate who is any sounder in mind, body, and spirit than Tom Eagleton. I am fully satisfied, and if I had known every detail that he told me this morning, which is exactly what he has just told you here now, he would still have been my choice for the vice presidency of the United States."[90]

Why did McGovern embrace Eagleton so unequivocally at Sylvan Lake? Why did he not wait for the press to break the story and then state that he needed "a few days for reflection, consultation, and evaluation of the public reaction?"[91] It was certainly not because Eagleton had in fact removed all doubts about his mental state, as the narrative will soon show. In part, McGovern was making a mistaken calculation that if his campaign got the story out before the press could expose it, and treated the mental problem as one that Eagleton had bravely conquered, the crisis would dissipate. For such a strategy, a half-hearted defense of his nominee would not do.[92] McGovern's decision reflected an impulsive streak, an inflated confidence in his own on-the-spot judgments. This quiet but powerful spark of ego had served him well in his long-shot pursuit of the Democratic nomination. It had served him less well in his dogged belief that he could talk Ted Kennedy into becoming his running mate, and now it was to be a key contributor to his undoing.

There was a further and more personal source of his support for Eagleton—a second hidden dimension of the whole affair. McGovern's instinctive sympathy was tinged with a father's experience of grief. One of McGovern's daughters, Terry, was shadowed by similar symptoms to Eagleton's. Only after her tragic death in 1994, brought about by alcoholism and depression, did McGovern make public the part her mental illness had played in his reaction to hearing Eagleton tell his story:

> As Eleanor and I listened to Tom's anguished discussion of the matter a week after his selection, we decided to stay with him. We reacted as we did in considerable part because Terry had been suffering from a clinical depression not unlike Tom Eagleton's. Despite our concern with Tom's problem and its impact on the national campaign and the subsequent problems that could arise if he became Vice President, I could not in effect punish him for being a victim of depression.[93]

Mankiewicz is convinced that the chief reason McGovern would not take his advice and jettison Eagleton right away was Terry: "He would in effect be saying to her, 'You're not fit.'"[94]

Both McGovern and Eagleton misgauged the impact of the revelations from the Sylvan Lake press conference. For many Americans, talk of a vice-presidential candidate receiving electric-shock treatments was frightening; to others, the disturbing element in Eagleton's story was that he had misled McGovern in order to gain a place on the Democratic ticket. A political firestorm began to spread around the country, increasingly intruding on the rustic McGovern encampment in the Black Hills. Leading newspapers, including the *New York Times* and the *Washington Post*, called on Eagleton to resign. Prominent Democratic politicians chimed in that the party's ticket, already saddled with McGovern's radical image, would be further dragged down by Eagleton's unreliability. Worst of all for McGovern were the pressures from within his own campaign. Finance director Henry Kimelman warned of a fundraising crisis: major contributors were backing off, and the direct-mail operation was frozen in place.[95] In a fusillade of phone messages and telegrams to McGovern headquarters in Washington, field workers in the McGovern grassroots army reported rumblings of mutiny. The ominous tone of many of these reports was evident in the terse communication from Rick Greg, McGovern campaign coordinator for Middlesex County, New Jersey: "Eagleton thing a disaster, has cut off money, ruined volunteer force, everyone demoralized."[96]

McGovern's political dilemma was compounded when the affair took two odd twists after he hastily sprang to his running mate's defense. The day after the Sylvan Lake news conference, McGovern was playing tennis when Carl Leubsdorf, a reporter for the Associated Press, showed up and asked him a few questions. According to McGovern, he responded to one about the public reaction to the Eagleton disclosure with a "'we'll have to wait and see,'" only to find that newspaper headlines misinterpreted his words to refer to a reconsideration of Eagleton's place on the ticket.[97] Furious about the implications, McGovern instructed his press secretary, Dick Dougherty, to tell the reporters at Sylvan Lake that the AP story was false. As Dougherty relayed the point to the press, McGovern called him again: "Dick, I want you to put in the statement that not only is that story wrong, but that I'm a thousand percent behind Tom Eagleton."[98] Leaving himself absolutely no wiggle room for a change of course, McGovern used a phrase that no presidential candidate should ever utter. His "thousand percent" equaled his "come home, America" as the most famous words that McGovern spoke in the 1972 campaign and became one of the most notorious gaffes in the lore of presidential politics.

The next day, in a second twist to the story, syndicated columnist Jack Anderson wrote that Eagleton had been arrested half a dozen times for drunken driving. Eagleton denounced the contents of the column as "'a damnable lie,'" and Anderson, unable to produce any evidence for his charges, had to offer an apology. The tempest over Anderson's unsupported allegations brought a surge of public sympathy for Eagleton. Previously on the defensive for deceiving McGovern in Miami Beach, he suddenly had the advantage of victimhood and became even more resolved to remain on the ticket. McGovern was now committed to a candidate who was not about to budge on his own.[99]

Even as Eagleton publicly campaigned to render himself irreplaceable, McGovern felt mounting pressure to be rid of him. Within two days of his "thousand percent" statement, he was hinting that Eagleton might have to resign from the ticket. The prevalent assumption at the time was that McGovern changed his mind about Eagleton purely for political reasons. Indeed, it was his reversal on Eagleton that shattered any vestiges of the "St. George" image and supplanted it with the perception that he was a commonplace political opportunist. In retrospect, it is somewhat surprising that political motives for removing Eagleton from the ticket drew such condemnation. Should McGovern have permitted a two-year campaign for the presidency to be destroyed out of loyalty to a running mate who had acted in bad faith? But political motives, although important to McGovern's change of course, were not the sole source for the decision to oust Eagleton. The third hidden dimension of the Eagleton affair (though McGovern and his aides dropped a few hints to the press in this instance) was that there were also medical reasons why McGovern changed his mind.

Eagleton had agreed to bring his hospital records to the Black Hills, but he arrived without them—and never did present them to McGovern or his staff. What the McGovernites did have in their possession was a memo from two Knight-Ridder journalists who had been on the trail of Eagleton's medical history, and in this memo was a phrase, seemingly quoted from a hospital file, about "severe manic depressive psychosis with suicidal tendencies."[100] McGovern and his advisers only had Eagleton's word for it that he was now in good health, and his caginess about his mental illness suggested that the full story was not yet available to them. Mankiewicz suggests that there was still another indicator that the truth about Eagleton's mental health remained elusive. In Mankiewicz's recollection of the conversation at Sylvan Lake, Eagleton, asked about medications for his illness, replied that he had taken one—Mankiewicz thinks it was Thorazine, an antipsychotic drug—but that the prescription was in his wife's name and could not be traced to him.[101]

With so many unanswered questions about Eagleton's mental health, Mankiewicz and McGovern sought advice from experts about whether someone with Eagleton's medical history could handle the stresses of the presidency. Even before Eagleton's trip to Sylvan Lake, Mankiewicz called psychiatrists he knew in Los Angeles and New York, and "without exception" they told him that "you can't have [Eagleton] in control of the bomb."[102] McGovern had not sufficiently attended to this information from Mankiewicz before his initial defense of Eagleton, but amid the growing uncertainty afterward about both Eagleton's political viability and his mental stability, he made some phone calls of his own, one of them to the eminent Dr. Karl Menninger. What McGovern heard from these psychiatrists was that it was not possible to be sure that Eagleton was beyond the risk of a relapse and that concern for the nation's security suggested that he leave the ticket.[103]

So by Friday, July 28, McGovern began to move diametrically away from his "thousand percent" support for Eagleton. In a clumsy maneuver that only exacerbated his new reputation in the media for deviousness, he used the reporters at Sylvan Lake as conduits and signaled that he was preparing to drop Eagleton, then on a trip to Hawaii and the West Coast.[104] But by this point Eagleton was in no mood to take any hints from McGovern. Convinced that he and not McGovern now had public sympathy in his corner, Eagleton was, in Mankiewicz's phrase, "breathing fire."[105] He told reporters in San Francisco, "The way this has turned out, I'm a distinct plus to the ticket. I'm going to stay on the ticket. That's my firm, irrevocable intent."[106]

After a confused and embarrassing weekend during which the impasse between the McGovern and Eagleton camps deepened, the two men finally met on Monday night, July 31, in a Senate room. Eagleton, still holding on to his hope of remaining on the ticket, finally gave permission for McGovern to speak privately on the phone to two of the doctors who had treated him for mental illness. According to McGovern's later account in his autobiography, neither doctor provided him with any reassurance that Eagleton could stand up to the burdens of the presidency.[107] McGovern was at last firm in his decision, and Eagleton yielded to it. At a joint news conference after their meeting, McGovern presented the reasons for Eagleton's resignation from the ticket:

> I have consistently supported Senator Eagleton. He is a talented, able United States Senator whose ability will make him a prominent figure in American politics for many, many years. I am fully satisfied that his health is excellent. I base that conclusion upon my conversations with his doctors and my close personal and political association with him. In the joint decision that we have reached tonight, health was not a factor. But the public debate over Senator Eagleton's past medical history continues to divert attention from the great national issues that need to be discussed.[108]

This statement nailed down the impression that Eagleton was capable of continuing on the ticket and had only been removed to serve McGovern's political interests. Its genesis was the fourth hidden dimension of the Eagleton affair. The words that McGovern read to the press were, he says, not his own; they had been drafted by Eagleton and his staff to ensure *his* political survival.[109] It was Eagleton who was behind the claim that health was not a factor in McGovern's decision. McGovern argues that since he had no authority to fire Eagleton, who was the nominee selected by the Democratic convention, he had no option but to accept Eagleton's terms, even with their high cost to his own reputation. As

McGovern puts it: "If I had said, 'Well, Tom, . . . I've got to explain to the country that you have an illness that is one that competent psychiatrists feel should keep you from occupying the highest office in the land,' he would not have stepped down." On the contrary, McGovern recalls, Eagleton threatened that if there was one word spoken by McGovern or his staff about the issue of mental health, "I'll stay on this ticket and fight you all the way to November."[110]

To the public, unaware of the hidden dimensions of the affair, Eagleton came out of it the victim and McGovern was viewed as the transgressor. The media was remarkably gentle with the senator from Missouri. *Newsweek* gave him three pages to tell his version of the story, *Time* a full page, and in neither magazine did Eagleton have to answer any questions.[111] Meanwhile, McGovern lacked a comparable opportunity—or the freedom—to present the full story from his side. Eagleton was off the ticket, but his political reputation, unlike McGovern's, was secure. According to pollster Patrick Caddell, "By the fall campaign, the most popular person in the country was not the President, or Senator Kennedy, or Senator Humphrey, or Senator McGovern—but Senator Eagleton. And his popularity was derived from the fact that people felt that he had gotten a raw deal."[112]

Under these circumstances, there was hardly any sympathy for McGovern except among his inner circle, who alone knew about the hidden dimensions of the affair. The effect of the Eagleton fiasco, *Time* commented, was "to make McGovern look either devious or weak or both, or at the most charitable, indecisive."[113] In the spring, McGovern had been the masterful commander of a stunning insurgency; thanks to the Eagleton affair, with its initial botched choice and subsequent clumsy reversals, he appeared to be a candidate of questionable competence. In the spring, McGovern had been a fresh voice of candor and integrity; thanks to the Eagleton affair, with his "thousand percent" support and then push of his running mate off the ticket, he appeared to be a candidate of dubious credibility. McGovernites expected to have a huge advantage over "Tricky Dick" Nixon in the matter of character, but it was their man whose character was under a cloud after the Eagleton affair. This event, McGovern lamented, "overshadowed the Watergate scandal as a subject of journalistic concern. It—not Watergate, not Vietnam, not the American economy—was *the* political story of 1972."[114]

It is conceivable that the Eagleton affair cost McGovern a good shot at the presidency—not in 1972 but in 1976. After the Democratic convention he was well behind Nixon, but Humphrey had nearly closed a similar gap against Nixon four years earlier. Even without his Eagleton burden, however, McGovern was not likely to make up ground as well as Humphrey had, considering the absence of Wallace from the race, the image of radicalism, the rift with the Democratic regulars, and the extensive assets of the president in 1972. Nonetheless, had McGovern selected a different running mate and thereby averted the fiasco that befell him in the last week of July, he might have run a more respectable race against Nixon. Some McGovernites speculate about a possibility that was precluded by the Eagleton affair. Frank Mankiewicz believes that "McGovern could have been elected in 1976 had he run a more accepted losing race in 1972."[115] Bob Shrum shares this view and spells out its logic: "If it had not been for the Eagleton affair, George would have carried 10 or 12 states; [he] still would have lost [but] would have got about 45–46 percent of the votes. And having been right about Vietnam and Watergate, he probably would have been the Democratic nominee for president and maybe the president in 1976."[116]

Conclusion

There was no real chance of the McGovern campaign ever recovering from the Eagleton affair. The impact of the affair itself, coming in the wake of Humphrey's attacks in the California primary and the chaos at the Miami Beach convention, was devastating enough. But after Eagleton, the press presented McGovern through a fatal frame: hapless loser. Dick Dougherty, McGovern's press secretary after the convention, wrote, "As a running news story, we were no longer Mc-Govern, the presidential nominee; we were McGovern-in-trouble . . . Had things gone the other way, had Eagleton never seen the inside of a hospital but been the attractive young politician he appeared to be, the story would have been entirely different."[117] Kirby Jones, Dougherty's predecessor as press secretary, concurs, "[The press] looked for events and incidents that reaffirmed this new perception of McGovern as a screw-up."[118]

Reporters did not have to look too far, and they soon had new tales to tell of a feckless Democratic nominee. McGovern's search for Eagleton's replacement became another farce in the eyes of the media, which portrayed him, in the words of *Newsweek*, as "the supplicant who couldn't find anybody of even middling-high reputation to run with."[119] Aware of McGovern's increasingly dim prospects, a string of Democrats, including Ted Kennedy and Hubert Humphrey, rebuffed an offer to join his ticket. The most embarrassing response came from Ed Muskie, who, in perhaps unconscious payback to McGovern for waylaying the frontrunner in the early primaries, insisted on holding a press conference to publicize his rejection. Finally, McGovern found a running mate: Sargent Shriver. A Catholic, a member-by-marriage of the Kennedy family, a veteran of the Peace Corps under JFK and the War on Poverty under LBJ, Shriver was a good substitute. But any positive press McGovern might have reaped from the choice was outweighed by the humiliation of the search process.

If the selection of a new running mate deepened doubts about McGovern's competence, a flap about Pierre Salinger shortly afterward renewed questions about his credibility. Salinger had headed to Paris after the Democratic convention, and McGovern had asked him to convey to the North Vietnamese delegation to the peace talks there the candidate's hope that they might release some

American POWs as a gesture of their desire to terminate the conflict. Three weeks later, while McGovern was on a campaign trip to the Illinois State Fair, he was asked by the press about a report that Salinger had told the North Vietnamese they would do better negotiating with Nixon than waiting for his possible election. Since this was not what he had instructed Salinger to say, McGovern denied the report. Worse, in what he called a burst of irritability—that also reflected his characteristic impulsiveness—he claimed to know nothing about the Salinger mission. The original press report had been incorrect, but McGovern's blanket denial was a further error of judgment that subsequently had to be acknowledged. As he wrote later, "In the network news and in the papers, . . . the story appeared as another McGovern reversal: the Democratic candidate first had denied and then confirmed assigning Salinger to contact the North Vietnamese."[120]

By mid-August, weeks before the traditional Labor Day opening of the presidential contest, the McGovern campaign was badly battered. Not all of the beating that McGovern was taking during this period was his fault: the bitter-end opposition of the regulars from the California primary through the Miami Beach convention, and the deception of his first running mate, were each a major contributor to his downfall. Yet McGovern's own weaknesses *were* on display in these months. He was accused of being indecisive and opportunistic, but these were not his actual flaws. His chief mistakes in these months stemmed from his inflated self-confidence, which led him to several impulsive and ill-considered decisions that later had to be rescinded.

"In retrospect," Gary Hart reflected, "[the] campaign was doomed when Eagleton was selected. We could not win with him or without him. There was no way out."[121] Hart's judgment was correct. Yet McGovern and his army, willfully but necessarily, shut out the harbingers of their imminent demise. The same self-confidence that drove McGovern to serious errors of judgment fed a steely determination to pull off a political miracle in the fall even more astounding than the one in the spring. McGovern and his army had, in their deep and passionate opposition to the war in Vietnam, a profound cause that inspired a continuing commitment. After the Eagleton affair, defeat was staring McGovernites in the face—but they were not going down without a struggle.

5

"A Long, Slow Crawl"

In mid-October 1972, George McGovern was delivering one of his standard speeches on Vietnam at the University of Minnesota when he interrupted his remarks to play a tape recording. As the campus audience listened, in the words of *Time*, in "stunned silence," an anonymous voice came through the loudspeakers:

> I am a Viet Nam veteran, and I don't think the American people really, really understand war and what's going on. We went into villages after they dropped napalm, and the human beings were fused together like pieces of metal that had been soldered. Sometimes you couldn't tell if they were people or animals . . . I condoned that. I watched it go on. Now I'm home. Sometimes I, my heart, it bothers me inside, because I remember all that, and I didn't have the courage then to say it was wrong.[1]

It is scarcely a commonplace for a candidate for the presidency to speak of American atrocities in a distant war. McGovern's aides were as shocked as the reporters covering his campaign when the tape came on, and some worried about the political fallout from the grisly and guilt-ridden portrait it painted. But McGovern's Minneapolis surprise did not attract a great deal of attention, since the Democratic candidate was, by this point in the fall campaign, perceived as so prone to gaffes and so hopelessly far behind that whatever he did was greeted with widespread indifference. That indifference may be the best explanation for McGovern's otherwise-odd violation of American political norms. Unable to make his message heard by any but his committed antiwar supporters, and confronted with the majority's seeming unconcern for the terrible violence being done in its name, McGovern was desperate enough to raise the stakes of political discourse. He still wanted to win the election, still clung to an increasingly fantastic scenario of a come-from-behind, photo-finish victory. Yet in some part of his mind, where the electoral reality had seeped in, he may have found compensatory satisfaction from this howl into the wind.

After the downward arc of the McGovern insurgency from the California primary through the Eagleton nightmare, the fall campaign against President Nixon was shadowed from the start by the specter of futility. For much of its course, many in the press, disenchanted with the insurgency after the convention and Eagleton, depicted McGovern and his aides as rank amateurs losing a lopsided game they could barely play. But as the end neared, some of the media began to express sympathy tinged with a trace of pity. *Time* dubbed McGovern's campaign "the hard-luck crusade," and *Newsweek* similarly observed that McGovern had been "luckless" since the primaries.[2]

Yet to depict McGovern's closing effort merely through the terms of pathos is to miss its deeper dignity. Brought low by a summer of disasters, and widely condemned as a conniving politician rather than a reformist "white knight," McGovern ran a fall campaign that eventually reestablished many of the virtues he had originally displayed in the spring, though few noticed or believed anymore. Among the journalists assigned to follow his campaign, William Greider of the *Washington Post* was the least inclined to join in the drumbeat of criticism about an inept candidate. To Greider, the McGovern campaign was not a farce but a tragedy. "This guy is trapped in events," went the essential storyline of Greider's coverage; "he's struggling heroically to overcome them, and he's not succeeding."[3]

Holding on to hope against an impending debacle that loomed ever nearer, McGovern had to endure blow after blow against his honor and his pride. At times, he had to struggle against perhaps the worst thing that can happen to an American political leader: becoming a subject of ridicule in place of respect. His fall campaign for the presidency was not without further stumbles, and years later he remembered it painfully as "a long, slow crawl."[4] In the end he righted himself and reclaimed his honor. Nonetheless, his not inconsiderable pride, well concealed beneath a mild and gentle exterior, was about to suffer a wound that would never quite heal.

McGovern among the Regulars

To many observers, the McGovern campaign against Richard Nixon in the fall of 1972 appeared fevered but formless, a bootless wandering in the political wilderness. The campaign had devoted some time to strategy for the fall before the Democratic convention, but its planning was limited to questions of the electoral college map, budgeting, and personnel.[5] Consumed by the California challenge, the convention battle, and the Eagleton affair, McGovernites paid little attention during this period to a larger thematic framework. As a result, Theodore White wrote with some scorn, everyone seemed to have his or her own plan for defeating Nixon, and the campaign shifted aimlessly from one of these to another.[6] Looking back decades later, some McGovernites recall even more of a strategic blankness. Frank Mankiewicz says that in contesting Nixon, "we had no plan as to how to run the campaign after the convention."[7] Harold Himmelman is even more critical of his comrades and himself: "This was a very innocent and inexperienced group of people who won something [the Democratic nomination] they had no idea what to do with once they won it."[8]

Nonetheless, it is possible to discern two distinct phases of the fall McGovern campaign, each occupying roughly half of the period from the end of the Eagleton affair until Election Day. While there was some overlap between these phases, there was also a significant shift in theme and tone midway through the fall contest. As one of McGovern's three speechwriters, Sandy Berger was in a good position to define this shift: "After the convention, there was a phase in which McGovern became Hubert Humphrey, a rather traditional Democratic candidate. We would do speeches on what . . . the bowling-alley audience wanted to hear . . . [Then], McGovern got his bearings back, maybe at the point at which he saw the gap [in the polls] was pretty yawning. The campaign became about the war and about Watergate."[9]

Courting Democratic regulars seemed imperative to McGovern after the bitterness of the spring and at the convention. In a sense, this courtship had always been integral to his strategy—the "center" stage envisioned two years earlier at Cedar Point after the wooing of the "left" in the early going. But the task now appeared far more daunting than McGovern had ever imagined. The difficulty was symbolized by the implacable opposition of AFL-CIO president George Meany, who refused McGovern the endorsement, money, and manpower of his federation. While many union leaders dissented from the official AFL-CIO line and rallied behind the nominee of their party, the hostility of Meany and his allies epitomized the roadblocks in McGovern's way as he tried to stitch regular Democrats together with his insurgent base.

Turning himself into another Hubert Humphrey was the recommendation that McGovern was receiving from many voices in the party establishment and the mainstream press. At a private dinner in St. Paul, Humphrey himself advised McGovern that he "ought to emphasize economic issues almost exclusively."[10] Ted Van Dyk advocated the same message in a strategy memo to the candidate, arguing that all of McGovern's campaign positions should be rolled into "one central theme." This theme, Van Dyk wrote, was simple: "Richard Nixon and the Republicans favor big business and special interests. George McGovern and the Democrats favor ordinary people and their interests."[11]

McGovern began his reconciliation campaign immediately after his selection of Sargent Shriver ended the Eagleton affair (though not its lasting damage to his image). At the mini-convention that ratified his choice of Shriver, a popular figure with the regulars, he held a series of "unity meetings" with elected Democratic officials. His first trip after the mini-convention, through New England and New York, was also designed to make up with party regulars as well as to regain some momentum. Yet the auguries were far from favorable. As *Newsweek* noted, "His New England swing was tarnished in Providence the second day by the conspicuous absence of the mayor (who sent word he was out of town) and the frostiness of the state chairman (who pledged sardonically to back McGovern '1,000 per cent')."[12]

Intensifying his efforts at reconciliation, McGovern made visits to the two figures that, more than any others, represented the wing of the Democratic Party that he had defeated through his insurgency. First up, late in August, was a pilgrimage to the Johnson ranch in the Texas Hill Country to obtain the blessing of the ex-president with whom McGovern had warred over Vietnam. Avoiding the subject that still divided them, the two men talked politics, and LBJ offered sage advice to McGovern to emphasize his World War II record of heroism and proclaim his gratitude for the opportunity that America had granted to him as a poor boy from the prairie. Considering their previous rift, the two men got along surprisingly well, perhaps because Johnson, in political retreat and failing health, and McGovern, battered after the Eagleton fiasco, were both wounded men. LBJ, with a white mane flowing down to his shoulders, even looked like a McGovern supporter.[13]

The next day, McGovern flew north to see Mayor Richard Daley of Chicago and repair some of the damage done when Daley's delegation had been rejected by McGovernites at Miami Beach. Badly needing to carry Illinois, McGovern was open to Daley-style political bargaining. "We had a meeting with Mayor Daley," McGovern recalls, "and he just put it to me straight. 'You back the county slate and the Illinois Democratic slate, you know, our candidates across the board, [and] I'll back you.' So I agreed to that readily."[14] Too readily, it turned out, because on Daley's slate was State's Attorney Edward Hanrahan, who had been in charge of the infamous raid that gunned down Chicago Black Panther leader Fred Hampton. In the language of politics, the quid pro quo that Daley demanded was reasonable, but in the language of moral reform that McGovern was touting, it was something of an embarrassment.

What Berger describes as the "bowling-alley audience" phase of the fall campaign went on well into September of 1972. McGovern enlisted not only Ted Kennedy but also two of his defeated rivals from the spring, Edmund Muskie and Hubert Humphrey, to join him for rallies on the campaign trail.[15] It was unconventional for a presidential candidate to share the limelight with other party leaders, but McGovern felt that he needed to borrow legitimacy from Kennedy charisma and Muskie-Humphrey orthodoxy. Another feature of this phase was a repositioning on the domestic issues that had brought McGovern the most trouble in the spring. In a speech before the New York Society of Security Analysts, McGovern dumped his notorious "demogrant" in favor of a more conventional welfare scheme and reshaped the tax reform plan that had brought cries of alarm from Wall Street. The speech was received favorably in the media, but to some voters the changes on welfare and taxes only furthered the post-Eagleton perception that McGovern was inconsistent and opportunistic.[16]

The initial fall strategy aimed to bring home disaffected Democrats, but a number of signs pointed to its inefficacy. In part, its message was overshadowed in the media by continuing difficulties within the McGovern campaign. The narrative frame that press secretary Dick Dougherty described as "McGovern-in-trouble," formed during the Eagleton affair and elaborated in the embarrassing search for his replacement and the flap over Pierre Salinger's mission to Paris, was further applied to an emerging tale of a campaign organization in disarray. Staff conflicts and resignations (or threatened ones) further blistered McGovern's reputation for competence, leading to the question of how he could ever manage the burdens of the presidency if he could not even maintain his own campaign in good order.[17] The worst personnel problem was the awkward standing of campaign "chairman" Larry O'Brien, whom McGovern had recruited for the fall as an ambassador to the regulars. This veteran of the Kennedy-Johnson era was, not surprisingly, uncomfortable with the guerrilla style of the McGovernites, and he intimated to a journalist that unless the campaign organization was refashioned to his liking, he might quit. O'Brien later denied that he ever actually threatened to resign, but his disgruntlement signaled to regulars that they could not work with the McGovernites and to reporters that McGovern was still at sea about how to run a presidential campaign.[18]

A disarray motif for the McGovern campaign fed beautifully into the plans of the opposition, because the Nixon campaign, reflecting its leader's obsessive hierarchical bent, was nothing if not organized. The Republican convention in late August, held, like the Democratic conclave, in Miami Beach, made for a dramatic contrast with the chaotic gathering that nominated McGovern and Eagleton. The GOP's celebration of President Nixon was, as *Newsweek* put it, "a clockwork convention." Through an accident, the press obtained a copy of a secret Nixon convention plan and learned that the Republicans' "democratic process was scripted right down to pauses for laughter and applause."[19] The reassuring imagery of order was intensified by the smooth-running organizational machine at the Committee to Re-Elect the President. To be sure, the Nixon operation had its own internal tensions, but the press was effectively shut out and the facade of masterful discipline upheld.

McGovernites protested in vain that the press was missing the real story of the Nixon organization. While journalists exposed every minute squabble at the wide-open McGovern offices, they neglected to point out the far more troubling conduct at Nixon's fortress-like headquarters. Dick Dougherty's campaign memoir noted McGovern's exasperation at press stories about his staff:

"Why's the press making so much out of these petty things? It's ordinary shakedown stuff you might get at the start of any campaign. What's it amount to compared to Nixon's campaign? We haven't had a John Mitchell quit as head of our campaign. We haven't had his wife telling about security men ripping her phone out and sticking hypodermics in her ass. We haven't had our people arrested in the dead of night with their rubber gloves on burglarizing and bugging the Committee to Re-Elect the President."[20]

As Nixon stuck close to the White House and cloaked his brass-knuckles political style with the constitutional dignity of his office, McGovern tried to cut into the president's huge lead during the first phase of the fall campaign through an exhausting travel schedule. Writing off the South, he tirelessly traversed the Northeast, Midwest, and Pacific Coast. As he recalled in his autobiography,

> Gary Hart, Frank Mankiewicz, and scheduling director Steve Robbins planned a relentless blitz, taking me by jet to three or four major cities a day. The days often began at the crack of dawn and ended at three in the morning. The Labor Day schedule set the pace. I started with two rallies in Ohio, flew to an early evening rally in Oakland, California, and then on to a late-night rally in downtown Seattle.[21]

McGovern rallies consistently drew large and enthusiastic crowds. But these were mostly composed of his youthful supporters; the traditional blue-collar Democrats that were the target of this phase of the fall campaign were not much in evidence. And as McGovern courted the center but had little to show for his efforts, Democrats on the left grew increasingly restive at his embrace of his former foes. His old allies began to warn him that his new solicitude for the likes of Lyndon Johnson and Richard Daley was threatening to alienate his base. Columbia University economist Seymour Melman wrote to McGovern in mid-September that "all around me, wherever I go, I am confronted by pro-McGovern people who are depressed and despairing, who have been turned off by the quality of your campaign since the national convention." Melman cited "the stamp of politics as usual" and the accommodation of the Humphrey Democrats as the source of liberal discontent with McGovern's centrist strategy.[22]

It was less the storm clouds on the left that prodded McGovern to shift his strategy in September, however, than the grim poll findings that his bread-and-butter appeal to Democratic regulars was getting him nowhere. With forgivable hyperbole, Gary Hart wrote that "the adverse public opinion polls . . . dropped periodically on the campaign like nuclear bombs on some devastated island."[23] The bomb blast was most extensive during the first phase of the campaign. For example, in three Gallup Polls, taken in early August, late August, and mid-to-late September, McGovern dropped from 26 points behind Nixon to 34 points behind him and then crept back up only to 28 points in the rear.[24] For the "center" thrust envisioned in the original McGovern strategy, which had already been bent almost beyond recognition from the primaries through the Eagleton affair, this was the final repudiation. The McGovern insurgency had been born on the left, and there, in the second phase of the fall campaign, it would take its last stand.

Grassroots and Media Politics

Overcoming such an enormous Nixon lead presented a problem of media as well as message. The McGovern insurgency had been propelled in the primaries, most of all, by its dedicated grassroots army. Yet in a general election, fought nationwide over a short span of time, strength in the field was necessarily secondary to the effectiveness of a candidate's self-presentation and thematic message on television and in print. The McGovern campaign still had experienced organizers and idealistic volunteers in abundance, but it was at a serious disadvantage in competing with the Nixon campaign, flush with nearly unlimited funds and expert at the art of attack, on the terrain of media politics.

The dispiriting events of the summer of 1972, especially the Eagleton affair, filtered down into the ranks of McGovern's army, but there were remarkably few desertions. To a considerable extent, the McGovern campaign remained a grassroots endeavor to the end. Gary Hart, the champion at McGovern headquarters of the grassroots approach, wrote with pride about its vigor in the fall even under the most discouraging of circumstances:

> Following the Eagleton nightmare, and then through demoralizing rumblings of power struggles and the Salinger incident, the work went forward in the field. Throughout August, hundreds of headquarters and storefront offices were opened, thousands of phones installed, millions of pieces of literature printed, hundreds of thousands of volunteers recruited . . . This massive, monumental organizational effort was the great unreported story of the fall.[25]

Perhaps most remarkable was the number of volunteers who continued to stream into McGovern offices across the nation even as the press disparaged his campaign and the polls demolished his prospects. Even if some of these volunteers were less certain about the candidate than they had been in the spring, the cause for which he stood remained undiminished in their eyes by the hostile treatment it was receiving. No accurate count of McGovern volunteers exists. But a sense of their numbers can be gleaned from a September Gallup Poll, which found that "15 per cent of registered voters who currently prefer McGovern over Nixon say they plan to work in the Democratic campaign."[26]

Out in the field, McGovernites threw themselves into their work and struggled against omens of futility. They were aware of the terrible polls—but were armed with a rationale for discounting their significance. As Ted Pulliam, one of the earliest McGovern campaign staffers, observes, the polls were equally unfavorable in the spring—and repeatedly falsified once McGovern's insurgency gained traction. So, Pulliam says, "we figured the polls were sort of meaningless."[27] Passionate, and often defiant in the rebellious sixties style, McGovernites held tightly to their belief in the fundamental decency of their candidate and the overriding urgency of putting an end to the war in Vietnam. Jamie Galbraith spent the fall working in Youngstown, Ohio, and he remembers, amid all the frustrations of the campaign, that there was "still esprit de corps."[28]

Yet as the end of the fall campaign approached, at least some McGovern field workers began to feel despair.[29] No matter how extensive or efficient the grass-roots army was in local political arenas, it could not compensate for disadvantages in the national media war. Even the guerrilla commanders of the spring insurgency were now reduced to bit players. Rick Stearns, the most brilliant of these commanders, observes that his role in the McGovern campaign during the fall was much diminished because "organizational work paled in importance [next] to what was happening on the candidate side and the media side of the campaign."[30] On the media side, McGovern's own grassroots style, so impressive back in New Hampshire and Wisconsin in the spring, was equally outdated. As Gordon Weil wrote, "McGovern was a superb campaigner. He actually enjoyed meeting average voters and worked hard at it. But people-to-people campaigning turned out to be far less important than national media coverage."[31]

Immersed in the frenetic campaign schedule of August and September, Mc-Govern and his top aides were unaware of how decisively they were losing the media campaign to Nixon. As McGovern tells the story, it was his wife, Eleanor, who delivered the news to him.

> She said, "George, Nixon's never on television except when they show him walking along the Great Wall of China [or] chatting with Chou En-Lai and Mao Tse-Tung. Or when they show him sitting in the White House with a nice soft blue shirt, he's in a rocking chair, and he's saying, 'yes, we're going to end the war in Vietnam, of course, but we're going to do it with honor'" . . . [By contrast], she said, "They flashed you, and you're on the back end of a truck out in Ohio somewhere. The wind is blowing, your hair is all over everywhere, you look like you need a shave . . . The lighting was bad, and you're just screaming into the wind."[32]

Wrapping himself in the dignity of his office, Nixon made himself an elusive target for the McGovernites. Slashing attacks on McGovern's incompetence and radicalism were left to a large stable of well-coached Republican surrogates and to state-of-the-art television attack ads. The president's greatest potential area of vulnerability, the Watergate scandal, was, of course, the focus of an extensive White House cover-up. Nixon rarely mentioned his own party; indeed, his own name was hidden beneath the slogan: "Re-elect the President." Sargent Shriver assailed Nixon's anonymity as a case for the psychiatrists, but the president's self-effacement was actually shrewd politics.[33] The McGovernites hoped that they could goad Nixon into coming out from the White House and engaging in a toe-to-toe battle with their candidate, which would remind the electorate of Nixon's aggressive character and his opponent's contrasting decency. It was an implausible scenario from the start.

The McGovern campaign challenged Nixon to a series of debates, but the incumbent had absolutely no incentive to take the bait. Debates between the presidential nominees of the two parties were not yet institutionalized (that would begin in 1976), and the only prior instance of one had proved very costly to Nixon. Running far ahead in the polls, it was easy for the president to ignore the clamor from the McGovernites that he must face their man.[34]

The McGovernites had pinned great hopes on the unpopularity of Richard Nixon, but the chief story line for the press that fall was the unpopularity of George McGovern. As George Lardner Jr. wrote for the *Washington Post* in late September, "With President Nixon sitting cannily in the White House, disdaining confrontation, McGovern is out in the field, all alone, trying to tilt with his opponent in absentia, but all too often shadow-boxing with his own image and style, in the greatest danger of suffering nicks and scrapes."[35] "The irony," a reporter for *Time* remarked a few weeks later, "is that the election so far is turning not on Nixon's character and credibility but on McGovern's."[36] Nothing depressed McGovern as much in the fall as the realization that the public rated Richard Nixon much higher than him not only as a leader but as a person. He was especially anguished by the findings from focus groups conducted by Haynes Johnson and David Broder for the *Washington Post*. Reading in their series of stories that the majority of Americans thought Nixon was more likely than McGovern to extricate the United States from Vietnam, McGovern says, "I had a hard time to keep from weeping in despair about this country." Johnson and Broder also reported that Nixon was far ahead of McGovern on credibility, thanks to the Eagleton fiasco. "I pondered that for a long time," McGovern relates. "How could Richard Nixon, who antedated Joe McCarthy, who was smearing peoples' character . . . how could he be the one who bested me even on credibility?"[37]

With the media war going so poorly, by mid-September the McGovern campaign began to receive suggestions from many quarters about bold new approaches. One of the most creative came from novelist Philip Roth. Roth proposed a series of television broadcasts in which McGovern would "face a panel of five American citizens (five new panelists each time) who oppose him. The goal here would not be to convert his opponents, or to 'best' them in argument, but rather to answer their objections, and thus to continue to clarify his position." For a candidate caricatured as both radical and inconsistent, Roth's little drama would allow him to address directly—and dispel—the doubts about his political identity that had mushroomed since Humphrey's attacks in California.[38]

Roth's clever but risky plan was not adopted, but a second suggestion of his— that McGovern should deliver several thirty-minute nationally televised speeches on the key issues—was exactly along the lines that McGovern strategists were already thinking. As McGovern observed in his autobiography, "By late September it was obvious that I had to reach the voters in a different way. Visiting three or four cities or towns a day was not enough, yet that brutal pace could not be stepped up. I had to communicate with more Americans in a shorter time."[39] The plan for switching the media strategy to "fireside chats" demanded a great deal of money and a large chunk of the candidate's precious time. Yet it also presented the first opportunity of the fall for McGovern to present himself and his ideas in his own terms rather than through the unflattering frame of journalistic coverage. The first of the national broadcasts, set for early October, would, naturally, be about the war in Vietnam. It was a chance for McGovern to recover his own voice and to revive the passions that had propelled his insurgency to its earlier successes. A second phase of the fall McGovern campaign was about to begin.

The Return of the Insurgent

In the second phase of his fall campaign, McGovern could no longer be mistaken for an updated version of Hubert Humphrey. In conflict with his gentle persona, he increasingly became a hard-hitting and harsh critic of President Nixon and of Nixon's America. Not only his Republican opponents but many members of the press as well complained that McGovern had crossed the line, sounding off as the self-righteous minister's son preaching to a congregation of American sinners. There was a tinge of political excess in this final McGovern, a reflection of his mounting desperation. But there were also many of the "hard truths" that McGovern had always promised to utter. The event that most clearly marked the opening of this second phase was McGovern's first nationally televised broadcast of the fall. On October 10, 1972, he spoke to the country about the war in Vietnam. The event was carefully staged to cloak McGovern with the dignity of his senatorial office and to buttress a claim called into question by the Eagleton affair—his consistency and conviction. The broadcast began with a shot of the Capitol dome and then cut to a Senate room, where McGovern sat quietly in a chair and looked into the camera with unmistakable earnestness.[40] His opening remarks reminded the viewers of how long and how fervently he had resisted the war:

> Under three separate presidents—two of them Democratic and one of them a Republican, I have opposed this war. During these same long years, Mr. Nixon has supported the war. This, I think, is the sharpest and most important difference between Mr. Nixon and me in the 1972 presidential campaign. Mr. Nixon has described the war as our finest hour. I regard it as the saddest chapter in our national history.[41]

McGovern's Vietnam broadcast highlighted both the material and the ethical costs of the war for Americans. "Since he came to the presidency," McGovern pointed out, "Mr. Nixon has spent $60 billion of your money on this war—$60 billion of your taxes to kill human beings in Asia instead of protecting and improving human life in America." He appealed to Americans to think not only of their own casualties but of the even greater suffering of the Vietnamese people. And he insisted that bringing an immediate end to this terrible war was not an ignominious retreat but a requirement of American patriotism: "As a bomber pilot in World War Two, like millions of you, I did what had to be done . . . I loved America enough to offer my life in war thirty years ago. And for nine years I have loved this country enough to risk my political life to call us home from a war in Asia that does not serve the interests and the ideals of the American nation."[42]

This speech may not have won McGovern many converts, but it did inspirit his antiwar base. It ended with an appeal for funds, and in response $1.5 million poured into McGovern headquarters.[43] With this speech, opposition to the war became the leitmotif of the McGovern campaign at the end, as it had been at the beginning of the insurgency. McGovern's "magnificent obsession" to end the American nightmare in Vietnam once more became the campaign's hallmark. As with the Vietnam veteran's tape recording that opened this chapter, the candidate's own discourse on Vietnam was unsettling. William Greider observed in the *Washington Post* that "McGovern's moral message is repugnant to a great many American voters who not only disagree with it, but are outraged that a major party presidential candidate should even be saying such things."[44] McGovern was quite willing to shock complacent Americans—but he also clung to the hope that after that initial shock, the essential decency of the American people might be reawakened.

McGovern did not abandon the bread-and-butter themes of the prior phase of the fall campaign. Ten days after his first nationally televised speech, he delivered a second, "Four Years and No Prosperity." In this broadcast, McGovern attempted to woo back blue-collar Democrats by invoking the class imagery of Franklin Roosevelt and Harry Truman. He cast President Nixon as the heir of Herbert Hoover: "Every single time this administration has faced an important economic choice, they have picked a policy that is right for the few and wrong for you." He cast himself as a Democratic populist, fighting for the interests of working people, yet pilloried almost beyond recognition by the falsehoods of the Nixon campaign.

Now the Nixon Administration seeks to blind you to their failures and their favoritism by scaring you about me. They know who you will support if issues like tax reform and jobs and inflation are honestly debated. They know your true interests are with the Democratic Party in 1972, but they do not want you to know. So they are trying to frighten you to vote against yourselves.[45]

It was the topic of McGovern's third televised speech—the historic corruption of the Nixon administration—that brought him the most extensive condemnation as a moralistic scold. McGovern's October 25 broadcast capped a month of sharply worded commentary on the unfolding Watergate scandal, which the *Washington Post*, alone among major newspapers, was vigorously pursuing at the time. Eleanor McGovern set the tone in an early October appearance on *Meet the Press* by charging that the Nixon administration was "the most corrupt in recent history." Her husband upped the ante the next day in a speech to a UPI editors' conference by removing the qualifying adjective. The break-in at the Watergate, he insisted, was only one instance of a broad pattern of corruption. The Nixon administration was indicted for its crass favoritism to privileged interests, its assaults on a free press and other First Amendment values, and its illegal war-making. It represented not only "the corruption of government but the corruption of America."[46] Just as with his heated rhetoric on Vietnam, McGovern's tough talk on corruption was widely castigated: a challenger was not supposed to speak such inflammatory words about a sitting president of the United States.

The critique of corruption that McGovern and his aides developed was both genuinely felt and politically calculated. So much had gone awry for the McGovern campaign since the California primary that the Watergate scandal appeared as an unexpected opening—a last chance to demonstrate the true nature of what the McGovernites were fighting. Frank Mankiewicz was particularly charged up by the political potential of the corruption issue. As he recounts, "We thought Watergate would be a much stronger issue than it was . . . [We talked a lot] about corruption. It didn't work. People were not that interested, then!"[47] In those innocent days before the secret history of the Nixon administration was revealed, it was hard for all but the Nixon haters to believe that the conduct of the president and his men could be so sordid. The McGovernites' talk of corruption was discounted as the desperate exaggerations of a doomed campaign.

Although there were few indications that the charges of corruption against the Nixon administration were sticking, the October 25 broadcast developed them into a comprehensive and detailed argument about the threat to American integrity. McGovern's speech laid out the then-available evidence about the misdeeds of the Nixon presidency. Challenging the view that McGovern's character was the real issue of the campaign, the speech attempted to shift the focus to the ethical mire in the Nixon White House. In words that were dismissed at the time as moralistic fulmination, McGovern drew a chilling conclusion: "Ambitious men come and go, but a free society might never recover from a sustained assault on its most basic institutions. And one can only ask, If this has happened in four years, to what lengths would the same leadership go in another four years, once freed of the restraints of facing the people for reelection?"[48]

The three televised speeches required McGovern to take some breaks from his rigorous travel schedule, but apart from these there was little slackening of his coast-to-coast campaigning. Modest improvement in the national polls during October gave encouragement to his overworked staff, as did the crowds at the candidate's appearances, which, Gary Hart noted, "ranged from good to spectacular, in both size and enthusiasm."[49] Hard-nosed political realism would have dashed the McGovernites' lingering hopes, telling them that the gap in the polls was too huge to close and that the crowds were mostly composed of the same passionate antiwar activists who had turned out for McGovern in the spring. But the McGovernites had pulled off miraculous upsets before and would not give up the ghost now. There was still enough of their faith left even to dream of a McGovern administration, and so they turned for advice on planning a presidential transition to men who had done it before. McGovern penned a note to himself: "Write Ted Sorenson [President Kennedy's closest aide] to begin setting forth a transitional plan—office procedure—staffing—task force—early problems for the period Nov. 8–Jan. 20."[50] Gary Hart enlisted a top LBJ aide, Harry MacPherson, for a similar undertaking.[51]

As McGovern and his aides jetted around the country, a journey that outside observers were writing off as desperate took on a strange air of gaiety. The McGovern campaign may have been the last gasp of the 1960s, but it would have some rebellious fun before it expired. A campaign that would treat Hunter Thompson as an insider was bound to be unique in the annals of modern American politics. McGovern himself had a rich sense of humor beneath his sober mien, but the mood on his campaign plane, *Dakota II*, was somewhat subdued by the depressing turn of events that the Eagleton affair brought.[52] On the second campaign plane, however, filled mostly with reporters and staffers, levity was the hallmark. Reporters christened it the "Zoo Plane," and as Timothy Crouse, author of *The Boys on the Bus*, described it, it resembled nothing as much as John Belushi's *Animal House*:

> The Zoo Plane had the look and air of the poorest but wildest frat house on a Southern campus. There were posters and campaign totems everywhere—a cardboard skeleton labeled Ms. Boney Maroni, a dandruff ad onto which had been pasted a picture of George McGovern with confetti in his hair, a Roosevelt and Garner poster, Polaroid snapshots of all the regulars, orange and black streamers for Halloween . . . The excitement of riding the Zoo Plane sprang from the fact that all rules had been totally suspended.[53]

Ardent followers and a spirited entourage provided McGovern with something of a cocoon for the last stages of the campaign. Yet a few supporters ventured to puncture persisting illusions of victory, perhaps out of a concern to prepare a man that they admired for the heartache sure to come. William Greider witnessed an incident in Detroit, where McGovern heard from "an earnest young man standing in a circle of admirers . . . 'I'm for you,'" the McGovern supporter told the candidate. "'We're all for you. But you're going to be extremely disappointed in this country. People just don't give a damn the way you do.'"[54]

McGovern did, as Sandy Berger remarks, get his bearings back in the second phase of his fall campaign. The televised speeches that were the centerpiece of this phase made up little ground for him against Nixon, but they articulated in depth and with detail what he had to say to the American people. These speeches can legitimately be interpreted in two opposite ways—as politics or as prophecy. In the first, McGovern was engaging in a calculated effort to break through the indifference of the public and jolt Americans into turning against the Nixon administration and all of its evils. In the second, his was a voice of impolitic alarm, saying not what might win him the election so much as what was on his pained American conscience.

"Kiss My Ass!": The Final Weeks

Challengers may hurl verbal brickbats at an incumbent president, but the man in the White House has the power to trump words with deeds. The day after McGovern appeared on national television to condemn the corruption of the Nixon administration, Henry Kissinger, the president's national security adviser and the media's darling, went before the cameras to proclaim that "peace is at hand" in Vietnam. According to Kissinger, only minor details needed to be ironed out with North Vietnamese negotiators in Paris before the war would be stopped. There was much uncertainty about the veracity of the claim and mounting suspicion that it was an electoral ploy. A week after the Kissinger statement, the president went on television and backed away from it. This notorious incident probably did not help Nixon's credibility on the war. But it effectively switched the subject from corruption, ensuring that the campaign would end with a concentration on the issue about which McGovern cared most passionately but upon which Nixon had the more popular position.[55]

Knocked temporarily off stride by the Kissinger announcement, McGovern and his aides became increasingly convinced that the talk of peace was merely a campaign gambit. The night after Nixon's television appearance, McGovern took to the airwaves for his final indictment of the president.

> The President may say peace, peace—but there is no peace, and there never was. For it is not the details but the central issues that are still in dispute. I

know that many Americans were struck by the coincidence that after four years of fighting and dying, the Administration announced just twelve days before the election that peace was in reach . . . But, like you, I wanted deeply to believe what we were told . . . Now this hope is betrayed.[56]

McGovern's speech contained more than anger and accusation. Near its end, he acknowledged with startling sadness for a presidential candidate that his obsession to end the war might not be shared by the majority of Americans.

I do not honestly know whether the war weighs as deeply on the minds of the American people as it does on mine. I do not honestly know whether the blunt words I have said tonight will help me or hurt me in this election. I do not really care. For almost a decade, my heart has ached over the fighting and the dying in Vietnam. I cannot remember a day when I did not think of this tragedy.[57]

The controversy over whether peace was actually "at hand" was the main event of the campaign's closing weeks. Otherwise, it ended with a blur of intense McGovernite activity on the campaign trail and in the field, and brought into stark relief both the affection and the animosity that the insurgent evoked. Already impressively large, the crowds at McGovern rallies grew bigger still as Election Day approached. At times, they seemed to take it on themselves to lift the weary and frustrated candidate. "People pushed crumpled dollar bills into his hands," Greider reported from Moline, Illinois. "Small children called him 'George,' and the teenagers told him he is beautiful. And, all along the fencerow, their words and faces sought to reassure him."[58] The flow of donations became so immense that McGovern's headquarters staff had to organize late-night "parties" to handle the towering mailbags full of money. Lacking the warm bath of friendly crowds that the candidate and his traveling party were enjoying, the McGovernites in Washington found therapeutic relief from their miseries by counting the small bills that signaled the hope and determination of so many of their supporters.[59]

Hostility as well as love tracked McGovern during the final weeks of the campaign. His rallies drew some hecklers along with the throngs of admirers, and their gibes finally snapped his patience. In Battle Creek, Michigan, as McGovern told the story in his autobiography, "an unusually obnoxious" heckler "started working me over. Eleanor was with me, and I was doubly angered. I motioned for the man to lean over the fence and whispered in his ear, 'Listen, you son of a bitch, why don't you kiss my ass.'"[60] The heckler related McGovern's words to a nearby reporter, and McGovern's profanity became national news. Some aides worried about the political effect, but McGovern, then and in later years, relished the remark.[61] Mistaken too often for a milquetoast, McGovern was a genuinely gentle man, but he could always hit as hard as he was being hit.

The accusation that most infuriated McGovern and his aides during the final weeks was not profaneness but piety. The final issue of *Newsweek* to hit the stands before the election contained a devastatingly contemptuous portrait of McGovern. Written by Richard Stout, who was covering the McGovern campaign, and Peter Goldman, the newsmagazine's premier stylist, the article opened with words seldom seen in a pillar of "objective" journalism:

> His eyes go flat and lifeless on television. His voice struggles for passion and sounds like grace at a Rotary lunch. His mandatory candidate's tan, in these last sunless hours before Election Day, is fading toward vellum. He looks less the politician than the schoolmaster, an assemblage of bony angles and stray wisps of hair and ill-at-ease smiles; even the junior staffers aboard his charter 727, the Dakota Queen II, refer to him with mixed affection and despair as McGoo. But George Stanley McGovern, in the waning weeks of his campaign, has turned more furiously evangelical than any major-party candidate since William Jennings Bryan . . . He is, in a sense, the preacher's boy from Mitchell, S.D., come home in the end to the politics of rectitude . . . With his polls stubbornly low and his own good-guy reputation tarnished by events, he has returned more and more to the old moral absolutes—and to the harshest rhetoric of any campaign in memory.[62]

Although other reporters with the McGovern campaign did not share the indignation that the Stout-Goldman piece provoked in the McGovernites, most of them did not, apparently, agree with the portrait either. According to Timothy Crouse, the majority of journalists traveling with McGovern may have pounced on his flaws, but they liked him and "most of them secretly wanted to see him beat Richard Nixon."[63] They witnessed McGovern in all of his complexity, yet only a few captured this effectively in their reportage. Radical, opportunist, bungler, and now sanctimonious prig—a succession of unflattering media images accompanied McGovern along the campaign trail. The candidate was not without fault in contributing to these caricatures. Nonetheless, he had a legitimate grievance that neither his character nor his message came through the media to the public without considerable distortion.

Conclusion

Like many celebrities, comedian Tommy Smothers actively campaigned for McGovern. In Chicago a week before Election Day, Smothers's remarks, taped by a

McGovern staffer, were completely at odds with his goofy television persona but were representative of the mood of apocalyptic dread that lurked just beneath so many McGovern supporters' willed hopefulness. "I was wondering," Smothers told the audience in at attempt to combat its defeatist air, "what happened to that passion that we all had a long time ago and how we felt so outraged and incredulous [at] things going down . . . When you get six years of Johnson followed by four years of Nixon, you've got ten years laying on your head, and now if Jesus Christ was running on the Democratic ticket, you'd say he was full of shit too." An opponent of the overweening establishment was bound to stumble, Smothers said, but even if McGovern was less than perfect as a candidate, voters should consider the awful alternative. Smothers concluded by citing an article he had just read by novelist Hans Koning: "He says the uglies of this world are watching this election. The uglies of the world from London to Johannesburg to Saigon to Peking, the facts of life guys . . . the moneychangers, the pigs . . . the Argentine torturers are watching and waiting to see confirmed that the only thing that pays on earth is to be an unscrupulous opportunist."[64]

Suppressing their inner dread, many McGovern staffers grasped for signs of a political miracle. The fervent crowds at the last-minute rallies, which were more enormous than ever before, were fodder for their fantasies. Jeff Smith, McGovern's aide-de-camp, remembers thinking that "the crowds were so big; how could these crowds be wrong?"[65] He conveniently forgot that McGovern's following was the antiwar activists and Nixon's was the "silent majority." McGovernites took heart too from the writing of liberal columnist Mary McGrory. Mentioning the huge crowds, the reinvigoration of antiwar passions, the hostility of Democrats to Richard Nixon, and, above all, the millions of first-time young voters, McGrory raised the prospect that "one of the greatest surprises in history may be in store for all of us."[66] McGrory offered Smith another ray of hope: "You say, 'Mary's no dummy. If she sees something, maybe we should see something.'"[67]

It also helped stave off despair that, as speechwriter John Holum observes, the McGovern staff was simply too fatigued by the end "to think clearly about what was going to happen."[68] Yet whatever illusions buoyed up the longtime McGovern workers, in another part of their minds the inevitability of their failure was sinking in. Many McGovernites were reconciling themselves to defeat as Election Day loomed. Some wondered if their candidate was the last to accept the obvious, or whether he was maintaining a façade of optimism to prop up his followers.

The last day before the election was a headlong sprint across the country, starting in New York, shifting to Philadelphia, then on to Wichita, Kansas, and Long Beach, California. McGovern continued to give his all to the campaign on its final day, as he had done for two exhausting years. Yet "somewhere between

Philadelphia and Wichita," he later wrote, "I admitted to myself for the first time that I was going to lose."[69] After a rally in Long Beach, where 25,000 supporters waited patiently into the night to cheer him, McGovern flew home to South Dakota to await the results. He now knew that he faced defeat, but he was still unprepared for the staggering dimensions of Nixon's impending victory. There would not be much solace to be found even in his home state, which, like every other state but Massachusetts, was about to reject him.

PART II

The Meaning of the McGovern Campaign

6

"Radical"?

Among the old McGovern campaign films in the archives of Guggenheim Productions in Washington, D.C., where I screened some of their footage in 2002, the television ad with the most arresting title was "Radical." Charles Guggenheim, a great documentary filmmaker, nominee for twelve Oscars and winner of four, had made his first film for McGovern for his 1962 run for the Senate, and for the 1972 nomination season Guggenheim produced a beautiful thirty-minute documentary on McGovern's life and cause. "Radical," shot in August, was a five-minute spot, similar in style to many others that Guggenheim produced during the 1972 campaign, but its subject matter was especially revealing, for it cut to the core of one of McGovern's greatest problems as a candidate for the presidency.[1]

The setting was a café in Menominee Falls, Wisconsin. Gathered around McGovern was a group of small-town residents, most of them small businessmen. And the question they had for the Democratic nominee concerned allegations that he was something completely alien to them: a radical.[2]

Unsurprisingly, the purpose of the TV ad was to prove a negative. "I'm not a radical," McGovern began. He immediately proceeded to associate himself with the most cherished American values, with the "first principles" of the Declaration of Independence and with the Judeo-Christian tradition. It was the government policies of recent years that had radically departed from the American way, not McGovern. The war in Vietnam, most of all, was "offensive to the ideals I was taught in a religious home."

People say, McGovern went on, that "I'm radical on taxes." But it was just "justice and common sense" to close tax loopholes favoring the rich. Nor was it radical to call for full employment, even if achieving this goal required the federal government to be the "employer of last resort." McGovern was being mistaken for a radical, he suggested, because he was an advocate of change. But every American leader of the past—McGovern cited Abraham Lincoln, Franklin Roosevelt, and John Kennedy—who had advocated change "has been called a radical." "After they die," he concluded, "they become heroes . . . A conservative is a worshipper of dead radicals."[3]

"Radical" was a skillful TV spot in dispelling the more hysterical portrayals of McGovern's ideology. It situated McGovern's positions in the campaign not in some foreign belief system or sixties left-wing rebellion but in the hallowed texts and symbols of the American political tradition. McGovern's own midwestern roots and modest demeanor signaled that he had much in common with these solid small-town Americans. If Republicans were pillorying him as a radical—in a preview of how they would portray his Democratic successors for decades to come—the political motive behind the canard was all too apparent.

Nonetheless, it is a mistake simply to dismiss the furor over McGovern's ideology as a case of conservative opponents blowing smoke to obscure his true stands. Although McGovern saw himself as a liberal and not a radical, his liberalism was of a different kind than the liberalism of his immediate Democratic predecessors (and his successors). It was a liberalism that was simultaneously old-fashioned and newfangled, reaching back to a time before the consensus liberalism of the Cold War era and reaching out to the advanced liberal thinkers and forces that, in the course of the 1960s, had moved to new ground beyond consensus. It was liberalism with a moral edge foreign to the pragmatic and technocratic bent of the Kennedy-Johnson years. It was a liberalism that, at least in its challenge to the conventions of postwar liberalism, might even be dubbed radical.

The ideology, rhetoric, and policy proposals of George McGovern in 1972 are worth serious examination—as much for their rejection by elite pundits and ordinary voters alike as for their substance. In the fate of McGovern's brand of liberalism there is much to be learned about political insurgency in the United States, about what can and cannot be said in the course of a campaign for the presidency. In the repudiation of what McGovern represented the identity crisis of contemporary liberalism is also implicated, for later Democratic candidates have been shadowed by the ideological apparition of "McGovernism." Before turning to look at what McGovern said and what he proposed in 1972, at his ideology, rhetoric, and programs, the most powerful attack on his ideas first needs to be considered: the charge of "radicalism."

"How Radical Is McGovern?"

The muddled state of the debate in 1972 about McGovern's ideas is nicely captured in a *Newsweek* article written shortly after his California primary victory put the insurgent candidate within reach of the Democratic nomination. The piece was titled "How Radical Is McGovern?" implying that the important issue was to evaluate just how much of a leftist McGovern was. This alarming headline was belied, however, by careful and thoughtful analysis in the body of the article, which concluded with the observation that McGovern's willingness to alleviate the concerns of moderates was "hardly the mark of a radical candidate."[4]

To McGovernites the charge of radicalism was, on its face, ludicrous. How, they asked then and continue to ask, could a politician repeatedly reelected in conservative, Republican-leaning South Dakota possibly be a leftist? McGovern himself dryly mocked the charge at the time: "Ordinarily, we don't send wild-eyed radicals to the United States Senate from South Dakota."[5] McGovern's long-time aide, John Holum, who also hailed from South Dakota, said much the same three decades later: "He is not a left-winger. He is not a radical. He is a very conventional, mainstream politician."[6]

The image of McGovern the radical was, in a sense, the invention of his opponents, and it is possible to trace when and how McGovern was saddled with this impolitic identity. It was a process in which his Democratic rivals and his Republican adversaries subtly collaborated. On the Democratic side, Scoop Jackson inaugurated the charge of radicalism in the Ohio primary, and Hubert Humphrey enlisted its full force for the California primary. But the single most damaging phrase in this line of attack came from the Republican minority leader of the Senate, Hugh Scott of Pennsylvania: McGovern, he alleged, was "the candidate of the 3 A's: acid, amnesty, and abortion."[7] Nixon strategists thus had plenty of ammunition, and at the president's direction they hammered away at the radicalism theme throughout the fall campaign.[8]

It was in the press, however, that the left-wing label was first attached to the insurgent candidate and provided wide circulation in the spring of 1972. The portrait of a radical McGovern was the handiwork, above all, of Rowland Evans and Robert Novak, whose syndicated and much-quoted newspaper column adopted the classic inside dope approach of a Drew Pearson and Jack Anderson but gave it a conservative slant, foreshadowing the right-wing media of today.[9] Their column soon after the Wisconsin primary, broadcasting the fear of Democratic leaders that McGovern is "the Barry Goldwater of the left whose nomination would be a Democratic calamity," was only their opening shot.[10] Before Scott associated McGovern with "the three A's," an Evans and Novak column quoted an anonymous liberal senator making a devastating—and largely false—claim to the same effect: "The people don't know McGovern is for amnesty, abortion, and legalization of pot . . . Once middle America—Catholic middle America in particular—finds this out, he's dead."[11] By the California primary, it only remained for Evans and Novak to applaud Humphrey for affixing to McGovern the image that they had first suggested: "Humphrey in California has finally made McGovern publicly defend his far-out positions which long ago won him impassioned support from the Democratic Party's left fringe."[12]

Most New Left radicals saw little affinity between McGovern and themselves apart from their shared hostility to the war in Vietnam. They viewed McGovern as an establishment liberal who had the good sense to recognize how the war was hurting "the system" but who was not otherwise keen to challenge it. As one underground newspaper editor put the argument, "If elected, McGovern will be heir to what has become an American Empire . . . The business of an empire is worldwide business . . . and from his past record there is little indication that McGovern sees anything wrong with U.S. imperialism."[13] New Leftists rejected the hopeful conviction of the New Politics crowd that fundamental change was possible through the electoral process, so they were distrustful of the younger McGovernites' beliefs and aspirations as well. For their part, the New Politics liberals who worked for McGovern did not regard themselves as radicals. At the higher levels of the McGovern campaign there were none of the bearded leftists of sixties fame; on the contrary, the McGovern staffer was most often what Alexis de Tocqueville had long ago identified as the pillar of an American conservative elite: a lawyer.[14]

Although the charge against McGovern of radicalism was politically inspired and patently exaggerated, a forerunner of the tactic that would later make not "radical" but "liberal" a label from which to flee, it was not altogether a fantasy. That McGovern was not the radical that his enemies conjured up does not mean that he was the conventional liberal that his supporters defensively claimed him to be. There was something about McGovern and his ideas that did set him apart from recent Democratic standard-bearers, something that could even appeal to the American left—or at least to that part of it that was not doctrinaire.

In 1972 Adam Hochschild, a "non-denominational radical," was a journalist working for *Ramparts*, the popular New Left magazine of the era. At the age of thirty, he had never voted. Casting his first ballot ever for George McGovern in the California primary, he assumed that McGovern would be denied the nomination by the powers that be. Surprised when McGovern won the nomination, Hochschild decided to volunteer for the fall campaign: it was the "first—and the last—time that I felt someone was running for president as a major-party candidate that I felt like working for." He left the Bay Area and moved to Washington, D.C., winding up in the McGovern voter-registration project at the Democratic National Committee. It was altogether characteristic of the McGovern campaign that within two months of first voting, Hochschild became its director of voter registration for seventeen states—though these were the ones judged "least likely to go for McGovern."[15]

To understand McGovern's difference from other liberal candidates and to fix his place in the American political tradition, it is helpful to consider some clues in what he has said over the years about his political forebears and heroes. In my interviews with him, he has several times cited his political models: Thomas Jefferson, Abraham Lincoln, Woodrow Wilson, and Franklin Roosevelt. His list is less interesting for what it includes—these are of course the "greats" of the liberal tradition—than for what it excludes: McGovern doesn't mention anyone after FDR. John F. Kennedy does not make the list, even though it was his appointment of McGovern as director of Food for Peace that made him a national figure. As he told me, he is grateful to Kennedy, but he never agreed with JFK's hawkish foreign policy.[16]

An even more illuminating clue is McGovern's admiration for former vice president Henry Wallace, who challenged President Truman's emerging Cold War policy with his Progressive Party candidacy in 1948, only to be linked to

Communist Party operatives and denounced as a fellow traveler. As a graduate student at Northwestern in 1948 McGovern was one of the campus activists who worked enthusiastically for Wallace, but later he was dismayed when he came into contact with the dogmatic Communists supporting the challenger to Truman.[17] It would be possible to write this episode off as a youthful indiscretion for a mainstream American politician if McGovern had ever repudiated his support for Wallace. But he never has.

When McGovern published his autobiography, *Grassroots*, in 1977, a Truman revival was flourishing in the post-Watergate climate. Merle Miller had a huge bestseller with his oral biography of Truman, *Plain Speaking*, and there was even a popular song by the group Chicago, "America Needs You, Harry Truman." McGovern wanted none of it: "Today Harry Truman is being elevated retroactively as a great President, whereas Henry Wallace is largely forgotten. But I believed in the late forties and I believe now that both the domestic health of the nation and the peace of the world would have been better served by the hopeful and compassionate views of Wallace than by the 'Get Tough' policy of the Truman Administration."[18] (Ironically, McGovern's support for Wallace in 1948 did not hurt him in 1972. According to William Safire, Nixon campaign strategists decided not to bring up this bit of McGovern biography, fearing that just as some conservative New Hampshire primary voters had supported Eugene McCarthy in 1968 because they confused him with Joseph McCarthy, so some conservative voters might actually vote for McGovern because they were likely to confuse Henry Wallace with George Wallace.)[19]

McGovern's list of liberal heroes ends with FDR, and he retains his admiration for the ideas and character of Henry Wallace, because he never subscribed to the dominant form of liberalism that developed after World War II (and was perhaps emerging even earlier, in the later years of Franklin Roosevelt's presidency).[20] Godfrey Hodgson in his classic *America in Our Time* lays out the "ideology of the liberal consensus" that flourished from the Truman era to the closing years of the Johnson presidency. At home, the "liberal consensus" jettisoned concerns about corporate power and economic inequality, embracing economic growth as the panacea that would establish social harmony amid shared prosperity. Abroad, it warred against global communism while bringing "the good tidings of the free-enterprise system to the rest of the world."[21] The political leaders and intellectuals who propagated the "liberal consensus" of the Cold War era were confident, indeed complacent, that they could bring about the good society without class conflict on the left or conservative mobilization on the right. They were defensive in their anxiety that symbols like "Munich" or "Yalta" could be hung on them unless they repeatedly demonstrated their patriotic toughness.

This was not McGovern's liberalism. His version was old-fashioned, looking back to an ancestry that stretched from Jefferson's Declaration of Independence to Roosevelt's New Deal but that had been obscured by the new ideology of consensus and Cold War. Perhaps the most important component of McGovern's old-fashioned liberalism was the tradition of antimilitarism and antiimperialism. McGovern can be placed in the lineage of Jefferson, who feared a professional military in a republic; Lincoln, the young congressman whose blasts at President James K. Polk's Mexican War resembled McGovern's blasts at the wars of three presidents in Vietnam; and William Jennings Bryan, whose attack on the U.S. imperial adventure in the Philippines was an eerie precursor to the New Politics attack on the war in Southeast Asia. In his critique of the Pentagon behemoth, he was reaching back to a perspective that had once characterized the common liberal faith but was now scarcely intelligible to most citizens of Cold War America, who could not imagine a president saying what Woodrow Wilson had said (to resounding applause from Congress) in December 1914: "We never have had, and while we retain our principles and ideals we never shall have, a large standing army."[22] McGovern was remembering the magnanimous spirit of FDR's "Good Neighbor Policy" toward less-developed nations.

Domestic issues were secondary to foreign-policy issues for McGovern, and he relied heavily on aides and outside advisers to formulate his economic program, but here too his views reflected the old liberalism. He did not believe—indeed it was increasingly difficult for many liberals to believe by 1972—that economic growth would, by itself, solve the central dilemmas of American domestic life. The accommodation with corporate power and the continuation of economic inequality that had marked the liberal consensus were now blatant and galling in the hands of the Nixon administration. Old liberal concerns about equity and power in the economy were of renewed relevance. Yet the ideology of economic growth had set down deep roots, and to raise the old questions about the economy was as risky as to raise the old questions about militarism and empire. That McGovern's economic proposals sent shivers down the spines of many on Wall Street was nothing new; stockbrokers' reactions in 1972 recalled the terror of Bryan in 1896 or the rage at Roosevelt in 1936. What was new, in the era of the liberal consensus, was that Wall Street hostility to McGovern did not impress the working class: on the contrary, in the new, George Wallace–style populism, which reserved its fury for government rather than business, Wall Street apprehensions about McGovern's redistributive plans only stoked the fear, even in blue-collar communities, that McGovern might be a radical.

By the 1972 campaign McGovern's old-fashioned liberalism was receiving a fresh infusion from a new left-liberalism that grew out of the turmoil of the 1960s. The liberal consensus of the Cold War era had cracked during the presidency of Lyndon Johnson, and a number of liberal politicians and thinkers, influenced by the persistence of poverty, the riots in black ghettoes, the egalitarian demands of the previously excluded expressed in new social movements, and the mounting disaster in Vietnam, were moving leftward under the pressure of events. These were the liberals who rallied behind McGovern's candidacy, and while the origins of his liberalism were different from theirs, he was open to their ideas. Feminism was a case in point. McGovern was hardly a feminist in 1972 and was sometimes ill at ease around militant women. Yet he instinctively sided with the feminists and made their cause part of his campaign. Inevitably, his association with the women's movement furthered perceptions of him as radical at the time, although the women's issues he was championing hardly seem radical today.[23]

McGovern's message in 1972 was a blend of old-fashioned and brand-new liberalism, but of the two, the old was uppermost. Amid the frenzied pace of the campaign, William Greider of the *Washington Post*, the journalist on the campaign trail with the most sympathy for McGovern, found it hard to get a fix on the candidate's thinking. Only afterward, Greider says, did he realize that McGovern was "really a New Dealer."[24] Greider's judgment can stand as a good nutshell description of McGovern's political faith. To some, this description will only suggest how antiquated McGovern's liberalism was in 1972. To others, it will suggest that McGovern's problems in being understood during the campaign were a sign of how much the liberal tradition had been compromised by the Cold War consensus, of how far it had fallen from its past moments of grace.

"Hard Truths"

The cloakroom in the Senate was buzzing on the day that former White House aide Alexander Butterfield exposed the existence of President Nixon's secret taping system. George McGovern was in a phone booth in the cloakroom, and he overheard several Democratic colleagues, unaware of his presence, talking about him. "Somebody," McGovern recalls, said that "'if we had just had these tapes, McGovern would have won that election.'" Senator Herman Talmadge of Georgia disagreed, and the reason he gave shook McGovern. "You know," said Talmadge,

> what was wrong with George in that campaign was that he gave the impression that he was mad at the country. He was condemning her policy in Vietnam and he was complaining about the poor and talking about women's rights, and it just seemed like everything he said indicated that he was mad as hell about this country. People aren't going to support a candidate like that. This is a great country. It makes mistakes, but by God if you get up there and preach day and night against America, you're not going to be elected.[25]

What most dismayed McGovern about Talmadge's characterization of his campaign rhetoric, he says, was that "I was trying to underscore my love for the country."[26] Yet if McGovern's love is readily apparent in the speeches he delivered during the 1972 campaign, so too is the passionate critique of an American society gone astray that Talmadge took as anti-American preaching. The best of these speeches were published two years after the election under the title *An American Journey*, and while it is hard to imagine finding much of value in a volume of campaign speeches by, say, Michael Dukakis or John Kerry, even after three and a half decades, many of McGovern's campaign speeches still make for provocative reading. Through his rhetoric, Sandy Berger observes, McGovern was engaged in "a fight for the soul of America. He felt it very passionately, and those around him did [as well]."[27]

From the late spring of 1972 until Election Day, McGovern's own power of expression was enhanced by a remarkable trio of speechwriters: John Holum, Sandy Berger, and Bob Shrum. All three were talented wordsmiths, all three were young enough to pull all-nighters during the hectic fall campaign, and all three were bound for distinguished careers in American politics. Holum, long a McGovern Senate aide, was nominally in charge of the speechwriting operation, but the three McGovern rhetoricians worked comfortably as a team. Berger had begun the 1972 campaign season writing for the aborted candidacy of Harold Hughes, switched to John Lindsay, and then came over to the McGovern camp; he may be, he jokes, "the only person in history to participate in writing three concession speeches in one [election] cycle."[28] Shrum started with Muskie, and it was a powerful antiwar speech that he composed for the senator from Maine that caught McGovern's eye and led to his hiring once Muskie "suspended" his campaign. Shrum's two colleagues quickly recognized the gift that soon made him a legendary Democratic speechwriter and gave him the lead role in drafting most of McGovern's speeches.[29] On Election Day, as the dimensions of his defeat registered, McGovern toasted his speechwriting team with affectionate humor: "There they are—the men who wrote the words that moved the nation."[30]

McGovern's campaign speeches were based on the premise that "Americans want a president who will tell them the hard truths as well as the easy ones—who will appeal not just to our selfish interests, but to what Lincoln called 'the better angels of our nature.'"[31] One of these "hard truths" was what the Cold War had done to America. Responding to the claim of pundits that the Democrats needed to nominate a mainstream candidate rather than an insurgent from the party's antiwar wing, McGovern loosed a fierce blast at the "establishment center." His indictment turned the conventions of Cold War liberalism upside down:

> Most Americans see the establishment center as an empty, decaying
> void that commands neither their confidence nor their love. It is the
> establishment center that has led us into the stupidest and cruelest war in
> all history . . . The establishment center has persisted in seeing the planet
> as engaged in a gigantic struggle to the death between the free world and

the Communist world. The facts are that much of the so-called free world is not free, but a collection of self-seeking military dictators financed by hard-pressed American workers. And most of the Communist nations are far more obsessed with their own internal divisions than they are with Washington, London, Bonn, or Saigon . . . The establishment center has constructed a vast military colossus based on the paychecks of the American worker. That military monster, now capable of blowing up the entire world a hundred times over, is devouring two out of three of our tax dollars. It inflates our economy, picks our pockets, and starves other areas of our national life.

McGovern imagined a post–Cold War America governed by a new center, which would "end senseless wars, offer jobs to the jobless, [and liberate] all people—black, brown, red, and white—male and female—young and old."[32]

Democratic as well as Republican presidents had been responsible for Cold War violations of America's founding principles. But the Republican whom McGovern was facing in the general election was particularly culpable for poisoning the political environment, aggrandizing the powers of the presidency, and subverting the constitutional order. As revelations of the Nixon administration's abuses trickled out in the press, McGovern tried to pull them together into a comprehensive account of corruption at the top: "The men who have collected millions in secret money, who have passed out special favors, who have invaded our offices in the dead of night—all of these men work for Mr. Nixon." The American people, McGovern insisted, faced "a moral and a constitutional crisis of unprecedented dimensions," a crisis sure to deepen over the next four years unless Nixon was defeated and the imperial presidency was overturned.[33]

McGovern lashed out at the undemocratic concentration of power in the economy as well as in the executive branch of Richard Nixon. Contrasting his economic plans with the president's, he invoked an economic populism not heard in Democratic presidential campaigns since the era of Roosevelt and Truman:

I do not want to soak the rich, but I want them to pay their fair share, and I want the government to stop piling new taxes on rank-and-file taxpayers. Mr. Nixon thinks it is right to have a depletion allowance for oil, but no depletion of a worker's back. Mr. Nixon thinks that it is right to have higher taxes for Americans who earn their living by hard work and lower taxes for those who live on stock market and property gains. I think that money earned by money should be taxed at the same rate as money earned by man . . . This election is more than a contest between George McGovern and Richard Nixon. It is a fundamental struggle between the little people of America and the big rich of America, between the average working man or woman and a powerful elite.[34]

Almost all of McGovern's campaign speeches were passionate, but the passion reached a peak when the subject was the war in Vietnam. Reading his heartfelt language decades later, the words can bring back the anguish that led millions of Americans to make ending the war their political mission:

What is it that keeps a great and decent country like the United States involved in this cruel killing and destruction? Why is it that we cannot find the wit and the will to escape from this dreadful conflict that has tied us down for so long? . . .

For what we now present to the world is the spectacle of a rich and powerful nation standing off at a safe distance and raining down a terrible technology of death on helpless people below—the most incredible and murderous bombardment in all the history of mankind . . . The air strikes come with new weapons and new techniques, and these weapons have a very special purpose . . . that is to kill and maim human beings.

We have the innocuous sounding "pineapple" with 250 steel pellets in the casing of each one . . . We have steel fleshettes that penetrate the skin and cannot be removed. We have napalm—jellied gasoline that sticks to the skin as it burns. We have white phosphorus that cannot be extinguished until it burns itself out.

Now, these are some of the weapons that produced that picture we saw in the press not too long ago of the little girl, Kim, running away from a school that had been hit by American napalm. She was naked, her clothing had been inflamed, and she was running directly into the lens of a cameraman nearby.

And I want to say to my fellow Americans that that picture ought to break the heart of the people of America.[35]

Herman Talmadge was not alone in describing this campaign rhetoric as "preaching." Even some observers who preferred McGovern over Nixon were troubled by his moralism. McGovern's candidacy seemed to them steeped in sanctimony. Garry Wills thus argued that McGovern's claim to deserve the power of the presidency was based not on popular appeal or political vision but merely on the pretension of superior rectitude. In Wills's stinging account, McGovern actually seemed to confuse himself with the character that the media had created: "Saint George."[36]

Wills caught a whiff of moralism coming off McGovern. But the moralizing posture that he attributed entirely to McGovern's personality was common to the entire protest generation. If the moral fervor of the 1960s and early 1970s was given to excesses of self-righteousness, nevertheless it was focused on a brutal war and an imperial presidency that deserved condemnation. A year after McGovern went down to a landslide defeat at the hands of Nixon, much of America was reacting to the Watergate scandal with its own moral outrage.

The shock of Watergate made it clearer that the "hard truths" McGovern delivered in 1972 were anything but anti-American. McGovern's campaign speeches were instances of what scholars have identified as the most distinctive American rhetorical genre: the jeremiad. A legacy of the Puritans, the jeremiad calls on a once-blessed people to face up to their fall into sin and to return to the path of redemption blazed by their ancestors. It has often been deployed for political as well as religious purposes. Even the cheery FDR sometimes made use of the chastising tropes of the jeremiad. The greatest speech in presidential history, Lincoln's Second Inaugural, took the form of a jeremiad.[37]

Yet Lincoln urged Americans to acknowledge their "humiliation" for the sin of slavery only after he was reelected.[38] In the midst of an election campaign, McGovern's speeches, especially on the war in Vietnam, were powerful and moving to his supporters, but for the majority of Americans their critical tone proved impolitic. No writer in 1972 so savagely depicted mainstream America as Hunter Thompson, but he was addressing the readers of *Rolling Stone*. McGovern, Thompson recognized, spoke to a tougher audience: "We are not a nation of truth-lovers. McGovern understands this, but he keeps on saying these terrible things anyway."[39] In 1972 McGovern was challenging Americans and Nixon was reassuring them. Anyone who wants to understand the difficulties of liberal insurgency in America ought to ponder the result: a large majority of Americans welcomed Nixon's message and spurned McGovern's.

One Issue

George McGovern was *the* antiwar candidate in 1972. His campaign slogan, "right from the start," called attention to the fact that his Democratic rivals were latecomers to the one crusade that fired up liberal activists. Apart from opposition to the war, however, McGovern's name at the start of the campaign season was associated only with agricultural issues (as a senator from South Dakota) and hunger (as former director of Food for Peace and current chairman of the Senate Select Committee on Nutrition and Human Needs), neither of which was on the election agenda. Labeled a "one-issue" candidate by the press, McGovern and his staff began, well before the first primary in 1972, to cultivate a broader political identity, aiming to expand his following beyond antiwar activists and to establish his credibility as a prospective president.[40]

Before the campaign, McGovern had worked out his positions on Vietnam—and on national security policy more broadly—with the assistance of his Senate aide John Holum, who in 1970 had drafted the McGovern-Hatfield Amendment to End the War. To develop an economic program he turned to another aide on his Senate staff, Gordon Weil. That still left huge gaps in his positions on the myriad issues likely to come up during the campaign. Shortly after Ted Van Dyk joined the campaign staff in 1971, he pulled nineteen-year-old Harvard student Jamie Galbraith away from his volunteer position with Students for McGovern and set him to work on creating a complete McGovern agenda. Galbraith, son of the famed economist (and a future economist himself), pored over the *Congressional Record* and McGovern's Senate files to figure out where the candidate stood on various issues. "In a few cases," he recalls, "we were creating [McGovern's] policy as we went along."[41] Under Van Dyk's supervision, Galbraith produced *McGovern on the Issues,* a booklet printed up in thousands of copies.

The announcement of comprehensive and often detailed proposals at first was advantageous, setting up a contrast between McGovern, the bold challenger, and Muskie, the bland frontrunner. After McGovern took over the frontrunner role, however, some of the same proposals became traps. Boldness brought accusations of radicalism; the unusual level of detail invited probing questions on matters like cost. Caring deeply about Vietnam and foreign policy but unexcited about most domestic issues, McGovern failed sufficiently to study his own program and was sometimes unable to rebut criticisms of it effectively. When Jamie Galbraith handed him proof sheets for *McGovern on the Issues,* the candidate made only one change, rejecting Van Dyk's attempt to limit his proposed cuts in the defense budget. After this initial perusal of the detailed platform his aides constructed, Van Dyk says, "I don't think George . . . went back and read it and found out what he thought."[42] A candidate who was not involved enough in domestic issues, including the bread-and-butter proposals that mattered most to traditional Democrats, was handicapped in articulating them with clarity and conviction.

In the end, then, for McGovern if not for all McGovernites, the campaign *was* fundamentally about one issue. As John Holum put it, "It really was at heart about the war."[43] And it was in talking about the war that McGovern most closely resembled the preacher, calling upon Americans to look to the state of their souls. Indeed, a few weeks before the election McGovern chose fundamentalist Wheaton College in Illinois, alma mater of Reverend Billy Graham, as the site for a flat-out sermon and described the Vietnam War as a crisis for American morals. If elected president, McGovern said at Wheaton, he could stop the war in a moment. But this political act would not get at "the attitudes that brought us to this war," would not make up for "the insensitivity of those who have given us weekly body counts" or "the tears shed over the death of Americans, while too many seem indifferent to death among the Vietnamese." Americans, McGovern said in words remarkable for a presidential campaign, must "change those things in our character which turned us astray, away from the truth that the people of Vietnam are, like us, children of God."[44]

Yet to notice only McGovern the moralist is to miss a great deal in his running campaign commentary on Vietnam. For McGovern also approached the war as an old-fashioned, antiimperialist liberal and as a historian of progressive bent.

Focused as he was on the horrifying particulars of this war, he nonetheless connected it to a larger context and viewed it as symptomatic of the misguided policies of the Cold War consensus. For more than two decades, under presidents from both parties, U.S. foreign policy, McGovern told interviewer Stanley Karnow, "has been based on an obsession with an international Communist conspiracy that existed more in our minds than in reality."[45] The United States had become entangled in Vietnam with over half a million of its troops because it was seen as the chosen battleground of the Sino-Soviet bloc for challenging American power and credibility. But now, McGovern pointed out during the campaign, the original premise of the war had been exploded: the Communist giants were at each other's throats and eager to cut separate deals with the United States. Even Richard Nixon, whose rise was owed to his anti-Communist ferocity, recognized the need—and the political advantage—of shedding old obsessions; the president gained in the polls "after he was wined and dined in the Communist capitals of Peking and Moscow."[46]

Although Nixon himself had paved the way for a post–Cold War foreign policy in the new relationships he was forging with China and the Soviet Union, he was clinging to hoary Cold War myths in his Vietnam policy. Systematically, McGovern shredded each of these myths. Nixon claimed that the United States was continuing the war he had pledged to end as a candidate in 1968 in order to maintain self-determination for the people of South Vietnam. But the government of General Thieu that Nixon was propping up was in reality an authoritarian and graft-ridden regime whose payback to the United States was the heroin its officials were peddling to alienated GIs. Nixon claimed that the United States was continuing the war to free its prisoners of war and obtain an accounting of its servicemen missing in action (MIAs). But in his four years as president, hundreds of additional U.S. forces had been imprisoned, and earlier captives stood no closer to release. Nixon claimed that the United States was continuing the war to preserve its honor in the world by demonstrating its unbowed determination. But the brutality of his course wasted lives and resources, estranged allies, and dishonored the nation's founding ideals.[47]

Ending the war as quickly as possible was the central pledge of McGovern's candidacy. He promised that on the day of his inauguration he would halt all acts of force by U.S. troops throughout Indochina. American forces would be withdrawn within ninety days, with residual air and naval elements remaining in Southeast Asia until the North Vietnamese fulfilled their own peace proposal, releasing American POWs and accounting for the MIAs at the same time that U.S. forces departed. The Vietnamese people would be left to settle their own political affairs, with international assistance for repairing the enormous damage caused by the war, while a McGovern administration would pursue a policy of reconciliation and generosity at home, guaranteeing Vietnam veterans either jobs or fully funded higher education and allowing draft resisters to return from exile. McGovern's jeremiad on the war, challenging Americans to reflect on how they had gone astray, ended in the ancient manner, with a vision of a people restored to their true way: "On the night when the last American soldier from Vietnam has landed in San Francisco, there will be a new birth of confidence and hope for all of us . . . On that night, America can begin to be America again."[48]

Once the United States put the war in Vietnam behind it, McGovern argued, it could move into a new era of international relations. His "Come home, America" theme was assailed by critics as a call for a new isolationism, but he insisted, in a major policy speech in Cleveland, Ohio, a month before the election, that his aim instead was a "new internationalism." McGovern's post–Cold War foreign policy was to emphasize peace, democracy, and economic development. With Cold War obsessions discarded, and with Communist powers open to negotiations, the United States could avoid "the kind of reflexive interventionism that has foolishly involved us in the internal political affairs of other countries." It could cease its support of dictators and apartheid regimes in the guise of anticommunism. A new foreign policy would emphasize multilateralism over unilateralism, with greater reliance on the United Nations, and would peacefully demonstrate the superiority of democratic over Communist methods by promoting economic and social development in the Third World. The "new internationalism" would even transform the presidency, lessening pressures toward executive secrecy and usurpation of power and restoring constitutional comity with the legislative branch. Above all, McGovern's program looked to reduce the reliance of foreign policy on military power, reverting to the American tradition that a "standing army," a massive and permanent military establishment, should not be the distinguishing characteristic of a free republic.[49]

It was his proposal for a large-scale cut in the Pentagon's future budgets that, even more than his position on the war in Vietnam, drew fire against McGovern as weak-kneed when it came to defending the nation. McGovern called for a defense budget for fiscal 1975 of $54.8 billion, about $32 billion less than the figure estimated by the Nixon administration for that year. He insisted that his budget "does not require major revisions in American commitments or a major scaling down in real American security interests." To be sure, some of the proposed reductions were dramatic—for example, sharply reducing the size of the aircraft carrier fleet and the U.S. force deployed in Europe. But McGovern emphasized that he was leaving ample funds in the budget to maintain the nuclear deterrent triad of land-based missiles, submarine-based missiles, and bombers, and to defend the United States and its allies. His justification for so large a defense cut was that the Pentagon budget had become a sacred cow, increasingly bloated over the years and routinely enlarged without debate. His alternative was "a zero-based budget, set by evaluating the threats which must be faced rather than by comparison with spending in the past." As threats were redefined, as the United

States disengaged from Cold War interventions and partnerships with dictators, the real security interests of the nation would prove much less costly.[50]

To McGovern, the Nixon defense budget represented not only the perpetuation of Cold War obsessions but the corruption of the military-industrial complex as well. Since Democrats from Truman through Johnson had largely made their peace with the military-industrial complex, McGovern was forced to invoke a Republican president, Dwight Eisenhower, as his mentor on the dangers of excessive defense spending.[51] Under the administration of Eisenhower's vice president, the military-industrial complex had become even more formidable in grasping at resources that thereby became unavailable for pressing domestic needs. McGovern attacked the enormous waste—and huge profits for defense contractors—in the Pentagon budget. He pointed out that the military establishment under Nixon was as riddled with privilege as the corporate establishment: the United States has "more colonels, Navy captains, generals, and admirals now—with two and a half million men under arms—than we had commanding twelve million men at the height of World War Two."[52] Before an unreceptive audience at a Veterans of Foreign Wars convention in Minneapolis, McGovern presented himself not as the pacifist many in the room mistook him for, but as a military reformer, seeking "a leaner, tougher, and more effective military force."[53]

Summing up the sorrow and the hope of the antiwar generation, McGovern's "idealistic" foreign and defense proposals of 1972 won him little respect outside of his political base. Yet McGovern's "new internationalism" was recognizably the forebear of liberal views of the world ever since: the human rights campaign of the Jimmy Carter years, the mass movements and congressional resistance against Ronald Reagan's nuclear buildup and Central America interventions, the multilateralism of the Bill Clinton administration, the opposition to George W. Bush's war in Iraq. Like McGovern, liberal activists could not forget the lessons of the war in Vietnam, could not grow comfortable with new wars or military muscle-flexing around the globe. They would likewise carry the burden that McGovern carried in 1972 and would repeatedly be thrown on the defensive by the charge that they were weak on national security. However much the horrors of the war in Vietnam are now widely acknowledged, it has been the heirs of Nixon who have had the upper hand on national security issues in subsequent presidential campaigns, and it has been the heirs of McGovern who have been caught up in an identity crisis of American patriotism.

Populism and the Ivy League

As a member of President Kennedy's Council of Economic Advisers, James Tobin was one of the architects of his "New Economics," which, by applying neo-Keynesian theory to the American economy, accelerated growth through tax cutting. A decade later, as one of the chief economic advisers to presidential candidate George McGovern, Tobin, a future Nobel laureate, was an advocate for a quite different approach: "Ten years ago it was correct to emphasize the need to get this country moving again . . . But it's time for McGovern's issues—income distribution, economic inequality, poverty, and fairness of the economic system—to have a bigger place."[54] During the 1972 campaign McGovern raised issues of economic justice that had been subordinated to the creed of economic growth that both parties had embraced by the late 1960s. With the assistance of some of the top experts in the nation, he updated populism and tried to stake out advanced ground on the economy. For his pains, he was derided as an impractical radical by the business community and as a zealot for the welfare state in blue-collar circles.

McGovern's program for a fairer distribution of income in the United States aimed to reverse a decade of tax cuts at the top and to raise taxes on wealthy citizens and large corporations. In his original tax reform package, announced at the beginning of 1972, one key proposal was a minimum tax on large incomes so that the wealthy could not escape taxes through the multitude of loopholes riddling the federal tax code. A second proposal called for rolling back corporate taxes to their effective rates in 1960—before they had been reduced by both Democratic and Republican presidents in the name of economic growth. A third proposal called for a steeper estate tax, with the rate reaching as much as 100 percent on inheritances over the then-considerable sum of $500,000 (this maximum rate was soon adjusted downward to 77 percent when McGovern's aides discovered, to their surprise, that workers disliked the complete confiscation of wealth); exceptions were to be made for family-owned businesses. Raising taxes on those who could best afford them was seen not only as a matter of justice amid persisting economic inequality in America but as a necessity if more was to be done for low- and moderate-income Americans.[55]

To redistribute resources to needier Americans, McGovern's chief aide on economic issues, Gordon Weil, drawing on the work of a maverick businessman and several professional economists, came up with the "demogrant," a proposal that became notorious as a political blunder of the highest magnitude. The principle behind the demogrant was to provide a cash payment to every American that would be kept by the poor, taxed gradually away up to middle-class levels, and completely returned to the Treasury in taxes paid by those above a median income. The demogrant was designed to replace the demeaning, bureaucratic federal welfare system with an income maintenance system that would improve the lot not only of the current welfare population but also of low-wage workers (since they would be able to keep a portion of the grant even while employed). Coupled with the tax reform proposals to raise rates on the wealthy and the large corporations, the demogrant was not supposed to cost the Treasury anything; it was to be purely a transfer from haves to have-nots. Weil wanted to keep the program general enough to postpone hard questions about detail, but McGovern, seizing on one illustration about how the demogrant might work, thought it would be more understandable to ordinary voters if the figure of $1,000 per person was specified. It proved a costly misjudgment.[56]

Although the tax reform and income redistribution platform attracted support for McGovern from blue-collar voters in the early primaries, both issues got him into trouble once his opponents began to focus on derailing his growing insurgency. Perhaps because the financial community had become accustomed to favorable treatment from Democrats and Republicans alike over the preceding decade, McGovern's call for tax reform set off a wave of alarm on Wall Street. Raising taxes on the wealthy and the corporations was taken as tantamount to the opening shot of a class war. In July, *Business Week* reported that among investors, "even those who claimed to be lifelong Democrats talked of 'opening Swiss bank accounts.'"[57] That same month, Eli Sagan wrote Frank Mankiewicz that many of the affluent people he knew "are convinced that George McGovern is going to send some blue-jeaned, long-haired young men to confiscate that Mercedes-Benz right out of the garage."[58]

The demogrant was only one of many income maintenance schemes floating around among economists and politicians in the late 1960s and early 1970s, and it was by no means the most radical. It was a cousin to President Nixon's failed Family Assistance Plan of 1969 and to the Earned Income Tax Credit (EITC) passed by Congress in 1975. But as Weil noted with chagrin, while the substance of the proposal was defensible, "it was a terrible idea to inject in a political campaign."[59] The demogrant was too unfamiliar and controversial for a campaign, a problem only compounded by the McGovern campaign's failure to prepare in advance for the likely economic and political objections that would be leveled against it. Even worse, as James K. Galbraith observes, "it was easy to make fun of."[60] It was also easy to distort. Because families up to a middle-class income would be able to keep part of the cash grant even after taxes, first Humphrey in his California debate with McGovern and then the Nixon campaign in its fall TV ads made the outrageous but politically effective charge that McGovern was proposing to put half of the American people on welfare.

With the financial community in an uproar and Humphrey scoring points with ordinary citizens against the insurgent's ill-starred demogrant, the McGovern campaign was compelled to rethink its economic positions as the fall campaign approached. Teams of tax and welfare experts were assembled, and McGovern himself, now fully aware of the political dangers, became more immersed in the substance of economic policy than heretofore.[61] In late August the campaign rolled out its new economic agenda in a well-received speech to the New York Society of Security Analysts. The demogrant was now dead: a frustrated McGovern earlier had told speechwriter Bob Shrum to "put a stake through [its] heart."[62] In its place was a conventional welfare plan, creating public-service jobs for employable welfare recipients; shifting aged, blind, and disabled welfare recipients to the Social Security System; and providing grants of up to $4,000 in cash and food stamps to those—largely women and their children—unable to work.

If McGovern was retreating on income maintenance, however, he was not backing down on his larger populist vision of economic redistribution, even before a Wall Street crowd. His new economic program still called for $22 billion in increased taxes on wealthy individuals and corporations, mainly through closing loopholes such as the preferential treatment of capital gains and the oil depletion allowance. At the same time that McGovern proposed to treat unearned income the same as earned income, he pledged to cut the maximum tax rate on all income to 48 percent. Combined with the $32 billion to be saved from his alternative defense budget, revenues generated by tax reform would finance an extensive agenda of redistributive measures. McGovern proposed a federal guarantee of a job to every American able to work, property-tax relief to hard-pressed homeowners, and stepped-up spending on such liberal staples as education, health care, and the environment.[63]

Ironies abound in the story of McGovern as the last real economic populist to run for president as the nominee of a major party. McGovern might be viewed as a prairie populist, the heir to such reformers from the plains as William Jennings Bryan and George Norris. This image is somewhat misleading, however, because while he was instinctively a populist, the substance of his populism was not an export from the West. Like most senators, McGovern was not a specialist on economic policy, and for the content of his economic platform he turned to professionals who supported him because of his opposition to the war.[64] His populist ideas were actually a product of the Ivy League. Their chief creators were economists from Yale, Harvard, and Princeton, along with MIT and Northwestern, among them such academic stars as James Tobin, John Kenneth Galbraith, and Lester Thurow.[65] The pedigree for McGovern's liberal, redistributive economic agenda was more prestigious than the pedigree for the conservative, supply-side economic agenda put forward by Ronald Reagan eight years later. Yet McGovern's economists, impressive for their commitment to economic justice as well as for their technical sophistication, resided at a distance not only from Wall Street but also from the precincts of the working class. Reagan's advisers may have advanced dubious propositions from the standpoint of the economics profession, but they were better attuned to the desire for gain up and down the economic ladder.

Some McGovern aides point out that his ideas on the economy, however widely derided in 1972, were prophetic of later policies adopted by the federal government, including EITC and the tax reform act of 1986.[66] In the main, however, what is notable about McGovern's economic agenda is how it stands as a counterpoint to the trend in economic policy since his defeat. Later Democratic presidential candidates have shied away from his talk of economic redistribution (with the notable exception of Carter's tax reform platform in 1976) and returned to the politics of economic growth. They have nonetheless been placed on the defensive in this endeavor by the Republicans' politically winning language of lower taxes. From Ronald Reagan's cuts in the tax rates of the wealthy and the corporations to George W. Bush's slashing of the capital gains tax, American economic policy has gone in the opposite direction than McGovern urged in 1972.

Early Skirmishes in the Culture War

The radical image that was hung on George McGovern revolved around issues of culture as much as foreign policy or economics. McGovern seemed an unlikely commander for the forces mobilizing on behalf of the new cultural values and practices associated with the movements of the 1960s. His small-town upbringing, modest midwestern demeanor, and conventional family life marked him as a pillar of traditional American culture. On the sixties spectrum from "hip" to "square," he was patently toward the square end. Jeff Smith, who started working for McGovern during his 1968 senate reelection campaign, recalls that when McGovern was in South Dakota he would sometimes wear "electric blue suits." But as the activists of the antiwar and women's movements embraced McGovern as their candidate for 1972, they helped to spruce up his style. McGovern grew fashionable sideburns and wore his hair longer, and when he visited Southern California, where he was the favorite of Hollywood liberals, he began to buy his suits in Beverly Hills.[67]

Younger McGovernites were much closer than their candidate to the new culture. They were not long-haired radicals, much less hippies, but in appearance and behavior they were poles apart from the straitlaced youth for Nixon. Visiting the headquarters of the two campaigns, Theodore White observed the manifest differences:

> The uniform at McGovern headquarters was slacks, bell-bottom trousers, sun-tans, open-necked shirts; on the grass embankment outside his headquarters, on a sunny day, students and volunteers ate quiche Lorraine, or beans and chili, or whatever the community's $2-a-plate special was that day . . . At the Republican Committee to Re-Elect, the uniform was the business suit, dark colors and pinstripes, 1950 Madison Avenue style, necktie neatly knotted, sideburns trimmed at mid-ear, and nothing more than coffee or Coca-Cola was served in the severe legal offices the Committee occupied.[68]

Through its identification with the new culture, the McGovern campaign had more social cachet than the Nixon campaign, but in the electorate there were many more square than hip voters. So from the moment that Hugh Scott labeled McGovern as "the candidate of the 3 A's: acid, amnesty, and abortion," his campaign was on the cultural defensive. Of the three unpopular positions ascribed to McGovern by this phrase, only *amnesty* was an accurate or fair representation of his stance. By pledging an amnesty for war resisters in jail or abroad once the Vietnam conflict was over, McGovern advanced a position consistent with his moral outrage on the war and advantageous in solidifying support on the campuses. Yet his pledge, he later pointed out, was hardly radical: President Nixon had spoken favorably about amnesty as late as the winter of 1972, and magnanimous amnesties after wars were in fact the American tradition.[69] When President Carter issued a general pardon for Vietnam resisters upon taking office in 1977, there was relatively little controversy.

Abortion as an issue made McGovern uncomfortable. Under pressure from his feminist supporters to take a strong stand, he resisted both out of political instinct and because he was not sure he personally agreed with the position of the women's movement. Actress Shirley MacLaine, one of those who pressed McGovern on women's right to control their own bodies, ultimately concluded that "abortion was an issue too explosive for him to handle."[70] Consequently, McGovern's campaign stance was a model of caution if not confusion. He told women that they should be free to make their own decisions in consultation with their doctors, but he also reassured opponents of abortion that he was opposed to federal action on the subject and would leave the issue to the states.[71] Less than three months after the election, the U.S. Supreme Court went much further on abortion rights in *Roe v. Wade* than anything McGovern had ever contemplated.

Acid (or LSD) was never the issue—presumably it made Scott's list only because of its alliterative value—but marijuana was, because it was the symbolic drug of the counterculture. At an early point in the campaign a McGovern policy document raised the possibility that marijuana might be regulated like alcohol. But this stance was clearly bound to be controversial, and McGovern instead adopted the common-sense position that possession of small amounts of marijuana should be treated as a misdemeanor and not a felony, and should not result in incarceration. His proposal disappointed those who favored a more liberal approach to personal experimentation with "soft" drugs, but it still left him vulnerable to the hard-line antidrug message of the Nixon campaign.[72]

The McGovern campaign worried that its identification with the new culture would cost it votes. Even though McGovern strategists successfully warded off minority platform planks on abortion and gay rights at the Democratic convention, the identification was made anyway. For the social movements backing McGovern, his campaign was the vehicle for their entry into Democratic Party politics, even when McGovern spurned key portions of their agenda. As Bob Shrum reflects, "The women's movement in many ways found expression in the campaign. The nascent gay rights movement found expression in the campaign."[73] Whether or not he chose the role, McGovern was a leader in the early skirmishes of the culture war.

McGovern was the first Democratic presidential nominee to stand for the new cultural values that had emerged in the 1960s. The openness of his campaign to young people, feminists, gays, and other activists for cultural change had lasting consequences: the Democratic Party was now a home—if not always a comfortable one—for these forces as they matured politically. The cultural issues that McGovern handled gingerly and often reluctantly in 1972 were ones that later Democratic candidates would have to face more squarely. In the culture war that still looms large in American politics, the McGovern insurgency was the campaign in which the contending forces, strategies, and tactics were initially put into play.

Conclusion

Several weeks after the 1972 election, James Wall, editor of the *Christian Century*, requested an interview with the defeated candidate. "You have elevated the political dialogue," Wall wrote to McGovern, "in a manner that few people presently realize." But when Wall inquired about the role of morality in American politics in their subsequent interview, the conclusions McGovern drew for the readers of a religious publication were hardly encouraging from a spiritual standpoint. "I would have to warn any future presidential candidate," McGovern said, "that regardless of how clear the moral imperatives might be to him, it is highly risky to assume that drawing an issue sharply in moral terms will win majority support. It might even repel large numbers of people who don't want to be disturbed in their lethargy and apathy and who prefer not to feel conscience-stricken about what the nation is doing." McGovern concluded that he had erred in assuming that he could rely on the fundamental decency of the American people. Asked by Wall what he would have done differently had he known better from the outset, McGovern replied, "I think I would not have put things on quite such a lofty level. I would have tried to combine morally sound positions with a greater emphasis on appeals to self-interest."[74]

Four years later, when Jimmy Carter achieved greater success with a moral message, McGovern updated his reflections on what a presidential candidate could or could not say in a campaign. In McGovern's view, Carter had learned from the 1972 campaign that moral critique might be effective in a presidential campaign—but only when blame was directed solely at the Washington establishment and coupled with praise for the virtue of the electorate.

> Carter saw the merits of that "Come home, America" approach, calling the country back to its first principles, but I think he also saw the danger . . . that

you can carry that to the point where people feel uncomfortable with it . . . So, Jimmy modified that message . . . The way I stated it, I want this country to be the great and good country it can be when it's faithful to the ideals of our founders. Now, Jimmy saw that as a very tall order. My God, are we going to have to be as good as Jefferson, and Tom Paine, and John Adams, and George Washington? So, he said, I want a government as good and decent as the American people are. Not that they can be. There's nothing wrong with the people, if we just have a government that is as good as the people are, we'll be fine. That lets the people off the hook.[75]

McGovern's reflections on the place of moral discourse in presidential elections can be read by skeptics as a belated recognition of political reality by a candidate who had been naïve in his original idealism. And of course they can be written off as sour grapes by those who regard him as steeped in self-righteousness. But they can also be taken seriously as the painful experience not only of McGovern himself but also of the leading McGovernites and the numerous liberal activists who worked in the 1972 campaign. These are cautionary thoughts about the limitations on liberal insurgency in American politics. They suggest that the majority of Americans don't want to be challenged in campaigns, don't want to be asked to examine their own practices, don't want to be reminded that they should live up to Lincoln's "better angels of our nature." McGovern's reflections suggest that campaign discourse is most effective on a superficial plane, targeting the failures of the opposing party but exempting everyone else from criticism. Self-interest—the currency of everyday politics in a pluralist system—must be the crux of the campaign, even though in a polity where the disadvantaged lack political clout it is seldom going to be a motor for fundamental change. The lesson for contemporary American liberals, then, seems to be that short of economic or political collapse under conservative rule, there are not likely to be many openings for the liberal perspective to receive a full hearing in presidential politics.

Characterizations of McGovern's ideology as radical also point to lasting issues for the political identity of liberal Democrats. The liberal positions for which McGovern was denounced would be ascribed, often with even greater distortion than in 1972, to his successors, even when they were intent on avoiding the liberal label. Like McGovern, later Democratic candidates would be charged with weakness on national security and doubt about the virtue of America's interventions abroad. Like McGovern, they would be charged with favoring the poor and the nonwhite while loading upon blue-collar whites the costs of a permissive welfare state. Like McGovern, they would be associated with the militant challengers to mainstream norms who threatened to subvert the institutions and values of traditional American culture. During the 1972 campaign, conservatives

developed a successful template for negative campaigning against their caricature of modern liberalism.[76]

McGovern was the last presidential nominee of the Democratic Party who
was genuinely an insurgent liberal. Since 1972 the insurgent impulse has often
reemerged in the party, and the desire for a more committed and far-reaching
liberal stance has remained strong among many activists at its base. Leaders such
as Ted Kennedy, Jesse Jackson, Tom Harkin, Paul Wellstone, and Howard Dean
have periodically given voice to the idea of reviving a full-throated liberalism.
But each time a call for pursuing an authentic liberal agenda is issued, the electoral disaster of 1972 is invoked by its critics, who summon the McGovern campaign as a specter to haunt liberal dreams.

Before New Hampshire: McGovern speaking in Milwaukee, December 1971 (Michael Lloyd Carlebach)

Connecting to blue-collar voters: a McGovern factory tour in New Hampshire, winter 1972 (Copyright © 1972 Diana Mara Henry/dianamarahenry.com)

Campaign manager Gary Hart in his headquarters office (© Keith Robert Wessel)

Rick Stearns,
McGovern's
wizard of the
new rules for
presidential
selection
(Michael Lloyd
Carlebach)

Jeff Smith, McGovern's aide-de-camp (Michael Lloyd Carlebach)

Morris Dees, McGovern's populist fundraiser (Michael Lloyd Carlebach)

Amanda Smith,
McGovern's
women's issues
coordinator
(Michael Lloyd
Carlebach)

McGovern campaigns with Julian Bond and Jesse Jackson before the California primary. (Michael Lloyd Carlebach)

Charles Guggenheim, head of McGovern's media operation, filming the candidate (Michael Lloyd Carlebach)

McGovern works on his acceptance speech at the Democratic Convention in Miami Beach. (Michael Lloyd Carlebach)

Women's liberation and gay liberation: Bella Abzug and Alan Ginsberg at the Democratic National Convention (Copyright © 1972 Diana Mara Henry/ dianamarahenry.com)

A young McGovernite: Bill Clinton on the floor of the Democratic National Convention (Copyright © 1972 Diana Mara Henry/dianamarahenry.com)

An ill-starred choice: Senator Thomas Eagleton with McGovern in the traditional convention pose (copyright © Diana Mara Henry/dianamarahenry.com)

Patching up relations with the regulars: Mayor Daley of Chicago endorses McGovern, August 1972 (Michael Lloyd Carlebach)

McGovern campaigns at the Illinois State Fair, Springfield, August 1972. (Michael Lloyd Carlebach)

McGovern campaigns in Ohio with somber union officials, Labor Day, 1972. (Michael Lloyd Carlebach)

Young McGovern supporters at a Philadelphia rally, September 1972 (Michael Lloyd Carlebach)

McGovern campaigns with Ted and Joan Kennedy in Pittsburgh, September 1972. (Michael Lloyd Carlebach)

A McGovern supporter tries to dismiss disheartening polls, fall 1972. (Copyright © 1972 Diana Mara Henry/dianamarahenry .com)

McGovern delivers his concession speech, November 1972. (Michael Lloyd Carlebach)

7

A Grassroots Army

"I trust this is the start of something big," Greg Craig wrote to national headquarters early in September 1972, as he took up a position as one of three Vermont state coordinators for the fall McGovern campaign. The McGovern insurgency had captured the state in the spring, shocking the "Neanderthals" who ran the Democratic Party machine in Chittenden County, Vermont's main population center. Craig thought a similar upset was possible in the general election since Richard Nixon was a questionable character who hardly represented "New England Republican values." He conceded that it would be an uphill struggle, especially in combating the prevailing image of the McGovernites. WCAX, Vermont's only television station, Craig reported, "will cover our events but will take pictures of hair, beards, beads, and booze, and will ignore the throngs of traditional, straight-laced Vermonters who also flock to McGovern happenings. As an example, we had a registration rally the other evening in a park in Burlington. The way it came over WCAX was like all the freaks in the hills had come down, mobilized to take over Vermont for McGovern."[1]

Craig was not one of the more prominent McGovern field coordinators. But he provides an exuberant account (in field reports and in an interview) of a McGovern campaign at the state level, an undertaking whose fugitive existence makes it difficult to reconstruct decades later. His story about one of the smallest states previews the larger and more diffuse story of an extraordinary grassroots campaign by what Gary Hart called "the McGovern army."[2] It captures many of the characteristic features of the McGovern operation in the field: the creativity and energy of its organizers, the dedication of its volunteers, the tensions with the regular Democratic Party, the participatory sixties ethos that could frustrate its own leadership, and the relationships with a national campaign whose support was consistent but whose mistakes eventually let it down.

In his background, Craig was similar to other McGovern organizers: he was a former campus leader (president of the student council at Harvard), a veteran of civil rights and antiwar crusades, a young activist shaped by the intense politics of the 1960s. But he stood somewhat apart because he had originally been an organizer for Muskie rather than McGovern, figuring that the senator from Maine was the candidate with an acceptable antiwar position who stood the best chance of winning the presidency. Craig's stint with the Muskie campaign proved an unhappy one: he found that the Muskie people were mostly Democratic regulars, that his natural comrades were working for McGovern and having much more fun, and that the McGovern field operation was vastly superior to those of the other candidates. So, like his former Yale Law School classmates Hillary Rodham and Bill Clinton (whom he served as counsel during the 1999 Senate trial), Craig joined the McGovern campaign for the fall. Postponing the start of his legal career, he returned to his home state to mobilize the masses for McGovern.

The McGovern campaign in Vermont was brimming with energy and enthusiasm, its storefront offices filled with volunteers, its "various witty events" raising money and spirits. But any hope of winning the state against Nixon rested on an alliance with the regular Democrats, particularly "ethnic, Catholic, patriotic Democrats" from Burlington who were hostile to McGovern. Craig was only twenty-seven years old, but he was more "reputable looking and deferential" than the other two McGovern state coordinators, so he became the emissary to the regulars. Seeking out Democratic machine leaders, who were several decades older than the McGovern organizers, he drank beer with them and talked about hunting and fishing. And he tried to induce them to visit the storefront offices so they might see for themselves how the McGovernites were bringing in new voters and creating the potential for traditionally rock-ribbed Republican Vermont to turn Democratic.

Vermont regulars had a strong gubernatorial candidate in 1972, Thomas Salmon, but in his campaign appearances he was studiously ignoring the Democrats' national ticket. The McGovern coordinators were angry at Salmon's snub of their candidate, and they sought a meeting with him to warn that unless he endorsed the insurgent in his speeches, the sizable army of McGovern volunteers would not vote for him in November. Greg Craig and Prentiss Smith, a state coordinator who was about twenty years old, thought it would be a private meeting with Salmon, but the whole McGovern office staff "marched in" and insisted, in the spirit of "participatory democracy," on having their say. Salmon was incensed by the public rebuke, but in a private meeting he subsequently sought with Craig and Smith he agreed to mention McGovern favorably in his appearances. Learning about the second meeting, the McGovern staff turned their anger upon their state coordinators for making a deal behind their backs. Grassroots democracy was flowering in the Vermont McGovern campaign, passionate and inspiring but difficult to discipline and nearly as suspicious of its own leaders as it was of opposing elites.

With its paltry three electoral votes, Vermont received little attention from the national McGovern campaign. Craig pleaded with the Washington headquarters for one of the "major four"—the presidential and vice-presidential candidates and their wives—to make a campaign stop in Vermont, capturing media attention and galvanizing a final push for Election Day. Shortly before the election, Eunice Shriver flew in to the state. Her visit turned out to be a microcosm of the stumbles that dogged the fall McGovern campaign. The first words she uttered to the reception committee at the airport deflated all of Craig's hopes: "I don't know why I'm here. Don't you think I should be in Texas? Texas is more important than Vermont."

The McGovern grassroots army in Vermont and other states could not overcome the national campaign's intractable problems in the fall. In the spring, however, observers viewed it as a marvel, the key to McGovern's astonishing ascent. As the McGovern army continued to multiply, from its emergence in the New Hampshire primary to its massive mobilization for the contest in California, it became the decisive factor in the battle for the Democratic nomination.

From his own experiences in South Dakota, McGovern appreciated the potential of a grassroots campaign better than did his rivals in 1972. Yet in his sparsely populated home state, organizing a party at the grassroots had been possible for a single individual; for a presidential campaign McGovern would need to build a field operation in which first tens, then hundreds, and finally many thousands would work for his candidacy. Fortunately for him, a grassroots philosophy, a pool of experienced organizers, and a legion of committed volunteers were created in the late 1960s, especially through Eugene McCarthy's insurgent effort of 1968. Until then, as Carl Wagner, one of McGovern's most talented organizers, put it, "The idea that individual citizens within communities became the backbone of a political venture hadn't existed."[3] The McCarthy campaign showed the possibilities of a grassroots mobilization for the presidency, but the McGovern campaign four years later elevated this brand of citizen politics to a much more sophisticated—and successful—level.

McGovernites were not alone in 1972 in believing that they had discovered in grassroots campaigning a decisive new force in American politics. Participatory democracy, the watchword of sixties activism, had moved off of the campuses and beyond the social movements and into electoral politics. With the McGovern-Fraser reforms in the Democratic Party, and with the resulting changes in state laws that affected the Republican Party as well, primary elections, caucuses, and conventions decided by the rank and file were now the only road to the White House. The youthful McGovern grassroots army, demonstrably superior in 1972 to aging party insiders in mobilizing voters for wide-open nomination contests, looked like an electoral equivalent of the great citizen armies in the English and French revolutions that transformed warfare.

In retrospect, however, the period from 1968 through 1976, with 1972 as the peak, was an interregnum in the modern history of presidential campaigns. The McGovern campaign was a grassroots junction between a past in which party elites selected candidates in closed meetings and a future in which professional consultants ran media-heavy campaigns financed by big money. It was a cause-driven junction between a past in which party loyalty was uppermost and a future in which candidate personality was in the spotlight. The McGovern campaign appears not as the signpost for a more participatory politics but as the road not taken, especially by the Democratic Party. The presidential campaign of 2004, featuring Republican superiority at locally based electoral mobilization, suggests that Democrats need to find this road again.

Organizers

McGovern had probably the best grassroots organization in the history of modern American politics. His operations in New Hampshire and Wisconsin established the campaign's basic approach to grassroots politics. The approach was much the same in each state, providing a model applied elsewhere in the field, but the organizers who developed it, Joe Grandmaison and Gene Pokorny, were not much alike.

Joe Grandmaison, twenty-eight at the time of the New Hampshire primary, was a party regular from a French-Canadian family with deep roots in the state's Democratic politics. Grandmaison was voluble and abrasive. He got his way by screaming and holding his breath if necessary. But he was masterful at building McGovern support around his state, deploying growing numbers of young volunteers inspired by antiwar passion that he did not especially share.[4]

Gene Pokorny, twenty-five at the time of the Wisconsin primary, grew up on a Nebraska farm. A Phi Beta Kappa graduate of the University of Nebraska, Pokorny was more cerebral and earnest than Grandmaison but equally as pragmatic and tough. A veteran of the 1968 McCarthy campaign, he was drawn to McGovern because the South Dakota senator represented to him the "wisdom and strength in rural America."[5] Pokorny moved into Wisconsin more than a year before its primary and began to build the McGovern operation from a small nucleus to an elaborate network.[6]

In the McGovernites' grassroots model, organizers began working early—a year or more before the date of the primary. Armed with lists of activists from the McCarthy and Kennedy campaigns of 1968 and subsequent liberal causes, they located potential cadres at the local level and recruited them one by one. These grassroots leaders set up McGovern committees in cities and towns across the state, and McGovern's own favorite device, the index card, became the means through which canvassers from these committees compiled massive lists of McGovern supporters. As primary day approached, the McGovernites unleashed their grassroots network in a mobilization that dwarfed the efforts of more highly rated presidential aspirants. The weekend before the New Hampshire primary, Grandmaison recalled, five thousand volunteers "leafleted the state in an hour and a half."[7]

Antiwar activists and campus volunteers comprised most of the foot soldiers of the McGovern grassroots army, but they were by no means its only troops. McGovern organizers concentrated in the primaries on generating support in blue-collar communities as well, capitalizing on widespread alienation in the working class and demonstrating that McGovern could potentially appeal to traditional Democrats. Carl Wagner, another of the most prominent McGovern organizers, was assigned to working-class areas in Iowa, Wisconsin, Ohio, and California. Uncommon among McGovernites, he had prior experience in blue-collar communities: before joining the McGovern campaign he worked for the Alliance for Labor Action, a progressive coalition of non-AFL unions. His specialty was to attract supporters for McGovern whose chief concerns were not directed toward ending the war in Vietnam.[8]

As Wagner observes, before McGovern became the frontrunner and was tagged as a "radical," working-class and ethnic constituencies were available to him through skillful organizing. At the grassroots level, the McGovern campaign was much more diverse than the stereotype of a youth crusade. Many working-class families backed McGovern in the primaries because he represented a populist alternative to prevailing probusiness policies.

After Wisconsin, as the number and frequency of state primaries accelerated, the McGovern campaign had to make adaptations to the model developed by Grandmaison and Pokorny. There was no longer time to get on the ground so early and build support gradually. But there were compensating advantages. McGovern now had visibility and momentum, and volunteers were pouring into the campaign and often organizing themselves at the local level. Moreover, a talented and experienced corps of McGovern organizers was in place, available to be dispatched from state to state as political opportunity beckoned. Harold Himmelman had been in charge of organizing Ohio for McGovern but was transferred to Massachusetts for a primary that looked more promising. When Pat Caddell's polls picked up a late shift toward McGovern in Ohio, however, Himmelman, who had just moved his wife and two children to Massachusetts, received a call from Gary Hart to return immediately to Ohio.[9]

Most McGovern organizers were young and not burdened by family responsibilities. The same was true of the McGovern advance team, headed by Steve Robbins, which organized rallies and scheduled appearances by the candidate and his most prominent backers. These itinerant McGovernites enjoyed none of the creature comforts of the well-paid professional consultants who run campaigns today; on the contrary, they were paid minimal salaries and expected to live off the land. Gary Hart depicted Robbins in New Hampshire, "sleeping on a cold linoleum kitchen floor covered only by a sheet during bitter winter weeks."[10] Advance man John Podesta, a future White House chief of staff, described how McGovernites on the road were "living off the buckets" passed around for small donations at campaign rallies. Advance men attended the rallies they had set up, Podesta explained, not just to assess the effectiveness of their work: "You wanted to be at the rallies because you could get your hand in the buckets and might eat that day."[11]

The climax of the McGovern grassroots campaign for the Democratic nomination came in California, where, according to Gary Hart, "the army that had started with a handful was now 50,000 strong."[12] Although McGovern's victory in the California primary was in one sense a triumph for his grassroots campaign, its narrowness was in a different sense a reminder of the limits to the bottom-up approach in presidential politics. Before the primary, McGovern adviser Fred Dutton told reporter David Broder that it was "questionable whether even McGovern's army of volunteers can communicate his message for him to the rootless, wandering voters of Los Angeles and its suburbs."[13] California, vaster than any state in which McGovern had previously run, was a preview for a national campaign in which grassroots organizing would lose some of its effectiveness. Humphrey did not have anything remotely resembling McGovern's army in California. But as Steven Roberts observed in the *New York Times*, the senator from Minnesota was out to scare people about the radical consequences of a McGovern candidacy, and "in this chaotic and unpredictable state, fear is a proven political weapon."[14] It was an observation already familiar to the shrewdest alumnus of California politics, Richard Nixon.

Volunteers

The McGovern army pulled in massive numbers of volunteers. At campaign headquarters in Washington, they mostly showed up on their own with growing frequency. Marcia Johnston, initially in charge of the volunteer operation at the headquarters, described the unpaid campaign workers as an "eclectic group of people," ranging from young teenagers to "retired ladies." One group called itself "Mothers for McGovern" and established one of the first in-house child-care centers in the nation.[15] And of course there were the young people: Sara Ehrman, the "Jewish mother" of the McGovern campaign, remembered the "starry-eyed" kids, full of "energy and purity," eating leftover sandwiches and sleeping in the headquarters basement. Scruffy-looking youth were so common at McGovern headquarters that Ehrman was irritated when she was called out of an important meeting to see one—wearing a torn T-shirt, cutoff jeans, and combat boots, with a scraggly beard and long hair—until he exclaimed, "Mom, you don't recognize me!"[16] Many of the young McGovern volunteers became "roadies," traveling to the primary states where the action was.

Universities and colleges were the most fertile territory for campaign volunteers, so McGovern's travel schedule before 1972 included many antiwar speeches on campuses. Cultivation of this newly enfranchised constituency paid off: the same Gallup Poll that showed McGovern as the choice of a discouraging 3 percent of Democrats at the start of 1972 indicated that he had the backing of 15 percent of college students.[17] One of the first special operations set up by the

McGovern campaign was National Students and Youth for McGovern. It appealed to student idealism but also to student pride that young people could decide the election and change the course of American history:

> Students and young people are the core of George McGovern's natural constituency. More than any other political figure of the past decade, George McGovern has spoken out and acted on the issues which concern and affect students . . . This year, for the first time, students have the vote. More than ever before, in 1972 the American people will be looking to the campuses for a sign of what the future holds.[18]

Student volunteers played a particularly crucial role in McGovern's New Hampshire and Wisconsin primary successes. The numerous universities and colleges in the Boston area were thoroughly organized by young McGovernites, with Harvard, MIT, and Boston University closely networked together for campaign work. As the New Hampshire primary approached, caravans of these students went north to canvass the state for McGovern.[19] Some at McGovern headquarters were sensitive to the appearance that the campus activists for McGovern were Ivy League elites.[20] Thus, there was a drive to organize New Hampshire colleges, like Keene State, for McGovern, so that local students would disprove the elitist image and promote McGovern within their families and in their communities.[21]

Although the McGovern army of volunteers was skillfully coordinated by the national and state campaigns at the grassroots level, many of the local McGovern committees were in fact self-organized. Local McGovern volunteers continued to come forward even through the fall, their enthusiasm undimmed by grim polls and prognostications. These short-lived committees left little in the way of records, but a letter from an anonymous California volunteer to Frank Mankiewicz in early October 1972 is illustrative of their spirit:

> I thought you might like a first-hand report from "Small Town U.S.A." I am in charge of a small store front McGovern headquarters in a very small town called Grover City in the south of San Luis Obispo county . . . I am so encouraged ... I thought it might help the spirit if I passed on a sample of the grass root movement. The building was given free; young men painted it at night, after a full day's work, free. The first night we worked here a very nice man came by and gave a check for $100.00 When we had open house 40 people came and left $65.00 in donations and a good list of volunteer workers . . . I have sent mailings out to six of my precincts . . . I just got my first report back on one and I can't believe my ears. Only 2 Democrats are going to vote for Nixon, the balance are McGovern supporters. I firmly believe there is a movement abroad that cannot or will not be measured by polls of any sort.[22]

Volunteers were the heart of the McGovern insurgency, but along with—and partly due to—their idealism and passion they presented difficulties for the campaign. In the top echelon of McGovern staff, Gary Hart was the most fervent champion of grassroots work, but he recognized that "one of the problems of a grassroots campaign is that by its very nature it's hard to control. It is not hierarchical."[23] Thrown into fierce competition at the local and state levels against old-line and prowar Democratic regulars, many McGovern volunteers were not inclined to be gracious in victory, no matter how badly the campaign needed the regulars in the fall. Jeff Smith tells the story of McGovern convention delegates in his home state of New Mexico. McGovern won the New Mexico primary, with Wallace coming in second, and neither candidate's slate of delegates to Miami Beach included the state's senior U.S. senator, Joseph Montoya. The national campaign asked for one of the McGovern delegates to step aside so that the unhappy Montoya could be placated. At a meeting of McGovern delegates, one rose and responded to this pragmatic concern: "I'll be God damned with this war going on and Montoya on the wrong side . . . if I'll kiss [his] ass to get him back on the delegation." At that point, Smith's mother "jumped up from the back and said, 'I volunteer. I'll kiss his ass if that's what it takes.' And she gave up her spot."[24]

Anger directed by volunteers at defeated regulars could be redirected against the McGovern campaign's own organizers for betraying the participatory ethos of grassroots democracy. A New Jersey delegate wrote to McGovern in July that the candidate was "becoming more and more isolated from your grassroots workers and from the 'street people' by your staff and the bureaucracy that through necessity has grown up around you."[25] Grassroots grievances of this sort were particularly common in California. A fall petition titled "What Is Wrong with the Southern California Campaign?" presented the suspicious questions of McGovern volunteers: "Why are constant power struggles within the campaign destroying our ability to gain the Presidential power it's all about? Why has less happened with the big bureaucracy than happened without it? Where have the grassroots people gone? THEY MOWED THE GRASS."[26] A September meeting of more than a hundred McGovern activists in Los Angeles bitterly complained of "a tragic lack on the part of the campaign leadership in involving the grassroots people in the campaign."[27]

Almost inevitably, some of the volunteers who had been attracted to a candidate whom they regarded as "Saint George" became critical of the political moves that McGovern felt he had to make in the fall campaign. Instead of political strategists on his staff leading him astray, foot soldiers in the McGovern army suspected that their commander himself was eager to compromise. If McGovern's problem with the electorate was that too many voters considered him too far to the left, some of his volunteers worried that he was not left enough. These complaints too emanated most often from California. Marin County activists warned national headquarters of disgruntled liberals who were saying that "the Senator is turning out to be 'just another politician' [and] that he no longer is the reformer 'if ever he truly was one.'"[28] Larry Diamond, the student body president at Stanford, reported that Palo Alto McGovernites were unhappy about the focus on bread-and-butter issues in the early fall and wanted to hear speeches on Vietnam "that have much more soul."[29] Riding the passionate politics of grassroots insurgency, McGovern found that its energy and conviction did not come without cost to him.

Managing an Insurgency

Despite these difficulties thrown up by the passions and suspicions of the volunteers, the grassroots effort was the greatest asset of the McGovern campaign. On the ground, in its decentralized operation, the McGovern campaign was a remarkable success that is still of relevance for presidential politics. Its top command, its centralized component, was another story. Reasonably effective in the nomination campaign, the centralized McGovern organization was beset by numerous failings in the fall. Some of these reflected the top staffers and their rivalries, which were not untypical of more orthodox campaigns. Even more, organizational failings reflected the questionable management style of the candidate himself. Deeper structural tensions were at work as well—the contradictory demands of managing an insurgency that tries to win in the conventional game of presidential politics.

We can trace the evolution of the central McGovern campaign organization, as it developed from a long-shot insurgency to the campaign of the Democratic Party's presidential nominee, through four stages. McGovern was so obviously a long shot that no high-level veterans of presidential elections were at first interested in joining his campaign. The initial staff in 1970, with Gary Hart, Rick Stearns, and a handful of others, only possessed campaign experience at a lower level, but that brought a compensating advantage: Hart and Stearns were not wedded to past practices and had unusual insight into a transformed nomination process in which an outsider like McGovern might upend all of the conventional assumptions. As Gary Hart wrote, the original McGovern staff was so "meager" that there was no real division of labor: "During this period we were all simultaneously and constantly political operatives and organizers, schedulers and advancemen, fund-raisers, name-gatherers, bodyguards, follow-up agents (whose duties included writing the indispensable thank-you notes), drivers, negotiators, magicians, and medicinemen."[30]

The only significant tension within the organization during this first stage was between the campaign staff and McGovern's South Dakota Senate staff. The South Dakotans, especially administrative assistant George Cunningham, were not at all happy about McGovern's run for the presidency. They resented the newcomers from the campaign staff commandeering McGovern's time and attention. Even more, they worried that a hopeless bid for the presidency would ruin the senator in his home state and cost them their jobs. As Jeff Smith, whom McGovern added to his Senate staff in 1968 with an eye to a presidential effort for 1972, sympathetically observed about the South Dakotans, "They had been with him through thick and thin, and then all of a sudden, [it's] like Cinderella; somebody else takes her off to the ball, and they're going, 'What about me?'"[31]

Young recruits, inspired by McGovern's antiwar stance, started to come aboard the campaign staff. Hart began to divide up responsibilities, including a system of regional desks at the national headquarters to facilitate and coordinate the grassroots campaigns in the states. Camaraderie was high among this group—and ambition was modest. Scott Lilly, desk officer for the border and central states, depicts "an environment that is rarely found in a campaign." It was, he says, "a very selfless operation. People were there because they were really committed to the cause. Presidential campaigns turn very ugly when people start thinking about the jobs and the fame and the glory . . . We were there because we thought it was important."[32]

When veteran political operatives Frank Mankiewicz and Ted Van Dyk joined McGovern's staff in the summer of 1971, they inaugurated the second stage in the development of the McGovern central organization and generated its first significant rivalries. Marcia Johnston expresses the ambivalence of the original McGovernites about the addition of Mankiewicz and Van Dyk: on the one hand, their arrival showed that the campaign was becoming "serious." But "on the other hand, these are the *old guys*. They don't get it. They're worried about bumper stickers and we're trying to change the world." For the original McGovern staffers, the generational divide was also a philosophical and strategic divide: this campaign was not like the ones in which Mankiewicz and Van Dyk had been high-level participants. This campaign would be won with "boots on the ground," not with the "party bosses."[33]

High-level struggles about strategy that were equally struggles about power now became a feature of the McGovern organization, although they did not, at this stage, undermine the cooperation that characterized most McGovern staffers below the top. There was some tension between Mankiewicz and Van Dyk, and Van Dyk was more peripheral to the main action than he had expected when joining the campaign. But the principal conflict was between Mankiewicz and Hart. Many staffers were now identified as Frank's people or Gary's people, the latter group more numerous.

At several points during the nomination campaign, Mankiewicz sought to take over top management, temporarily persuading McGovern to place the less-experienced Hart at a lower position in an organizational hierarchy. But

Hart rallied his forces and convinced the candidate to retain him in his post as official campaign manager.[34] As Hart recalls, "I had the original organizers with me who wanted to stick to the original plan . . . The phone began to ring off the hook when the word got out [that Hart was to be demoted], from Pokorny and Grandmaison and people like that, essentially saying, 'if Hart goes, we go.'"[35] So McGovern left Hart and Mankiewicz in an uneasy state of blurred authority, and whatever rivalry continued to simmer between them, it was not so intense as to prevent them for collaborating for the campaign's good.

Primary victories in the spring of 1972 brought a new influx of McGovern staffers and a third stage in the evolution of the campaign organization. These new recruits came mainly from the Muskie campaign as it collapsed. When Muskie's prospects plummeted, it was natural for the New Politics activists who had opted to work for the original frontrunner—including Anne Wexler, the Podesta brothers (Tony and John), and Bob Shrum—to join the original McGovernites, many of whom were friends from previous insurgent campaigns.

Absorption of the former Muskie operatives into the campaign was easier than the incorporation of Washington pros had been. McGovernites appreciated that they needed the new talent to win the Democratic nomination and make a serious run at the presidency. Initially, however, there was some understandable resentment toward the recent arrivals for their previous choice to place realpolitik (with Muskie) ahead of idealism (with McGovern). Original staffers had buttons printed up reading FMBNH—For McGovern before New Hampshire. The newcomers, sharing the youthful bravado and humor of the McGovernites, soon dissipated the tensions. As John Podesta relates, he and his brother had buttons of their own printed up that "said FMBRI—For McGovern before Rhode Island— and wore them quite proudly."[36]

McGovern's impending capture of the Democratic presidential nomination initiated the fourth—and most conflict-ridden—stage in the development of the campaign organization. To run a national campaign, the McGovern organization brought in a few high-level figures with electoral experience and connections to the major constituent groups of the Democratic Party. But these late recruits were not liberal insurgents, and the personal ambitions, traditional practices, and special agendas they introduced into the campaign brought tension and disarray that often outweighed the strengths that they added. Rob Gunnison remembers sarcastically remarking about some of the latecomers to the staff that came into the campaign with personal agendas, "Geez, I thought we were all working for George McGovern!" (But Gunnison also recalls that even the original McGovernites played "fantasy games" about future jobs if McGovern was, improbably, to win.)[37]

A few of the original McGovern staffers felt shoved aside by the heavyweights. Kirby Jones, McGovern's press secretary during the spring, was replaced for the fall by the veteran journalist Dick Dougherty, who had earlier resigned from the press position when the campaign looked hopeless. As Jones reflected, most of the younger McGovernites "didn't see what was coming," didn't anticipate that experienced people looking to future jobs would "come out of the woodwork now that McGovern was the nominee." For Jones, it was an eye-opening demonstration of "power politics."[38] The problems of this final organizational stage ran deeper than the hurt feelings of several committed, longtime McGovernites relegated to the sidelines. As major new players were added to the mix—Jean Westwood as McGovern's choice for chair of the Democratic National Committee; Lawrence O'Brien, past DNC chair, as chairman of the campaign; Congressman Frank Thompson as head of voter registration—power centers within the organization were multiplied beyond the earlier Hart-Mankiewicz divide. In precisely the period when the candidate himself was absorbed in escalating crises of credibility that demanded his full attention, his organization became a hydra-headed beast.

Disorganization at McGovern campaign headquarters became a recurring press story in the fall. Congressman Thompson resigned his post because his voter-registration operation did not receive the full funding it had been promised. Chairman O'Brien was reported to have threatened that he would not stay unless the campaign changes he was suggesting were adopted. Longtime aide Gordon Weil quit in frustration, only to rescind his resignation after the story hit the newspapers and he wanted to spare the campaign further embarrassment. Unknown to the press, there were even more threatened departures: Ted Van Dyk resigned temporarily, and Jean Westwood offered to resign to ease McGovern's organizational burden. Coming on the heels of the Eagleton fiasco, the management problems of the McGovern fall campaign buttressed skepticism that McGovern had the competence to be an effective president.[39]

McGovern was bombarded by memos from senior staffers in this period, all of them recommending that he put one person in charge of the campaign organization. Reporting that "the headquarters is a shambles," Weil told McGovern that the cause was "a failure to have any single person who can see what needs to be done and then sees that it is done."[40] George Cunningham mapped four distinct organizational fiefdoms:

> Morale is low at the campaign office and there is uncertainty in the field
> basically because of the confusing lines of authority that exist in the higher
> echelons of the campaign. We have the following situation at the top:
> Gary Hart, Manager, National Campaign
> Frank Mankiewicz, Director, National Campaign
> Larry O'Brien, Chairman, National Campaign
> Jean Westwood, Chairman, Democratic National Committee
> Decisions which are made at a secondary level, if adverse to one party
> or another as they inevitably must be, can be, and are, bucked to one of

the above, frequently on a rotating basis, until a favorable decision to the protestant is made. All of this slows everything up.[41]

Although published reports of disorganization damaged his stature—and although members of his staff, frustrated by the confusing authority structure, felt that this was one press criticism that was warranted—McGovern never did put one person in charge, and the disorder within his campaign persisted to the end. Among McGovernites at the top of the campaign, various explanations were offered for McGovern's shortcomings at campaign management. Frank Mankiewicz believed that McGovern was "too nice a fellow. He couldn't come to grips with the idea of one tough person running the whole campaign." In this view, McGovern was reluctant to demote or dismiss anyone who had loyally served him. Mankiewicz thought that if McGovern had been compelled to pick a single campaign head, he would have been the choice, but "Gary had been there early, and George wanted to reward him for that."[42]

A second explanation focused on the theme of participatory democracy. Morris Dees noted in bemusement that "there will never be another campaign like the McGovern campaign. Any critical strategic meeting could be attended by anybody."[43] Gordon Weil felt that his own reputation among McGovern staff as an abrasive character came because he bucked the liberal fetish that decisions had to be made in a participatory fashion. In Weil's view, McGovern backed the liberal view and rejected an orderly hierarchy for the campaign because he believed in a participatory and open politics.[44]

Weil also argued that McGovern did not recognize the need to pick one of his staff as the top campaign manager because he mistakenly thought he could be his own manager. This third explanation was echoed by such close observers of McGovern as Gary Hart and John Holum.[45] It was couched in its most accusatory form by press secretary Dick Dougherty, who advanced a "theory of the one-man band." According to Dougherty, McGovern believed that

> he could do anything his staff did and do it as well or better. This was
> understandable in a way. When he started out as the poorly paid executive
> secretary of the South Dakota Democratic Party in 1953 he was his own
> speechwriter, fund-raiser, press secretary, organizer, typist, driver,
> mimeograph operator. Name any function in politics, and he had done
> it . . . A man for whom staff couldn't do much was likely to be not just
> undemanding of staffers but, implicitly at least, contemptuous of them . . .
> The truth was that there was only one strategist, one theoretician, and one
> man in the inner circle—George McGovern.[46]

In light of the abundant criticism of McGovern as manager, I asked him why he had never given one person—presumably either Hart or Mankiewicz—the authority to impose discipline upon the campaign. While considering Hart his campaign's manager, McGovern readily admitted that some people within the staff "found confusing" the "dual focus" of Hart and Mankiewicz. But he was satisfied with this arrangement: "It helped bring us to the nomination. Why change at that point?" McGovern acknowledged that it was a "legitimate criticism" of him that he had not shifted to a clearer authority structure for the national campaign in the fall. But he still believed it was too easy to say that his organizational problems would have been solved by having "a strong person take over" after the Democratic convention. "Who would it have been?" he asked. Any way he turned—elevating either Hart or Mankiewicz or choosing someone entirely new—would have presented new difficulties and might have opened new rifts.[47]

McGovern's defense against the criticism was not sufficient, for he paid a high price for his campaign's disarray in its final stage. He deserves much of the blame that many McGovernites, otherwise so fond of him, bestow on him for failures in campaign management. However, whether one sees too much softness, or conversely too much hubris, in McGovern's personality to arrange for effective management once his candidacy moved to the highest level of the presidential game, the problems at the apex of his campaign reflected more than a flaw in the man. Throughout the election season, and especially in the fall, McGovern was attempting to combine two opposing political approaches—a decentralized grassroots campaign and a centralized mainstream campaign. He was hoping to mobilize insurgents but also to win over insiders. Needing both constituencies to gain the presidency, he needed the top staffers who represented each—Hart for the grassroots, Mankiewicz for Democratic elites. Offering either of these men the complete command of his campaign and demoting the other risked alienating half of his forces. The management weaknesses of the McGovern effort ultimately transcend the candidate, suggesting organizational tensions in the politics of insurgency quite different from those found in more conventional presidential campaigns.

"A Million-Member Club"

There *was* one centralized function in the McGovern campaign that was a striking success, even in the fall: fundraising. Ironically, what made this centralized operation work so well was fervor at the grass roots. Although the McGovern campaign brought in some money in the orthodox fashion, by soliciting large contributions from the wealthy, most of the funds that financed the campaign came through direct-mail solicitations of small donations. In the annals of campaign finance, 1972 is famous for the enormous cash pile of the Nixon campaign and the secret, illegal contributions that built it. But the McGovern campaign produced a more encouraging story for a democracy: of clean money, collected in an open fashion, from ordinary citizens who wanted changes in government policies and not favors for themselves.

As a long-shot effort, the McGovern insurgency in its early stages was cash-starved and resource-poor. Press secretary Jeff Gralnick complained to Ted Van Dyk in October 1971 that he was expected to mail out seven hundred copies of a document and yet the campaign headquarters possessed only a single mimeograph machine.[48] In the dark winter months before McGovern's surprising showing in the New Hampshire primary belied the terrible poll numbers, the insurgency often seemed on the verge of collapsing for want of money; Gary Hart called this time "the Valley Forge of the McGovern campaign."[49] During the New Hampshire grassroots operation, a financial angel appeared in Miles Rubin, who pulled cash out of his ski parka to float media and phone-banking that had previously been unaffordable.[50]

Well into the primary season money remained, in the words of campaign treasurer Marian Pearlman, "a constant crisis." Typical for the McGovern campaign, Pearlman was a young lawyer with no background in accounting; her sole qualification for handling the day-to-day money flow was that she had grown up in a family that owned a small business. Funds flowed into the McGovern campaign mostly in mail bags full of envelopes containing small bills. "We never knew each day," Pearlman recalls, "how much money was coming in." She was constantly running to the bank to deposit the day's receipts, hoping to cover the checks that had already gone out to field operations with the highest priority. But as McGovern's successes in the primaries began to mount, the mail bags full of money began to increase commensurately and the cash crisis eased.[51]

The small bills and checks were a response to a direct-mail operation that was one of the McGovern campaign's greatest points of pride. Estimates by McGovernites of the total of small donations generated through its mailings run between $20–25 million, not enough to match Nixon's unprecedented mountain of funds but sufficient to finance a campaign that did not fail for lack of money. Tapping into the passionate antiwar feelings of its grassroots base, the McGovern campaign mobilized an extraordinary number of contributors and aimed for even more. In his acceptance speech at the Democratic convention, the candidate drew the contrast between his funding and Nixon's: "Let the opposition collect their $10 million in secret money from the privileged. And let us find one million ordinary Americans who will contribute $25 each to this campaign—'A Million-Member Club' with members who will expect, not special favors for themselves, but a better land for us all."[52] The McGovern campaign did not reach the million-member mark, but its final list of donors included about 600,000 names.[53]

The central figure in this democratic fundraising was another of the McGovern campaign's rich cast of characters, Morris Dees. Born in 1936, the son of an Alabama cotton farmer, Dees inherited from his father a largely defunct southern tradition of progressive white populism. As a college student he was briefly a volunteer for the then-populist candidate for governor, George Wallace. With a friend, Dees started a mail-order business while still in college, soliciting parents to send their children who were away at school a custom-baked birthday cake. Branching out into other ventures, especially publishing, even through his years in law school, Dees developed one of the most profitable direct-mail businesses in the country, and when he sold his company for $6 million in 1969, he was a wealthy man still in his early thirties. Returning to the practice of law, he began the Southern Poverty Law Center early in 1971 to fight for racial justice in the South. At about the same time, he became an unpaid consultant to the McGovern campaign.[54]

McGovern asked Dees to put out a direct-mail appeal right before his early announcement for the presidency, hoping to generate enough of a response to fund the building of a campaign organization. Dees drafted a long letter, based on his reading of McGovern's speeches, which political veterans advising the candidate rejected in favor of a one-page appeal. Knowing from his successful experience with direct mail that to sell a product you need to tell a story, Dees says that he ignored the instructions from headquarters and sent out a seven-page letter on his own. McGovern was upset about this act of defiance—until the money pouring in proved Dees right and allowed the campaign to get under way.[55] After this success, no one in the campaign ever challenged Dees again on his mastery of direct mail.

Over the course of the campaign, Dees, assisted by Jeff Smith and Tom Collins, devised a succession of inventive techniques to raise money from ordinary citizens. Beginning with those who sent in cash or checks in response to the original seven-page letter, the direct-mail operation launched a McGovern for President Club, with each member requested to contribute $10 a month. Once more the response rate was phenomenal, with many accompanying their donations with heartfelt letters and giving more than they could really afford. Small donations never made the campaign flush with funds, but they did keep it afloat even as McGovern seemingly remained a hopeless dark horse. Once he surged to the front, the direct-mail undertaking rode ascending hopes with fervent appeals. In one imaginative venture in the summer of 1972, small donors on the rapidly growing mailing list were supplied four checks to fill out, each to be dated on the first day of the four months remaining before the election. Supporters of modest means thus were allowed to stretch out the impact on their personal finances, while the McGovern campaign was saved the time and expense of repeatedly contacting them while being guaranteed a higher sum per donor.[56]

Most of the money that financed McGovern's insurgency came from people with modest incomes—but by no means all of it. A small number of wealthy antiwar liberals made sizeable contributions or loans to the campaign even in its early stages. McGovern's top financial aides, Henry Kimelman and Miles Rubin, developed ambitious plans for a program of "large gifts" to finance the campaign against Nixon.[57] Starting with the California primary, a group of wealthy contributors was approached to make loans or donations to the campaign of $1,000 or more, and a significant number, according to Rubin, gave at the $25,000–$50,000 level. To McGovern's critics, including syndicated columnists Evans and Novak, the presence of these "fat cats" in the background of the McGovern campaign undercut its populist image and created a financial equivalence with the Nixon campaign.[58] Yet as Rubin points out, there was a huge difference between McGovern and Nixon "fat cats": McGovern's big donors, motivated principally by their despair over Vietnam, did not expect him to win and were not looking for any personal benefits as payback for their contributions.[59]

Another source of large sums for McGovern was the celebrity concerts produced by Warren Beatty. John F. Kennedy may have been the first presidential candidate to attract a large number of movie stars to his campaign, but his appeal to Hollywood lay in his glamour. McGovern was devoid of glamour, but he drew the stars—"sparklies" in the argot of the McGovernites—because he was the champion of the antiwar cause, and his campaign became a watershed in the history of Hollywood liberalism. Beatty put together a series of legendary concerts: shows in the spring of 1972 at the Forum in Los Angeles and Madison Square Garden in New York each drew almost 20,000 people and together raised about $700,000 for the campaign. The lineup of performers was spectacular—Barbara Streisand, Carole King, and James Taylor in Los Angeles; Simon and Garfunkel, Peter, Paul, and Mary, and Mike Nichols and Elaine May in New York—and those who purchased expensive tickets (cheaper ones were available for the "kids") were escorted to their seats by ushers like Jack Nicholson, Goldie Hawn, and Dustin Hoffman. (Wandering into the upper section of Madison Square Garden, usher Paul Newman was nearly mauled by fans and had to be rescued.) The concerts were not Hollywood's only contributions to the campaign; as was noted earlier, many celebrities—Beatty and his sister, Shirley MacLaine, foremost among them—donated large amounts of their time to hitting the campaign trail for McGovern.[60]

Wealthy liberals and media superstars aided McGovern out of their own idealism, but in the end it was the dedication of ordinary donors that was most remarkable. Even as McGovern's prospects grew increasingly bleak through the fall campaign, the flow of small donations did not diminish; in fact, it intensified right up to the end. During the final weeks of the campaign, so many mail bags containing modest sums arrived at McGovern headquarters in Washington that they strained the capacity of campaign volunteers to open them and count the cash. Some of the last-minute donors were steadfast in their hopes; others, aware of the impending defeat, gave as an act of defiance, putting their money behind a conception of their country that they knew the majority was about to reject.[61]

The grassroots financing of McGovern impressed Larry O'Brien, the old party pro who was otherwise skeptical of the insurgency, as "the highlight of the campaign."[62] It was a highlight as well for the possibility that presidential elections might be financed in a manner that furthers rather than undermines the influence of ordinary citizens. And it was an intriguing reminder that citizens can give a great deal of themselves when they see a candidate and a cause in which to believe.

Media and the Grassroots

Grassroots campaigns and media campaigns are normally seen as opposites. In the first, ordinary citizens in large numbers actively shape the dynamics of the campaign; in the second, a handful of professional consultants fashion slick messages to move—or manipulate—a passive electorate. But this dichotomy was not true for the McGovern campaign: only a few McGovernites were involved in creating television ads and handling relations with the press, but they partook too much of the spirit of insurgency to run a conventional media operation. The McGovern campaign's television ads were positive and shone with authenticity, and its press relations were unusually forthright. For these very reasons, they were at a competitive disadvantage against the textbook media manipulation of the Nixon campaign.

For the nomination season, Charles Guggenheim set out to display in a biographical film the qualities of character that had attracted him to George McGovern as a person and as a political leader. Guggenheim believed that if people knew the real McGovern—his heartland roots, his moral convictions, his all-American story—they would support him.[63] He presented McGovern's life in powerful yet unadorned images, with an air of authenticity evocative of the rebellion of innovative filmmakers of that era against Hollywood glossiness and gimmickry. It was a brilliant production—"so good," Hunter Thompson wrote with a bit of his usual hyperbole, "that even the most cynical veteran journalists said it was the best political film ever made for television."[64]

Guggenheim's biography framed McGovern's life in terms of his profound commitment to peace. Its early shots—pictures of McGovern's father as coal miner and then minister, images of the Dust Bowl, a photo of the young pilot leaving his wife to go to war—established McGovern as a quintessential son of the American heartland. Its treatment of his political career established his boldness in bucking the Republicanism of his home state and his liberal lineage as the friend and heir of Robert F. Kennedy. The narrative took on even more dramatic punch as it turned to the war in Vietnam: McGovern appeared as a man who enjoyed the love of a happy family and the rewards of a successful career and yet was compelled by his conscience to take an unpopular stand against a "policy of madness." Announcing his antiwar candidacy for the presidency, he was ignored by the press, but he sought out and listened to the concerns of ordinary citizens, and "slowly the people came to know he was there." The final frames of the biography, showing McGovern speaking against a backdrop of images of America, clinched the message that here was an American patriot of the finest kind.[65]

Most McGovernites loved Guggenheim's work. When I interviewed the much-honored documentary filmmaker six months before his death in October 2002, I was therefore surprised to hear him say that McGovern might have been better served if someone else had produced his campaign commercials. Guggenheim described himself as "fundamentally a filmmaker," but by the time of the 1972 election, he suggested, campaign media were increasingly the domain of specialized "spin doctors" who fashioned commercials on the basis of market research. Resistant to screening longer campaign films in prime time, television stations now wanted short spots instead. Too brief to tell Guggenheim's positive stories of character, these spots were more suited, he said, for "hit-and-run" accusations against the opposition. Nixon's media specialists were way ahead of Guggenheim in mastering the new format with pioneering attack ads (which I discuss in Chapter 10), and a specialist on McGovern's side who was similarly attuned to the changes in campaign television might have made for a more even contest on the air.[66]

Yet Guggenheim's resistance to following the approach of the Nixon ads was more than a matter of his vocation or even his personal distaste for going negative. As McGovern fell far behind Nixon in the fall of 1972, some members of his campaign organization began to press for attack ads against the president. They pointed out that while McGovern was starting to deliver sharply worded speeches on the duplicity and corruption of the Nixon administration, his campaign commercials stuck to positive portrayals of the Democratic candidate.[67] Guggenheim's retort was that Nixon's character was not a secret to the American people, who liked the president's strength in foreign policy but did not like him as a person. The real issue in the fall, he felt, was "the competence of George McGovern," especially in the wake of the Eagleton affair, and so television ads that displayed McGovern's leadership qualities were more important to air than reminders about "tricky Dick."[68]

Eventually, toward the very end of the campaign, Guggenheim lost the argument over negative ads. Adamant that he would not make this kind of commercial, he stepped aside as the McGovern campaign brought in another television producer. The last-minute attack ads of the McGovern campaign were not exactly distinguished for their originality. In one, ordinary-looking people appeared reciting a litany of complaints about Nixon—corruption, spying, inflation, coziness with fat cats, and more—and then the screen flashed the name Nixon in all capital letters with colors that kept changing. In another, charging the president with undermining the soundness of American currency, the portrait of Washington on the dollar bill morphed into the face of Nixon.[69] Guggenheim felt grim vindication when pollster Lou Harris informed him that McGovern's negative TV ads only put him further behind.[70]

Guggenheim's films for McGovern in 1972 are a testament to the possibility that campaign advertising might honor the reasoning capacities of the American electorate. At the same time, Guggenheim's experience in the fall campaign speaks to one of the disturbing paradoxes of presidential campaigning today, especially for insurgents: Americans want more integrity and authenticity in their candidates, yet a campaign that emphasizes the positive is most often trumped by an opposition that, like Nixon in 1972 and his subsequent imitators, has perfected the art and science of the negative.

The Perils of Openness

No diatribe against the press in American political history is as notorious as Richard Nixon's rant after he lost the California gubernatorial race in 1962. When the 1972 election was over, however, it was McGovern who had a complaint about press coverage:

> During the campaign, I was subjected to the close, critical reporting that is a tradition in American politics. It was not always comfortable, but it is always necessary. Yet Mr. Nixon escaped a similar scrutiny. The press never really laid a glove on him, and they seldom told the people that he was hiding or that his plans for the next four years were hidden. Six days after the Watergate gang was run to the ground, Mr. Nixon invited reporters into his office, and submitted to the only interrogation his managers allowed during the fall campaign. Not a single reporter could gather the courage to ask a question about the bugging and burglary of the Democratic National Committee. Much of this can be blamed on the incestuous character of the White House press corps itself.[71]

This complaint should not be dismissed as merely expressing the frustration of a loser: McGovern, unlike Nixon, was not paranoid about the press, and several observers of American journalism in 1972 seconded his allegation about bad habits in the media's coverage of presidential campaigns.

The McGovernites were hardly innocents at press relations—not with Frank Mankiewicz, press secretary to Bobby Kennedy, in charge of handling the media. Mankiewicz charmed reporters with his humor and affability—and spun them with aplomb. Edgar Berman, an associate of Hubert Humphrey, groused about how the Mankiewicz touch distorted coverage of the contest between his candidate and McGovern: "During the Humphrey-McGovern debate . . . in California, Mankiewicz had the press clapping their flippers every time he threw them a sardine."[72] Kirby Jones, a Mankiewicz protégé, recalled how in each of the primaries Mankiewicz, working in conjunction with pollster Pat Caddell, shaped favorable media interpretations of election results by pointing the press to key precincts where the McGovern campaign—but not the journalists—had known in advance that it was likely to exceed expectations. Jones also remembered Mankiewicz's lesson that the care and feeding of reporters was taken as a test of a campaign's seriousness: when the inexperienced young aide was suddenly thrown into the breach as press secretary, the sole words of advice that the veteran media handler offered were: "Don't lose the bags of any of the journalists."[73]

Although McGovernites were not innocents in their relations with the press, they were insurgents, grassroots democrats who believed in a more open politics. In the absence of a single authority figure imposing message discipline, everybody in the campaign talked to the press.[74] Speaking to big-time reporters was an especially heady experience for young McGovernites, who were seldom loath to share their thoughts and even their gossip. For the journalists, covering the McGovern campaign was equally an unusual occurrence. William Greider of the *Washington Post* remembers it as the last presidential campaign that was "fun" for a reporter. "It was wide open," says Greider. He could stroll into the McGovern headquarters in Washington at any time. There was no security guard posted; instead, the reporter encountered a day-care center in the hallway. Greider felt free to drop in on any of the McGovern staffers in their offices, and they were generally eager to chat with him about how the campaign was going.[75] Little about the McGovern campaign was concealed from the press, even its dirtiest laundry.

By contrast, the Nixon campaign was, in Greider's phrase, "buttoned down."[76] Nixon's aides were tight-lipped, and the president himself was unavailable to reporters. While the journalists following McGovern had plenty of material for stories about disarray within his organization, those assigned to Nixon rarely called attention to how little they knew about the inner workings of his campaign. Cassie Mackin of NBC News caused a brief sensation by reporting that "the Nixon campaign is, for the most part, a series of speeches before closed audiences, invited guests only," in which the president made false charges against McGovern.[77] "Before the Nightly News was off the air," Timothy Crouse wrote, "Herb Klein [a Nixon press strategist] was on the phone to NBC, demanding corrections."[78] Cognizant of the administration's history of intimidating the press, no other reporter covering Nixon followed Mackin's lead and produced critical stories about how closed and deceptive his campaign was.

The Nixon media operation positioned the president high above the fray. In his place it used a stable of surrogates—cabinet members, senior White House staff, Republican senators and governors, and of course the administration's ace political hit man, Vice President Spiro Agnew—to come at McGovern from all directions and on nearly every imaginable issue. Adhering to the journalistic canon of objectivity, the media gave the surrogates' attacks extensive play without commenting on the stratagem they represented. The normally unflappable challenger could not contain his outrage: "The Nixon-Agnew intimidation of the networks has worked to the point where every Republican who pops off is given equal time with George McGovern . . . I don't think the President ought to be allowed to sit there in the White House and have these lackeys of his running around the country getting equal time with me every day."[79]

The McGovern campaign's press problems in the fall were partly of its own making. Even with Mankiewicz's skills, the McGovernites remained a largely inexperienced and undisciplined bunch in a fight with professionals who were masters at message control. Blabbing to reporters is never a prescription for electoral success, and the McGovern campaign might have recognized that there are legitimate limits to openness even for insurgents committed to greater public transparency. These weaknesses perhaps were not unique to the McGovernites, and they may even be an occupational hazard for political insurgencies. The very authenticity and spontaneity that make an insurgency like McGovern's a fresh force in American politics open it up to the critical scrutiny of journalists accustomed to reporting the circumlocutions of professional politicians and their handlers. If an insurgency is raising unfamiliar issues and testing the ideological limits of conventional politics as well, it is all the more a tempting target for the media to caricature.

Whatever the failings of the insurgents, the press hardly did itself proud in covering the contest between McGovern and Nixon. As Crouse observed, journalistic objectivity was a failure in 1972, producing a "staggering inequality between the coverage of the two campaigns." While reporters assigned to McGovern took advantage of his campaign's openness to probe into its weaknesses, "the White House reporters were failing to get across the obstacle course that the White House had set up; indeed, they were not even trying."[80] The shortcomings of objectivity as a guide to journalistic behavior were, however, only the beginning of the problem. A deeper distortion was the deference typically given to an incumbent president. In the 1972 campaign that deference was mixed with fear: a timorous White House press corps was not about to cross a vindictive chief executive whom it was sure would be around for another four years. What its coverage in 1972 ultimately revealed was that the press did not know either how to credit forthrightness or how to expose deceit.

Conclusion

Some McGovernites took solace after their overwhelming defeat by pointing to their role as grassroots pioneers. Gary Hart compiled a list of the campaign's innovations:

We had introduced some revolutionary concepts and methodologies to American politics that would continue to have an impact regardless of the outcome of this campaign. There had been the emergence of the massive volunteer army. There had been a high degree of technical skill combined with ideological commitment and motivation. We had introduced democracy to political campaigning. We had decentralized authority and decision-making, encouraging local authority and control. There was also our program of popular, broad-based campaign financing.[81]

Understandably, Hart highlighted the genuine successes of the grassroots campaign and left out its difficulties: the inexperience and mounting disarray at the top, the indiscipline and bouts of suspiciousness at the base. There was a further problem with his prophecy: the grassroots revolution that he saw the McGovern campaign as commencing, although perpetuated in a more modest form in the Carter campaign of 1976, the Kennedy campaign of 1980, and his own presidential bid in 1984, petered out by the middle of the 1980s, at least for the Democrats. Campaigns run by professional consultants, requiring big money to pay for slick media, became the state of the art. Looking back, James K. Galbraith observes with regret that at the time he had thought the McGovern campaign "was actually the beginning of a much larger form of American politics. It turned out to be the high-water mark of participatory politics in America."[82]

Turning away from grassroots campaigning was not only a loss for citizen participation in the democratic process; it also marked the abandonment of a potentially powerful political tool. Democrats began to rediscover the importance of grassroots mobilization in the 2000 and 2004 presidential elections. Yet Steve Robbins, McGovern's chief scheduler, argues that they have yet to match the McGovernites at the grassroots. "There has never been a field operation since," says Robbins, "as good as the McGovern field operation." Unlike the Democrats' popular mobilization in 2004, the McGovern grassroots operation had been built up over time and was largely an indigenous undertaking, with local volunteers out canvassing months before the day of an election. The McGovernites used phone banking on occasion, but they did not rely heavily on any technology of communication. As Robbins puts it, "There is no substitute for walking—and I don't think anybody's walked as well as we did."[83]

Much has changed since 1972 in grassroots politics, most obviously in the uses of technology. Yet the McGovernites' conception of a volunteer army with "boots on the ground" remains valuable, especially for the organization and intense involvement of activists in their own communities that an Internet mobilization is hard-pressed to equal. Those hoping to revive the Democratic Party at the local level can do worse than studying the successes of McGovern's grassroots army.

8

Democratic Insurgency

Ted Van Dyk was at the CBS studio in Los Angeles when Hubert Humphrey lambasted George McGovern as an impractical and dangerous radical in a debate on *Face the Nation*. Returning to the McGovern campaign's hotel, he encountered the candidate's daughter Terry. "Terry was crying," Van Dyk remembered, "and she said, 'Did dad get to talk to Uncle Hubert after the debate?'" McGovern and Humphrey had been next-door neighbors in Chevy Chase, Maryland, for twelve years, and the two men and their families had grown close. Van Dyk continued: "I recall, when I worked for Humphrey, seeing his children's handprints and the McGovern children's handprints in the patio outside his house."[1]

Expecting "a gentlemanly debate"—the first of three scheduled right before the critical California primary—with his old friend and mentor Hubert, McGovern "wasn't prepared for him to open up right out of the box with a series of attacks on everything I had stood for."[2] Emphasizing that both men had supported appropriations for the military, Humphrey suggested that McGovern had been as wrong about Vietnam as he had been. On every other issue he claimed a gaping distance between his moderate positions and McGovern's wild radicalism. On national security: "I submit that the McGovern defense proposals cut into the very muscle of our defense . . . without any regard as to what kind of negotiations you can make with the Soviet Union." On Israel: "If you start cutting the Sixth Fleet, with the Soviet buildup of its fleet in the Mediterranean . . . [the Soviets] can overrun Israel." On welfare: "[the] welfare proposal that Sen. McGovern makes today is not only a horrible mess. It would be an unbelievable burden on the taxpayer . . . It's an estimated $72 billion cost to put 104 million Americans on welfare." This last charge provoked McGovern to a costly blunder. Disputing Humphrey's exaggerated numbers, he retorted: "There's no way . . . that you can make an exact estimate on [my] proposal."[3]

When Humphrey launched his initial salvo against McGovern in the May 28 debate, Gary Hart recalled, "It was the first time, and the only time, that Senator McGovern's jaw almost literally dropped, because he could not believe what was happening."[4] What startled McGovern was not only the ferocity of the attacks on him but also their substance. Briefing papers for the California debates prepared by his aides informed McGovern that Humphrey had in previous years called for defense cuts and welfare increases comparable to those McGovern was now proposing.[5] Top McGovern staffers were equally nonplussed. As Eli Segal, coordinating the McGovern campaign in the California primary, put it, "We were all stunned . . . I felt that the whole thing was going to slip away."[6]

McGovern entered the initial debate in a conciliatory frame of mind. He assumed that the two men's longstanding friendship would constrain Humphrey. He figured that Humphrey had already lost any realistic chance of winning the Democratic presidential nomination for 1972 and would remember how McGovern had rushed to support him after he won the 1968 nomination. Besides, McGovern thought he had more to gain from a benign colloquy with Humphrey: confident that his campaign was bound to win the California primary and take the Democratic nomination, "the one thing we needed to avoid was alienating the Humphrey supporters. We needed them after Miami." Hence, he wanted "to come across as a reasonable and somewhat restrained person, with respect for Hubert as a senior statesman."[7]

Perhaps McGovern should not have been quite so surprised and ill prepared for the attacks, for there had been several ominous signs of what Humphrey had in store for him in the weeks before the two men debated. Rowland Evans and Robert Novak, no friends to McGovern, had written in their nationally syndicated column of May 15, "A backstage decision by Senator Humphrey's campaign to finally take off the gloves against Sen. McGovern will become clear within the next week . . . 'We are going to show that McGovern is a radical, just like Goldwater was in 1964,' one highly placed Humphrey operative told us."[8] Desperately short of campaign funds for paid media, Humphrey followed the attack script in his frenetic California campaign schedule. Four days before the first debate, appearing in front of 6,000 Lockheed Aircraft workers, he assailed McGovern's alternative defense budget: "I'm not going to be seeking the office of the presidency at the expense of this nation's security and I'm not going to go out and buy votes at the expense of America becoming a second-rate power."[9]

McGovern had been advised to attack rather than conciliate Humphrey by someone who remembered, with vitriol, the Humphrey nomination steamroller of 1968. Adam Walinsky, a speechwriter for Robert Kennedy, held a view of Humphrey equal in savage contempt to anything found in the pages of Hunter Thompson. Walinsky wrote a ten-page memo of warning to McGovern:

> The most important thing to do—indeed, the one essential thing, more important even than presenting your own program—is to *cut Hubert's nuts off* . . . There is no way to compete with that windbag on the "merits" of program. He has a program for everything; he had one ten years ago; if he didn't he will say he did and no one, including himself, will know the difference. He is, as Jeremy Larner once said, the Dagwood Bumstead of politicians: anything good he hears from anything else, he will cram into his sandwich of speech, spread it with a layer of schmaltz, and gulp the whole

thing down. The only way to show what a fool and opportunist he is, is to pin him with his record—hard.[10]

Humphrey's attacks on McGovern in their first debate (the next two debates were anticlimactic) were not sufficient to save his failing campaign by stopping the insurgent frontrunner. Patrick Caddell's postdebate poll for the McGovern campaign suggested that California voters preferred McGovern's calm to Humphrey's shrillness. The real damage done to McGovern lay on a larger political stage. The nationally televised debate had been many Americans' first serious exposure to McGovern; they had now seen this fresh face in presidential politics painted with the color of radicalism, and they had heard him awkwardly struggling to rebut the former vice president's charges. Nixon campaign strategists had been handed a huge cache of ammunition for the fall campaign, all the more explosive because it carried the imprimatur of the standard-bearer for the Democratic Party establishment. Looking back on McGovern's landslide defeat in November, Eli Segal saw the fatal turn of events coming in California: "We were doomed from the debates on."[11]

The friendship of McGovern and Humphrey was never the same after their debate in California, but the two later achieved a reconciliation of sorts. Among their aides, however, the event continued to rankle—and to evoke contradictory ethical judgments. In the eyes of the Humphrey camp, it was McGovern who was responsible for the rupture between the two men. Well before the debate, Max Kampelman, Humphrey's closest political adviser, complained to Frank Mankiewicz that McGovernites in California were "distributing a scurrilous anti-Humphrey piece by Pete Hamill . . . suggest[ing] that Hubert Humphrey is a war criminal."[12] McGovern's insurgency, by denying Humphrey the chance for a rematch against Richard Nixon, struck Kampelman as an act of ingratitude: "I thought it was a lack of loyalty that McGovern ran. McGovern would have had no career had it not been for Hubert Humphrey."[13] For the McGovern camp, the moral onus was squarely on Humphrey. Hart spoke for many McGovernites in calling the Humphrey of the California debate "a man who is so ambitious he'd do anything in desperation." His attack on McGovern, Hart said, was the "betrayal of a friendship."[14]

The McGovern-Humphrey debate in California was a battle of erstwhile brethren. But this bitter conflict was much more than personal, for the two men led—and symbolized—the forces contending for control of the Democratic Party. Theirs was a fight over power and a contest of ideology. It was even a clash of cultures: to Humphrey supporters, the McGovernites were the long-haired kooks, while for the McGovernites Hubert Humphrey and his friends were as egregious an example as Richard Nixon of what was wrong with America. Like most instances of fratricide, the McGovern-Humphrey battle left both sides bloodied. The Old Guard, the Democratic regulars who looked to Humphrey as their last hope, could not destroy McGovern's insurgency. But they could grievously wound it.

Insurgents

Who were the McGovern insurgents that so rattled the Democratic regulars? In an immediate sense, they were the kind of Democrats that had come to dislike Hubert Humphrey, once a great liberal hero, because he had become a mouthpiece for the war in Vietnam, and who admired George McGovern for his early and passionate opposition to it. Yet although protest against the war was the leitmotif of the McGovern campaign, there were deeper historical and sociological roots to the McGovern insurgency.

McGovern's campaign for the presidency was an insurgency by necessity. As the longest of long shots, stuck at 2 or 3 percent in national polls as the 1972 election season began, his candidacy had no prospect in the early going of attracting the endorsements or dollars flowing to more plausible contenders; a grassroots uprising of outsiders was the only alternative open to McGovern. But the McGovern campaign was also an insurgency by choice. The McGovernites were the Democratic Party's reformers, the dissidents who, outraged by Humphrey taking the 1968 nomination without running in a single primary, had demanded a more open and participatory selection process. They were the party's critics, the left-liberals who were appalled by what the Democratic establishment had wrought in the 1960s. Their insurgency was, as Frank Mankiewicz put it, "a struggle to take over the Democratic Party . . . and take the Democratic nomination away from the war people."[15]

McGovernites relished their identity as insurgents. Some liked to imagine themselves, in keeping with romantic sixties imagery, as the guerrilla fighters of the American electoral system, living off the countryside while encircling a decrepit elite in the capital. Of course, they had their own campaign headquarters in Washington, D.C., but it was different from the campaign offices of the "Establishment" candidates. As Hart pictured it, the small McGovern office on First Street, "on the socially marginal fringe of Capitol Hill," was a symbol of "our continuing awareness that our campaign was unconventional and nontraditional; that to take headquarters in the commercial/professional heart of Washington, as most Presidential campaigns did, would somehow jeopardize its mood of classlessness, democracy, and insurgency, its spirit of parity and egalitarianism, its élan."[16] When the office was moved after McGovern won the nomination to a much larger space in the former Muskie headquarters on K Street, in "the commercial/professional heart of Washington," some McGovernites felt that the change of address brought a deflation of élan. Jeff Smith lamented that in the new headquarters, occupying an entire eight-story building, there was "no more action." Everybody was "in their own little cubby holes, in their own little worlds, and they didn't see each other all day long."[17]

The McGovern insurgency was multigenerational. It won support from some of the surviving left-liberals of the New Deal era, like Chester Bowles and Archibald MacLeish. More important as its senior generation was the Stevenson liberals of the 1950s. As was noted earlier, McGovern himself had been attracted to political activism by Adlai Stevenson's presidential campaign of 1952, and he was typical of many well-educated, middle-class Democrats in responding enthusiastically to Stevenson's eloquent call for a public-spirited liberalism.[18] Stevenson Democrats were party reformers; as E. J. Dionne has pointed out, the conflict within the party between regulars and reformers that grew so destructive in 1968–1972 actually began in the 1950s.[19] Yet from the standpoint of the late 1960s and early 1970s, Stevenson had been a fairly conventional politician on the issues of race and the Cold War. So it was a fifties liberal cadre driven further to the left by the civil rights struggle and the war in Vietnam that was drawn to the McGovern insurgency.

Although some important McGovern activists—and a considerably larger percentage of financial supporters—were middle-aged liberals from the suburbs, the characteristic that most dramatically marked the McGovernites was youthfulness. The top McGovern staff had some mature figures, such as Mankiewicz, Kimelman, and Rubin, but they were the exceptions. A remarkable number of the individuals who led the McGovern insurgency were under age thirty-five. In my interviews of major McGovernites, about two-thirds had been between twenty-five and thirty-two during the campaign. Hart, who became a handy symbol for the media of McGovernite youthfulness, was actually something of a senior statesman in his mid-thirties. The young McGovernites were classic representatives of the sixties activist generation—or at least of that segment of it that continued to believe that fundamental change was possible within the established channels of American politics. Most had previously been involved, on and off the campus, with the hallmark causes of the 1960s, civil rights and the war, and had campaigned for either Gene McCarthy or Bobby Kennedy in 1968.

Out in the field, in the insurgency's grassroots operation, key McGovernites were often even younger. New York was a case in point. The McGovern campaign's coordinator for the June primary in New York, directing a volunteer force of 25,000–30,000 canvassers, was Ed Rogoff, who was twenty at the time. Though he was a veteran of New York City Democratic wars, Rogoff had never held a full-time job prior to the McGovern campaign.[20] When Joe Grandmaison, already a legend among McGovernites for his extraordinary organizing in New Hampshire, arrived in New York in July to run the fall campaign in the state, he employed Jimmy Bailinson as the paymaster who reimbursed field organizers for their expenses. Bailinson was all of twelve, and his extreme youth caught the media's eye. His picture appeared in the *Washington Post*, and the *Los Angeles Times* ran a feature story about him. But when CBS called McGovern headquarters in New York to arrange a televised interview with Jimmy, it was too late: at his mother's insistence, he had left the campaign in order to attend summer camp.[21]

Youth was an obvious factor, but of comparable importance in understanding the McGovern insurgency are gender and education. Men continued to play the dominant roles and to hold a disproportionate share of the positions in the McGovern camp, but women were more involved and influential in this campaign than in any previous major-party presidential campaign. Active in the antiwar cause and in the emerging feminist movement, young women were mobilized as never before, and a number of them gravitated to the McGovern insurgency out of conviction and because it was so open to their participation. Thus, it was natural for McGovernites to think in terms of gender as well as age and to define their opponents in the Democratic Party as middle-aged males.

Higher education was the most common denominator for McGovernites and most clearly set them off from Democratic regulars based in the unions and the urban machines of the old New Deal coalition. The McGovernites were an impressively well-educated bunch. Of the aforementioned McGovernites interviewed, all had attended college (although a few dropped out to engage in political action) and most had done postgraduate work. About a third had attended the nation's top law schools, including Harvard, Yale, Columbia, Penn, NYU, and Michigan. What was true for top McGovernites was also evident in the entire McGovern insurgency. A study of representation at the two parties' national conventions in 1972 found that McGovern delegates had the highest percentage of B.A. degrees and far exceeded any other campaign in recipients of M.A. and Ph.D. degrees.[22]

Demography is not destiny—but it cannot be disregarded in explaining the decline of the Democratic regulars and the rise of the McGovernites. As political scientist Everett Carll Ladd observed, the New Politics and the Old Guard wings of the Democratic Party that contended for power in 1972 were drawn from "ascending and declining strata" in American society.[23] Labor unions, the core of the blue-collar Democratic Party since the New Deal, had slowly been losing members since their peak in the mid-1950s, falling from 33.2 percent of the nonagricultural workforce in 1955 to 27.4 percent in 1970. Urban machines, their usual partner in the party, were crumbling even more rapidly apart from a few bastions like Chicago: urban Democrats had contributed 21 percent of the Democrats' presidential vote in 1952, but by 1968 their percentage had dropped to 14 percent. During this same period, higher education in the United States was experiencing extraordinary growth. When World War II began, fewer than 1.5 million students attended American universities and colleges, but "between 1960 and 1974," Ladd noted, "the college population *increased* by 5 million."[24] By

1972 there were vastly more Americans with higher education than at the heyday of the New Deal coalition. And compared to the small college cohort of the earlier era, the college-educated of 1972 were more liberal and more likely to vote Democratic.[25]

The highly educated New Politics liberals who flocked to the McGovern campaign were more issue-oriented and ideological than the blue-collar Democrats of the Old Guard. Ending the war in Vietnam was their guiding passion, but they also cared deeply about civil rights, women's rights, the environment, and the participatory democratic reform of American politics in general. Significantly, and with ominous implications for the success of the Democratic Party, the one area where most cared less than did the Old Guard was the bread-and-butter issues of economic policy.[26] The fact that the activists of the McGovern campaign were motivated more by the social and global issues of the 1960s than by the distribution of material benefits did not, however, make them political naifs. As McGovern recalled, his forces were led by "pragmatic idealists—people who were idealistic but also had a good hard-headed practical sense as to how you get organized and win elections."[27]

A fitting emblem for the young McGovern insurgents (although he was less idealistic and even more pragmatic than most) was Rick Stearns. Stearns attracted less notice from the media in 1972 than did the charismatic Gary Hart, the wisecracking Frank Mankiewicz, the talented organizer Gene Pokorny, or the *Wunderkind* pollster Pat Caddell. Among McGovernites, however, no one else drew such universal accolades. To Ted Van Dyk, Stearns was "the best person we had in that primary campaign." As Amanda Smith put it, "Rick Stearns really invented an awful lot of the McGovern campaign." While the rest of the McGovern staff was embroiled in internecine conflicts at one time or another, Kirby Jones observed, "nobody screwed around with Rick Stearns—he was in charge of that delegate thing, period." Hart paid the highest compliment of all: asked how McGovern pulled off his long-shot capture of the Democratic nomination, he replied: "I think it was credit to one person, and one person alone. That's Rick Stearns. Rick was, I think, the smartest person at what he did in American politics."[28]

Born in Los Angeles in 1944, the son of an airline pilot, Stearns matriculated at Stanford, took off two years to attend the American University in Beirut, later spent a year as vice president of the National Student Association, and eventually completed his B.A. degree in Palo Alto. Selected as a Rhodes Scholar, he departed for Oxford, where he became a close friend and traveling companion of Bill Clinton. Stearns was, Clinton observed in his autobiography, "probably the most politically mature and savvy of our group [of Rhodes Scholars]."[29] Stearns had campaigned for McCarthy in 1968 and attended the tumultuous Chicago convention as a McCarthy aide. Later, he interned at the commission that was, under the leadership of McGovern, rewriting the rules of Democratic nomination politics. Intrigued by the new election process taking shape, he collected original materials and began extensive research that would ultimately inform the thesis he wrote for his Oxford degree. Few academic papers have been so consequential: Stearns's research placed him ahead of anyone else in understanding how to play the new game of presidential politics.[30]

Perceiving that the new selection process was so wide open that an antiwar insurgency could win with the proper strategy and execution, Stearns offered his expertise to the only campaign that was interested in what he had to say. Despite his youth he became a mainstay of the McGovern inner circle. McGovern staff were in awe of Stearns's encyclopedic knowledge of the selection process; one of them quipped, as Gordon Weil recalled, that if "George Wallace had had Rick Stearns, he might have been able to get the nomination."[31] Yet it was no accident that Stearns's expertise was devoted to the candidacy of McGovern, even apart from his own opposition to the war. Stearns had never paid his dues as a Democratic loyalist, and he lacked the party experience and connections required for high positions on the staffs of other candidates in 1972. But he did have the intellectual mastery and the analytical tools to vanquish party veterans at the new game that most only dimly understood. Abstract sociological theories about the rise of a new intelligentsia in a postindustrial United States found concrete validation in the strategic success of Rick Stearns in 1972.

The McGovern insurgency beat the regulars in the 1972 nomination game, but it never intended to destroy them. From the outset, McGovern and his strategists knew that to win against President Nixon they would need the support of the Old Guard. They tried, with their left-center strategy, to walk a political tightrope, mobilizing an insurgency to oust the old party power holders without alienating them. As Hart noted, "We would occasionally hear something about some upstart coordinator . . . somewhere saying we're going to trounce the old guys in the party, and we'd shut them up."[32] McGovern thought he could walk the wire without falling, telling an interviewer in the spring of 1972, "I think I've got the skill and common sense to quiet the fears of these people and bring them on board at some point."[33]

Hart and McGovern underestimated the depth and passion of the opposition from many Old Guard Democrats. The most implacable in their hostility to McGovern were the aged barons of organized labor: George Meany, president of the AFL-CIO, and his chief political lieutenant, Committee on Political Education (COPE) director Al Barkan.

Implacables

For all of the harsh accusations that he had hurled against George McGovern in the primaries, Hubert Humphrey endorsed his old friend after he won the Democratic nomination and campaigned for him in the fall. But Humphrey's most powerful backers, the aging leaders of the AFL-CIO, were unrelenting in their opposition to McGovern's presidential effort. The sixty-three-year-old Al Barkan was, in McGovern aide Scott Lilly's description, the "evil genius" behind the stop-McGovern movement, which forced the insurgents to fight for the nomination all the way to the convention floor in Miami Beach.[34] Barkan's boss, seventy-seven-year-old George Meany, called a special meeting of his executive council immediately after McGovern took the nomination, at which the AFL-CIO decided, for the first time since the American Federation of Labor merged with the Congress of Industrial Organizations in 1955, not to endorse the Democratic candidate for president. Proclaiming a policy of neutrality between McGovern and Nixon, on the grounds that the labor rank and file disliked both men, Meany enforced it vigorously until Election Day, cracking down on state and local labor federations that attempted to rebel against the union hierarchy and support McGovern.[35]

Meany's was a peculiar definition of "neutrality." Before the election season began, he had been a vociferous critic of President Nixon's wage-price controls as biased toward business and had resigned in protest from the president's Pay Board when it slashed wage gains that unions had negotiated with management. Once McGovern was nominated, however, Nixon's sins against working people were no longer of great concern to Meany, who happily went golfing with the president and members of his cabinet.[36] Meanwhile, the AFL-CIO president refused to meet with McGovern and would not even take his phone calls; instead, he went out of his way, in speeches before labor assemblages and on national TV, to denounce the Democratic nominee. As with the battle between Humphrey and McGovern, the conflict between Meany and McGovern was personal (although this time the intensity of feeling was mainly on Meany's side). Yet once again a deeper dynamic was evident, reflecting forces that transcended the personalities of the two men, and it worked to drive the McGovern insurgency apart from the blue-collar and ethnic constituencies that had been the cornerstone of the New Deal Democratic coalition.

Why did Meany nurse such implacable hostility toward McGovern? Since Meany had stated in 1971 that McGovern would be acceptable to him as a Democratic candidate, it may have been Barkan, Gordon Weil speculated, who fed the AFL-CIO president's increasing ill will toward McGovern.[37] Whatever the relative fierceness of their animosity toward McGovern, both Meany and Barkan disparaged him as a double-crosser for a 1966 incident: McGovern had promised to vote in favor of cutting off a conservative filibuster against a labor-backed measure to repeal Section 14B, the notorious right-to-work provision of the Taft-Hartley Act, and then had switched his vote, which would not have affected the outcome, out of concern for the fallout among his state's voters. Although the labor leaders' persisting anger about this incident appears genuine, it was too slim a basis to explain their all-out opposition to McGovern's candidacy. McGovern had apologized to Meany for the vote switch as a bad mistake in an otherwise impressive prolabor voting record—93.5 percent favorable according to COPE's own scorecard—for a senator from a farm state with few union members. Besides, Meany's AFL-CIO had endorsed John Kennedy in 1960 and Lyndon Johnson in 1964 even though their transgressions against labor interests while in the Senate were far more serious than McGovern's. It was less McGovern's character that concerned Meany and Barkan than what he represented: a threat that encompassed power, ideology, and cultural values.[38]

The McGovern insurgency was a major blow to the power of the AFL-CIO leadership. Rarely in American history had a major interest group suffered such a rapid drop in power as did organized labor between 1968 and 1972. In the earlier year, the AFL-CIO had appeared at the peak of its influence within the Democratic Party. When Lyndon Johnson announced that he would not be a candidate for reelection, leaving the Democratic field temporarily to the insurgencies of Eugene McCarthy and Robert F. Kennedy, it was Meany, along with his aide Lane Kirkland, who went to visit Vice President Humphrey and prevailed upon him to enter the race. Labor officials rounded up delegates in the big industrial states for Humphrey, who eschewed the primaries altogether, and they stood behind him at Chicago as he claimed the Democratic nomination. In the fall, as a weakened and divided Democratic party floundered in supporting Humphrey's candidacy, it was the AFL-CIO that stepped in with an unprecedented mobilization of manpower and money that nearly closed the gap with Nixon by Election Day.[39]

Over the next four years, however, organized labor's political stock crashed. By opening up the nomination process to new forces, the McGovern reforms closed down the backroom venues in which organized labor had been dominant. AFL-CIO leaders were at sea in the new process, and their inept strategy of putting forward noncommitted labor delegates in primaries and caucuses was easily trumped by McGovern insurgents. Organized labor came to the Democratic convention of 1972 with its numbers reduced and its influence minimized. It had little say on the party's platform and had no hooks in the party's nominee. In the eyes of Meany and Barkan, the man responsible for bringing organized labor so low was McGovern.[40]

If the political loss to labor weighed most heavily with Barkan, the ideological threat of McGovern mattered more to Meany. Although far closer to McGovern than to Nixon on most economic issues, Meany disliked McGovern's stands on welfare and busing. But it was foreign policy that drove Meany to despise McGovern. As an anti-Communist of the old school and a zealous advocate of the war in Vietnam, Meany was horrified by the collapse of the Cold War consensus. He was almost as unhappy with Richard Nixon for his trip to China as for his wage-price controls. Compared to Nixon, however, George McGovern was beyond the pale. Appearing on *Face the Nation* on the Sunday before Labor Day, 1972, Meany shot one of the most feared darts in American politics at a candidate struggling to recover from the Eagleton disaster: "When I look at a man who's a candidate for the presidency of the United States, I've got to look at him not only as a trade unionist, but as an American. And frankly, when I read the things that George McGovern stands for . . . and I find out that he's become an apologist for the communist world, I just . . . " (he did not complete the sentence).[41] AFL-CIO researchers, presumably at Meany's direction, compiled and circulated an anonymous photocopied document titled "Let's Look at the Record," which painted McGovern in even more alarming tones than did Republican campaign materials. The tenor of this document can be gleaned from such section headings as "Blind Trust in Moscow," "Russia Peaceful, So Let's Reduce Our Arms," "Capitulation to and Apologies for Hanoi," and "All Out for Castro."[42]

McGovernites offended Meany as much as did their leader. To a labor chieftain born in 1894, the baby boomers of the McGovern insurgency were insulting the most revered values of authority and propriety. Even before the Democratic convention, as an unnamed labor official told the *Washington Post*, "McGovern smells to [Meany and his associates] of kids and beards."[43] The convention itself sent the labor hierarchy into even greater paroxysms of cultural disgust. After it ended, Barkan traveled to labor gatherings to warn them against any affiliation with the "kooks and nuts" of the McGovern campaign who had seized the Democratic Party.[44] It fell to Meany, speaking before a convention of the United Steelworkers, to express most vividly the revulsion of a cultural conservative at the new social forces that had displaced organized labor on the floor of the convention:

> We listened for three days to the speakers who were approved to speak by the powers-that-be at the convention. We listened to the gay lib people— you know, the people who want to legalize marriages between boys and boys and legalize marriages between girls and girls . . . We heard from the abortionists, and we heard from the people who look like Jacks, acted like Jills, and had the odors of Johns about them.[45]

In his animus toward the McGovern campaign, Meany did not speak for all of labor, but he did voice the hostility of that segment of it from which he himself had come: the building-trades unions. Meany got his start in organized labor in his father's South Bronx plumbers' local, and it was the craft unions of the old AFL, historically the most conservative element in the union movement, that were his original political base. Here were to be found the unionists least likely to accept McGovern: the "hardhats" who beat up antiwar protestors in New York in the spring of 1970 were construction workers from the building-trades unions. These unions, wrote Taylor Dark, "were composed of workers who were likely to be culturally conservative and disdainful of the movements of the sixties that challenged existing attitudes toward sexuality, race, and patriotism."[46]

The war that Meany and Barkan were waging against him bewildered and frustrated McGovern. He had tried ingratiation, writing to Meany in April 1972 to hail him as "Mister American Labor" and to applaud him as "a fighter for the underprivileged all your long life."[47] He and his advisers presumed that the AFL-CIO leadership, once it failed to block their insurgency, would be pragmatic enough to play ball with it. When Meany's executive council refused to endorse McGovern, he defiantly retorted that he could circumvent the labor leadership and appeal successfully to their membership.[48] But he was badly stung and rightly worried. After Meany denounced him on *Face the Nation,* McGovern scribbled in rage on the back of a hotel envelope, "[Mr. Meany] is behaving like a political bully . . . When he calls me an apologist for communism, he knows that it is so much rubbish. He's beginning to sound more like his golfing partner Richard Nixon than a spokesman for the working people of America."[49]

McGovern's bewilderment and frustration were shared by many labor leaders who were not part of the Meany machine. Protests against the AFL-CIO policy of neutrality continued to mount for weeks after it was announced, and in the next month, many leaders of national and international unions, which were not bound by the AFL-CIO edict as were the state and local labor federations, formed the National Labor Committee for McGovern-Shriver. The dissenters represented mainly industrial, service sector, and public employee unions in the AFL-CIO, thirty-five in all, along with the independent—and progressive—United Auto Workers, which had thrown its support behind McGovern in the spring. Some members of the National Labor Committee were opposed to the war in Vietnam; a larger number felt that McGovern was so obviously superior to Nixon on issues important to trade unions that the refusal to endorse him was irrational.[50] At a meeting of COPE at which Barkan tried to impose the ban on support for McGovern, Eugene Glover of the machinists' union, which joined the dissenters, forcefully rejected his case for culture war. "Hell," said the union leader, "we used to complain that the young people were running around the streets, demonstrating to no effect, and rejecting the 'system,' whatever the hell that is. But now they have come into the political system. We get mad because they have outsmarted us . . . What are we afraid of? They are our sons and daughters."[51]

In fighting the New Politics forces of the McGovern insurgency, Meany and Barkan hurt themselves by stimulating movement toward a New Politics in organized labor.[52] Nonetheless, the wound they inflicted on the McGovern campaign was deep enough. The AFL-CIO's formidable resources of manpower and money, which had provided Humphrey a fighting chance to catch Nixon in 1968, were refused to McGovern in 1972. Equally important, the animosity toward McGovern from the most well-known figure in organized labor dealt a blow to his image among working people. As organizer Carl Wagner counted the cost, "the AFL-CIO and Meany taking no position on this race dramatically influenced the perception of McGovern."[53]

There are abundant materials in the historical record to characterize the top AFL-CIO leadership, in its attacks on an insurgency whose desire for change echoed the labor movement's own fabled youth, as an out-of-touch gerontocracy. A photograph of an AFL-CIO gathering in this period shows an all white (with one exception), all male, over sixty, overweight officialdom.[54] Joseph Golden, author of an unauthorized biography of Meany published in 1972, told a television interviewer, "You look at the AFL-CIO executive council and it looks like an old folks home. The average age is way above sixty . . . I could talk to labor people for hours on end without ever hearing one fresh idea."[55]

Yet if it is hard not to make Meany and Barkan the villains of this piece because they wounded the McGovern insurgency so vengefully, it is important not to miss the significance of Meany's own wounds. Six weeks after the Democratic convention of 1972, in a speech to the International Association of Bridge, Structural, and Ornamental Iron Workers, Meany laid bare his pain alongside his fury. Pulled down from their political eminence by the McGovern insurgency, representatives from organized labor had been relegated, Meany said, to their pre–New Deal status as "second class citizens at the convention." The well-educated—college professors, teachers, professionals, even students—now ruled over the working class: Meany, a high-school dropout at the age of fourteen, appeared particularly bothered that "thirty-nine percent of the delegates at that convention held postgraduate degrees." What pierced the AFL-CIO president the deepest was the disrespect that he perceived: "During the pre-convention period and during the convention itself, those people running the show repeatedly indicated their contempt, and I mean this, their contempt for the trade union movement and for the people we represent."[56]

Voicing distress at the displacement of and scorn toward labor's aging leadership by the ascendant intelligentsia that had coalesced behind the McGovern insurgency, Meany expressed sentiments that resonated with many working-class and ethnic voters. The gulf between the new Democratic Party that the McGovern campaign was introducing and the core constituencies of the old blue-collar coalition forged in the New Deal was substantial. Bridging this gap—maintaining working-class and ethnic loyalty to the Democrats—was one of the most daunting challenges facing the McGovernites. Election Day statistics show that in this critical task they largely failed.

McGovern's Blue-Collar Problem

George McGovern's blue-collar problem was part of a general problem for Democrats that was obvious to political observers of all stripes in 1972. While John Kennedy had attracted 66 percent of union voters in 1960 and Lyndon Johnson had polled a remarkable 80 percent in 1964, Hubert Humphrey, though a longtime ally of organized labor, had fallen to 51 percent in 1968 against the conservative populist assaults of Richard Nixon and George Wallace.[57] But as an antiwar candidate, backed by long-haired youth, militant feminists, and black activists, McGovern had a particular problem with working-class and ethnic voters. He needed to draw votes in blue-collar precincts in order to win the critical Democratic primaries. He needed to demonstrate his ability to appeal to blue-collar communities to prove himself a credible prospective opponent against President Nixon.

Along with campus visits to excite his base and recruit student volunteers, McGovern's campaign schedule in the early going targeted working-class locales. "We went out of our way," explained Steve Robbins, McGovern's scheduler, "to go to blue-collar communities." McGovern's appearances there were designed with an eye to visuals for television or newspaper photos: plant tours in which McGovern could be shown conversing with factory workers played up his concern for the issues facing working people. For the Massachusetts primary McGovern was sent to the home of a low-income Irish-American family in South Boston, "with linoleum on the floor and no carpets," to talk about its problems. "We understood," said Robbins, "the importance of identifying with the historic FDR party component."[58]

At first the McGovern campaign seemed to succeed with this approach. Its vote totals in blue-collar neighborhoods in the New Hampshire, Wisconsin, and Massachusetts primaries surprised journalists and pundits and stoked their belief that the McGovern insurgency was a rising force in American politics. In the watershed Wisconsin primary, David Broder of the *Washington Post* was particularly struck by the election returns from the industrial cities of Racine and Kenosha: the blue-collar voters who were supposed to provide the base for establishment candidates Muskie and Humphrey instead preferred the rival voices of populist alienation, McGovern and Wallace.[59]

Once the attacks on McGovern for his alleged radicalism started, however, and reached a crescendo with Humphrey's campaign in California, the McGovern blue-collar strategy faltered. Carl Wagner had enjoyed considerable success in organizing blue-collar voters behind McGovern in Milwaukee, but he found the task more difficult in working-class southeast Los Angeles: people were watching the TV news, and Humphrey's charges against McGovern registered "dramatically."[60] After the California primary, matters only got worse: televised images of the tumultuous Democratic convention, the bitter rejection by George Meany, and the departure from the ticket of Senator Eagleton, an urban Catholic with strong trade union ties, further tarnished McGovern in the eyes of blue-collar voters. The McGovern campaign could not hope to go back to the symbolism that had first established a tenuous connection with working-class and ethnic communities. Factory floor tours, for example, were no longer feasible,

Robbins lamented, because the horde of reporters now following McGovern would "trash the event."[61]

During the fall campaign, McGovern's hopes to repair his connection with the working class occasionally flickered. Asked for a recollection of an encouraging moment on the campaign trail, he singled out an event in Pennsylvania where, accompanied by Ted Kennedy, he appeared before a labor audience. In response to a questioner, McGovern began to speak passionately about his doctoral dissertation on the Ludlow, Colorado, coal strike of 1913–1914, and how his research on the brutal treatment of the miners "had given me a lifelong sympathy for the problems of labor." From that moment on, the audience grew increasingly warm toward McGovern; when he finished, there was "a sustained standing ovation and people clapping each other on the back—here's a guy that finally understands what blue-collar workers are up against."[62]

In a few states and cities, McGovern had help in repairing the connection. He received a higher percentage of the working-class vote where individuals or organizations respected by blue-collar constituencies vouched for him. In Massachusetts, the only state McGovern won, ties to ethnic organizations forged in the primary campaign and the backing of the Kennedy clan bucked the national trend among blue-collar voters. Michigan was a somewhat similar story, since the powerhouse union in that state, the United Auto Workers, enthusiastically endorsed and labored for McGovern. Even insurgent campaigns need friends in high places.[63]

For the most part, though, the connection between McGovernites and blue-collar voters was increasingly frail. Most young McGovern staffers and field organizers, products of the nation's top universities and colleges, had no prior experience with working-class life and did not know how to talk to workers. McGovern and his running mate, Sargent Shriver, could not compensate for this inexperience because their own feel for a blue-collar constituency was deficient. Scott Lilly, one of a handful of McGovernites with a background in labor politics, accompanied Shriver to a working-class bar in Baltimore. The vice-presidential candidate blew the intended symbolism of the event by ordering a Courvoisier ("le Cognac de Napoleon"). Bar patrons clustered around the patrician Shriver asked in puzzlement, "What did he say?"[64]

On the defensive against the image of radicalism that stuck to McGovern, and verging on desperation, the McGovern staff strained for analogies between their candidate and working-class heroes of the past. Eli Segal promoted a campaign flier pitched in form and content at blue-collar voters:

I remember when I was a kid
The things the Republicans used to say about FDR
The bosses were afraid of Roosevelt

and the banks were afraid
And they called him some kind of name . . .
You know who reminds me of FDR?
This guy McGovern
He talks straight and he cares about the average working family
He'll do something about our health care
and job safety and jobs
And he scares hell out of the Republicans
Just like FDR
I guess that's why they lie about him
The same way they lied about Roosevelt
Because McGovern, he's on our side.[65]

There were in fact affinities between McGovern's economic proposals and Roosevelt's in the benefits they directed to working-class voters, but McGovern did not sing his economic tune with the same feeling as when the war in Vietnam was the subject. Neither the substance of his message on the war nor the moral judgment it pronounced on American conduct in Vietnam played well to a blue-collar audience. Richard Krickus, the most stinging critic of the McGovernites' failure to understand workers and ethnics, wrote: "McGovern's statements that the war was an 'immoral one' and a 'frightful waste of men and money' were not bound to win him votes in those working-class communities where the young men went to Vietnam and not college or Canada."[66] So in the end, McGovern did not remind many blue-collar voters of FDR. Working-class defections from the Democratic presidential ticket of 1972 were unprecedented since the beginning of the Great Depression, and they constituted the single most devastating electoral blow to McGovern's candidacy.

Overlapping McGovern's problem with working-class voters was his difficulty winning support from white, mostly Catholic, ethnics. The McGovernites recognized their weakness with the working class from the start, but in the case of ethnics they remained obtuse for the entire campaign. While Nixon and the Republicans were relentlessly courting and pandering to white ethnics, the McGovern campaign was flat-footed in its approach to this vital, traditionally Democratic bloc of voters.

The insurgents' problem was glaring: a widespread sentiment among white ethnics that McGovern, first as party reformer and then as presidential candidate, cared about incorporating blacks, women, and college students into his coalition but not Irish, Italian, Polish, or other self-identified ethnics. One of the most widely cited campaign commentaries in 1972 was a piece by Chicago newspaper columnist Mike Royko in which he addressed Alderman William Singer, cochair with Jesse Jackson of the pro-McGovern, reform Illinois delegation to the Democratic convention:

I just don't see where your delegation is representative of Chicago's Democrats . . . As I looked over the names of your delegates, I saw something peculiar . . . There's only one Italian there. Are you saying that only one out of every 59 Democratic votes cast in a Chicago election is cast by an Italian? And only three of your 59 have Polish names . . . Your reforms have disenfranchised Chicago's white ethnic Democrats, which is a strange reform.[67]

Two McGovern staffers, Gerald Cassidy and Kenneth Schlossberg, took it upon themselves to press for a campaign operation geared to white ethnics. Cassidy's background set him apart from most other McGovernites: his roots were in the world of Catholic ethnics, he had attended a Catholic university (Villanova), and his loyalty to McGovern came from having served as his general counsel on the Senate Select Committee on Nutrition. In requesting resources for a headquarters staff and field operation expressly directed at ethnic constituencies, Cassidy and Schlossberg presented a penetrating analysis: "The heavy emphasis in the press during and since the convention on voter registration of youth as the secret key to your victory in the fall contains what we see as a very dangerous side-effect—the appearance of deliberately dividing the electorate into 'us' and 'them.' The 'us' being the accepted McGovern constituency—the young, the black, the poor, the women's libbers, etc.—and the 'them' being the rest of white middle-class working America, including Catholic-Ethnic America."[68]

By the time the request was written, Cassidy recalls, it was already too late to reach the ethnics. And even though the Cassidy-Schlossberg ethnic operation was established, it never obtained the resources it had initially been promised. Cassidy ascribes the neglect of the ethnic-Catholic world to the thinking of the McGovern campaign's high command. To Hart and Mankiewicz, he alleges, any focus on white ethnics was "inappropriate." Ethnic politics represented the old politics and not the new. In the eyes of issue-oriented reformers, it was "grungy."[69]

As an experienced politician, McGovern himself had no ideological aversion to ethnic politics. But a political career in South Dakota had hardly prepared him for it, and it was clearly not one of his strengths. Shirley MacLaine observed that McGovern was awkward in the company of ethnic voters: "He insisted, even after a waitress warned him not to, on having milk with chopped chicken liver in a Jewish delicatessen. He never knew how to act with Mexicans or Puerto Ricans or Italians or wild Irish intellectuals. He seemed uncomfortable with people who were overt or aggressive."[70] Cassidy argues that if McGovern's top staff had propelled him in that direction, he could have made the connection: having grown up in a small town, with "wonderful values, among hard-working people," and with a record as a war hero, he "could have spoken from those values and crossed ethnic lines and reached those people."[71]

McGovern and the McGovernites can be seriously faulted for their failure to solve their blue-collar problem, and their experience presents powerful lessons, especially for their liberal descendents in the contemporary Democratic Party. Scott Lilly sums up the failure:

> It was very important to reach out and attract young, idealistic, educated people . . . but it should never have been done at the expense of ordinary working-class people who had been the purpose of the party since its formation. There were a lot of people in the McGovern camp that were not sufficiently sensitive to the ethics and the values and the perceptions of the world that ordinary working people had.[72]

Insufficiently attentive to blue-collar communities, especially to ethnics, sometimes tone-deaf in style, and too worried about losing its supporters on the left to rein them in when they behaved in ways offensive to working-class voters, the McGovern campaign revealed a fundamental flaw in the New Politics that it heralded as the liberal future. Yet one also comes away from this story with a sense of how exceptionally difficult it would have been to make matters turn out much differently. The heart of the McGovern insurgency was a passionate drive to end the war in Vietnam and free America from its Cold War obsessions, but in blue-collar communities, patriotic sentiments were predominant. The energies that drove the McGovern insurgency came from the social movements and well-educated youth who were the most celebrated products of the 1960s, but that decade had a contrary meaning to the culturally conservative and racially fearful white working class. Bound together, but only loosely, by traditional Democratic economics, the new McGovernites and the old Democrats were profoundly at odds on the character and direction of American society. It was often said at the time that only a candidate with charisma—meaning only a Kennedy—could have held together such discordant political forces. By 1972, even that scenario had become more fantasy than possibility.

McGovern's Jewish Problem

A few weeks before Election Day 1972, Frank Mankiewicz wrote to a supporter, "This talk about the Jews moving to Nixon is just that—talk, and utter rubbish."[73] But the extensive correspondence in Mankiewicz's papers about McGovern's Jewish problem suggests that neither he nor anyone else in the campaign regarded the matter as "rubbish." Whereas the "Catholic-ethnic" problem that Cassidy and Schlossberg were highlighting received limited attention from McGovern's top staff, the Jewish problem was the focus of much anxious strategizing. The Mc-

Govern campaign even added a special adviser in this area, Richard Cohen of the American Jewish Congress. Comparatively few in numbers in the national electorate, Jewish voters were critical in several of the largest states, especially New York, California, and Illinois, and Jewish contributors were vital for the financing of a competitive campaign. Losing this traditionally Democratic group was unthinkable if McGovern was to have a prayer of winning.

The Jewish problem came at McGovern from both sides. Humphrey initiated the Old Guard Democrats' assault on McGovern as allegedly unreliable on the safeguarding of Israel during the California primary, and it was this Humphrey charge that seemed to do the most damage to McGovern, hurting the insurgent among Jewish voters, particularly those of moderate income or seniors, in Los Angeles. Nixon, vigorously courting the Jewish vote, presented himself as Israel's best friend, and he had assistance in this portrayal from the Israeli government, especially Itzhak Rabin, then Israel's ambassador to the United States. McGovern was charged by both the Humphrey and Nixon camps with weakness on the defense of Israel, most notably for voting against the sale of Phantom jets to Israel when it came before the Senate as part of a military appropriations bill that also included money for the war in Vietnam. He was charged with undue concern for Israel's foes, as when he suggested compensation for Palestinian refugees who had been displaced during the formation of the Jewish state. In short, McGovern was in trouble with Jews because he was viewed as departing from the traditional, orthodox posture of Democratic presidential candidates on support for Israel.[74]

Rick Stearns became a pariah for some Jews when McGovern's foes circulated reports that five years prior to the campaign, Stearns, in his role as vice president of the National Student Association, had signed a newspaper ad expressing support for the rights of Arabs. Jews suspicious of McGovern called on him to fire Stearns, and the young McGovernite began to receive death threats. McGovern was not about to dump Stearns, to whom he owed so much, and his spokesmen tried to fend off the attacks by pointing out, accurately, that Stearns had nothing to do with the policy side of the campaign.[75]

Faced with the potential for a high level of defection from Jewish Democrats, McGovern went to great lengths to repair his reputation among them. As Gordon Weil observed, "He courted the Jews, speaking to rabbinical councils and, as Mankiewicz quipped, where there were no rabbinical councils, we created them so that he could speak to them."[76] Throughout 1972 McGovern was rigorously orthodox: as he recalls, "The position I took [on Israel] during the campaign was right down the line with what . . . the Jewish organizations wanted." Yet he was aware that despite a long record of support for Israel, he could not obliterate the traces of his past questioning of orthodoxy. One of a group of liberal Democrats who had begun to think that "we had to keep the door open to the Palestinians and to the Arabs as well" and adopt "a more even-handed position" in the Middle East, McGovern suspects that "some of that showed through" in the public statements he had made about Israel before 1972.[77]

Questionable orthodoxy on Israel was not McGovern's only problem in the Jewish community. Some affluent Jews voiced alarm at his redistributive tax proposals. Among Jews of more modest means, unhappiness with McGovern centered on his alleged advocacy of "quotas," an ugly word to a people whose admission to elite institutions had historically been curtailed by numerical limits. Critics of McGovern invoked the party reforms that popularly bore his name, assuring representation to minorities, women, and youth at the Democratic convention, and recalled reports of his pledges to blacks and Hispanics that he would provide them with federal jobs in numbers equal to their proportions of the population.[78] McGovern's defenders shot back that it was President Nixon who was actually pushing affirmative action for minorities and that "Senator Mc-Govern rejects the quota system as detrimental to American society."[79] The irony in the heated accusations that McGovern's candidacy was biased against Jews was that Jews were just as well represented on his campaign staff as on those of other Democratic candidates and that more Jews had been delegates at the convention that selected McGovern than at previous Democratic conventions.

For all of the efforts that it expended, the McGovern campaign met limited success in winning back disaffected Jewish Democrats. Defections by these traditional Democratic voters were only a small contributor to the landslide that buried McGovern in November 1972. Their scale was nonetheless significant: exit polls showed that Nixon had doubled his percentage from 1968 and taken slightly more than a third of the Jewish vote.[80] Unlike the situation with blue-collar voters, subsequent Democratic presidential candidates faced nothing as severe as the Jewish problem that plagued McGovern in 1972. Perhaps this was in part because the lesson of the McGovern campaign was so plain: deviation from orthodoxy here, especially on Middle East policy, is dangerous ground for any Democrat running for president.

Retreat from the South

Although the McGovern campaign leadership nurtured hopes until the end of recapturing disaffected Democrats from blue-collar and Jewish communities, it had few illusions about the no-longer-solid South. It recognized that the Democratic Party had been losing strength in the South since the presidential election of 1948, principally on the issue of race but also because of the region's growing economic and cultural conservatism. McGovern made a token campaign swing through Arkansas, Georgia, and South Carolina shortly before the Democratic convention to demonstrate that he was a national candidate, but his campaign's leadership knew that any electoral-college map upon which he might win a majority would not likely include the South. As Jeff Smith relates, "We used to joke that McGovern's southern strategy was when he went out to National Airport in Alexandria [Virginia]."[81]

Actually, the McGovern campaign did have a southern strategy—but only for the nomination contest. Ted Pulliam, a native of North Carolina with an accent rare in McGovernite ranks, was placed in charge of the campaign's regional desk for the South. Pulliam trolled for southern support in states that picked their delegates to the Democratic national convention in local caucuses and conventions, mobilizing McGovern supporters to turn out in force for these otherwise sparsely attended events. He paid special attention to pockets of liberal politics in the South, especially in cities like Atlanta and college towns like Chapel Hill.[82] Often forming coalitions with blacks to contest Democratic regulars, liberal McGovernites scored some startling victories in the battle for southern delegates. In Louisiana, Mississippi, and Virginia, a majority of the state contingent that went to the convention was composed of McGovern delegates.[83]

A few young McGovernites hoped for even more. Twenty-two-year-old pollster Pat Caddell, who had grown up in Jacksonville, Florida, wrote late in June, "After nearly four years of political and cultural research on the South, I am convinced that there is a strong potential for McGovern in the South." Citing as precedents the recent victories of "New South" reformers, Caddell saw "a chance to combine alienated Wallace whites, liberals, and blacks to produce new winning coalitions in some states."[84] Civil-rights leader Julian Bond, a Georgia state legislator, sent along the advice of an associate that McGovern could win over some of the Wallacites through an unexpected appearance at Nashville's Grand Ole Opry: "The media thrust of this whole trip is gutsy George goes into the heart of enemy territory and wins over masses to his cause."[85] But a veteran McGovern strategist deflated these balloons with a trademark wisecrack: "I do not believe," Frank Mankiewicz wrote to Eli Segal, "[that] George McGovern could carry Florida even if he were an alligator and alligators could vote."[86]

Elected Democratic officials in the region, Old Guard and New South alike, were antagonistic to McGovern's candidacy. "Democratic leaders across the South," William Greider wrote in the *Washington Post* as McGovern stood poised to win the California primary, "are sounding alarm bells over the prospect of 'devastating' losses in their region if Sen. George McGovern rolls on to win the party's presidential nomination."[87] When McGovern had to fly out of California on the eve of its primary to confront a firestorm among Democratic governors assembled in Houston for a meeting of the National Governors' Conference, southern executives were the most vocal in their complaints. Taking the lead in outspoken opposition to McGovern was an archetypal New South leader, Jimmy Carter. Subsequently, Carter cordially invited McGovern to stay at the executive mansion in Atlanta during his southern swing but then held him at arm's length for the remainder of the campaign.[88] Four years later, some McGovernites still resented this snub.

With the South such inhospitable terrain in the fall, the McGovern command only put up much of a fight in Texas, which Humphrey had narrowly carried four years earlier, sending in its two best southern-bred organizers, Taylor Branch and Bill Clinton. The Texas campaign was a futile venture, and McGovern was shellacked by a 2–1 margin in the state. It was scant comfort there that the results were even worse elsewhere in the territory of the old Confederacy: McGovern lost to Nixon by more than 2–1 in most southern states and by as badly as 4–1 in Mississippi. Perhaps the most staggering statistic is that this son of a Protestant minister received only 14 percent of the votes of southern white Protestants.[89] In the short run, the main effect of McGovern's repudiation by the South was to boost the attractiveness among Democrats of a southern favorite son for the next election. In the long run, the obvious yet powerful implication was that the South would be in the forefront in the hostility toward liberalism that would shape Democratic defensiveness for decades.

"They Didn't Do Squat"

McGovern's hopes to reconcile the regulars to his insurgency and reunite the Democratic Party for the general election were undercut almost immediately after he won the nomination when he had to jettison Senator Eagleton, a running mate chosen with an eye to pleasing traditional Democrats. His subsequent forays at peacemaking avoided another disaster. Yet they remained deeply problematic, as was evident in the reaction to his visits with Lyndon Johnson and Richard Daley.

McGovern's peacemaking with Johnson and Daley predictably upset his insurgent forces. They were dismayed to see the great dissenter against the war in Vietnam consorting with the president who had escalated the war and the mayor who had dispatched his police to club antiwar protestors. Yet these gestures for unity in the Democratic Party against Richard Nixon were not nearly potent enough to win the regulars' hearts for McGovern. As McGovern wrote in his autobiography, "After the convention, the conventional wisdom was that my first task would be to reunite the party and reassure the electorate about myself. Yet each step toward those goals seemed to be frustrated or counterproductive."[90]

Embracing the regulars of the Democratic Party brought further awkward moments for McGovern. While he was condemning the corruption of the Republicans under Nixon, McGovern's campaign brought him into contact with Democrats whose own ethical and legal standing was none too high. Ted Pulliam, pulled off of the southern desk for the fall campaign and reassigned to several northeastern states where there was still a hope of winning, prepared a briefing paper for McGovern's swing through northern New Jersey in late September. Previewing a meeting McGovern was scheduled to attend in populous Hudson County, Pulliam noted that many of the Democratic mayors who would be present were under a cloud of scandal. "Also present," he added, "will be various state representatives . . . most of whom are in some way tainted through past dealings. The group will be one short due to a shooting this past weekend in which he was the victim."[91]

McGovernites in the field had similar frustrations in the effort to reunite Democrats against Nixon. In some states McGovernites and regulars were successfully integrated in campaign operations during the fall. In others, however, mutual suspicion between the two sides persisted. Many regulars, shocked by their primary defeats at the hands of the upstart McGovernites and further inflamed by the bitter-end struggle up to the convention to deny McGovern the nomination, were never reconciled to his candidacy.[92] Besides, they could read the postconvention polls and calculate that they would not have to subordinate themselves to McGovernites for long. For their part, McGovern campaign staffers were skeptical of more than just the motivation of the regulars. "A lot of those guys," Lilly points out, "the reason we rolled over them as easily as we did [in the spring] is that they weren't very good, they didn't work very hard . . . Their idea of organizing was spending the night at the bar at the Ramada Inn, talking with their buddies and picking up a $150 bar tab."[93]

The McGovern campaign's superb field operation, with its talented young organizers and horde of enthusiastic volunteers, carried it through the fall. But the contribution of regulars to the Democratic presidential campaign was small. In the memory of the McGovernites, the regulars' role in the fall is recalled mainly through images of their shirking. Miles Rubin quips, "You could have shot a cannon" through McGovern headquarters "and not hit a Democratic Party regular."[94] Harold Himmelman, coordinator for the fifteen eastern states during the fall, chaired a meeting shortly after the Democratic convention at which top Muskie, Humphrey, and Jackson operatives were asked to work for McGovern. "Boy, they hated us," Himmelman says. They had come to the meeting to "cover their ass" and maintain the appearance of cooperation. In the fall, "they didn't do squat."[95]

Conclusion

In the preface to his chronicle of the McGovern campaign, *Right from the Start*, Gary Hart noted with amusement the suggestion by Washington superlawyer Edward Bennett Williams that he title the book *Heist* instead.[96] For sixties veterans of clashes with the "Establishment," an outlaw image was appealing. To Hart himself, it may have suggested a political twist on the role of bank-robber

Clyde Barrow, as portrayed by Hart's buddy on the campaign trail, Warren Beatty.

In later years, though, it was more in fashion among conservative critics of the McGovern campaign to employ such images. The McGovernites, conservative Democrats and ex-Democrats alleged, had stolen the party from its rightful owners. Wrecking a majority coalition that had governed most of the time from 1932 to the late 1960s, the McGovernites had put into power an elite minority who dragged the party down to one defeat after another. In his gloomy history of the Democrats' "demise," ex-leftist turned neoconservative Ronald Radosh's account of 1972 is titled "McGovernism and the Captured Party." Radosh mourns the failure of the Democrats in 1972 to turn to the one figure that might have saved them from disaster: the white knight of neoconservative Democrats, Scoop Jackson.[97] The McGovern campaign is, for the neoconservative version of Democratic Party history, the prime piece of evidence for the argument that "we didn't leave the Democratic Party; the Democratic Party left us."

Yet if we imagine the McGovernites as a gang that robbed the bank of the Democratic Party, it was a bank that had previously laid off its security guards and shut off its security cameras. The neoconservative attack on the McGovernites rests on a static and ahistorical account of party politics that neglects to notice the atrophy of the New Deal coalition. Historian Herbert Parmet observes that by the end of the 1960s the structure of the Democratic Party was "abysmally weak."[98] The urban machines had almost all crumbled by that point, and the labor unions were well along in the process of decline that has been one of the most transformative facts in modern American politics. Postwar prosperity had undercut the appeal of a class-based politics, even among blue-collar voters.[99] Meanwhile, the rise of college-educated professionals in a postindustrial economy was reshaping the contours of the political landscape. As progressive reformers, the McGovernites would not have stood a chance of winning the Democratic presidential nomination if the regulars had not grown so decrepit. And their success in 1972 in bringing a new agenda to prominence in their party was hardly a novel phenomenon: New Deal liberalism itself had been shaped not by Democratic Party politicians but by the network of progressive New Dealers, some of them former Republicans, who had left their law schools and other elite institutions to work for FDR in Washington.[100]

The Democratic Party would have missed out on a much-needed revitalization if it had not become a home for the committed and talented young activists who rallied behind McGovern in 1972. Nevertheless, these representatives of a rising social class fell well short of a majority, and their aspirations were often at odds with the beliefs and values of traditional blue-collar Democratic partisans. Overcoming the division within the Democratic Party, a serious crack in the 1968 election and a chasm in 1972, has become the obsessive focus of Democrats ever since. Historian Steven Gillon calls it "the Democrats' dilemma"—to "retain the allegiance of blacks while winning back southern whites and working class ethnics"; to "arouse the enthusiasm of liberal activists at the same time that it courts more conservative voters."[101] Excepting Jimmy Carter in the wake of Watergate, no Democratic candidate for president successfully resolved this dilemma until Bill Clinton, twenty years after he worked in McGovern's Texas campaign.

Clinton was fortunate, however, to face weak opponents in his two presidential races. And the uncertain ideological substance of his eight years in the White House left many activist Democrats disappointed, much as they were disappointed with the blurry campaigns of Mondale and Dukakis before him and Gore and Kerry after him. In reaching out to conciliate the more conservative Democrats whose past defections have hurt the party, its nominees and incumbents have presented a muffled message. They have not figured out how to win without compromising or concealing fundamental convictions. Many rank-and-file Democrats, especially the liberals, erupt in frustration election after election that their party, unlike the Republicans, does not stand for firm principles. Originating in the trauma of 1972, the Democrats' identity crisis reflects a party afraid it will pay the kind of price that George McGovern paid if, like him, it says what it believes.[102]

9

Mass Movements and McGovernites

On the opening day of the 1972 Democratic convention in Miami Beach, the women's caucus gave George McGovern a standing ovation. Its meeting was packed, with 700 female delegates in attendance, exuberant over their numbers at the convention—triple the representation from four years earlier—and their new clout in presidential politics. Of all of the presidential candidates appearing, only Shirley Chisholm, the first African American woman to run for president, was greeted with enthusiasm comparable to the warm reception for McGovern. Most of the women at the meeting were fervently antiwar and respected McGovern for his early and courageous stance on Vietnam. But the size of the gathering attested to another of McGovern's achievements: his chairing of the reform commission that had rewritten the Democratic Party's rules on delegate selection, leading to the huge leap in the representation of women. As Liz Carpenter, a former White House aide to LBJ, put it when introducing McGovern, "We know we wouldn't be here if it hadn't been for you."

Expressions of affection for McGovern did not last long this day. Indeed, they did not survive his first words to the caucus. Trying to fend off the praise with self-deprecating humor, McGovern quipped that the credit for women's presence at the convention "would have to go to Adam." Hisses and boos filled the room, and one woman sporting a McGovern button called him "George the pig." In an instant, McGovern had gone from a champion of feminism to a typical clueless male. His feeble attempt to apologize for his blunder—"Can I recover if I say Adam and Eve?"—did not improve the audience's mood.

As McGovern delivered his prepared remarks to the caucus, he was interrupted by shouts from the floor. "We know about the war," one woman complained. "What about abortion?" Some of the gibes at McGovern on the issue of abortion may have come from delegates backing other candidates, but the sentiments they voiced were shared by almost all of the women in the room. McGovern had embraced a long list of feminist goals, but he balked at endorsing the one item on the women's agenda that generated the most passion. Limping to the end of his remarks, McGovern only drew cheers when he pledged to support the caucus's challenge to the credentials of the South Carolina delegation because of its gender imbalance. It was a pledge that his campaign was about to break.[1]

The McGovern insurgency is indelibly associated with the mass movements of the 1960s: civil rights, antiwar, students, women, gays. More than any other presidential campaign, it was the bearer of the hopes of these movements that the nation would move in a new direction, toward equality at home and peace in the world. Such symbiosis between mass movements for social change and a grassroots campaign for the presidency remains an appealing prospect for many progressives, who dream of new coalitions—feminists, minorities, environmentalists, peace activists, and others—that will put both muscle and motivation behind a liberal presidential campaign in the future.

Yet if there is genuine inspiration to be found in the story of mass movements and McGovernites, there is also a more complicated and troublesome dimension of the relationship that needs attention. Mass movements and insurgent presidential campaigns can cooperate and advance mutual interests. But their collaboration is bound to be thorny, because each has a different agenda. Mass movements may embrace a presidential candidate who favors their goals, but they will not subordinate their cause to the needs of that candidate. Insurgent campaigns may believe in the same ideals as the mass movements that support them, but they will not pursue these ideals if the electoral costs are likely to be high. Movement activists and partisan insurgents also have distinct political identities. Activists define themselves by their causes, insurgents by their candidates, and the loyalties of each to comrades and leaders are potentially in conflict.

In this instance, the McGovern campaign was an authentic vehicle for the aspirations of sixties movements. But it never advanced them with the complete commitment of the movements' own activists. McGovern's reception at the women's caucus was emblematic of the relationship that developed between his insurgency and movement politics: some genuine warmth and solidarity, but also frequent tensions, moments of mutual disappointment, and even occasions for bitterness and recriminations. The experience of the McGovern campaign suggests that insurgent campaigns, both on the left and on the right, connect more deeply with movement politics than conventional campaigns, but the relationships between the two forces for change are, for that reason, more tangled and harder to negotiate.

Mass movement activists that supported McGovern for president perceived him as more sympathetic to their grievances and aspirations than other white male candidates. But they also regarded him with wariness, suspecting that he and his top strategists were all too ready to sacrifice movement goals to electoral expedience. And while McGovern was well versed in the movement language of "empowerment," in the eyes of movement activists it seemed evident that he continued to run the show and keep members of previously excluded groups in their old role as subordinates. To Bella Abzug, the behavior of McGovern and his strategists at the Democratic convention was "another episode in the continuing political saga of men in power ignoring or underestimating women and abandoning their commitments to them."[2]

The McGovern strategists interpreted the same episodes in a radically different light. They found it hard to comprehend why movement activists could not refrain from the militant demands and outbursts that only diminished McGovern's public standing and ultimately redounded to the benefit of President Nixon. Frank Mankiewicz viewed the relationship as "a serious problem: how to deal with these emerging wild men and women while recognizing our affinity with them—but not seeming too close, because they were crazy, many of them."[3] Gary Hart was equally perplexed: "It was just bizarre. We were fighting Richard Nixon, and the movement groups kept wanting to push McGovern farther and farther toward their particular interests rather than win the election. And the more we responded to their demands, the more extreme . . . or more out of control the campaign looked."[4]

The mass movements that produced the most perplexity for the McGovern campaign were not the landmark causes of the 1960s: the civil rights and antiwar movements. The civil rights movement had created a crisis for the Democrats in 1964 over the issue of seating the Mississippi Freedom Democratic Party at the convention, but by 1972, four years after the assassination of Martin Luther King Jr., civil rights forces were divided and drifting. The antiwar movement was at the center of the Democrats' explosion at Chicago in 1968, both in the convention hall and in the streets outside, but by 1972, with the draft ending and the radical protest wing of the movement a spent force, what remained of the antiwar cause was largely absorbed into the McGovern campaign. The problematic movements for the McGovernites were new arrivals that had not been present even as recently as the 1968 convention: the women's rights and gay rights movements. It was in the McGovern campaign that these movements made their first appearance in presidential politics. It was the dawn of a new phase of movement politics—a "politics of identity"—and the initiation of an ongoing dilemma for the Democratic Party—a "politics of culture war."

Of the two brand-new causes, it was the women's movement that was most powerful—and most vexing for the McGovern campaign—and thus receives the fullest treatment in this chapter. The story of feminists and McGovernites has two distinct parts: the relationship between the campaign and women's political groups, and the issue of gender roles within the campaign organization itself. Much of this story has never been told before. Replete with high ideals and low resentments, it is a revealing tale about the politics of insurgency and the transformation of liberalism from the 1960s to the present.

Feminists and McGovernites

At the 1968 Democratic convention in Chicago, 13 percent of the delegates were women, and the party's platform did not discuss women's issues. Four years later, at the Democratic convention in Miami Beach, 39 percent of the delegates were women, and the party's platform included a fifteen-point Rights of Women plank, everything feminists had requested save a statement on reproductive rights.[5] As chair of the party's reform commission, McGovern reaped credit from women for this remarkably swift increase in their representation. But the driving force for the change was a new feminist organization: the National Women's Political Caucus (NWPC).

Between the two party conventions, a militant women's movement had erupted onto the scene. The famous Atlantic City demonstration against the Miss America Pageant, which inaugurated the new public face of feminism (and gave rise to the myth of bra-burning), took place only a month after the 1968 Democratic convention. As a new generation of feminists published startling manifestos and shattered traditional proprieties, the media was fascinated by the most militant groups, highlighting the radicals (the Redstockings) and the antimale separatists (including the colorful WITCH—Women's International Terrorist Conspiracy from Hell).[6] Less noticed was a more conventional political project: to adopt the methods of the pressure group for the goal of women's equal inclusion in electoral, legislative, and presidential politics. This project attracted the leading figures in mainstream feminism, including Betty Friedan and Gloria Steinem. If any individual leader can be singled out for spearheading women's organization for political influence, it was Congresswoman Bella Abzug.[7]

The NWPC was formed in July 1971 as more than 300 women convened at the Washington Hilton to establish an independent political organization that would advance women's search for equality. The group struck gold with its very first undertaking, as it turned its attention to the reform process already under way in the Democratic Party, the McGovern-Fraser Commission. The NWPC won a swift and stunning victory: that November, only four months after the group was founded, a delegation of its leaders met with Lawrence O'Brien, chair of the Democratic National Committee, and secured his agreement to rewrite the party reform guidelines for the upcoming national convention. In place of the existing general language on increasing representation for women, minorities, and youth on each state's delegation, the revised rules now stipulated explicit numerical targets (quotas in all but name). The tripling of female convention delegates from 1968 to 1972 and the progress in woman's political influence that it portended can be traced to this agreement.[8]

As an insurgent, McGovern was keenly attuned to the rapid emergence of women as an important new constituency. In the hunt for a majority at the Democratic convention, women would, under the new rules, comprise the largest single bloc of delegates. Women's rights were a natural theme for an insurgent campaign that was challenging the retrograde "Establishment center." Moreover, the McGovern campaign believed that a gender gap was developing in American politics. Shirley MacLaine, who took over the role of coordinator for women's issues for the fall campaign, wrote to the campaign leadership, "A study of the attitudes of women suggests that they are a natural constituency for McGovern. As voters, women tend to be more idealistic than men, and more committed to humanistic values."[9]

McGovern himself was not a feminist—few men were this early in the women's-rights revolution. But as Amanda Smith, MacLaine's predecessor as the campaign staffer assigned to women's issues, put it, he did possess "a wonderful instinct for fairness."[10] His task of appealing to women was complicated, however, by the candidacy of Shirley Chisholm. Many women in the NWPC wanted to endorse Chisholm on feminist grounds, even though they knew she had no chance to win the nomination.[11] Even Gloria Steinem, a longtime friend and supporter of McGovern, chose to run in the New York primary as a Chisholm delegate.[12]

Facing this obstacle, the McGovern campaign made a series of smart moves in the early stage to attract feminist support. McGovern organizers were directed by Smith to contact NWPC organizers in their states and to "express Senator McGovern's full support for their goal of political equality, solicit their support, offer information on delegate selection, etc."[13] McGovern demonstrated his seriousness about the reform rules when his own delegate slate from Illinois turned out to contain a large preponderance of older white males. As Scott Lilly recalls, "McGovern blew a gasket and directed that [his workers] go and get people who had circulated petitions to get on the ballot to withdraw so that women and minorities could be put on the ballot."[14]

McGovern was far out in front of other male candidates in the symbolic politics of women's rights. In February 1972, he sent a public letter to the president of National Airlines:

> I am astonished that National Airlines is persisting in an advertising program which many women find insulting. I refer, of course, to the tasteless and suggestive "I'm Cheryl, fly me to Miami . . . " An equally personal and more impressive campaign than your present one would be . . . making clear, if indeed it is true, that there are competent women at every professional level of National Airlines . . . Unless you are changing this program, it will indeed affect my choice of airlines during the coming weeks, when the Presidential Primary will take me often to Florida.[15]

McGovern's threatened boycott of a sexist business brought him kudos from feminists, with one NWPC official thanking him profusely for the "beautiful letter you sent National Airlines."[16]

Once McGovern emerged as the frontrunner for the Democratic nomination, feminists began to demand more of him. They were especially frustrated by his cautious stance on abortion. Feminists thought McGovern was merely playing politics with what was, for them, the transcendent issue for women, taking a hedged position out of a fear of offending traditionally Democratic Catholic voters. They were not aware that the insurgent was personally conflicted about the subject and wanted to downplay it as much as possible.[17] Twenty members of NWPC met with the candidate at his home a few weeks before the Democratic convention to pressure him on their issues. Afterward, the *Washington Post* reported, the women were "'disappointed' with the stand Sen. George McGovern is taking on abortion and other women's issues and threatened to 'sit on their hands' after the conventions if no candidate is 'taking a leadership role' on those issues."[18]

McGovernites and feminist activists arrived in Miami Beach with preoccupations and emotions that clashed more than they overlapped. For the party insurgents in the McGovern campaign, victory in their long march to the Democratic nomination was so close that they could almost taste it. Yet the "Anybody but McGovern" regulars were girded for their last desperate stand, and in the showdown vote over the California delegation challenge the McGovern campaign would either triumph or die. If it did survive to take on President Nixon, the last thing it needed was to adopt controversial positions that would confirm the dangerous reputation for radicalism with which it was already saddled. To the feminists of the NWPC, in contrast, the story of the convention was about their coming out as a political force. Rooming together at the aptly named Betsy Ross, a fleabag hotel where the cockroaches were "so big they could carry the chairs," female activists were fired with the "spirit of sisterhood and purpose."[19] Although many favored McGovern's candidacy, the strategic concerns of his campaign were not their concerns.

The jeering of McGovern at the opening meeting of the women's caucus was a preview of what was to come. McGovern had promised at the meeting to back the women's challenge to the gender makeup of the South Carolina delegation. But fearing that a successful point of order by the stop-McGovern coalition on the South Carolina ballot would prove fatal for the upcoming ballot on California, McGovern's chief floor strategist, Rick Stearns, dumped enough votes in a disguised maneuver to scuttle the women's challenge.[20] When the feminists began to realize what had happened on the South Carolina vote, they were outraged. As Phyllis Segal of the NWPC saw it, McGovern's pledge had been conveniently scrapped in the interests of "realpolitik," and infuriated feminists quickly made plain to the McGovernites their "sense of betrayal."[21] For their part, McGovernites saw the feminists as obtuse to political reality. In Gary Hart's recollection,

> I came back the night after the South Carolina challenge to the hotel
> about four in the morning, and there sat the late Bella Abzug and Gloria
> Steinem. And they were angry. We had spent time with them explaining the
> parliamentary situation—that if we supported the South Carolina challenge

and lost, the precedent established would also unseat our California delegation. But they didn't want to hear it. They were focused totally on South Carolina as a symbol, and they could have, it seemed to me, cared less about the nomination. Our focus was on the nomination. We worked for it for over two years, and for them the symbol of South Carolina was more important than the nomination.[22]

A similar situation developed on the following night of the convention as it considered the party's platform. The 1972 Democratic platform had an unprecedented Rights of Women section, calling for a priority effort on behalf of the Equal Rights Amendment, strong antidiscrimination and equal pay measures, and the appointment of women to high-level positions in every branch of the federal government. But it omitted the one commitment about which feminists most cared. The NWPC activists promoted a minority plank on abortion, conservatively worded so as to substitute "choice . . . in matters relating to human reproduction" for the most politically charged of the three "A" words. Fresh from victory on the California challenge and now more in charge of convention dynamics, Stearns and other McGovern campaign strategists again ensured that the feminist position did not prevail on the floor. There was no violation of a pledge in this instance: McGovern had never yielded to feminist pressure on the issue of abortion. Yet the feminists were perhaps even more furious over their second defeat than their first, coming as it did on their most deeply felt concern. It especially enraged them that McGovern's women's-rights spokesperson at the convention, Shirley MacLaine, while herself pro-choice, appeared on the rostrum to argue against the minority plank. It enraged them as well that the McGovernites granted a right-to-life delegate time to speak against their plank.[23]

Feminist anger at the McGovernites poured out in full public view. Crying with rage, Steinem lit into Hart and the other McGovern convention managers: "You promised us you would not take the low road, you bastards."[24] Abzug scolded MacLaine: "A sister never goes against a sister." MacLaine defended herself: "Sisters have a right to have pragmatic politics as well as personal principles."[25] Bad feelings from the battles over the South Carolina challenge and the abortion plank did not fade away. Writing later about the convention, Steinem put in a dig at Hart as "one of the arrogant young men who have made life miserable for women working in the campaign."[26] In Stearns's recollection, "Abzug never forgave me. I remember being at a luncheon at the issues convention two years later in Kansas City . . . She and I were at the same table and she made it a point to turn her chair around and sit with her back to me for the entire lunch."[27] McGovern himself was exempted from most of the feminists' persisting anger, perhaps out of respect for his record on the war and party reform and from the need to maintain enthusiasm for his contest with Nixon. Abzug even set aside her feud with MacLaine and became cochairwoman with her of a National Women's Advisory Council for McGovern.

One factor that made the recriminations flowing between feminists and Mc-Governites so intense was the close personal ties across the two camps. Nowhere was this more ironic than in the story of the Segals, Eli and Phyllis. As legal counsel to the McGovern-Fraser Commission it was Eli who gave his wife, then a law student at Georgetown, the inspiration and the access to data to write a research paper on women's underrepresentation as convention delegates—a document that later became the basis for the NWPC's successful project to rewrite the rules of the Democratic Party for presidential campaigns. At Miami Beach, Phyllis was an NWPC staff member, organizing women whose formidable numbers at the convention owed much to her past work, while her husband was a top McGovern strategist coping with the consequences. During the convention, Phyllis relates, the couple remained at "arm's length," with Eli staying at the comfortable headquarters hotel and Phyllis living with her "sisters" at the low-rent Betsy Ross. Helping to spearhead the women's challenge to the South Carolina delegation, she had no inside information from her husband about the maneuvers that the McGovernites were planning and thus "was as totally blown away as everybody else" by their deception. She and her husband "had our words afterwards. The betrayal felt personal as well as political." Her anger was assuaged by her recognition that the motives of the McGovernites were not "malign" and were shaped by the pursuit of the larger goal she and her husband shared: electing McGovern and ending the war.[28]

After their disheartening defeats on South Carolina and abortion rights, the feminists at Miami Beach bounced back with a last-minute effort to promote Sissy Farenthold for the vice-presidential slot on the McGovern ticket. Farenthold, who had run a surprisingly effective campaign in the spring for the Democratic gubernatorial nomination in Texas, was in some ways an odd choice for NWPC activists: as Jane Pierson relates, she was a "slow-talking" southern lady who was used to being treated as a "princess."[29] Yet Farenthold had charisma, and feminists saw her as a vehicle, NWPC activist Doris Meissner recalls, for their desire "to assert, in the face of the party hierarchy," women's will and aspirations.[30] With McGovern strategists occupied with their eventual selection of Senator Thomas Eagleton, the women organized with dispatch and produced 420 votes for Farenthold, almost a quarter of the total that McGovern's choice received. A symbolic show of new strength on the part of the women, the Farenthold candidacy also had an unintended yet damaging effect on the McGovernites: the length of the convention proceedings on the vice-presidential choice was the principal reason that McGovern's acceptance speech was disastrously delayed until the middle of the night.[31]

Feminists found some satisfaction at the end of the convention when Mc-Govern selected Jean Westwood of Utah as chair of the Democratic National

Committee, the first woman to hold such a post in either party. But tensions between feminists and McGovernites continued into the fall. The chief flash point for conflict was gender inside the McGovern presidential campaign. McGovern had more females on his staff than previous nominees, with some of the women holding important positions. But the feminists insisted that there should be complete equality. Sara Ehrman tells a story of a group of militant women, led by Abzug and Steinem, who walked into the campaign headquarters one fall day "in a phalanx" and "were raising hell." The feminists "literally shoved me against the wall and wanted to know where the women in the campaign were."[32]

To McGovernites, especially the men, this demand by feminists was yet another mark of their willful indifference to the insurgents' political needs. "We were fighting for our lives" in the fall, Hart says. But the feminists—and activists from other social movements as well—"began to position themselves apart from the campaign and constantly challenged the campaign." The issue of what Hart calls "quantitative affirmative action" in staffing was particularly "a no win. If the McGovern campaign had said, 'okay, give us ten women to hire, or ten blacks, or ten Hispanics,' they may or may not be experienced people and we probably didn't have the payroll to pay them. So we would have had to fire some experienced people to put them on. And then the press would have said, 'This campaign is a sponge, it has no backbone, it caves in to everybody, and that's the way, if McGovern were to win, the administration would be run.'"[33]

Contrary agendas drove feminists and McGovernites, despite many shared values and personal bonds, into recurrent conflict. Understanding the circumstances for the two sides—the McGovernites' increasingly difficult political straits, the feminists' militant awakening in the first flush of a great social transformation—sympathy is more warranted than assignment of blame for failures in collaboration. At their principal site of confrontation, Miami Beach, the McGovernites appeared to have the upper hand, dealing the feminists stinging defeats on gender balance in delegations and on abortion rights. Covering the convention for *Harper's Magazine,* the radical Australian feminist Germaine Greer, famous for her book *The Female Eunuch,* depicted it as an embarrassment for the feminist cause: "The miserable fact was that the women's caucus was not a caucus in any meaningful sense: the McGovern machine had already pulled the rug out from under them." In Greer's account, feminists came to Miami Beach exultant about the arrival of "womanpower," only to be swiftly turned into patsies by McGovern's strategists, who knew that for liberal women there was no alternative but their man. With a sarcastic sentence that begged to be quoted, Greer summed up her indictment of American feminists, who lacked her own radical edge: "Womanlike, they did not want to get tough with their man, and so, womanlike, they got screwed."[34]

It can be argued, however, that rather than getting "screwed," feminists came out of these clashes in better shape than did the McGovernites. The McGovernites, as Hart observed, were fighting for survival in Miami Beach and thereafter, and whatever brief triumphs they savored from the convention were soon swept away by the Eagleton fiasco. For feminists, in contrast, the Democratic convention of 1972 not only established lasting precedents on women's rights and gender equality but also stimulated a sharpened political consciousness. With women's representation in the selection of Democratic presidential candidates rapidly rising toward parity with men, with many of their goals endorsed by the party's platform, with a female heading the national committee, and with the solidarity and strength displayed in the Farenthold boomlet, feminists moved past their losses at Miami Beach and counted their gains.

Looking back on their encounter with the McGovern campaign, the early NWPC activists recognize a watershed in the political history of the women's movement. For Doris Meissner, the first executive director of the NWPC, after the struggles of 1972, women "didn't have to fight these kinds of battles anymore"; from then on, "women had to be at the table" and campaigns were expected to place women "in senior positions."[35] For Phyllis Segal, the experience of Miami Beach was both "enraging and empowering": feminist frustration "became an engine to build the movement," and thus "1972 reflected a time when women started [developing] an independent voice as a political force."[36] As Jane Pierson puts it, the 1972 campaign "was a turning point for the women's movement because it became a much more powerful movement after that." Subsequent to 1972, "the Democrats had to deal with women, [and] it changed the party." In the end, she believes, "the McGovern campaign was the ideal vehicle for women."[37]

Because the McGovern insurgency inaugurated a new phase of feminist politics and an altered relationship between women and the Democratic Party, the issue of women's participation was bound to come up inside as well as outside the campaign organization. On the McGovern staff, the emerging role of women in politics was never a central focus, but it was an unavoidable subject.

A Gender "Laboratory"

"It is Senator McGovern's policy," Amanda Smith wrote in a memo to the campaign organization, "that there should be no separate Women's Division, feeling that women will make a greater contribution to the campaign if they are integrated directly into general campaign operations."[38] The use of civil rights–era language in this statement was deliberate, echoed as well in McGovern's statement to Gloria Steinem in the fall of 1971 that his campaign had adopted "the philosophy of no 'Separate But Equal' women's division."[39] Yet if a pioneering egalitarian approach to gender in presidential politics was an official directive for the campaign staff, its top figures were all men, and their attitudes on the role of women in politics had been formed in the prefeminist era. Gender relations within the McGovern campaign thus were caught up in the same unsettling social transformation that marked its larger connections to the feminist movement. The campaign staff was, in Smith's phrase, a "laboratory" for new gender relations in politics, for an experiment in which the women would be more interested than the men and from which they would derive more instructive lessons.[40]

Amanda Smith was the principal experimenter. Born in 1940, Smith had master's degrees in education from Harvard and political science from Columbia, and she came to the McGovern staff by way of the campaign for the McGovern-Hatfield Amendment to End the War. As one of his earliest staff members, she was originally assigned to be McGovern's scheduler, a position at which she was soon replaced by the more experienced Steve Robbins. She was asked to be in charge of women's issues as well, about which she also lacked much of a background, but she was told that this would not be a full-time matter. Smith believes that her hiring was not just due to her credentials but also because "I had long blond hair to my rump, I had blue jeans, [and I had] lots of blue eye-shadow."[41]

According to Smith, she soon found out that regardless of McGovern's official policy on gender equality within the campaign, the men at the top did not take the issue—or her—very seriously. She complained to Sara Ehrman, an older woman on McGovern's senate staff: "'Sara, they treat me like a child.' And Sara looked up at me and said, 'Amanda, you look like a child. You need to put your hair up.'" Smith responded not only by adopting a more professional look but by reading about gender relations, and she "became a feminist very quickly." She began to work on women's issues full-time, seeing her labors as a "two-sided job. On one hand, I was supposed to attract voters and workers to the McGovern campaign because of the candidate's stand on [women's] issues. On the other hand, I was supposed to make it come true." Smith never gained admission to the inner circle of the McGovern campaign, but she did find ways to encourage other women to take a more assertive role. In the summer of 1972 she left her position with the national McGovern campaign to accompany her fiancé, political scientist James David Barber, as he took up a position at Duke University. (Barber became famous that year for his book *The Presidential Character*, which predicted that President Nixon's damaged psyche would eventually lead him down the path of political disaster.) Shirley MacLaine took her place.[42]

Smith was not alone in perceiving the men at the top of the campaign, especially Hart and Mankiewicz, as uninterested in the concerns of feminists. Ehrman characterizes the attitude of the staff's male leadership toward women's demands for equality: "Placate them. Don't rock the boat. [It was] not a serious issue. It was a serious issue for McGovern."[43] Ehrman shares Smith's view that the liberalism of male McGovernites, the candidate excepted, did not extend to the subject of gender. "One of the interesting things we learned in the campaign," Smith relates, "was that your [position] about women's issues seemed to have very little, at least in those days, to do with your other stances on political issues

. . . The trouble with those good liberal men was that they were so sure that they were right on the issues that they did not think that they needed to think about women's issues . . . You got surface acceptance but not a real engagement."[44]

Although most male McGovernites fell short of their candidate's public commitment to full equality within his campaign, it might be said in their defense that there was no precedent in presidential politics for a campaign organization in which women played parts equal to men's. The feminist revolution was so new that even many of the women who had significant positions within the campaign were not focused on women's issues. Most female McGovernites were motivated by the drive to end the war in Vietnam rather than by the feminist revolution. Some, like Marcia Greenberger, had previously attended law schools where they had been accustomed to being one of only a few women in a male environment, and so they did not find the McGovern campaign's gender imbalance at all unusual. For Greenberger, who later founded the National Women's Law Center, awareness of women's distinct issues was only beginning to germinate.[45]

It was among the women of the McGovern campaign more than the men that Smith concentrated her consciousness-raising efforts. What she was learning from her work was that subtle cultural attitudes of both sexes were more of an obstacle to women's political equality than the overt sexism of the men:

> It's true that we had sexists then who wanted to push aside women . . . It's true that we had self-important men who wanted to push aside anybody. And, yes, it's true that some women weren't competent. But all three of those categories of people were relatively small . . . I got interested in the way that women and men had been socialized differently so that male behavior tended to end up with males in power and female behavior tended to end up with females out of power.[46]

An example Smith gives of this syndrome in the McGovern campaign was the response to failure. When men made a mistake, they didn't tend to regard it as important and drove themselves even harder. When women made a mistake, they questioned their own competence and allowed men to take over the task from them.

One woman, a state cochair for McGovern, wrote to Smith that she had been mortified that she was not invited to stand near the candidate in front of the television cameras when he won the primary. Smith reflected on the scene the night that McGovern captured Wisconsin and realized that "the ones who ended up on the stage, next to him, had not gotten there by invitation, they'd gotten there by elbow." Inherited patterns of male aggressiveness and female passivity were the root of the problem, so Smith began to advise other high-level women in the campaign to push themselves forward to a position at the candidate's side.[47]

If men at McGovern headquarters in Washington paid lip service to the campaign's ideology of gender equality, McGovern women in the field typically faced unabashed patriarchy. Barbara Holum (Barbara MacKenzie during the campaign—she subsequently married McGovern's longtime aide John Holum) was sent by the Washington office as its representative to a meeting of Democrats in a Midwest state who were planning a local McGovern event. Walking into the meeting, she encountered a group in which everyone was white, male, and over forty-five. The man chairing the meeting was "livid," she recalls, because the McGovern campaign had sent a "girl" to talk to them. He pounded the table and yelled at her, "'What do you know? You don't know anything!'" Not a single man in the room reacted to her presence with sympathy. Holum initially thought that she should be replaced with a male for a subsequent meeting of this group, but when she decided to stick it out, the national headquarters was completely supportive. In the end, she says, the group's event was a huge success and "they loved me!"[48]

Betsy Wright's encounter with sexism in the Texas campaign did not end so well. Fresh from working for Sissy Farenthold's gubernatorial bid in the spring of 1972, Wright, the top young liberal organizer in Texas, was recruited to help the McGovern coordinators, all of them from out of state, in the fall campaign. With the younger coordinators, Taylor Branch and Bill Clinton, and with Clinton's girl-friend, Hillary Rodham, Wright struck up lasting bonds. Years later, she served Clinton in Arkansas as his chief of staff. Despite the importance of the campaign in her life, she recalls it as an unpleasant experience. The main reason was an older McGovern state coordinator who directed at her, as the highest-ranking woman at McGovern headquarters in Austin, the brunt of his sexist condescension. Wright was regularly greeted by this official with "How are your hormones today?" When she expressed unhappiness with his attitude, she was told that "you just need to get laid." Having recently read feminist authors, Wright's sensitivity to patriarchal behavior was at a peak, and she could not abide the sexist patter. The lesson she drew from the McGovern campaign was that women needed political power, and after it was over she went to work for the NWPC in Washington.[49]

Among the women working in the McGovern campaign, there was sufficient discontent about gender issues that when Abzug and Steinem led their "pha-lanx" of feminists into the national headquarters, Ehrman notes, the female staffers present were "cheering them on."[50] Yet in a historical sense, the McGovern campaign was, for women in political campaigns as much as for women in the feminist movement, a breakthrough. Smith sums up the campaign's accomplishment for women:

> When McGovern said, "Women will be equal," nobody understood what a complicated statement that was. Everybody's response was yes, yes, sure . . . One of the things that was so interesting was that by the time of the convention, McGovern women had more power, more authority, more titles,

more salary, more anything than had ever been the case in any political campaign . . . And they were furious. The reason that they were furious was that . . . they got a good look at how far that was from true parity.[51]

Recent Democratic campaigns for the presidency have come much nearer to gender equality, with women occupying positions at the very top of the organization. Instead of figures like Frank Mankiewicz and Gary Hart, managers such as Donna Brazile for Al Gore and Mary Beth Cahill for John Kerry now run operations. It was in the McGovern insurgency, however, that women's road to real power in presidential campaigns originated.

Gay Liberation and the McGovern Insurgency

A mass movement for gay and lesbian rights was even newer to the American political scene in 1972 than was the feminist movement. It took a riot—the physical resistance by patrons of the Stonewall Inn, a gay bar in New York's Greenwich Village, to a police raid in June 1969—to launch the gay liberation movement in the United States. (In this period the word *gay* was used for both male and female homosexuals.) Once gays began to smash their way out of the closet, however, long-simmering tensions fueled a fast-growing mass movement. With examples of movement-building widely available after the civil rights, antiwar, and feminist struggles of the 1960s, Gay Liberation Fronts sprang up almost overnight throughout the country (and internationally as well). Like feminists, gays were a new constituency that was mobilized for political action and impassioned about its goals. Far more than in the case of feminists, however, whichever presidential candidate could capture gays' allegiance would also assume the risks of identification with the most stigmatized minority in the country.

Several gay liberation organizations approached the Democratic presidential campaigns before the opening of the 1972 primary season, seeking to determine their positions on gay issues. Forwarding a questionnaire on gay rights to the McGovern campaign, Guy Charles, representing *The Advocate*, a "homophile newspaper," presented a typical case for taking the gay community seriously as a political force:

> The year 1972 marks the first occasion that [homosexuals] have the
> opportunity, under Gay Liberation, to really unite and be a part of the
> election process of the country. Gay women and men are already becoming
> a part of the political scene as campaign workers, party workers, election
> officials, and even candidates for office. It was shown, during the last
> Congressional elections in New York, as also on the West Coast, that the Gay
> vote can help to decide who will go to Washington . . . The Gay Community

. . . is now estimated to be in excess of 10% of the voting population, [and the] voting power of the Gay minority will be shown and felt, as it was in the case of the Black minority.[52]

Although the figures on gay political strength were inflated, the McGovern campaign, an insurgency committed to a sixties liberal vision of equality, could not ignore such pressure. McGovern's left-center strategy for capturing the Democratic nomination required him to stake out advanced positions on cultural matters. Moreover, from the vantage point of the early nomination game, the climactic primaries would come in California and New York, the two states where gays were becoming a visible political presence. Beyond any political calculations, the openness and participatory spirit of the insurgency made it difficult for McGovernites to exclude even unpopular groups. Whatever the likely risks of supporting the gay movement, Bob Shrum observes, "We didn't know how not to allow it some space" in the campaign.[53] The expansion—and then the contraction—of that space forms another story of mass movements and McGovernites that has not been told before.

Responding to the growing clamor from an assortment of gay liberation groups, a statement and a list of six proposals were issued on McGovern's behalf—but not directly by the candidate—in San Francisco on February 2, 1972. This document represented his campaign's strongest pledge on gay rights and was a key to the substantial gay support that it subsequently received. Senator McGovern recognizes, the statement reads, "that certain assumptions of the majority concerning homosexuals have been used as a rationale for harassment and denial of their elementary civil liberties. As for other stigmatized minorities, Senator McGovern pledges the full moral and legal authority of his presidency toward restoring and guaranteeing first-class citizen rights for these individuals." Of the six proposals that followed, the first was the boldest and most controversial: "Sexual orientation should cease to be a criterion for employment by all public and governmental agencies, in work under federal contracts, for service in the United States armed forces, and for licensing in government-related occupations and professions."[54]

Remarkable for its time, McGovern's forthright position on gay rights had the desired effect. Ronald Alheim, a gay activist from Albany, New York, took the lead in forming Gay Citizens for McGovern and recruited about forty organizers around the country for the group, which received official recognition from McGovern campaign headquarters.[55] This group was probably the first of its kind for the presidential campaign of one of the major parties. In the course of building support for the California primary, Ann Marcus, the McGovern coordinator for Southern California, found considerable enthusiasm for her candidate in the gay community. She worked with gay activists on producing a brochure targeted at their community and distributed in the gay bars. McGovern's picture was on the front of the brochure, and Marcus noticed that it had been "ever so slightly doctored. McGovern could have been gay." She made sure that the candidate and his national staff did not see the brochure.[56]

As the McGovern campaign successfully moved from the fringe of the Democratic Party and contemplated a contest with the Republicans, its original left-center strategy dictated a search for safer political ground. The cause of gay liberation was the most unsafe of all—indeed, as Norman Mailer remarked, endorsing this cause in 1972 was "political suicide."[57] At a meeting of the Democratic platform committee in Washington prior to the national convention in Miami Beach, the McGovern forces, in a dominant position on the committee, rejected the inclusion of a plank on sexual orientation (along with a plank on abortion). This plank incorporated some of McGovern's earlier proposals on gay rights, but it went further, urging "repeal of all laws, federal and state, regarding voluntary sex acts involving consenting persons in private, laws regulating attire, and laws used as a shield for police harassment."[58] The vote against the plank was 54–34, with many of the McGovern representatives appearing sympathetic to its sentiments and opposing its adoption only because they had been so instructed by the leadership of the campaign.[59]

At Miami Beach, the McGovern campaign was again able to downplay the gay rights issue. The minority plank on sexual orientation was debated on the floor, in front of the television cameras, but the debate was delayed to the pre-dawn hours and the plank was defeated by a voice vote. Nonetheless, words and images of a sexuality not addressed before by a major political party had been broadcast to the nation, and they added an important piece to the emerging portrait of the McGovern campaign as an uprising of the marginal and the strange. Scott Lilly comments on the political impact:

> A lot of the groups that got floor time at that convention were the kind of people that [many Americans] had never seen before. It was the first time that they saw people get up and say they were gay . . . and liked to kiss other men. That's a much less shocking thing today than it was then . . .
> In the summer of 1972, people couldn't believe they were seeing some of the things that were on television. And McGovern didn't need to have it on television. He needed to have pictures of the bombs dropping out of a B-28 on television.[60]

The gay rights issue, Barbara Holum points out, was so unfamiliar and unsettling in 1972 that any association with it was "offensive" to old-line Democrats.[61] Even some in the McGovern camp were upset about ties between their candidate and the gay liberation movement. According to Sara Ehrman, at Miami Beach "the South Dakota folks [from McGovern's senate staff] were in a rage about it." George Cunningham, McGovern's senate chief of staff, and another South Dakotan "picked a gay guy up bodily and threw him out of the hotel." The South Dakotans were worried about how McGovern's identification with gay liberation might hurt him back home, but even more important, in Ehrman's view, was the fact that the gay cause "was abhorrent to them."[62]

Gay organizations took their convention setback more in stride than did the feminists. During the fall campaign there was some alarm among gay activists about even further backtracking on McGovern's part toward their issues. Two leaders of Gay Citizens for McGovern sent the candidate an urgent telegram in mid-October 1972, requesting clarification about McGovern's "apparent retraction" a few days earlier of the six-point program on gay rights originally issued in February. They warned McGovern that because word of this supposed retraction was spreading, "gay support for your candidacy is rapidly deteriorating in major urban centers."[63] But by this point in the fall, the McGovern campaign was in such deep trouble on other fronts that it did not worry much about the potential defection of gay voters. Gay discontent barely registered in the memories of the McGovern campaign's high command. With so much else marring McGovern's political standing against Nixon, Frank Mankiewicz observes, at least "the gay and lesbian issue was nascent" enough that it did not become a major headache for the campaign.[64]

From a contemporary standpoint, the McGovern campaign may appear instrumental and timid in its relationship with the gay-rights movement, pulling close to the movement as it sought the Democratic nomination and then distancing itself as it moved toward the center for the fall election. Considering how novel the gay cause was in 1972, however—and, even more important, how politically explosive it was—the very fact of the relationship remains historically important. Ronald Alheim of Gay Citizens for McGovern ascribes the candidate's early support for gay rights to "political convenience." Nonetheless, he concludes, McGovern was "more progressive" on issues of sexual orientation than other political leaders of the era, "even some [elected officials] who were closeted gays."[65]

The McGovern campaign did not make gay rights one of its banner concerns, but it did grant the gay cause its initial recognition in a presidential election. In a slim paperback handed out by the campaign, McGovern: The Man and His Beliefs, gays come at the end of a list of oppressed groups. "I hope for the day," reads the quote from McGovern, "when we do not need to specify that 'Liberty and Justice for ALL' includes blacks, Chicanos, American Indians, women, homosexuals, or any other group. ALL means ALL."[66] This was a cautious recognition and a tentative first step, but gays were now on the civil-rights map in presidential politics. This fateful political move, like so many others that remain seminal to the enduring identity crisis of the Democratic Party, began with the McGovern campaign.

"Brother McGovern"

Unlike the feminist or gay liberation movements, the African American civil rights movement was an aging force in 1972, past its heroic prime and hampered by severe internal divisions. The other two movements cared as much about what was in the platform (the abortion plank for women, the sexual orientation plank for gays) as about their political representation. But with the landmark achievements of the civil rights struggle behind them, black activists were primarily focused on representation in 1972, and they were determined to obtain real positions of power from the Democratic presidential nominee. The relationship between McGovernites and black activists was hardly free of stresses and tensions, but the differences between the two sides, revolving principally around distributive political goods, were more easily negotiated than were the controversial policy issues around which feminists and gays pressed their demands on the campaign.

Hoping for the power of black unity, African American leaders instead floundered in factionalism during the Democratic presidential selection process. Shirley Chisholm was the first black candidate to run for the presidential nomination of one of the two major parties, but her campaign drew more support from feminists than from black activists. Chisholm could not obtain the endorsements of major black political organizations. She blamed the resistance to her candidacy within her own community on the sexism of the established black leaders; they complained that she didn't consult them before announcing for the presidency and predicted—correctly as it turned out—that she would attract scant electoral support and tarnish the image of a formidable black voting bloc. Among the black organizations there was little agreement beyond the rejection of Chisholm's candidacy. The Congressional Black Caucus could not reach a consensus on whom to support in 1972, nor could the more nationalist Black Political Convention, which met that spring and issued a long list of mostly militant demands.[67]

Winning black support was an uphill struggle for the McGovern campaign during the nomination process. McGovern possessed a strong Senate voting record on civil rights legislation, he was its foremost leader on issues of hunger, and he could claim a close bond with Robert F. Kennedy, a revered martyr to the black community. But his record was unfamiliar to this community, and his signature stand, in passionate opposition to the war in Vietnam, placed him at a distance from the domestic priorities of most African Americans.

Recognizing that he would have to devote considerable efforts to drawing black votes in the primaries, McGovern made Yancey Martin one of his first campaign staff hires in 1970. Martin had been deputy director of the Democratic National Committee's Minorities Division and, before that, head of the black caucus among Community Action Program directors in the War on Poverty. He brought to the campaign his wide contacts in a national network of black political activists. That McGovern was not well known to the members of this network was, Martin says, actually a plus, because it allowed him to argue that the senator from South Dakota was an "empty vessel" on minority issues who could be filled in by the black leaders who got behind him. Martin coached McGovern on the niceties of black politics—that, for example, it was imprudent to arrive at a black gathering flanked only by white aides because it conveyed disrespect for black capacities.[68]

So long as Edmund Muskie, the frontrunner, was McGovern's main worry, his lack of minority appeal was a minor matter; the senator from Maine was no stronger than McGovern in black America. Once Hubert Humphrey became the competition, however, McGovern was at a substantial disadvantage. Humphrey boasted (often) of one of the brightest and longest civil rights records in American politics, and many black politicians, who had made large strides during the Kennedy-Johnson era, were enthusiastically backing him. Even as the McGovern campaign took off after its win in the Wisconsin primary, Humphrey's stellar reputation in the black community threatened to prove a potentially fatal weakness for the McGovern campaign. A field report from the Michigan primary tersely highlighted the problem that McGovern encountered in all of the early contests: "Black support: Humphrey clearly strongest among rank-and-file. McGovern relatively unknown."[69] After the Michigan primary, *New York Times* reporter R. W. Apple Jr. pointed out that the question of black support still hung ominously over the McGovern insurgency: "Can Senator George McGovern, whose political base is a state with only 1,844 blacks, whose personal style is the very antithesis of soul, sell himself to the black electorate? So far, the answer is no. In Miami, Pittsburgh, Baltimore, the Hough district of Cleveland—almost everywhere he has tried, except Boston—Mr. McGovern has failed to make major inroads into the black support of Senator Hubert Humphrey."[70]

Yet McGovern had a valuable asset in his bid to increase his share of the black vote for the climactic primaries in California and New York. Several of the younger black leaders, closely associated with the glory days of the civil rights movement, endorsed him and campaigned for him: Julian Bond, Jesse Jackson, Coretta Scott King. In California, McGovern also had the early endorsement of the state's rising black political star (and a former attorney for civil rights demonstrators in San Francisco), Willie Brown. As Hart observes, "The whole country was split along generational lines . . . Younger blacks were angrier about the war . . . and much more vocal on civil rights."[71] With the backing of these younger leaders, "Brother McGovern," as Jesse Jackson dubbed him, could campaign in the black community as a leader of greater contemporary relevance than the outdated Humphrey.[72] Fashioning McGovern publicity for the California primary, Charles Guggenheim emphasized that handbills and fliers targeted at the black community should emphasize that "the 'with it' Blacks are behind McGovern.

[For example,] 'Why Jesse Jackson thinks McGovern is our man.' 'Why Julian Bond thinks the old leadership can't move it anymore.'"[73]

In the California primary, McGovern finally caught up with Humphrey in the competition for black votes, with the two running about even. Humphrey was ahead in the black community in Los Angeles, but McGovern took the preponderant share of black votes in the Bay Area. McGovernites ascribed their candidate's victory among Bay Area blacks to talent and organization. As Eli Segal and Sandy Berger reported to headquarters in a review of McGovern's California primary campaign, "The effort in the North was far superior to the effort in the South, largely because of the presence of Willie Brown as a clearly identifiable and respected leader. In fact, there was considerable canvassing in the Northern black areas, while there was virtually none in the South."[74] The Humphrey camp had an alternative hypothesis to explain McGovern's new success among blacks: desperately short of funds, their campaign could not match the McGovernites in the "street money" distributed in the Bay Area.[75]

California brought the McGovern campaign another minority success story, in this case with the critical Chicano vote, which McGovern won, according to a survey done for the *Washington Post*, by a 2–1 margin.[76] By 1972 Mexican American activists were emerging from underneath the shadow of African American politics, and California was their chief bastion of strength. The McGovern campaign made a significant push for Chicano votes; thus its slate of convention delegates was 18 percent Mexican American. Most important, it gained the backing of the most admired Chicano leader, Cesar Chavez. "As a result of the Chavez endorsement," Segal and Berger reported, "we received the help of about a thousand farm workers who volunteered full-time in East LA and other Chicano communities. This effort was put together by Dolores Huerta [vice president of the Farm Workers' union] and Tony Podesta [an Italian American McGovern organizer who passed as Mexican American during the campaign] and had a dramatic impact on our visibility and activity in the Chicano areas."[77] Huerta became one of the three cochairs of McGovern's California delegation at Miami Beach.

With the "Anybody but McGovern" party regulars mustering their forces for a last-ditch effort at the convention, the McGovern camp looked to uncommitted black delegates as a bloc of votes that might put its candidate over the top on the first ballot. Through intricate negotiations, including promises of federal appointments, the McGovern campaign struck a deal late in June with Walter Fauntroy, the nonvoting congressional representative of the District of Columbia, which added almost 100 uncommitted black delegates to McGovern's total, bringing him to the verge of a first-ballot victory at the convention.[78] The deal was shaky, however, and it almost fell apart at the convention amid the swirling dynamics of black politics. Appearing before a session of the Black Caucus, Shirley Chisholm passionately appealed to black delegates not to sell their votes and to stick with her for the first ballot, and in the emotions of the moment she received a more favorable response than she had from African American voters in the spring. Her maneuver threatened to wreck McGovern's hopes for a first-ballot victory and throw wide open the contest for the nomination. But the McGovern campaign squelched her scheme by arranging an endorsement from California congressman Ron Dellums, heretofore Chisholm's most eloquent champion among black leaders.[79] A left-liberal ideologically close to the McGovernites, Dellums likely was concerned that Chisholm's gambit played into the hands of the party conservatives out to stop McGovern.

Too divided to have much impact on the nomination or the party's platform, black leaders found a vulnerable spot in McGovern at the very end of the convention, in an incident that foreshadowed the difficulties later Democratic presidential nominees would have in the face of black pressures. Since Larry O'Brien had earlier indicated to McGovern that he did not want to stay on as chair of the Democratic National Committee (he had second thoughts about this during the convention), McGovern rewarded a key supporter and pleased the feminists by picking Jean Westwood for the position. His choice for vice chair of the DNC was Pierre Salinger, JFK's press secretary and an early adviser to McGovern. When the presidential candidate presented his choices to a meeting of the national committee, however, black members objected to seeing a white woman but not an African American elevated to party leadership and proposed that Basil Paterson of New York be substituted for Salinger. McGovern and Salinger were both stunned by the black rebellion but saw no option except to accede to the switch. Two Kennedy men, O'Brien and Salinger, were thus replaced by representatives of the feminist and black movements, a change of guard that hardly warmed the hearts of already disgruntled Democratic regulars. McGovern's failure to insist on his way at the DNC was, Mankiewicz acknowledges, "a weak moment," a signpost of how dependent the antiwar insurgent was on a black electorate whose enthusiasm for him was far from certain.[80]

Inside the McGovern campaign, dominated by white male activists, some black staff members had complaints similar to what some of the female staff expressed. Although Yancey Martin had been one of McGovern's first staff hires, the top command of the campaign did not regard him highly or consider him part of the inner circle, as Martin learned when he was excluded from the first meeting held after Mankiewicz came aboard. Feeling slighted, especially by Hart, and then coming under attack from black rivals, including Jesse Jackson, Martin prepared a letter of resignation after the Democratic convention and delivered it to McGovern in person. Worried that the resignation of his top black aide would only compound the public-relations disaster of the Eagleton affair, McGovern asked him to stay on for the fall. Martin acceded, only to experience further frustration when he could not obtain campaign funds for organizing or for street money in the inner city.[81]

Marie Brookter, a black advance woman, published a memoir shortly after the campaign that charged white male McGovernites with arrogance and racial insensitivity. Brookter wrote that she "felt like a fly in a bowl of milk—the only black advance surrounded by whites, and a woman at that." She claimed that McGovernites viewed her "not as a responsible, experienced colleague but as a sort of showpiece—something to prove that Senator McGovern was sensitive to his black and female constituencies."[82] Brookter singled out her boss, scheduler Steve Robbins, as the principal source of her tribulations. But his hard-edged treatment, which she interpreted as a racial slight, was also directed at the white McGovernites who worked with him.[83]

Despite these tensions, the McGovern campaign managed to mount a reasonably effective appeal to black voters. The prominent civil rights leaders supporting the insurgent were dispatched to black communities in the large states to drum up enthusiasm for "Brother McGovern." A fragment of transcript from a tape recording of Willie Brown, relating an interchange in Houston, captures the panache with which he made the case for McGovern to the "brothers" on the street. Brown told his listeners that "no black man can justifiably support Richard Nixon." A man in the crowd had to be convinced even further.

I said to the brother, "You know, for the first time in our lives we are trying to elect a human being to the Presidency—a peoples' candidate." He said, "How do you mean that, brother?" I said, "Can you imagine anybody making a homemade sign that says 'Viva Nixon,' or 'Right on, Nixon.' Can you imagine that—no way, no way?" And the way I closed on the brother . . . was, I said, "Brother, can you imagine any day of the week, or month, or year when Richard Nixon will come out on the streets and say to the brothers, give it to me? No way. No way. But with George McGovern, now there is a man."[84]

African American voters came through for "Brother McGovern" in the end, at least compared to other traditional Democratic constituencies. A Gallup Poll in September, taken after McGovern's worst month of the fall campaign, found that blacks were much less likely to have held his miscues against McGovern than other Democrats.[85] African American votes in November accounted for about 20 percent of McGovern's national total. Reflecting his support from younger black leaders, he polled especially well among college-educated blacks and blacks under age thirty.[86] However, Nixon doubled his minuscule support in the black electorate over 1968, and turnout was down in ghetto precincts.[87] The commitments that the Democratic Party had made during the 1960s on racial justice helped to carry McGovern with African American voters (although they helped Nixon more with whites), as did the support of major black figures like Julian Bond and

Willie Brown. In addition, McGovern's brand of liberalism was more appealing to blacks than it was to most whites. The McGovern campaign navigated a difficult course through the currents of black politics. It could take some satisfaction from the fact that this was one important social group whose loyalty it did not lose.

The Illusion of Youth

Youth were the least troublesome of the progressive social groups in the eyes of McGovernites. They viewed the activist young as McGovern's natural constituency and as the most energetic foot soldiers in his grassroots army. Compared to feminists, gays, blacks, or Chicanos, youth were relatively unorganized and were already receiving so much consideration that they could hardly demand more. Best of all, with the demographics of the baby boom and the fortuitous enfranchisement of 18–20-year-olds in the Twenty-sixth Amendment, ratified in 1971, their numbers in the electorate were swelling dramatically. As Carl Wagner recalls, "The 18-year-old vote, we thought, was our salvation."[88] There was only one problem with the hopes that McGovernites placed in youth: youth as a mass movement—or even as a coherent social group—was an illusion.

The illusion of youth as a decisive force for progressive change was common to both leftists and liberals in the 1960s and early 1970s. As the cutting edge of mass movements for civil rights, student rights, and an end to the war in Vietnam, young people were the center of attention for superficial media commentators and erudite social theorists alike. On the New Left, militant youth were conceptualized as an alienated mass increasingly forming itself into a self-conscious and mobilized class, the revolutionary replacement for a co-opted and complacent proletariat.[89] Among liberals, there was enthusiasm about the post-materialism of youth, the quest for authenticity and moral commitment that rejected the blandishments of the consumer society in search of a just society.[90] Fred Dutton, an adviser to McGovern in 1972, predicted the year before that the number of eligible first-time voters would double from 1968 to 1972, "including over 10 million eighteen-, nineteen-, and twenty-year-olds." This new segment of the electorate, Dutton claimed, "could come crashing in as a great political tidal wave."[91]

It was not hard during the 1972 campaign for McGovernites to perceive progressive youth, who were supposed to provide them with the electoral edge, mobilizing before their eyes. Young people were one of the three groups—along with women and minorities—singled out by the McGovern-Fraser reforms for enhanced representation in the Democratic Party, and at the convention in Miami Beach there was a separate youth caucus (revealingly, its organizers expected 700 to attend its first meeting, but only eighty showed up).[92] They were also one of the principal categories used by McGovernites in their extensive voter registration drive in the fall; the mantra for this effort was "blacks, browns, and young people."[93] It was primarily young people who knocked on doors for McGovern in the fall and turned out in droves for the massive rallies that buoyed his campaign's spirits until the end.

Yet evidence continued to mount during the fall campaign that there would not be any tidal wave of youth voting for McGovern. Polls showed Nixon actually pulling ahead of McGovern among the younger cohorts. McGovern led in these surveys among college students, but they comprised less than a third of the 25 million potential new voters. And even among liberal youth, his luster was fading; more captivated than their elders by the image of "St. George," they were more disillusioned by the Eagleton affair. The Nixon campaign had its own youth effort, and with its enormous financial advantage it was able to outspend the McGovern campaign in registering young voters on its side.[94]

The youthful McGovernites made an all-too-frequent mistake for their times: they projected themselves and the people they knew into an entire generation. Their critics were all too eager to flay them for their hubris, but in this instance the attack was legitimate. Richard Krickus skewered the illusion of "youth as a class": "Those youngsters who did not attend college did not view the world through the same counterculture lens that students at Berkeley or Cambridge did. A growing number of working-class youngsters smoked pot, wore long hair, and favored mod clothes, but in most cases they were as straight as their parents on other matters and those who were politically discontented were probably more inclined to vote for a George Wallace or Richard Nixon than a George McGovern."[95]

On Election Day, McGovern was, as predicted, the preferred candidate of the age cohort enfranchised by the Twenty-sixth Amendment. But the 18–20-year-old electorate only gave him 55 percent of its votes, and its turnout rate was the lowest of any age group. Even in the next oldest group, aged 21 to 24, Nixon had the advantage.[96] Young voters as a whole were more progressive than their elders—but only slightly so. They were a constituency worth fighting for, but their loyalties, rather than reliably on the left, were up for grabs in 1972 and would remain that way for future presidential elections.

Conclusion

Many McGovernites may have been naïve about the progressive inclinations of youth, but some of them were more realistic in recognizing that mass movements could be a hindrance as well as a boon. It was imperative, these strategists believed, that the boundary lines between movements and insurgents remain distinct and that the campaign not be captured for purposes that undercut its electoral aims. In the nonprimary states, Rick Stearns notes, he was careful not to construct a coalition of "already organized groups" because the inevitable result would be that those "with the most radical agendas" would set the tone. "I always put a premium," he recalls, "on trying to recruit into the campaign people who were there for George McGovern and not because they were looking to empower whatever group it was they were associated with."[97]

It was during the period in which the McGovern campaign grew from a small band of outsiders to become the presidential standard-bearer of the Democratic Party that the conflicts between party insurgents and movement activists grew intense. To Gary Hart, movement activists were baffling in their short-sighted behavior. "Each special-interest group or caucus," Hart wrote, "seemed to want to possess the campaign. There seemed to be an unwillingness to accept the fact that the McGovern campaign was an entity unto itself, that we solicited support (which was long withheld in crucial periods) from many quarters—blacks, Chicanos, women, youth—and made a supreme effort to seek involvement and participation in decision-making, but that we were not the creation or creature of any group."[98] These mass movements could not accept the fact that the McGovern campaign was not their movement, indeed not a mass movement at all.

With its trademark openness, the McGovern campaign unintentionally put on display some of the structural stresses in the relationship between social movements and political insurgencies. Even as the two forces coalesced in the service of shared goals, the fact that their basic objectives were not at all the same led them to circle each other warily. The activists in the mass movements never doubted their own idealism. The McGovernites at times resisted them in the name of pragmatism, yet they believed that this was necessary for the electoral pursuit of the highest ideals of liberalism. Perhaps the most fitting emblem for the relationship between the two was the heated exchange on the duties of "sisters" between Bella Abzug and Shirley MacLaine on the convention floor in Miami Beach. Movement activists like Abzug wanted to see McGovern in the White House, but their loyalty was to their own cause. For party insurgents like MacLaine, sometimes torn between personal values and political commitments, loyalty had to be given to the latter regardless of the discomfort.

Yet out of these troubled dealings between mass movements and McGovernites there grew some important advances. To be sure, the gains were mainly for feminists and gays—and for blacks and Chicanos to a lesser extent. The McGovern campaign won some additional votes from women, gays, and minorities, but its association with their groups was costly among white males. Whatever the scorecard for 1972, the foundation was laid in the McGovern campaign for the increasing identification of women and gays with the Democratic Party—and for the mix of potential and problems that flowed from the new commitment to social equality.

As the mass movements that erupted in the late 1960s have aged, as they have turned into organized interest groups rather than the disorderly uprisings at their inception, they have become inclined to a pragmatism closer to—but still not identical with—the thinking of Democratic Party activists. The McGovern campaign had the good fortune to ally with emerging mass movements in their opening burst of activism and energy. It had the bad fortune to be interlocked with them at the stage in which their demands and their behavior were the most militant and controversial.

10

A Textbook for Attack Politics:

The Master vs. McGovern

The three campaign commercials ended with the same tag line: "Paid for by Democrats for Nixon, John Connally, Chairman." The president did not appear in any of them. These were classic attack ads, their effectiveness attested to by their target:

> Those three spots were hammering three things. Number one, George McGovern is a man that can't make up his mind. [They had] me flipping like a coin. One day, he's a thousand percent for his vice-presidential running mate, the next day he's a thousand percent against him . . . The second spot that they alternated with this one showed me wiping out half of the defenses of America. [It] shows American soldiers here, Russian soldiers here, and my hand comes down and wipes out half of the Americans. Half the tanks are knocked out, half the ships, half the airplanes, and the Russians are going stronger and stronger. So, he's not only a wobbly, undependable, change of mind artist, he doesn't believe in American defense . . . Thirdly, they have a worker up on a steel girder, maybe forty stories in the air, he's got a hard hat on and a hammer. He looks down and everybody else is on welfare. A thousand dollars to everyone . . . Why work if you've got this? And he's thinking, "You know, what is this McGovern all about? He wants to put everybody on welfare. I still believe in the right to work. I believe it's sacred . . . "
>
> They played around the clock. I think that it finally got to the point where they were playing every twenty minutes. [Democrats for Nixon] had unlimited money.[1]

"Ostensibly autonomous," *Newsweek* disclosed, "Democrats for Nixon in fact operates as a satellite of the Nixon campaign, which designed its television spots and lent it $180,000 for newspaper ads. Connally consults almost weekly with Mr. Nixon, campaign manager Clark MacGregor, and his predecessor, John Mitchell."[2] The Democrats whom Connally enlisted were further to the right than the regulars that had battled McGovern into the convention. As columnist Clayton Fritchey observed, among these party defectors were a number of "ex–Southern

Democratic governors, most of whom, like Connally, have been crypto-Republicans for years."[3] Several had been vocal segregationists.

Democrats for Nixon was a vehicle for defining McGovern in terms devised in the White House. In its television spots, as in the rest of the campaign ostensibly run by the Committee to Re-elect the President (CREEP), Nixon's dark personality vanished behind the constitutional dignity of his office even as McGovern's distorted features as both radical ideologue and feckless politician were sharply etched in the public view. Connally's front group was only one of several facades behind which Richard Nixon, the grand master of attack politics in modern American political history, orchestrated his opponent's defamation.

There was an ironic consequence to Nixon's hidden manipulations of the 1972 election. While floating high above the fray in the role of "the President," behind the scenes he called the shots for his campaign. As biographer Stephen Ambrose observed, Nixon "never let his associates, whether Haldeman and Ehrlichman and Colson and the rest in the White House, or Mitchell and Magruder and the rest at CREEP, forget that he was *the* expert, that this was *his* campaign, that he would make *all* the major decisions."[4] Yet when the campaign was over, he worried that he had done so good a job in covertly exacerbating the McGovern campaign's own weaknesses that liberal reporters and liberal historians, determined never to give him credit for his political genius, would ascribe his landslide victory entirely to McGovern's failure. Nixon told his staff that their postelection spin should turn attention away from McGovern and that they should spread the word that "it was the case of RN winning the election."[5] Yet so much of Nixon's ruthless brilliance was concealed in 1972 that he was bound never to receive the accolades for the campaign for which he hungered. The presidential campaign of 1972 is remembered primarily for the break-in and cover-up of the Watergate affair and secondarily for the blunders of George McGovern. Few recall the strategic mastery of Richard Nixon.

But the campaign players knew. The McGovern staff despised Nixon from the start and grew increasingly concerned about some of the techniques through which his agents were out to sabotage their efforts. Yet decades later, even after all of the revelations about Watergate and related crimes, when McGovernites compare Nixon's smooth-functioning and hard-hitting campaign machine to their disorderly organization, they cannot help but be a bit in awe. John Holum speaks for a number of McGovernites in acknowledging that "the Nixon people ran a brilliant campaign."[6]

And Nixon's subordinates knew even better. Many of the senior figures at CREEP and in the White House later went to prison, but for younger Republican operatives working in the campaign the experience was a revelation. The Nixon campaign, understood from the inside, was a veritable textbook for attack politics, written by its indisputable master. Here were inscribed lessons on the manipulation of public policy, the elaboration of wedge issues to fracture the opposition's coalition, the concealment behind surrogates, the countering of criticism by scurrilous charges, and the media politics of relentless attack. With smart students like Lee Atwater and Karl Rove, Nixon's 1972 text has been put into practice by Republican presidential campaigns ever since.

In this chapter I shift the focus from the McGovern campaign to its opposition. A consideration of how Richard Nixon and his agents went about the destruction of George McGovern is necessary to gain a full picture of the McGovern insurgency. Bringing Nixon into the story does not erase McGovern's errors or dissolve the structural dilemmas of an insurgent campaign. But it does make clear what McGovern and his supporters were up against in 1972.

"Kick Him Again"

Mutual loathing best characterizes the feelings of George McGovern and Richard Nixon toward each other in 1972. McGovern is not a man given to hatred of political foes, but his opponent in 1972 was an exception. In his autobiography, he wrote, "I have loathed Richard Nixon since he first came on the national scene wielding his red brush in 1946, but I especially resented his cheap insults to Adlai Stevenson—my first genuine political hero. It remains the mystery of my life that this unscrupulous man could deceive so many Americans for so long."[7] This sentiment was shared by McGovern's staff, for like most liberals of that era, they were accustomed to thinking of Nixon as the denizen of the political gutter immortalized in the cartoons of Herblock. For Frank Mankiewicz, distrust of Nixon was the habit of a lifetime: as a young man he had chauffeured Helen Gahagan Douglas during the 1950 California Senate campaign, in which Nixon, her opponent, labeled her "the pink lady."[8]

Detesting Nixon, McGovern and his associates presumed that most other Americans at least must dislike him, and so they were predisposed to underestimating him. Planning his run for the presidency, McGovern figured that the hard part would be the campaign for the Democratic nomination, but that should he be successful with his party, "it should be comparatively easy to defeat Richard Nixon by appealing to the decency and common sense of the American people."[9] Mankiewicz says that little attention was paid by the campaign leadership to the problems of competing with the president, and that "if we thought about it," the unquestioned assumption was that Nixon would be easy to beat.[10]

Convinced of their prospective rival's vulnerability, and completely immersed in their grueling struggle for the Democratic presidential nomination, the McGovernites were largely oblivious to the fact that the first six months of 1972 were the most successful months of the Nixon presidency. While they were slogging from the New Hampshire primary to the California primary, Nixon traveled to China, bombed Hanoi and mined Haiphong harbor in response to a North Vietnamese offensive without scuttling a planned summit in Moscow, and signed the SALT I agreement with the Soviets there. Gallup polls recorded the president's growing popularity: stuck at 49 percent for the three months ending in January 1972, Nixon soared to 61 percent after the Moscow summit concluded late in May of the election year.[11] Although his standing in the polls subsequently dipped a little, he was a more popular incumbent by the fall of 1972 than the McGovernites realized.

For his part, Nixon's comments about McGovern, in conversations with or memos to his aides, were uniformly hostile but oddly inconsistent. Sometimes McGovern was depicted as a dangerous radical ideologue, a "Communist sonofabitch."[12] At other times, he was an effete liberal, scorned as "soft" and "weak."[13] In the president's character analysis, his challenger could sound less like the real McGovern than like Nixon himself. Rejecting the common claim that McGovern would prove to be a "Goldwater of the left," Nixon wrote to John Mitchell, "McGovern is more clever and less principled than Goldwater and will say anything in order to win."[14]

The president and his aides were delighted to run against McGovern, considering him to be the weakest candidate in the Democratic field. Nixon wrote in his memoirs that "to me, his steady climb [in the primaries] was as welcome to watch as it was almost unbelievable to behold."[15] Of course, the Nixon White House did more than watch McGovern passively; it secretly attempted to provide his insurgency with a boost, putting out false poll numbers to make him look stronger.[16] Once McGovern became the likely nominee, however, it was time for the all-out attacks to commence.

A few days after McGovern won the California primary, Nixon informed his top aides, H. R. Haldeman and John Ehrlichman, about the approach to be taken toward the challenger. Ehrlichman reproduced Nixon's instructions in his memoir:

> There should be more "savage attack lines" in our literature. McGovern advocates amnesty for draft dodgers. Put in there that it may cost a billion dollars just to buy enough white flags for this country. You, John, must coordinate all of this. We must put out an attack on McGovern in the foreign field, too. Pick four major thrusts . . . For example, McGovern's for surrender. He's for amnesty . . . He's for left-wing extremism. And he is for increased taxes.
>
> McGovern must be handled with attack. Agnew, Connally, and the other surrogates must attack him. Don't create too many issues; drum three or four major themes . . . Attack McGovern on his wildest, most radical position. We must always stay with his worst positions, keeping him over on the left. He is always to appear to be a fanatical, dedicated leftist extremist . . . Abbie Hoffman, Jerry Rubin, and Angela Davis [the first two Yippies,

the last an African American Communist] are around his neck . . . The issues
are radicalism; peace-at-any-price; a second-rate United States; running
down the United States; square America versus radical America.[17]

Not long after Nixon directed his minions to go after McGovern with "savage
attack lines," the McGovern campaign began to run into imbroglios of its own
making. A stickler for order, Nixon watched the unruly Democratic convention
with amusement, particularly delighted by the impression made on television
by its parade of "women, blacks, homosexuals, welfare mothers, [and] migrant
farm workers."[18] He followed the Eagleton affair closely, speculating with his
aides about its probable outcome. In Nixon's textbook for attack politics, a crisis
for the competition was a signal to the smart campaigner to redouble his attacks.
The White House taping system captured Nixon's instructions to Haldeman and
Ehrlichman at McGovern's lowest point: "When you've got a fellow . . . who is
under attack like this, who has fallen on his ass a few times, what you do is to
kick him again. I mean, it's like Dempsey going for the kill with Firpo. I mean, you
have to . . . keep whacking, whacking, and whacking."[19] It was also a maxim of
the master strategist never to become complacent, never to let up no matter how
far ahead you were. Two weeks before the election, with polls showing Nixon
cruising to a landslide reelection, he told his aides to "step up attacks."[20]

For the Nixon school of political campaigning, no tactic was too brazen. When
Arthur Bremer shot George Wallace in Laurel, Maryland, in mid-May, Nixon and
aide Charles Colson discussed planting literature in Bremer's Milwaukee apartment that would link the would-be assassin to McGovern. Howard Hunt was
directed to fly to Milwaukee for this purpose, but the mission was aborted before his departure because the FBI had already sealed Bremer's residence.[21] A
month later, as the White House watched to see if the Watergate affair would
become a major issue in the campaign, Nixon and his aides considered how to
tie it to McGovern. Their most promising angle was the Cuban connection. Four
of the five men arrested for the Watergate break-in were anti-Castro Cubans, and
McGovern was known to favor the normalization of U.S. relations with Castro's
regime. Five days after the arrests, Nixon told Haldeman that "the main thing
is the Cuban thing," and Haldeman replied that "what the Cubans are going to
say and starting to say is that they're scared to death of McGovern."[22] Four days
later, continuing to hope that the Watergate break-in could be portrayed as an
initiative of the Cubans and not of the Nixon campaign, Haldeman suggested the
public-relations line to be used: "[The Cubans] got carried away. They're emotional people who were afraid of what McGovern's going to do. Why the hell
would anybody care what was happening at the Democratic Committee?"[23]

Attack politics was Nixon's motif in 1972, but it was only one of his electoral
assets. As the incumbent, he could use public policy proposals to neutralize troubling issues, thereby denying them to his electoral opposition. He could devise

programs and shape symbols as political wedges, widening fissures in the other party's traditional electoral coalition. He could utilize the vast executive establishment as his tool, employing an array of surrogates to carry the burden of demeaning his competitor while he stood aloof and appeared "presidential." And he had unprecedented sums at his disposal, over $60 million in campaign funds, some of it illegal contributions solicited—or extorted—from large corporations. Every president uses the powers of incumbency to enhance his prospects for reelection. No other president has used them as systematically and as relentlessly as did Richard Nixon in 1972.

For the Reelection of the President

In his White House memoir, William Safire has a chapter on Nixon's effort against McGovern entitled "The Campaign That Never Was." Safire's title has a double meaning. Compared to any of his previous runs for office, Nixon's own campaigning in 1972 was minimal, deliberately deflecting the media's focus to McGovern's problems. Compared to previous presidents, however, what Safire regarded as Nixon's actual campaign—before the fall of 1972—was anything but minimal. His entire first term, especially the two years since the 1970 elections, paved the way to his reelection.[24]

A Democrats for Nixon ad portrayed McGovern as a flip-flopper because of his awkward reversal in the Eagleton affair, and the president, by contrast, posed as a pillar of firmness in 1972. Yet McGovern was a more consistent figure in his political career than Nixon had been. The startling opening to China by the fervent anti-Communist was only the most obvious of Nixon's reversals. His presidency was a field for almost continual political zigzagging. The critic of government interference in the free market at the start of his term was the initiator of wage-price controls in 1971. The advocate of affirmative action in his Philadelphia Plan of 1969 was a sharp critic of racial quotas in 1972. The champion of a more humane welfare system in 1969 was a stinging critic of "the welfare ethic" in 1972.

Nixon had conservative instincts, but he lacked conservative principles. Looking back at his presidency from the vantage point of the Reagan years, when conservative principles were ascendant, a number of "revisionist" historians began to claim that Nixon had been, of all things, a liberal.[25] They pointed to his ambitious Family Assistance Plan, his proposal for national health insurance, his plan for affirmative action in the construction unions, his innovative record on the environment. As Joan Hoff, the most prominent of the "revisionists," put the argument, even if politics may have been the propelling motive, Nixon was staking out advanced liberal ground during his presidency by his willingness "to move beyond the twin boundaries of the New Deal and Great Society."[26]

The "revisionist" thesis about Nixon is flawed, however. It makes Nixon look liberal by taking him out of his historical context, in which government activism was still popular, and examining him within the context of Reaganism. It slights the fact that many of Nixon's proposals were responses to even stronger measures proposed by the Democratic majority in Congress. It credits Nixon for executive actions whose sources were genuine liberals—for there were still liberal Republicans then—in agencies like the Department of Health, Education, and Welfare and the Environmental Protection Agency. And it downplays the ephemeral existence of so many of Nixon's domestic initiatives. Jonathan Schell observes that "the productions of the Nixon Administration emerged from nowhere and sank back into nowhere when their usefulness was at an end."[27] "Usefulness" was the key—and the usefulness of liberalism for Nixon, like the usefulness of conservatism, lay in electoral payoffs and not in ideology.

Environmental policy illustrates the electoral focus behind so much of Nixon's domestic policy. Because he supported the Environmental Protection Act, the Clean Air Act of 1970, and a number of other environmental measures, he is often seen as a surprisingly progressive president in this field, especially against the backdrop of the anti-environmental turn later taken by Republicans. But Nixon's policies were primarily responses to the upsurge of the environmental movement at the end of the 1960s, which placed his administration on the defensive. In the Senate, Edmund Muskie of Maine and Scoop Jackson of Washington, both of whom were expected to challenge Nixon for the presidency in 1972, were competing with one another for the role of environmental champion. As historian J. Brooks Flippen comments, the president's advisers told him that "the administration should embrace the new environmentalism, take the offensive, or risk being run over on an issue that increasingly appeared politically potent."[28] It was in this context, Flippen observes, that Nixon, "a man with no environmental background, interest, or expertise, [became] committed to a program of environmental protection."[29] The commitment shrank once the incentives changed: believing in 1972 that environmentalism was fading, Nixon vetoed water pollution legislation.[30] But the record he had compiled in the meantime was sufficient for the 1972 campaign. Environmental protection was one liberal issue—others included health care and social security—that McGovern could not effectively employ against Nixon.

Economic policy was the domestic area in which Nixon feared he was most vulnerable. The president's calculated use of social and cultural wedge issues in the 1970 congressional elections had been overshadowed by economic problems, hurting Republican candidates and underscoring the Democrats' traditional advantage among blue-collar voters on bread-and-butter issues. Nixon was determined that by the time he had to face the voters in November 1972, the economy would look as good as he and his advisers could possibly make it. Inflation was one of his main worries. In August 1971, this foe of government controls took a dramatic step that he personally disliked: he instituted the first system of peace-time wage-price controls in the nation's history. Although the controls generated discontent in the ranks of organized labor, they did the trick for Nixon's electoral prospects. The rate of inflation, running at 4.4 percent for the first half of 1971, fell to 3.2 percent for the election year. McGovern hit hard on the issue, but with the problem of rising prices seemingly coming under control, it did not help him much in the election. Two months after his landslide victory, Nixon relaxed the wage-price controls that had kept inflationary pressures under wraps through the election and, exacerbated by soaring food and energy prices, inflation took off again.[31]

Recession was an even larger contributor to Republicans' electoral disap-pointment in 1970 than inflation. In 1972 the Nixon administration drove the economy hard toward an expansionary surge. The president ordered govern-ment departments to spend money as quickly as they could during the first half of the year, when the effects would be felt by Election Day. The Federal Reserve helped out with an easy money policy. By the fall the economy was booming, with real GNP growing by 8.1 percent in the final quarter of the year.[32] Taking no chances, the Nixon administration also directed as much money as it could into voters' pockets during the months immediately preceding the election. In a classic work of social science analysis, *Political Control of the Economy*, Edward Tufte used Nixon as his prime example of how incumbents can manipulate eco-nomic factors before elections. He demonstrated how transfer payments—Social Security benefits, veterans' benefits, and federal grants-in-aid to state and local governments—"accelerated in late 1972 and decelerated after the election."[33] So, in 1972, voters had a choice between a dangerous, radical populist and a safe, mainstream incumbent who was spreading prosperity far and wide.

Nixon cared about foreign policy in ways that he never cared about domestic policy. His global moves in 1972 with respect to China and the Soviet Union were dictated primarily by the geopolitical design that he and Henry Kissinger were following. He was even willing to take electoral risks when his global strategy ne-cessitated them. Had his bombing of Hanoi and mining of Haiphong harbor re-sulted in Soviet cancellation of the Moscow summit, for example, it would have handed the Democrats the potent campaign argument that Nixon was jeopardiz-ing peace on a global level to prop up a failed regime in South Vietnam.[34]

Nixon fancied himself to be a master of diplomacy, but he was too much the political master to minimize the electoral implications of foreign policy. Playing the China card against the Soviets was a geopolitical gambit; traveling to China was more of a televised spectacle for the electorate. Nixon wanted the voters of 1972, as much as the historians of the future, to view him as a great statesman. Striking at Hanoi and Haiphong in the spring of 1972 positioned him as the tough and decisive commander in chief, committed to "peace with honor" instead of McGovernite "surrender."[35] Resuming negotiations with the North Vietnamese in the summer of 1972 positioned him as a shrewder negotiator than a pacifist like McGovern could ever be. McGovern owned the issue of Vietnam when he competed with a large field of rivals for the Democratic presidential nomination. But in a Gallup Poll in the fall, Nixon led McGovern by 58 percent to 26 percent on the question of who would "do a better job of dealing with the Vietnam situation."[36] McGovern's "one issue," the American disaster in Southeast Asia about which he felt the deepest anguish, belonged in electoral terms to Nixon.

Positioning on policy to serve reelection was one component of Nixon's four-year campaign for a second term. With some luck and a lot more of design, Nixon's policy choices worked in tandem in the election year to serve his interests and sink McGovern's hopes. Not all of Nixon's policy stances were designed to neutralize liberal issues so that Democrats were unable to exploit them or to burnish the president's credentials for bringing prosperity and peace. Some had a different aim: to break apart the traditional Democratic coalition and draw its disaffected constituencies over to the president's side, even if they had to share space there with their traditional adversaries.

Constructing the Nixon Majority

From the beginning of his presidency, Nixon aimed to capitalize on the divisions within the Democratic Party that had been so glaring in the 1968 campaign. He was out to construct a new majority, less for his own party than for himself. The campaign to reelect the president, eager to pull in Democrats disenchanted with McGovern, eschewed the Republican label and did almost nothing to assist the party's congressional candidates.[37]

The most notorious of Nixon's maneuvers in search of a personal majority, his "southern strategy," is so well known that it only requires a brief discussion here. The racial appeal of George Wallace, running as a third-party candidate, almost cost Nixon the election in 1968, and he was intent on wooing the Wallace voters for 1972. A number of his early presidential moves were designed to convey the message that Nixon was the South's true friend. His Department of Justice and Department of Health, Education, and Welfare delayed court-ordered school desegregation. He sought, unsuccessfully, to weaken the enforcement mechanisms of the Voting Rights Act. In another legislative failure that nonetheless enhanced his stature in the white South, he nominated two southern judges in succession for a Supreme Court vacancy and accused the Senate of "regional discrimination" when it rejected them. The "southern strategy" paid off in 1972: once Wallace had to quit the presidential race, the South was Nixon country.[38]

The president also had what can be termed a "northern strategy" to benefit from racial conflict. Busing was the charged racial issue in 1972, its impact felt more strongly in the North than in the South, its electoral potential evident in

Wallace's strong showing in several northern primaries. Nixon's goal during 1972 was not to take decisive action to block busing for racial balance but to keep the issue bubbling and on the minds of anxious white voters. Speaking out frequently against this unpopular remedy for segregated schools, he called on Congress in March 1972 to impose a moratorium on court-ordered busing. That summer, when the House Rules Committee appeared ready to support his moratorium, Nixon told his legislative aides to keep it bottled up in committee so that he could continue to exploit the issue. Decrying congressional inaction that he covertly promoted, he talked about a constitutional amendment to ban busing for civil rights purposes.[39] The symbolic appeal of a constitutional amendment that was unlikely to pass in Congress was another of his campaign stratagems that later Republican presidents running for reelection would emulate.

Nixon was no more a natural adept at ethnic politics than was McGovern. Where the McGovern campaign slighted ethnic politics, however, Nixon plunged into them, seizing a critical opportunity as the New Deal Democratic coalition crumbled. His approach to ethnics was a matter of calculation and not of sympathy. Richard Krickus, a perceptive analyst of white ethnics, captured the contradiction between the private Nixon and the president fishing for votes. On the White House tapes Nixon could be heard telling Ehrlichman, "The Italians, they're not like us . . . They smell different, act different . . . The trouble is, you can't find one who is honest." On the campaign trail in Maryland, he told a crowd that "every time I'm at an Italian-American picnic, I think I have some Italian blood."[40]

Although Nixon did little campaigning in the fall of 1972, ethnic audiences received a good share of his tightly budgeted time. A campaign trip to New York City in late September was revealing for the politics and symbolism of the new majority that Nixon was assembling. His first stop, designed for the evening news on TV, was a ceremony at the Statue of Liberty, where, as *Time* magazine reported, "he was greeted by an honor guard of exuberant children in parochial school uniforms and yarmulkes. The signs proclaimed CATHOLICS FOR NIXON or JEWS FOR NIXON." At a subsequent stop, he met privately with conservative Jewish leaders. Nixon's day ended with a $1,000 a plate dinner in Manhattan that raised $1.6 million for his campaign.[41]

Nixon had two issues that were aimed at the Catholic (and the orthodox Jewish) ethnics: parochial school aid and abortion. The president's right-wing advisers, Patrick Buchanan among them, urged him to go after moderate-income and socially conservative Catholic voters by endorsing what William Safire dubbed "parochaid." Nixon agreed, and he emphasized his position before Catholic audiences even after the Supreme Court had ruled such aid to be unconstitutional. On abortion, which was just then emerging as the religious flashpoint in American politics, Nixon sent a letter to New York's Terence Cardinal Cooke in spring 1972, hailing the cardinal's effort to repeal the state's recently liberalized abortion statute. Contrary to Nixon's insistence on devolution and states' rights in other policy areas, he saw no problem with opposing state legislation on the subject of abortion. The campaign appearances and the targeted issue appeals paid off at the polls in 1972: Nixon doubled his support among Jews from 1968 and pulled majorities among Catholics and white ethnic groups.[42]

Along with race and religion, Nixon used class to construct his new majority. To appeal to the white working class, the cornerstone of the New Deal coalition, he exploited the issue of welfare. The Nixon presidency was a historic moment of transition in the politics of welfare. At the start of his term the president attempted, with his Family Assistance Plan, to outdo the Democrats in solving the problem of poverty in America. But once his income support program stalled in Congress, mistrusted by liberals and conservatives alike, and once he sensed that many white workers were increasingly resentful of welfare benefits, especially for minorities, he reversed course and used the issue to blast McGovern. In his first campaign speech on radio, written by Safire, Nixon aligned himself with the "work ethic" ingrained in traditional American morality while associating McGovern with the slothful "welfare ethic" of the 1960s.[43] His campaign ads, run through Democrats for Nixon, drove home the contrast with arresting visuals.

Unlike his feigned identification with ethnics, Nixon's turn to the working class was not purely instrumental. Although he had been a lifelong probusiness and antiunion Republican, his reaction to the 1960s was similar to that of the more conservative labor leaders, and he shared many of their resentments. As the McGovern insurgency brought college-educated activists, many from the top universities, to power in the Democratic Party, Nixon sought to move his own party in the opposite direction. In a memo to Haldeman on administration appointments, the president directed him to "quit recruiting from any of the Ivy League schools or any other universities where either the president or faculty have taken action condemning our efforts to bring the war in Vietnam to an end."[44] The 1960s confirmed Nixon's longstanding hostility to the Eastern "establishment" but brought him a new feeling of affinity with working-class leadership. He wrote in his diary in September 1972,

> The American leader class has really had it in terms of their ability to lead. It's really sickening to have to receive them at the White House as I often do and to hear them whine and whimper and that's one of the reasons why I enjoy very much more receiving labor leaders and people from middle America who still have character and guts and a bit of patriotism.
>
> The meeting with the labor leaders was the best of all. They were friendly, all out, and I hope we can find a way to see that this alliance is not broken immediately after the election . . . Frankly, I have more in common with them from a personal standpoint than does McGovern or the intellectuals generally.[45]

Nixon's strongest official ally in the ranks of organized labor was Teamsters president Frank Fitzsimmons. Fitzsimmons loyally backed and amply rewarded the president for his friendly stance toward the crime-riddled union, including a pardon for its imprisoned ex-president, Jimmy Hoffa, who still had nine years to serve on his sentence for jury tampering.[46] But the most important, if covert, union ally of the president in 1972 was the head of the AFL-CIO: George Meany. Even as Meany cut off communication with McGovern, he used Secretary of the Treasury George Shultz as an intermediary to contact Nixon. A month before the Democratic convention, Meany informed the White House through Shultz that he would not support McGovern in the fall under any circumstances.[47] Nixon cozied up personally to Meany with golf, drinks, and cigars after the convention. The White House, delighted by the "neutrality" of the AFL-CIO, kept up its courtship of Meany. After the union chieftain blasted McGovern as an apologist for communism in a television interview, White House aide Charles Colson, Nixon's top player at political hardball, sent a handwritten letter of appreciation. "Having watched your performance on *Face the Nation* yesterday," Colson wrote to Meany, "I simply would like you to know that I consider you a great patriot— one of the greatest of our times—and a man of honesty, courage, and conviction."[48]

The McGovern campaign bore some responsibility for the Democrats' loss of working-class voters. Yet it was up against a president who publicly manipulated white working-class resentments of the poor and the black and who colluded in private with labor leaders who slighted their members' economic interests in their anger about opposition to the war in Vietnam and the cultural upheaval at home. The unprecedented defection of blue-collar voters from the Democratic presidential ticket in 1972 was a key marker of McGovern's problems, but it was also a testament to the strategic accomplishment of President Nixon.

Pulling many of its constituent elements—the white South, white ethnics, Catholics, conservative sectors of organized labor—away from the New Deal coalition, Nixon constructed a personal majority for the 1972 election and beyond. He did not have the opportunity to take advantage of the rise of evangelical Christians; that would come later and became integral to the Reagan revolution in 1980. Yet with the exception of this constituency, for which he had laid essential groundwork with his antiabortion stance, his personal majority was ripening to become a Republican majority. What McGovern faced in 1972 was the forerunner of what his Democratic successors, starting with Carter in 1980, would have to face.

The Dirty Campaign

With President Nixon inaccessible to the press, secure inside a campaign cocoon, his team of "surrogates" mounted a steady attack on McGovern. Republican surrogates accused McGovern of so many follies and failings that anyone believing all of their words would have concluded that the Democrats had nominated a crackpot for president. Secretary of Defense Melvin Laird dubbed McGovern's defense proposals a "white flag surrender budget," reflecting a "philosophy of give away now, beg later."[49] Secretary of State William Rogers claimed that McGovern's position on Vietnam would give "our adversaries exactly what they want without any negotiation."[50] Secretary of Health, Education, and Welfare Elliot Richardson described McGovern's revised welfare proposal as "both costly and scatterbrained."[51]

While these scattershot charges were flying at McGovern, Vice President Agnew leveled a broadside against the Democratic insurgent in his inimitable fashion. McGovern, in Agnew's words, was "one of the greatest frauds ever to be considered as a presidential candidate by a major American party." The senator from South Dakota was a second Neville Chamberlain, "an apostle of appeasement." In a McGovern presidency, Agnew predicted, the United States would not have much of a national defense, but "there'd be plenty of pornography . . . and plenty of pot."[52]

Once McGovern sought to pick up campaign momentum from the Watergate affair, Robert Dole, the chairman of the Republican National Committee, became one of Nixon's most visible spokesmen. In essence, Dole's role was to muddy the waters by suggesting that McGovern's claims about White House involvement in the Watergate break-in were unproven—and that even if some of his talk about corruption in the Nixon administration turned out to be true, he was just as guilty of the same kinds of misdeeds in his own political career. In mid-September, when only the seven men first implicated for the Watergate crime were indicted, Dole demanded that McGovern and his campaign staff apologize: "As we knew all along, and as the grand jury has now determined, there is no evidence to substantiate any of the wild and slanderous statements McGovern has been making about many high officials in the Nixon administration. I would expect McGovern to stop trying to make a political issue out of this matter."[53]

As McGovern was about to deliver his nationally televised speech on Nixon's corruption in late October, Dole launched a preemptive strike with a flurry of allegations about the challenger's own supposed skeletons. His lead charge was the result of a series of conversations in the Oval Office two months earlier. Unhappy about press reports of illegal contributions to his campaign, Nixon asked Haldeman and Ehrlichman, "Are we looking over McGovern's financial contributors? . . . Who is running the IRS? Who is running over at Justice Department? What I mean is, with all the agencies of government, what in the name of God are we doing about the McGovern contributors?"[54] The three men soon fixed on Henry Kimelman, finance director of the McGovern campaign, as their chief target. The wealthy Kimelman had extensive business interests in the Virgin Islands, and in the search for a scandal, Ehrlichman obtained an Interior Department file on Kimelman and pored over it.[55]

A Republican National Committee press release, headlined "Dole Questions McGovern Credentials to Lecture Nation on Morality in Government," featured the fruits of Ehrlichman's "research." It stated that "Henry Kimelman, Senator McGovern's chief fundraiser, closest political adviser, and personal confidante, is a multimillionaire who was caught up in conflict-of-interest charges resulting from his tenure as personal assistant to former Secretary of the Interior Stewart Udall." Alleging that Kimelman had influenced Udall to make a decision on the site of a new airport for the Virgin Islands that increased the value of the finance director's property holdings, Dole complained that "Senator McGovern has never repudiated Kimelman for his direct activity in trying to bilk the taxpayers for personal profit." Following the purported Kimelman scandal was a hash of half-baked charges against McGovern. Some reached so desperately for intimations of immorality that they became unintentionally comic. Dole cited a 1971 column by Jack Anderson that reported that "Senator McGovern exchanged a used Chevrolet for a brand new Pontiac in 1965 without paying any difference in cost." He stated that "McGovern forces once bribed an Indian chief to have a vision favorable to McGovern's 1968 re-election campaign." In his conclusion Dole warned prospective viewers of McGovern's television broadcast that "we are going to get nothing but massive cover-up activities to gloss over a record of highly questionable conduct in personal and political affairs."[56]

This drumbeat of defamation was the public side of the attack on McGovern by Nixon's minions. The underside of the Nixon campaign was the work of its dirty tricks operatives. The political sabotaging of the Muskie campaign and the political surveillance of the Democratic National Committee offices at the Watergate complex receive most of the attention in the numerous accounts of the Watergate scandal. But once McGovern emerged as Nixon's likely opponent late in the spring of 1972, he and his campaign organization came in for their share of clandestine assaults by the president's agents. With plenty of its own troubles to handle after the California primary put it in reach of the presidential nomination, the McGovern campaign also had to cope with spying, sabotage, and the subversion of its message.

As a liberal insurgency, committed to a more open politics and teeming with volunteer workers, the McGovern campaign was especially vulnerable to dirty tricks. Even when McGovernites grew suspicious of some of the people in their midst, they lacked the time or the means to mount more than a primitive system of campaign security. After the election, when Frank Mankiewicz, researching a book on Nixon, wrote to his former colleagues for suspicious incidents, Harold Himmelman responded with one that highlighted the McGovernites' security difficulties:

In late May [or] early June, a very strange looking person appeared in the 410 First Street headquarters for a couple of days. He appeared to be casing the place. We had him watched by the private security guard we had hired (not terribly effective) and I think he finally disappeared. We did not have the fellow thrown out because if all strange looking people who worked in that headquarters were thrown out we would have lost 90% of the staff.[57]

The Nixon campaign's spying operation, greased by a huge slush fund, was more extensive than the McGovernites realized, although it was not always effective. About the time of the episode recalled by Himmelman, G. Gordon Liddy reconnoitered McGovern headquarters, planning a break-in so that he could plant a bug. Before he could put his plan into effect, however, he was ordered to concentrate on the DNC offices of Lawrence O'Brien.[58] One of Howard Hunt's young operatives, a plant in the Muskie campaign early in the campaign season, was shifted to McGovern's headquarters once his insurgency took off. However, as Haldeman related to Nixon, this young man "finally broke off with Hunt because he refused to bug Gary Hart's telephone."[59] A more successful Nixon spy against McGovern was Lucianne Goldberg. Hired by Murray Chotiner, Nixon's mentor in hardball politics, and paid $1,000 a week for her services, Goldberg posed as a journalist for the Women's News Service and traveled with the McGovern campaign in the fall. She provided a bizarre link between the troubles of McGovern and the troubles of his Texas co-coordinator, Bill Clinton, a quarter-century later: she was Linda Tripp's confidante and literary agent as Tripp collected material to expose the scandalous affair between President Clinton and Monica Lewinsky.[60]

During and after the campaign the McGovernites compiled a substantial list of possible sabotage by Nixon operatives. Quotations of an embarrassing nature appeared in the media, supposedly from unnamed McGovern aides but not traceable to anyone on the campaign staff. Someone impersonating Gary Hart phoned AFL-CIO headquarters and rudely insisted that he be put through to George Meany. Another imposter, posing as McGovern's buyer of television airtime, called CBS hours before a scheduled McGovern broadcast and claimed that his campaign was canceling the event.[61] Sabotage of McGovern campaign transportation was often suspected. According to scheduler Tony Podesta, an unknown caller persuaded the company supplying McGovern's buses in Dallas to change the arrival time at the campaign's hotel from 8 A.M. to 8 P.M., and the candidate's trip was "completely screwed up."[62] According to another campaign aide, William Heckman, someone tampered with the engines of fifteen to twenty buses parked outside the Cow Palace in San Francisco, site of a massive McGovern indoor rally, resulting in "a fantastic traffic jam."[63]

Probably the most significant element in the often petty subversion of the McGovern campaign was the fabrication of radical images to support Nixon's definition of his challenger's political identity. McGovern staff in California came across one scurrilous publication reporting that Charles Manson had endorsed the insurgent and a second depicting Abbie Hoffman and Jerry Rubin, the leftist Yippie pranksters, "pitching in" to assist McGovern.[64] The candidate himself noticed many odd occurrences during his campaign appearances that he now believes to have been "orchestrated by the dirty tricks people." At a televised rally at American University, "right behind me was a couple carrying a big banner with hammer and sickle, saying 'McGovern for President.' That had to be a Nixon operation . . . There would be no bona fide McGovern supporters that would hold up a hammer and sickle."[65] Nixon had told his aides that McGovern must never be allowed to come across as a moderate and must "always appear to be a fanatical, dedicated leftist extremist." Crudely, but not without effect, his agents carried out his orders.

Conclusion

Theodore White's final volume in his *Making of the President* series was marred by an Establishment insider's palpable admiration for Nixon and disdain for McGovern. Yet White was correct in claiming that it was Nixon who captured "the spirit of the times" in 1972.[66] With American involvement in Vietnam declining and with ghetto riots and campus revolts receding into the past, the tumult of the 1960s was almost over, and the McGovern campaign, representing that decade's last rebellious upsurge, encountered an electorate whose majority seemed tired of change. The public, William Safire wrote with satisfaction, "wanted stability after years of shocks . . . and that is what Nixon was giving them, not what McGovern promised them."[67] President Nixon elicited little love—leaders with the harsh features of order seldom do—but he supplied the majority of Americans with what they preferred in 1972.

Nixon would have defeated McGovern even if he had run the cleanest of campaigns. Indeed, the president's electoral assets proved to be so formidable that, as most commentators agreed afterward, he would have beaten anyone in the original Democratic field. Where his attack politics mattered was in driving up the margin of his victory over McGovern to historic dimensions. Since it was the landslide, and not the mere fact of defeat, that stigmatized McGovern and his wing of the Democratic Party, the repercussions for the reputation of liberalism were considerable.

Despite the enduring fascination of the Watergate scandal, McGovern continues to draw almost all of the criticism for what went wrong with his campaign in 1972. The mistakes that he and his staff made cannot be explained away, but they can be placed in the context of the extraordinary opposition that plagued him. Nixon's strategic mastery—and utter ruthlessness—need to be reckoned with when we assess McGovern's insurgency. They do not remove blame from McGovern's shoulders. But they do mitigate his failings.

Reconstructing Nixon's strategy for 1972 is essential for more than a reevaluation of the McGovern campaign. The master's campaign against McGovern became a seminal text for attack politics. It taught his Republican successors how to neutralize or co-opt issues normally belonging to liberals. It instructed them on how to play the cards of race, religion, and class to divide the Democrats and pull together a Republican electoral majority. It demonstrated the value of distancing the upstanding presidential candidate from surrogates who could slime his opponent (it was surrogates who disseminated the Willie Horton ads in 1988 and the Swift Boat ads in 2004). Several of McGovern's Democratic successors—Dukakis, Gore, and Kerry particularly come to mind—searched for the political center to avoid what happened during the liberals' moment. They were blasted nonetheless by attacks modeled on the ones that helped to do in McGovern during his 1972 campaign.

PART III

The Identity Crisis of the Democratic Party

11

Excavating the Landslide

By Election Day 1972, George McGovern and his campaign aides knew that they were going to lose to Richard Nixon. But none of them anticipated that they would be trounced in one of the largest landslides in the history of presidential elections. How the news reached McGovern—and how he took it—is the subject of a tragicomic anecdote in his autobiography:

> At six o'clock, I decided to take a nap in my room at the Sioux Falls Holiday Inn. I asked Jeff Smith [his aide-de-camp] to wake me when the returns were showing a clear trend. Less than two hours later, his eyes brimming with tears, he knocked on the door and told me that it was all over—that I would probably lose every state except Massachusetts and the District of Columbia. I hugged Eleanor and then tried to console Jeff. "No one really loses an effort in which he has stood up for what is decent," I told him. "Well," he replied tearfully, "that's easy for you to say, but what about the rest of us?" I have been teasing him about that response ever since.[1]

McGovern maintained his composure throughout this moment of bitter defeat. In a graceful concession speech, he paid tribute to the insurgency that had carried him to surprising success before humbling collapse:

> It does hurt all of us in this auditorium and many others across the country to lose, but we are not going to shed any tears tonight about the great joys that this campaign has brought to us over the past two years . . . We have found the greatest outpouring of energy and love that any political effort has ever inspired, at least in my lifetime.

And he held onto the faith that even in defeat the campaign had promoted its highest goal:

> There can be no question at all that we have pushed this country in the direction of peace, and I think each of us loves the title of peacemaker more than any office in the land . . . I want every single one of you to remember, and never forget it, that if we pushed the day of peace just one day closer, then every minute and every hour and every bone-crushing effort in this campaign was worth the entire sacrifice.[2]

On the plane returning to Washington the next day, McGovern was still laboring to cheer up his followers. Aide Rob Gunnison had his picture taken with McGovern and his wife; he doesn't remember what McGovern said to him that instant, but he does recall—and the picture shows—that McGovern "had me in hysterics . . . he cracked me up . . . The man was unbelievable to be able to do that . . . You would have thought he just whipped Nixon by fifteen points."[3]

For the mostly youthful McGovernites, their leader's composure was beyond their reach. Some reacted to the galling defeat with defiance. Organizing for McGovern in Youngstown, Ohio, Jamie Galbraith assured a large throng at the local campaign headquarters that "we would carry on . . . We had been defeated but we had not been deterred."[4] Defiance, however, could easily give way to despair. Many McGovernites considered the campaign a crusade to end the war and drive out a genuinely evil president, and now on election night, as Jeff Smith put it, "it's fucking Nixon in there again for another four years. I mean, how can this be? Will the country survive?"[5] The nightmare of "four more years" of a Nixon presidency was only compounded by the depressing revelation that a large majority of Americans favored it.

Most of all, there were copious tears shed for the collapse of their dreams. Barbara Holum, one of the original McGovernites, was horrified that night that there would be "four more years of Nixon and Kissinger and these awful, dishonest people." Holum—a Clinton appointee as a commissioner of the Commodities Future Trading Commission when I interviewed her in 2002—told me that she "went into the back room and cried," and as she relived the experience its emotions came back in her eyes and voice.[6] Another early McGovern aide, campaign treasurer Marian Pearlman Nease, invited young volunteers to her apartment to watch the election returns, and she "spent the whole night consoling all these inconsolable people who had worked their hearts out and couldn't understand how this could possibly have happened." She was only thirty-two, but that night "I felt like I was a hundred years old."[7]

McGovernites were devastated by the landslide defeat, but they were mostly young and bounced back quickly, with a significant number heading for important careers in public life. The pain remained with the one who had hidden it best on election night: the candidate. Chief speechwriter John Holum observes that the massive defeat "affected [McGovern] afterwards profoundly. It was a crushing personal blow, to be defeated—and to be defeated in South Dakota. That hurt him a great deal."[8] Several decades later, one can still feel the pain in McGovern's words when he discusses the election's outcome:

> There are some things that are worse than losing an election. It's hard to think what they are on Election Day . . . On election night all you can think of is the loss. What I could see for days after that were those hands reaching up, you know, on a platform or the back of a train or on the back of a truck.

Just to touch you. Or people holding their children up. That's what you see, and you think, I've let them down.[9]

The Dimensions of Defeat

Few McGovernites felt that their candidate had let them down. But many other Democrats, especially those who had opposed his nomination, charged McGovern with this failing, both at the time and in later years. McGovern's landslide defeat in 1972 became a negative touchstone for Democrats, a grim warning sign of what would happen to the party if it let its liberal wing prevail again.

The presidential election of 1972 was among the most one-sided contests in history, with Nixon's win comparable to the massive victories of Franklin Roosevelt over Alf Landon in 1936 and Lyndon Johnson over Barry Goldwater in 1964. Yet 1972 was, in another dimension, oddly unlike these predecessors. In the presidential balloting, Nixon pulled 60.7 percent of the popular vote to McGovern's 37.5 percent, with minor candidates receiving the remainder. The margin in the Electoral College was equally overwhelming: Nixon took 521 votes and McGovern 17. Massachusetts and the District of Columbia alone went for the Democrat, and in only three additional states—Minnesota, Rhode Island, and South Dakota—were the results even reasonably close.[10]

However, 1972 was not a landslide victory—indeed not a victory at all—for the Republican Party below the presidential level. In FDR's and LBJ's reelection cakewalks, their party had shared in their successes, racking up major gains for Congress, in which they already held majorities. By contrast, Nixon's triumph was a solitary one. Democrats in Congress retained solid majorities in both chambers in the 1972 elections, with Republicans picking up only twelve seats in the House and actually dropping two in the Senate.[11] The president enjoyed no party mandate in 1972 for a new political agenda. On the contrary, he still faced hostility from a Democratic Congress that was about to look into those peculiar events at the Watergate during the campaign.

These split results in 1972 only added to McGovern's embarrassment. To be sure, dire predictions by his adversaries at the convention that he would drag the Democratic ticket down from top to bottom had not been vindicated. Even so, the fact that other Democrats survived or even flourished while McGovern was floundering made his rejection by the voters appear all the more personal. Coming after Humphrey's defeat in 1968, in which he had polled only 42.7 percent of the popular vote, it was clear that the problems of the Democratic Party in winning presidential elections were not limited to McGovern. Nonetheless, the much larger size of McGovern's loss made him a certain target for recriminations. In the immediate aftermath of the election, the dominant tone in verdicts on his candidacy was one of scorn.

Scorn

Since Richard Nixon elicited little admiration from most pundits, the brunt of commentary on the election results was not to praise the president's clever re-election strategy but to dwell on McGovern's defects as a candidate. McGovern stood accused not merely of proving an inept campaigner but of possessing an unappealing personality as well. As columnist Chalmers Roberts wrote, in a not untypical assessment, two days after the election, "It was a lackluster affair, heavy with boredom." What had been advertised by both candidates as one of the clearest choices of the century between conflicting ideologies had, instead, descended into a comparison of personal characteristics, and in this comparison it was McGovern who was found sadly wanting. No wonder, Roberts opined, that so many voters had tuned out the race, resulting in the lowest turnout—55 percent—for any presidential election year since 1948.[12]

Most in the media swiftly wrote off McGovern as a loser. When he or his campaign managers put forward exculpatory evidence, pointing to the forces that had combined against them to generate a landslide, their arguments were dismissed as "alibis."[13] A rare exception to the general condemnation of McGovern's campaign was the editorial page of the *New York Times*, one of the few newspapers that had endorsed him: "In defeat, Senator George McGovern remains an admirable and respected figure. He waged a gallant and often lonely campaign, never losing confidence in his own prospects or, more important, in the rightness of his vision of America."[14]

The most predictable putdowns of McGovern came from gleeful Nixon men. An op-ed piece in the *New York Times* by Nixon speechwriter Aram Bakshian Jr. dripped with contempt:

> George McGovern's future as a national candidate die[d] on Nov. 7, but so did McGovernism—the New Left philosophy behind the man. Both perished from the same cause . . . because so much of the McGovernite philosophy goes against the grain of the American character . . . It was a basic "gut" feeling on the part of the electorate that the McGovernites rejected a number of root social and moral values shared by most Americans . . . Ever since the Puritans lost their grip on New England . . . our people have been suspicious of individuals or movements that bustle about telling us all how rotten we are (and by implication, how morally superior our denouncers are). As the McGovernites grew more and more shrill in their attacks on the President, men and women who were never avid enthusiasts of Richard Nixon began to take offense.[15]

Bakshian's blast at the McGovernites foreshadowed a generation of Republican rhetoric about unpatriotic and snobbish liberals. Nonpartisan critics avoided his sweeping judgment of Democrats, but they were often nearly as scornful of

McGovern personally. In a postelection column, David Broder of the *Washington Post* elaborated on the common theme that McGovern was the Democratic Barry Goldwater. Expressing his view that McGovern's most profound flaw was his naiveté, Broder's analysis ended with an argument about the presidency that would prove painfully quaint once the Watergate scandal exploded a few months later.

> What Goldwater and McGovern had in common—and what defeated both so resoundingly—was that in the course of their campaigns, the voters came to the same conclusion that political and journalistic Washington had previously reached: that they were lightweights in the heavyweight division of presidential politics. They were men of good heart and good spirit, open and honorable, whose failing was their tendency to see public questions in one-dimensional, almost simplistic terms. And because the presidency is a place where only the complex, multi-faceted questions come to decision, it is a place where moralizing and oversimplification are terribly dangerous. Somehow, the American people know this and reject those who lack the essential subtlety, skepticism, and—I suppose—deviousness the presidency requires.[16]

Theories of Disaster

Once campaign participants and outside observers had time to review the events of the contest and pick through the data generated on Election Day, they arrived at several different though sometimes overlapping explanations for the Nixon landslide. Nixon supporters and Old Guard Democratic opponents of McGovern took part in the disputes about what had happened—and what it meant—but the most anguished theoreticians in examining the disaster were the McGovernites themselves. The conflicting theories advanced important insights into the 1972 election, but they also were, inevitably, colored by personal interests and ideological biases.

McGovern's opponents favored an ideological explanation for the landslide. The Democratic insurgent, argued both Republicans and regular Democrats, had misread the mood of the American people and mistakenly offered them a left-wing vision alien to their values and aspirations. Speaking at a conference on the campaign held at Harvard in January 1973, Ben Wattenberg, Scoop Jackson's top adviser and a fierce critic of the McGovern wing of the Democratic Party, argued that the electorate, rather than being bored and indifferent in 1972, had made a thoughtful decision:

> I would say that what happened substantively in this election was that there was the equivalent of a referendum in this country. It was a referendum on

the so-called cultural revolution that has been going on allegedly for four or five years in this country. It involved many, many facets—busing and defense and welfare and all sorts of things—and a perception of whether this country was doing pretty well or teetering on the brink of failure. If there was going to be an election on something in this country, this was a pretty good thing to have an election on. And the American people voted no on what the whole "new politics" movement was about.[17]

In the McGovern camp, the candidate and political director Frank Mankiewicz also tended to explain the electoral outcome in ideological terms—albeit much darker ones that cast the worst onus elsewhere. In postelection interviews, McGovern acknowledged that his platform had only appealed to a minority among the electorate.[18] But he continued to assail Nixon, as he had during the campaign, for playing upon "the fears and anxieties of the people."[19] The most potent of these fears and anxieties concerned race. "There wasn't a lot of talk about racial prejudice," McGovern told Hunter Thompson, "but I think it was there. There were all kinds of ways . . . of tapping that prejudice. The busing issue was the most pronounced one, but also the attacking on the welfare program and the way the President handled that issue. I think he was orchestrating a lot of things that were designed to tap the Wallace voters, and he got most of them."[20] Mankiewicz concurred with this analysis, telling a television interviewer that the main reason blue-collar ethnic voters had turned against McGovern, as they had against other Democratic candidates before him, was the racial tension of the past decade, skillfully exploited by Nixon.[21]

An alternative theory out of the McGovern camp explained the landslide, as Thompson put it, in "two words: *Eagleton and competence*."[22] Campaign manager Gary Hart and pollster Patrick Caddell believed that it was negative perceptions of their candidate, emerging after the Democratic convention, that destroyed his chances. "I'll go to my grave," Hart said at the Harvard conference, "thinking that this election was decided on the issue of who was competent, who had those characteristics of leadership that people generally think should be in the White House."[23] Caddell emphasized the devastating fallout from the Eagleton affair: his surveys suggested that it had prevented disgruntled Democrats from coming back to their party at the end of the campaign, as happened in 1968, and particularly alienated young voters who lost faith in McGovern as a different kind of political figure.[24]

Two other factors besides ideology and personality received some attention in the postelection debate, although both were seen as supplemental and not central in explaining the landslide. The first was the advantages of incumbency. As Gordon Weil observed, only two incumbent presidents in the twentieth century, William Howard Taft and Herbert Hoover, had been defeated for reelection, and the circumstances that had undermined them—a party bolt for the first and a depression for the second—were absent in 1972. On the contrary, "Nixon had reversed most of the failures of his first three years in office in his last year."[25] A second contributory cause for McGovern's downfall was the fracture within the Democratic Party. As Weil pointed out later, too many regular Democrats were never reconciled to McGovern's candidacy; content to see him lose, they "sat on their hands" during the fall contest.[26]

These competing theories about the 1972 landslide can be at least partially tested by empirical evidence. Before doing so, however, it is worth pointing out that each theory was, in a sense, a mode of self-justification: in putting forward their explanations, the participants in the debate deflected blame and preserved the positions they personally favored. The ideological theory advanced by conservative Democrats like Wattenberg and by Nixon Republicans had, as will be seen shortly, considerable support in the election data. But public perceptions of McGovern as far to the left were, in part, a product of the shrewd and sometimes crass efforts from the Jackson and Humphrey campaigns in the primaries and from the Nixon White House in the fall to construct a radical caricature of the senator from South Dakota. The focus on racism, although important, left in the shadows the nonracial aspects of McGovern's liberalism that the electorate might have rejected. The personality theory, too, had substantial support from the data, but it was also useful in pinpointing McGovern's character as the problem and leaving his aides and his ideology without much tarnish. Talk of incumbency advantages and hostility from regular Democrats, regardless of its validity, was exculpatory evidence if one wanted to let McGovern and his followers off the hook.

Testing the Theories

Fortunately, abundant data exist to test the relative validity of these competing theories. The most extensive empirical investigation of the 1972 election, upon which I have drawn heavily, was conducted by political scientist Arthur H. Miller and three of his colleagues at the University of Michigan, and published the following year as *A Majority Party in Disarray: Policy Polarization in the 1972 Election*. The seventh in a series of such studies of presidential elections from the Michigan Survey Research Center, the 1972 research sampled 2,705 eligible voters, interviewed once during the fall contest and a second time right after Election Day.[27] Other political scientists and political analysts, using the Michigan research or other data sets, have also added to our knowledge of what the electorate was saying in 1972.

Major historical events seldom have single causes, and so it is not surprising that all of the competing theories advanced after the 1972 election find empirical support in the data. As its title suggested, the Michigan study, like the conservative critics of McGovern, placed primary emphasis on ideology. "Not only was this an issue election," wrote Miller and his coauthors, "but it may more appropriately be labeled an ideological election."[28] The critical ideological split, they observed, was not between Democrats and Republicans but between liberals and conservatives within the Democratic Party. It was the defection of self-identified Democrats, variously estimated by scholars at a 37–42 percent rate, that doomed McGovern to a landslide loss. And for these defecting Democrats, one striking finding of the research was that they placed themselves considerably closer to Nixon than to McGovern on an ideological scale and on most issue scales.[29] Political scientist David G. Lawrence argued on the basis of his data examination that it was the "Democratic lurch to the left [that] produced a situation in which the party was ideologically out of touch . . . with centrist Democrats."[30]

Racism, suggested by McGovern and Mankiewicz as a hidden key to the scope of the landslide, is not as evident in the data. As Lawrence observed, the explicitly racial issues that had played so large a part in the presidential elections of 1964 and 1968 were less visible and salient by 1972. Apart from busing, civil rights was not a prominent question before the electorate in the Nixon-McGovern contest.[31] However, a racial component to the landslide cannot be dismissed merely because it does not stand out in the survey research. That most of the voters whose first choice in 1972 was Wallace eventually went for Nixon is suggestive. So, too, is the finding that the Democrats were perceived as quite far to the left on race in 1972, indeed as more radical in supporting racial change than in the changes they were proposing in foreign policy or cultural matters.[32]

"Eagleton and competence," highlighted by Hart and Caddell as principal sources of the disaster, were also prominent factors in the data. In the Michigan study, 69 percent of respondents judged McGovern's handling of the Eagleton affair negatively, and three-fourths of these voters supported Nixon. The Democrat's overall campaign performance was also viewed critically, especially among the oldest and youngest age cohorts and the less educated. McGovern was exceptionally unpopular among Wallace voters. He was, as Miller and his coauthors noted, "the least popular Democratic presidential candidate of the past twenty years. Even among Democrats the overall reaction to McGovern was not positive, but neutral."[33]

One problem in assessing the relative weights of ideological and personality factors in explaining the landslide is that neither explanation paid sufficient attention to the role of Richard Nixon. Although some of Nixon's advantages as an incumbent were noted by all sides, the complete array of his electoral assets was known only to the president and his minions until the Watergate cover-up unraveled. Even in what was in full public view, the president's strengths were underestimated by most commentators at the time. It was common in 1972 to claim that the public had been forced to choose between two unlikable candidates. By the time of the election, however, Nixon was a relatively popular president. Using the measuring stick of a "feeling thermometer," which registers the emotions of a sample of voters, the Michigan political scientists found that he was the most well-liked political leader in the country in 1972, a full ten degrees above Ted Kennedy, in second place, and sixteen degrees above McGovern.[34]

The impact of the bitter divisions within the Democratic Party was poorly measured by the survey research for the 1972 campaign. Interview respondents were not asked about how they reacted to the controversial Democratic convention at Miami Beach. Working-class Democrats, who defected from their party in unprecedented numbers, were not questioned about the significance of Hubert Humphrey's attacks and George Meany's diatribes on McGovern.

In the end, the clash of theories about the 1972 landslide, although it generated some valuable light on the event, was somewhat artificial. All of the theories, it might be concluded, were interconnected. In fact, there was a circular flow between them. McGovern's left-center strategy, as argued earlier, had the unintended effect of shaping an image of inconsistency and vacillation. Even the Eagleton fiasco, insofar as Eagleton was a hasty choice at the convention by a candidate and staff exhausted by diehard opposition from the Old Guard of the party, had its roots in the ideological passions of the internecine conflict. Perceptions during the fall campaign of McGovern as indecisive and inept only made Nixon more popular by comparison, emphasizing his strong leadership and relegating his reputation for deviousness and rancor to the background. In turn, Nixon had ample means, from money to covert action, to paint McGovern in the most lurid ideological colors possible. McGovern's ideology and character, racial animosity, the president's strengths, the Democratic Party's weaknesses—all of them combined in 1972 to generate a landslide victory for Nixon.

Omens

Data from the 1972 elections can be examined not only to interpret the Nixon landslide but to search out omens for subsequent elections. One ominous sign for Democrats in the data was the defection of blue-collar and ethnic voters, especially Catholic ethnics. Drawing from exit polls, *Newsweek* reported a large drop in the Democratic presidential vote among the Italians and the Irish.[35] Political scientist Richard Rubin observed that McGovern "received only 46 percent of the Catholic vote and 48 percent of the labor union vote—the first time since the New Deal that these two key electoral groups supported a Republican over a Democratic presidential candidate." But if the old New Deal coalition was crumbling, the ideology and personality of McGovern were hardly the sole sources. "McGovern's candidacy," Rubin continued, "can only share the responsibility for losses among Catholics and organized labor, since the support of these core groups of the New Deal realignment has been weakening for over two decades."[36] Many blue-collar and Catholic ethnic voters were soured on the Democratic Party in 1972, the data suggested, not because of economic issues but due to the salience in that election of patriotism and cultural controversy.

A second and equally ominous trend for Democrats that accelerated in 1972 was the partisan transformation of the South. In 1968 Humphrey had lost every ex-Confederate state but Texas, but after four years of Nixon's "southern strategy," McGovern did not come close even there. With Wallace off the ballot in 1972, and with the vast majority of his southern supporters switching to Nixon, the South was the president's strongest electoral bastion. Theodore White noted that "of the eight states which gave the president 70 percent of their vote or better in 1972, all but Nebraska and Oklahoma were in Dixie."[37] McGovern's remaining Democratic supporters in the South were mostly black. An anecdote in Bill Clinton's autobiography is apropos: flying south as a McGovern staffer, Clinton conversed with a young man from Jackson, Mississippi, who announced disapprovingly: "You're the only white person I've ever met for McGovern!"[38]

Racial issues played a more subsidiary part in 1972 than in the three previous presidential elections, but the electorate was no less racially divided. In a post-election survey, pollster Louis Harris found that whites had broken 2–1 for Nixon and blacks had voted over 4–1 for McGovern.[39] Democratic support for the civil rights movement during the 1960s had given the party a moral claim on black voters. Now, with so many whites deserting the Democrats, loyal blacks had a claim of their own to make on the party.

Democratic problems with workers, ethnics, the South, and race were apparent to almost every political observer in 1972. But there were more subtle indicators in the data that almost no one noticed until much later. The McGovern insurgency brought emerging social forces to power in the Democratic Party, and compared to the old New Deal coalition these new activists, not only younger but more highly educated and more gender-inclusive, represented the Democratic coalition of the future. In their 2002 book, John Judis and Ruy Teixeira argue that what they predict will be *The Emerging Democratic Majority* can be considered "George McGovern's revenge." The working-class defection from McGovern in 1972, they show, was gendered: working women, a fast-growing demographic, favored McGovern by 13 percent more than did working men. Highly educated professionals, another category whose proportion of the electorate was rising, were also in the process of shifting toward the Democrats in 1972: McGovern received 42 percent of the vote from this constituency, well above his overall percentage and 6 percent better than Humphrey had done among professionals four years earlier.[40]

The data also contained important information about the issues that most mattered in 1972 and thereafter. Although McGovern had come under fire as a radical populist for his tax reform and guaranteed job proposals, on the issue of economic management the surveys suggested that he actually held the advantage.[41] Nixon may have pumped up the economy for 1972 and staunched inflation with wage-price controls, but it appears that some voters still held his shaky record as an economic manager against him. Republican gains in this area awaited Jimmy Carter's travails and Ronald Reagan's tax-cut elixir. That McGovern did reasonably well on economics despite the downward trajectory of his campaign was an indication that the Democrats' long-standing image as the party of working people continued to possess appeal.

Foreign policy, however, was more salient than economic policy in the 1972 contest, and on this subject Nixon held a substantial lead in the surveys over McGovern.[42] International affairs had tended to favor Republican over Democratic presidential candidates since the time of the Korean War. With Nixon's trips to the People's Republic of China and the Soviet Union, with his calculated mixture of peace overtures and military punishment in Vietnam, with his talk of McGovern as an apostle of "surrender," the normal Republican advantage was compounded in 1972. Since McGovern led the Democratic Party in a historic break from Cold War liberalism, ceding hard-line foreign policy to the Republicans for the generation to come, the Republican success with foreign policy in this election was a harbinger for themes that would play especially powerfully in the 1980s and again in the post–September 11 era.

Cultural conflict was another issue area where McGovern suffered with the electorate. The direct impact of cultural controversies on the electorate was not as great as with foreign policy or economic matters, but the indirect effect of slogans like "the three A's" presumably was present in the widespread perception of McGovern as unacceptably far to the left. Using questions on such issues as women's liberation, marijuana use, and political protest, the authors of the Michigan study constructed an index that divided voters into those who favored the "counter-culture" and those who favored the "traditional" culture. For 1972, they found that 27 percent of their sample was in the first group and 73 percent was in the second.[43] The "culture war" was just beginning in 1972, and the Nixon campaign was a pioneer in selecting issues and coining slogans that would turn it to Republican advantage. Cultural conflict thus contributed to McGovern's difficulties in being understood and respected by the electorate. In this regard, he was one of the "culture war's" first casualties.

Conclusion

On January 21, 1973, the day after President Nixon's second inauguration, McGovern delivered a lecture at Oxford University. Neither abashed by defeat nor reconciled to "four more years" of Nixon in the White House, the losing candidate in 1972 remained very much the moralist, speaking through British auditors to a home audience that had just rejected him, and trying, one more time, to summon it to the ancestral standards of the American political tradition. Assisted by his most talented campaign speechwriter, Bob Shrum, McGovern drafted an unsparing indictment of Nixon, not in his downfall to come but at the zenith of his power.[44]

The most provocative passages of the lecture went beyond even what McGovern had said about the president during the heat of the fall campaign. Treating the previous day's inauguration as a coronation, McGovern compared Nixon to Britain's most foul royal line: "You have been spared a King Richard IV. We seem to have him—for four more years." Indeed, the country that had once kicked out England's king was now in danger of undoing the most important consequence of the American Revolution. In the lecture's most oft-quoted line, McGovern said, "I am convinced that the United States is closer to one-man rule than at any time in our history." The evidence for usurpation was everywhere—in the abuses by the president of executive privilege, of war-making, of the power of the purse. Grieved more than anything else by the nightmare of Vietnam, McGovern saw the final insult to democracy in Nixon's postelection spree of violence. "Just before Christmas," he observed, "the President, in the flush of his electoral landslide, unleashed the most barbarous bombing of the war without even forewarning the Congress. He then refused to explain it or to permit any of his subordinates to explain it."

McGovern did not reserve all of his condemnations for the president. Other American institutions, counted on by the nation's constitutional founders to hold a president in check, instead were, he alleged, supine before Nixon. "Fundamentally," he claimed, "we have experienced an exhaustion of important institutions in America. Today only the presidency is activist and strong, while other traditional centers of power are timid and depleted." Congress was "exhausted by executive encroachment and legislative paralysis." The Republican Party had become a vassal of the White House, while the Democratic Party was becoming the party of congressional incumbency, "a party with no principles, no programs, living only from day to day, caring only for the perquisites of office." And "perhaps the most discouraging development of recent years is the exhaustion of the institution of the press. Under constant pressure from an administration that appears to believe that the right of a free press is the right to print or say what they agree with, the media have yielded subtly but substantially."

The remedy for this accelerating American crisis, argued McGovern, did not lie in the hope of electing a better president than Nixon four years hence. On the contrary, he wanted to wean Americans, especially liberals, from the romantic post–New Deal myth of the heroic presidency. McGovern suggested, in an ironic commentary on his own recent quest, that it was now time "to ask whether American progressives should continue to rely on a quadrennial chance to capture what is becoming an elective dictatorship." He urged instead a restoration of the original American system of shared power, especially through the reform and revivification of Congress. During the remaining years of "Richard IV," it was Congress that needed to take the lead in bringing Americans back to the values of the Declaration of Independence and the Constitution. In McGovern's mind, those values were fundamentally liberal. "The challenge of the American future," he proclaimed in his closing line, "is to revive our institutions and resume our progress at home while we act abroad with 'a decent respect for the opinions of mankind.'"[45]

Back home, reactions to McGovern's Oxford lecture were predominantly hostile. His animadversions on Nixon, it was widely remarked by American commentators, were sour grapes, in particularly poor taste because of the timing and foreign audience. But what came across to many as graceless whining in January 1973 read as powerful prophecy a few months later.[46] Well before a flood of Watergate books and articles poured out over the next year and a half—among them *The Imperial Presidency* by McGovern's friend and supporter Arthur Schlesinger Jr.—he had diagnosed the malady and prescribed the remedy that would soon become the conventional wisdom of a country shocked out of its political complacency. Indeed, McGovern's Oxford lecture has stood the test of time and still sounds a valuable warning about the dangers of presidential power for American democracy.

Shortly after Nixon resigned the presidency in August 1974, Pat Caddell, surveying voters for the 1974 congressional elections, asked his respondents for whom they had voted in 1972. Amused by some of his poll findings, Caddell phoned Frank Mankiewicz, who recalled their conversations: "[Caddell] said, 'You know, a very interesting thing is going on . . . We carried a lot of states that you don't know about.' I remember he called me one day and he said, 'We just carried Texas!'"[47] In this brief post-Watergate moment, Nixon's disgrace caused many Americans to forget what they had rejected in McGovern. Otherwise a prophet largely without honor, it was, for him, one small measure of vindication.

12

The Legacy of the McGovern Campaign

Richard Nixon's landslide victory in 1972 blasted the presidential hopes of George McGovern and tarred his reputation ever afterward. Yet for the young McGovernites who had rallied behind the candidate and his cause, the campaign proved to be a launching pad for careers in national politics. Far from slinking away in defeat, this talented campaign staff became key players in the Democratic Party for the generation to come. Two of them—Gary Hart and Bill Clinton—were presidential candidates. James K. Galbraith, who, like his father, became an activist liberal economist, says: "This community—the McGovern campaign—essentially dominated Democratic Party politics for the next twenty years at least."[1] Robert Shrum, a top strategist for the Kerry presidential campaign in 2004, concurs: McGovern "created an extraordinary cadre of people who've gone on to have huge influence in American political life . . . It's hard to think of anyone of my age who has had an impact in the Democratic Party . . . who wasn't involved in that campaign."[2]

The later careers of the McGovernites are the most obvious legacy of the McGovern campaign. Their political odysseys from 1972 to the present are the subject of the next chapter. My focus in this chapter is the more subtle impact of the McGovern insurgency in struggles over power, policy, presidential campaigns, and the identity of the Democratic Party itself.

At the core of the history of the Democratic Party since 1972 is a paradox: the party could run away from the liberal image of the McGovern campaign, but it could not run away from its liberal values. Many Democratic leaders, among them McGovern campaign alumni, were drawn after 1972 to the pragmatic position that the party must shed its association with liberalism to survive in the emerging conservative era. Yet for most Democratic activists, the convictions articulated so passionately in the liberals' moment of 1972 remained their essential convictions, even as they became increasingly anxious about admitting to them. The centrists' alternative, pioneered by Jimmy Carter and perfected by Bill Clinton, provided scant relief for the Democrats' ambivalence, since the guiding values of centrism were never made clear. Torn, defensive, and drifting in the wake of the electoral disaster of 1972, Democrats wrote a sad coda for their party's proud history in the twentieth century.

After 1972 there would be no more liberal moments like the McGovern campaign when the Democratic Party picked its presidential nominees. Fearing the price that McGovern paid for carrying the liberal label, the party picked non-liberals or liberals who adopted political disguises. Jimmy Carter was a proto-typical New Democrat, whose cause was morality and good government, the latter in need of downsizing. Walter Mondale was a Hubert Humphrey heir, and his most controversial campaign position, in response to Ronald Reagan, was a tax increase. Michael Dukakis tried fecklessly to fend off the charge of liberalism by insisting that his campaign was about competence and not ideology. Bill Clinton and Al Gore, erstwhile leaders of the centrist Democratic Leadership Council, proclaimed their Third Way, neither liberal nor conservative. And John Kerry came up with yet another mask for a Massachusetts liberal: the warrior Democrat. Election after election, Democratic presidential candidates presented conflicted, confused, or fuzzy identities. No wonder that, save for the personal magnetism of Bill Clinton in 1992, the party experienced a passion deficit compared to its Republican foe.

Although the Democratic Party tried to read the McGovern campaign out of its historical development, the party was fundamentally changed by the insurgency of 1972 and the forces that it brought to prominence. The old Cold War liberals did not regain their hold over the party; on the contrary, by the end of the 1970s many of them were turning in disgust toward an insurgency more to their liking, headed by Ronald Reagan. McGovern's passionate critique of the war in Vietnam, preceded by the antiwar insurgencies of Eugene McCarthy and Robert Kennedy, and followed by the revelations from the Church Committee of Cold War abuses and crimes, became the property of the majority of Democrats, who echoed his ideas and values as they opposed Ronald Reagan's arms buildup and Central America interventions and George W. Bush's war in Iraq. The new cultural forces—feminists and gays—that joined the Democrats in 1972 under McGovern's banner became important, and controversial, fixtures in the Democrats' presidential coalition. Even the struggle in 1972 between older black leaders committed to Humphrey and younger black leaders committed to McGovern went in the latter's direction: it was Jesse Jackson, cochair of the McGovern Illinois delegation, who became the most influential African American in the party over the next two decades.

No individual so neatly captured the ambiguities of the McGovern legacy as Bill Clinton. Clinton was a Texas organizer for McGovern in the 1972 campaign, and many members of the far-flung network that later advanced his presidential ambitions had first come to know him during that campaign. Yet when he ran for the presidency, it was as a centrist Democrat with a Third Way philosophy that repudiated McGovern's liberalism along with the older New Deal variety and Reaganite conservatism. Clinton's two presidential terms transformed the fuzzed identity of the Democratic Party into a personal art form—but they only passed along the persisting identity crisis of the party to less talented successors.

Counterinsurgency

The most immediate impact of the McGovern insurgency was to generate its opposite: a conservative counterinsurgency in the Democratic Party. Able to damage but not defeat the McGovernites, the stop-McGovern coalition lived on after the 1972 Democratic Convention in Miami Beach. It spawned two related projects to take back the party for the Old Guard after McGovern's anticipated—and, for many, welcomed—loss in November. The first and more short-term project, aiming at a recapture of the Democratic National Committee, was successful. The second and longer-term project, aiming to restore the Cold War liberals to dominance in selection of the party's future presidential candidates and formation of its ideology, was unsuccessful in its objectives. Nonetheless, it was of considerable historical significance: the counterinsurgency against "McGovernism" was a watershed in the political evolution of the neoconservatives.

The day after the Democratic convention's opening session, at which the McGovern forces, having won the critical California delegation challenge, ensured a first-ballot nomination for the insurgent candidate, anti-McGovern leaders met over lunch to plan their comeback. It was bitter-enders from the Humphrey campaign, the Jackson campaign, and the AFL-CIO leadership who began a series of meetings that day that continued throughout the fall campaign. Senator Muskie and his staff, less ideologically averse to McGovern, declined to take part.[3] The counterinsurgents soon had a strong candidate to replace Jean Westwood, McGovern's choice, as chair of the DNC: party treasurer Robert Strauss, a Texan with longstanding ties to the LBJ camp. Although a contest at the DNC would not take place until after the November election, Strauss announced his candidacy right after the convention, making it plain that "I sure didn't like what was going on" in the party.[4]

Old Guard Democrats with a special dislike of McGovern lined up behind Strauss. "Scoop Jackson forces," Strauss recalls, "were very responsible for my being elected chairman." Other key supporters of Strauss were Mayor Richard Daley of Chicago and Al Barkan from the AFL-CIO.[5] What made Strauss anathema at first to McGovernites was not just this brigade of their adversaries within the party, but his friendship with John Connally. As the head and mouthpiece for Democrats for Nixon during the fall campaign, Connally was, in the eyes of McGovern supporters, the arch traitor who, even more effectively than Vice President Agnew, had done a hatchet job on McGovern.[6]

Jean Westwood struggled to retain her post as DNC chair after McGovern's defeat, but she made a handy target for recriminations over the landslide. When the DNC convened a month after the election, Westwood narrowly survived a motion to remove her from office and was allowed to resign to save face. McGovern supporters on the committee threw their support behind two alternatives to Strauss, Charles Manatt, California state chairman (and a future DNC chair);

and George Mitchell, a top Muskie aide (and a future senator). But Strauss had the votes to win a majority on the first ballot. "The party's old guard," reported *Newsweek*, "had their way, ridding themselves of the last living symbol of the McGovern debacle—and seating one of their own, Robert Strauss of Texas, in her place."[7]

In accepting his new post, Strauss pledged to leave the McGovern-Fraser reforms in place even though he was personally opposed to them. A self-proclaimed centrist who believed the party had lurched much too far to the left in 1972, Strauss was nonetheless more pragmatist than ideologue. Understanding that the Democratic Party needed the McGovern wing in its future, he set out, he says, to play the role of peacemaker, hoping to demonstrate to McGovernites that he was not "the devil incarnate."[8] Over time, he largely succeeded, winning appreciation for his efforts from McGovern himself. In their ongoing relations, McGovern says, Strauss "couldn't have been more thoughtful. I didn't feel that we were penalized as a movement within the party."[9]

There was one matter, however, where some McGovernites were deeply unhappy with Strauss. In the course of the 1972 McGovern campaign, Morris Dees and Jeff Smith compiled a massive list of small donors, numbering around 600,000 individuals. After the election, there was speculation in the press that McGovern and his supporters would keep this valuable list for their own purposes and not share it with the Democratic Party.[10] Subsequent to Strauss's election as DNC chair, though, Smith delivered the list of names and addresses, which was in the form of tapes, to him on McGovern's behalf. As Smith tells the story, "I said, 'The Senator wants you to have these for the party,' and he sort of said 'yadda, yadda, yadda.' And it turned out later that he had basically put them on a shelf and never mailed them."[11] Strauss says that he has "no recollection of anything like that one way or the other."[12]

Why might the new DNC chair have failed to use the McGovern donors list for fundraising? The most charitable explanation is McGovern's: as the top executive at the national committee, Strauss might not have been involved in the details of implementing a fundraising plan.[13] Several McGovernites, however, share Smith's suspicion that Strauss's motive was to diminish the influence of McGovern supporters in the party and that he said to subordinates about the names on the tapes, "Those are just those issue-oriented people, let those people go."[14]

While this incident may appear minor, its implications for the subsequent development of the Democratic Party were enormous. Instead of building on the McGovern campaign's success in establishing a mass base of donors sending in small amounts, the Democratic Party was tied to the model of soliciting large contributions from the wealthy, a familiar practice in Strauss's wing of the Texas Democratic Party. Fearful that the Democrats might remain insurgent and liberal in character, the Old Guard shut down the democratic approach to fundraising and yoked the party to more affluent—and moderate—contributors. "Probably the greatest tragedy of the McGovern campaign," argues Scott Lilly, "was that Morris Dees and Jeff Smith built this fantastic list of contributors, and had the Democratic Party exploited that list in a systematic way, I think the balance between the two parties would be entirely different today . . . I think that Bob Strauss did not want the McGovern campaign to make a contribution [and] deliberately ignored the availability of those tapes."[15]

Taking back the DNC was only one part of a larger thrust by the stop-McGovern coalition to restore the Old Guard to its accustomed place atop the Democratic Party. The Miami Beach conclave of counterinsurgents also laid plans for their future as the Coalition for a Democratic Majority (CDM). As the sympathetic Rowland Evans and Robert Novak reported a few days after McGovern's downfall in November: "A broad-based organization of anti–New Politics liberal Democrats, privately conceived during last summer's McGovernite orgy at Miami Beach and secretly nurtured ever since, is surfacing as a cutting edge in the struggle for the soul of the Democratic Party."[16] To recruit members for the CDM, Norman Podhoretz, editor of *Commentary*, and his wife, Midge Decter, wrote a manifesto whose title—"Come Home, Democrats"—satirized McGovern's acceptance speech at Miami Beach and asserted the counterinsurgents' claim to rightful occupancy of the party. The CDM united McGovern's principal Old Guard foes from the spring. Hubert Humphrey and Scoop Jackson became honorary cochairs, but the guiding lights of the new group were top aides of theirs, including Max Kampelman for Humphrey and Ben Wattenberg for Jackson, along with Penn Kemble, an assistant to George Meany. Wattenberg became the group's chair and spokesman.[17]

The CDM believed that it represented rank-and-file Democrats who, deserted by the left-wing elitists of the McGovern insurgency, had defected in droves in 1972. Yet like its successor a decade later, the Democratic Leadership Council, the CDM itself was decidedly an elite—a collection of party leaders and associated intellectuals that made no effort to organize this mass base. Describing the group, Ben Wattenberg quotes another of its members, Jeane Kirkpatrick, to the effect that "CDM is a state of mind, not an organization."[18] CDM members were to the right of the McGovernites on a wide array of issues, but foreign policy was the most important. For this assemblage of Cold War liberals, the emphasis was now on the adjective and not the noun. Nothing galvanized them as much in 1972 as McGovern's opposition to the war in Vietnam and his critique of Cold War militarism. To counter what it regarded as a dangerous tendency among liberal Democrats toward neo-isolationism, the CDM formed a Foreign Policy Task Force, headed by Eugene Rostow, who, like his brother Walt, had been a Vietnam hawk in the Johnson administration.[19]

At the moment of McGovern's landslide defeat, prospects seemed bright for the Old Guard Democrats. But events soon undercut their project. The unfolding Watergate scandal vindicated many of McGovern's campaign charges and exposed the dangerous proclivities of the Cold War presidency. Nixon's resignation triggered a further flood of exposés about the secret history of the Cold War. It was the revelations of the Church Committee and other post-Watergate investigations about U.S. involvement in foreign coups and assassination plots, Gary Hart believes, that did the most to awaken Americans to the excesses of Cold War policy.[20] On top of these dramatic developments at home, the inglorious collapse of the South Vietnamese military and government in 1975 brought down the curtain on the signature fiasco of the Cold War liberals. Within the space of three years, the CDM appeared to represent less a resurgent majority in the Democratic Party than a beleaguered minority.

With momentum running in their adversaries' favor, the Cold Warriors of the CDM looked for allies outside the party. Eugene Rostow took the lead role in organizing, and became the chair of, the Committee on the Present Danger (CPD), formed in 1976. The CPD was a bipartisan operation, bringing together hawkish Democrats opposed to McGovernite foreign policy with hawkish Republicans opposed to Henry Kissinger's strategy of détente. Repudiating the foreign-policy approaches of both of the presidential candidates in 1972, the CPD aimed to bring back the original Cold War philosophy, emphasizing the evil global ambitions of the Soviet Union and the saving grace of American nuclear superiority. Members of the CPD were not much happier about the national security policies of the candidates in 1976, and when the winner, Jimmy Carter, rejected all fifty-three of the names proposed by the CPD (in conjunction with the CDM and the AFL-CIO) for the national security bureaucracy, its adherents on the Democratic side were all the more alienated from their party. Some remained Democrats, while others gravitated toward the Republicans, but most were attracted to the one presidential candidate on the scene who agreed with their views. Ronald Reagan, himself an ex-liberal Democrat who foreshadowed their migration two decades earlier, became the lodestar for a Cold War revival in which McGovern's opponents from 1972, reborn as neoconservatives, played an indispensable role.[21]

Jimmy Carter and the McGovern Legacy

Contrary to initial indications, Jimmy Carter was not one of the counterinsurgents. Carter was a leader among southern Democratic governors in attempting to block McGovern's nomination, and he delivered a nominating speech for Scoop Jackson at Miami Beach. Yet he had little in common with the Humphrey-Jackson wing of the party and its Cold War past, and at Miami Beach his staff, apparently with his tacit approval, angled to have him considered for the part of McGovern's running mate.[22] In Carter's run for the presidency, and during his administration, there was no animus toward McGovernites. His outsider campaign for 1976, which was only possible because of the McGovern-Fraser reforms, recruited two fellow southerners who had been instrumental in the successes of the McGovern campaign: Patrick Caddell as pollster/strategist and Morris Dees as fundraiser.

Most McGovernites, however, saw important differences between their insurgency in 1972 and Carter's outsider campaign in 1976. On matters of ideology and issue positions, liberal candidates Morris Udall and Fred Harris were more natural fits. And Carter, despite coming up with his own version of McGovern's pledge of truthfulness, raised suspicions among some of the insurgents of 1972 about the authenticity of his convictions. Pat Caddell recruited Bob Shrum, a friend from the McGovern campaign, to write speeches for Carter during the 1976 primaries. After less than two weeks with Carter, Shrum resigned from his campaign, writing the candidate: "I share the perception that simple measures will not answer our problems; but it seems to me that your issues strategy is not a response to that complexity, but an attempt to conceal your true positions. I am not sure what you truly believe in, other than yourself."[23]

Carter's domestic program resembled McGovern's in one area: tax reform. In his 1976 campaign he pledged to close tax loopholes, eliminate tax shelters, and remove the biases toward the rich that riddled the federal tax code.[24] But Carter was unsuccessful in achieving tax reform—and his failure on this front wrapped up perhaps the last effort that the Democrats would make in pursuing policies worrisome to wealthy interests. Elsewhere, Carter ran—and, even more, governed—as a domestic centrist, with policies remote not only from McGovern's proposals four years earlier but from the New Deal approach of a Hubert Humphrey as well. Long before the neoliberals of the 1980s or the New Democrats of the 1990s, Carter called for fiscal austerity and critiqued big government and bureaucracy. Perceived by many Democrats as veering to the right, he united in opposition leaders who had been on different sides in 1972. Ted Kennedy, an enthusiastic supporter of McGovern during the fall campaign, and George Meany, McGovern's most bitter critic on the Democratic side, thus shared the stage in 1978 to attack Carter's timidity on national health insurance.[25]

The story about Carter was different in foreign affairs, at least at first. The global policies that Carter advocated during his 1976 campaign and at the outset of his presidency were closer to McGovern's in 1972 than to those rivals of his that echoed the verities of the Cold War. McGovern and Carter derived their approaches to international relations from different sources: McGovern was a long-time critic of the Cold War steeped in the Jeffersonian tradition of anti-militarism, while Carter, a newcomer to global politics, was influenced by the post-Vietnam global managerialism of the Trilateral Commission, of which he and his top national-security advisers were members. In practice, however, their policy stances were similar. Human rights, which were the centerpiece of Carter's foreign policy, were an expression of American idealism and a rejection of Cold War realpolitik. Carter also started with skepticism of the military-industrial complex: he called for a $5–7 billion cut in the defense budget during his campaign and canceled production of the B-1 bomber in his first year in office.[26] His most controversial statement on foreign policy in 1977—"We are now free of that inordinate fear of communism which once led us to embrace any dictator who joined us in that fear"—could have come from one of McGovern's campaign speeches.[27]

By the end of his term, however, Carter's foreign policy was closer to the Cold War liberals than to McGovern's in 1972. The president came under intense pressure from the right, especially the Committee on the Present Danger, which was highly effective in lobbying to block ratification of the SALT II treaty. The twin disasters of the Iranian Revolution and the takeover of the American embassy in Tehran pushed Carter toward a more militant stance in world affairs. So, too, did a new burst of Soviet activity in Africa and Central Asia, culminating in the Russians' disastrous invasion of Afghanistan at the end of 1979. The president became something of a born-again Cold Warrior: he issued the Carter Doctrine to warn the Soviets against threatening the Persian Gulf and its oil, called for a sizeable increase in the defense budget, imposed a grain embargo on sales to the Russians, boycotted the 1980 Olympic Games in Moscow, and instituted draft registration for young men.[28]

Although Carter moved toward the position of Scoop Jackson, he did not impress Jackson's acolytes, who by this point were confirmed in their neoconservatism. The president could not out-tough Ronald Reagan, the new hero of most of the old Cold Warriors in the Democratic Party. Meanwhile, New Politics liberals were distressed by Carter's belated Cold War posture, which, coming on top of their disgruntlement with his approach in domestic affairs, pushed them into overt opposition. Disillusionment with Carter, Rick Stearns observes, was felt most intensely by the McGovernites.[29] Stearns, along with such fellow alumni of the McGovern campaign as Steve Robbins, Bob Shrum, and Carl Wagner, became key activists in Ted Kennedy's 1980 challenge to Carter for the Democratic presidential nomination. Kennedy's campaign was bungled, and Carter enjoyed a rally in popular support thanks to the Tehran hostage crisis. But there was not much of a future in the Democratic Party for hawkishness—especially after Cold War militancy became the property of the Republican who unseated Carter.

Eighties Echoes of the New Politics

Ronald Reagan extended and deepened the paradoxical legacy of the McGovern campaign. The election successes of Reagan and his handpicked heir in 1980–1988 demonstrated the vulnerability of liberalism and repeatedly showcased the ability of Republicans to caricature and discredit it. At the same time, Reagan's conservative policies in economics, social life, and international affairs so outraged most Democrats that they served to keep alive the themes of social justice and international cooperation that had been the leitmotifs of the McGovern campaign.

The Democrats' election disaster of 1980, encompassing the Senate as well as the presidency, sparked one of what would become a seemingly endless series of ideological self-criticism sessions within the party. In the early Reagan years, the talked-about new ideological approach was neoliberalism. Neoliberals claimed that they still shared liberal ends but had become skeptics about traditional liberal means. *Washington Monthly* editor Charles Peters, who coined the term *neoliberal*, wrote of this new public philosophy that "we no longer automatically favor unions and big government or oppose the military and big business. Indeed, in our search for solutions that work, we have come to distrust all automatic responses, liberal or conservative."[30] Breaking from both the New Deal liberalism of a Hubert Humphrey and its more populist cousin as articulated by George McGovern, neoliberals asked their party to dump its shibboleths about guiding the economy through centralized bureaucratic agencies and to place greater emphasis instead on entrepreneurship, appropriate technology, and globalization. If neoliberals did have a recent Democratic hero, it was President Kennedy (but not his brothers), the advocate of economic growth who cast a cool eye on the cant of economic redistribution.[31]

Although the neoliberal movement, with its cerebral pragmatism, seemed a far cry from the vocal idealism of the New Politics that had reached its apogee in the McGovern campaign, there were affinities between the two below the surface. Prominent neoliberals mainly hailed from the Northeast and the West, the regions most advanced in economic and technological development; they stemmed from the same college-educated stratum of political activists that had risen to power in the Democratic Party in 1972, with the passions of the antiwar cause now stilled and the complexities of public policy now of greater concern. That Gary Hart, McGovern's campaign manager, was now the single most visible figure in neoliberal circles made the common roots in postindustrial society even plainer. Furthermore, as products of the postwar boom in higher education, neoliberals shared most of the cultural and global values of the earlier McGovernites. While they did not talk much about such issues, they were supporters of women's rights and gay rights. And, as Peters wrote, most neoliberals "differ little from traditional liberals on such matters as the insanity of the nuclear arms race, the importance of foreign aid to the Third World, and our antipathy to exercising our military power abroad."[32]

"Insanity" seemed rampant to most Democrats in the early Reagan years, and the neoliberals joined their more traditional adversaries within the party in contesting the president's policies on nuclear weapons and Central America. Supporting a nuclear freeze and opposing Reagan's backing for *contra* rebels in Nicaragua and a right-wing regime in El Salvador, most Democrats sounded more like McGovern than like a Humphrey, Jackson, or Carter (at the end of his presidency). In fact, in the early 1980s, unlike 1972, rejection of traditional Cold War politics was the position even of the Democratic establishment. In September 1983, DNC chair Charles Manatt officially put his party on record in support of a "mutual and verifiable nuclear freeze."[33] Democratic leaders in the House echoed the language of the McGovern insurgency in assailing the irrationality of the Cold War arms race. House Speaker Tip O'Neill, speaking in favor of the freeze, thundered: "The world is racing toward catastrophe . . . The brakes have not been put on. Instead, the foot is on the accelerator."[34] Foreign Affairs Committee chair Clement Zablocki answered McGovern's plea at Oxford for a reassertion of congressional will against executive usurpations: "What the Congress is saying is that arms control is too important an issue to be considered exclusively a concern of the Executive when, in essence, what we are talking about is the fundamental issue of survival of all our peoples."[35]

Debates in Congress over Reagan's anti-Communist interventions in Central America were even more redolent of the impassioned views of the antiwar movement and the McGovern insurgency. In adopting the Boland Amendment to forestall the Reagan administration from funding and arming the *contras* in Nicaragua, and in urging a regional diplomatic solution to the multiple crises in Central American affairs, congressional Democrats tried to head off what they feared would be a second Vietnam. McGovern had been ousted from the Senate in 1980, the target of a successful conservative campaign to go after the liberals, but it could have been his voice that was heard discussing Central America a few years later in Congress. Congresswoman Barbara Mikulski of Maryland warned that "we are about to precipitate a regional war in Central America . . . What we should be doing is identifying with the struggles of the people. The reason there are national liberation movements is because we support the bullies, and we support the bullies because they say they are anti-Communist."[36] Congressman George Miller from California put it more simply: "This is a first step of our Vietnam. Some of us came here to stop Vietnam. And here is a chance to stop the new one."[37]

As the 1984 presidential season approached, Democrats wrestled with the conflicting impulses of dramatizing their profound differences with Reagan and muting them in view of his recovering popularity. Walter Mondale, the putative frontrunner, was inclined by instinct to mute the party's resurgence of antiwar passion. Democratic centrists would later couple Mondale with McGovern as feckless liberals who brought electoral disaster on the party, but in reality Mondale kept his distance from its McGovern wing. Unlike McGovern, Mondale never broke from the mold of their common mentor, Hubert Humphrey. Although Mondale, like many Democrats, had been gravitating toward a more populist liberalism in the late 1960s and early 1970s, McGovern's defeat sent him hustling back toward the center. As biographer Steven Gillon observes, "The 1972 election resulted in what friends referred to as the 'homogenization of Walter Mondale'—a conscious attempt to make him more acceptable to the middle class by downplaying his recent past."[38] Running for the Democratic nomination in 1984, Mondale was the choice of party regulars. Two other facts highlighted even more glaringly his dissimilarity from McGovern: before the primaries began he was officially endorsed by the AFL-CIO, headed by George Meany's heir, Lane Kirkland, but he was weak among young voters, who regarded him as a stale symbol of old-fashioned interest-group politics.[39]

That Mondale came to be regarded as a liberal rather than a centrist in 1984 had a lot to do with the pressures upon him from a party that had been transformed by the McGovern insurgency and infuriated by the Reagan revolution. Gary Hart, borrowing a page from the McGovernites' strategy against Muskie in 1972, offered the most effective challenge to Mondale's nomination, blasting the former vice president as the candidate of "the establishment past . . . , brokered by backroom politics and confirmed by a collective sense of resignation."[40] But Jesse Jackson was also a burr in Mondale's side during the nomination season, pressing him hard on minority issues. And then there was George McGovern, a candidate of boldness in 1984 in contrast to Mondale's caution.

The presidential bug had never completely left McGovern's system. In 1984, however, he understood that his chances were remote, and in campaigning for the presidency his principal motivation was to influence the Democratic debate by combating the tendency of the leading contenders to compromise with the Reagan revolution. Not really playing to win, McGovern had the luxury in this campaign of ignoring the painful lessons of 1972, some of which he had drawn himself after that contest. Once again, he positioned himself to the left, laying out a ten-point program. The changes in foreign and domestic policy that he advocated were no less sweeping and provocative than his stands a dozen years earlier. But this time, with no one taking his prospects seriously enough to have an interest in cutting him down, instead of being denounced as a "radical" he was saluted by many commentators as the "conscience" of the Democratic Party.[41]

Friends and admirers initially feared that McGovern would embarrass himself by his candidacy in 1984. But he was greeted with affection by Democratic audiences, and he won admiration from journalists for his peacemaking role at televised debates between the Democratic contestants. With little money or staff, he put up respectable numbers, coming in third among the eight candidates in the Iowa caucuses, virtually in a tie with Jesse Jackson for fourth place in New Hampshire, and barely behind Mondale's second-place finish in Massachusetts. McGovern dropped out of the race after the Massachusetts primary, having found at least some salve for the lingering pains of 1972.[42]

The 1984 Democratic convention in San Francisco was something like what the 1972 convention at Miami Beach might have been if the stop-McGovern conservatives had been magically removed. Abortion rights and gay/lesbian rights were championed in the party platform. Whereas disgruntled feminists had put up Sissy Farenthold as a symbolic vice-presidential candidate in 1972, in 1984 Geraldine Ferraro was Mondale's choice for a running mate. The Democratic Cold Warriors of 1972 were now mostly in Reagan's camp, so the party's positions on global affairs in 1984 were firmly against the president's revival of Cold War conflict. Mondale favored the nuclear freeze that had been passed by House Democrats, and his camp accepted a platform amendment from Hart that expressed the party's reluctance to send U.S. forces into Third World hot spots save under exceptional circumstances. As journalist Hedrick Smith observed, "Among Democrats at the convention, the McGovern legacy of resistance to military spending and American involvement abroad was apparent in the Hart plank, in signs calling to 'end the war in Central America,' and in the opposition of Mr. Mondale and his running mate, Representative Geraldine A. Ferraro, to developing the MX missile, the B-1 bomber, nerve gas, and anti-satellite weapons."[43]

Mondale's fall campaign was as doomed as McGovern's twelve years earlier. The former senator from Minnesota was even burdened by a vice-presidential imbroglio—this time over the questionable finances of Ferraro's husband. Once again, however, the forces aligned against a Democratic challenger ran deeper than a poor vetting of a running mate. Riding an upsurge of prosperity and a wave of nationalism, Reagan's team devised a feel-good theme for the president that easily routed the drab Mondale, whose gray campaign did little to arouse Democratic activists. The president cruised to a landslide reelection. Mondale won only Minnesota and the District of Columbia, allowing McGovern to tease him in later years that he had eclipsed the record set in 1972 for the worst Electoral College performance in history by a Democratic presidential candidate.

Democratic Backlash

Mondale's landslide defeat initiated a new stage in the worsening identity crisis of the Democratic Party. After 1984 the challenge to the liberalism of the "San Francisco Democrats" was more thoroughgoing and intense than the criticisms from neoliberals in the first years of the decade. Battle lines over Democratic identity were now drawn that are still visible two decades later.

Shortly after the election, in February 1985, a cadre of elected officials formally launched a new centrist organization called the Democratic Leadership Council (DLC).[44] Unlike the neoliberals, based mostly in the Northeast and the West, the bulk of the DLC came from the South. Like the neoliberals, the centrists of the DLC proposed that the party stand for the "national interest" rather than "special interests" such as the unions, and concentrate on economic growth through more business-friendly policies. Reflecting its conservative southern base, however, the DLC also challenged the cultural and foreign-policy stands that neoliberals largely shared with more traditional liberals, calling on the party to distance itself from the demands of feminists, blacks, and peace activists, and to commit itself to a "strong" national defense.[45] In the view of the DLC leadership, Kenneth Baer writes, "the Democratic Party at the national level had become a New Politics liberal party. The mainstream of the national party was not in the mainstream of the Democratic rank and file or of the general electorate."[46] It was the mission of the "New Democrats" of the DLC to move the party back into this moderate mainstream.

Reagan's 1984 "Morning in America" triumph owed more to personality, symbolism, and economic growth than to ideological advantages. Some survey evidence suggested that voters had actually preferred Mondale's positions over Reagan's on the majority of domestic issues.[47] Nevertheless, to the architects of the DLC the woes of the Democratic Party could all be traced to the unpopularity of liberalism. Mondale had been the standard-bearer for the party establishment, but that establishment had fallen under the sway of New Politics liberals. He was the heir of a party diverted disastrously to the left by McGovern in 1972, and DLC strategists came to link the two men together through the rhetorical construction of a "McGovern-Mondale tradition."[48] The DLC claimed Gary Hart, in his neoliberal rather than his McGovernite incarnation, as a kindred spirit. Hart recognized the shared passion for challenging encrusted Democratic patterns. But he did not join the new centrist organization, in part, he says, because it was "seen as a vehicle to get away from McGovernism."[49]

The identity crisis of the Democratic Party played out in tragicomic form during the 1988 presidential campaign season. Massachusetts governor Michael Dukakis was too much a conventional Northeastern Democrat to attract the DLC, but he shared its assumption that the liberal label was fatal for electoral purposes. Rejecting self-identification as a liberal, Dukakis insisted that he was really a conservative because he, by contrast to Reagan, produced balanced budgets.[50] In a major foreign-policy speech in advance of the Democratic convention, Dukakis asserted that he was a gradualist in global affairs and "not another George McGovern."[51] The signature passage in his acceptance speech at the convention reflected his attempted flight from ideology to managerialism: "This election is not about ideology. It's about competence."[52] As Sidney Blumenthal commented, it was a misguided flight: "Dukakis did not want a grand debate about national purpose. He hoped to avoid that. At his crowning moment he demonstrated in any case that he did not know how to make a larger argument. It was his notion that we would elect a president on bloodless, instrumental grounds, precisely where he believed that he was strongest."[53]

With ample assistance from the campaign of Vice President George H. W. Bush, Dukakis managed to come across to the electorate as *both* an emotionless technocrat *and* a starry-eyed liberal. Desperate to blunt Republican charges of softness on national defense, Dukakis strategists devised what proved to be the *reductio ad absurdum* of Democratic evasions of liberal identity: dressed in a flak suit and a helmet with his name inscribed, and clutching a machine gun, with the soundtrack from *Patton* playing in the background, the presidential candidate rode around a field in an M-1 tank as the cameras clicked. Attempting to escape a McGovern-like vulnerability on national security, Dukakis only enhanced it. The sight of him in the tank was so ludicrous that it became fodder for a Republican campaign ad and not a Democratic one.[54]

Meanwhile, Bush's campaign manager, Lee Atwater, updating Nixon's 1972 text on attack politics, used the Pledge of Allegiance and the American flag to pin Dukakis as unpatriotic and the sinister story of black rapist Willie Horton to tar him as squishy soft on crime—in sum, a hapless spokesman for what Bush called the "L-word."[55] No matter how frantically Dukakis and his Democratic successors shed the liberal label, Republican campaign professionals were equally intent— and generally more effective—at reattaching it to them. Ahead in the polls after the Democratic convention, the Dukakis campaign collapsed under the combined weight of its own blunders and Atwater's barrages. Only in the last two weeks of the fall campaign, when he literally rolled up his sleeves, proclaimed himself a traditional Democratic populist, and even admitted, though only for a day, that he was really a liberal, did Dukakis make up ground and lose by a more respectable margin than McGovern or Mondale (albeit to a weaker opponent).[56]

Whatever Dukakis's ideological evasions, the leadership of the DLC chalked up his defeat as yet another fiasco for liberalism. The party needed to be fundamentally remade, the DLC argued after 1988, attracting back the lost elements of the old New Deal coalition—northern workers and ethnics and southern white Protestants—by tamping down the forces of the New Politics and driving Democrats back to the center. DLC intellectuals sketched a full-blown public philosophy for these "New Democrats" in contradistinction to post-1972 liberalism. But DLC leaders realized that it was not enough to contest for the identity of the party on the terrain of ideas. DLC ideas would only take on practical effect in the hands of an appealing presidential candidate who identified himself as a "New Democrat."[57] It did not take long to locate a suitable figure for the role. Ironically, for a group that decried the "McGovern-Mondale tradition," its man was a former McGovernite.[58]

Confusions of Identity

The DLC picked both the right and the wrong man in Bill Clinton—the right candidate because Clinton was the most talented Democratic performer in a generation, the wrong candidate because he was too protean a character to be contained in a DLC mold. Clinton had moved in a centrist direction much earlier when a defeat after his first term as governor of Arkansas underscored the electoral backlash in the South against liberal programs and values. In the spring of 1989, Al From, the dominant figure in the DLC, invited Clinton to become the organization's next chairman, holding out the enticement that the position would provide him with a strong platform and resources for a presidential bid. Clinton took the job in 1990 and became an articulate spokesman for the political vision of the New Democrats.[59] He stood for what he called a Third Way in American politics, "neither liberal nor conservative but both and different."[60] Clinton's formulation was creative for more than its invocation of the skepticism toward liberalism that had marked the neoliberals and, more vehemently, the New Democrats. What was especially clever about it was its capaciousness—it committed Clinton to almost nothing and permitted him almost everything. With Clinton and his two successors as Democratic presidential candidates, the identity of the Democratic Party would become all the more fluid and indistinct.

It is not surprising in this light that the DLC was bound to be disappointed by Clinton's first two years as president. To be sure, Clinton's early agenda contained many items from the DLC platform, including the North American Free Trade Agreement and the crime bill. As president, however, Clinton was more concerned with uniting the Democratic Party behind him than reshaping it in service to an abstract public philosophy like that of the New Democrats.[61] He was careful to incorporate into his agenda items that would play to the interests of liberals, an indispensable component of his electoral coalition. Besides, fearing a repeat of Jimmy Carter's ruinous isolation from the more liberal Democratic leaders of Congress, Clinton aligned his priorities with theirs. Perhaps worst of all from a DLC standpoint, Clinton and his wife were, through their personalities, friendships, and political ties, closely connected to the same identity politics that Democratic centrists argued were driving white men out of the party. It was a nightmare for New Democrats as much as for the president that the most-publicized controversy of his first days in office concerned gays and lesbians in the military.

The DLC liked the remainder of Clinton's presidency much better. A stinging defeat in the off-year elections of 1994, which liberated Clinton from the burden of placating a liberal congressional majority and induced him to revert to a New Democratic posture, produced a presidency that the DLC was proud to claim.[62] It is questionable, though, whether Clinton's two terms produced a clear-cut, postliberal identity for the Democratic Party. His turn to the moderate middle to block the Gingrich Republicans, political scientists Paul Quirk and William Cunion wrote, was not a "principled centrist approach" but an "opportunistic centrist strategy," based on the crafty "triangulation" of amoral adviser Dick Morris rather than the sober political philosophy advanced by DLC theoreticians.[63] Moderation for Clinton also meant a commitment to popular entitlements that the DLC associated with traditional liberalism: the president's most effective issue in besting Newt Gingrich was the protection of Medicare and Medicaid against Republican assault. Nor was Clinton delinquent in looking to the interests of minorities and women as he mounted a successful defense of affirmative action. The DLC had wanted to bring white men back to the Democratic Party, but Clinton's most devoted supporters, both in the 1996 election and the 1998 impeachment battle, were African Americans and women. In short, Bill Clinton had multiple identities as president, bequeathing to his successors no particular identity at all.[64]

Al Gore was one of the founders of the DLC and had been its preferred candidate for the presidency in 1988. Yet when the vice president became the Democratic nominee in 2000, the continuing ideological uncertainty of the party was on painful display. Gore shied away from what might have been the most politically profitable identity—heir of Bill Clinton and helpmate in his accomplishments—because of the moral fallout from the Monica Lewinsky scandal. He also shied away from his own identity as a passionate environmentalist, and thus from the convictions and commitments that might have signaled authenticity, out of fear of defection from voters in border and southern states. Instead, his campaign was a case study in rampant identity confusion.[65] The Gore of 2000 sometimes appeared to be playing an ensemble of off-kilter Democratic campaign characters: the fuzzy persona (Carter), the experienced but wooden vice president (Mondale), the tedious policy wonk (Dukakis), and the smug elitist (new in 2000 but reprised by John Kerry four years later).

Ironically, the one campaign tune that brought Gore the largest boost in the polls—the populist strains of "Fighting Al" as performed at the Democratic convention—reached far back before his time to the traditional Democratic model of Harry Truman. Even though the Gore campaign eventually scrapped this populist motif as well, the Democrats were strong enough and the Republicans weak enough in 2000 to give the vice president a tiny majority in the national popular vote. But in the conclusive contest over Florida ballots, George W. Bush and the Republicans, surer of their identity and more relentless in their pursuit of victory, had the upper hand over Gore and his less resolute partisans.

Somewhat akin to Ronald Reagan, George W. Bush made the McGovern legacy visible again. When the Bush administration invaded and occupied Iraq, Democratic officials reacted cautiously while the party's base erupted in fury. The stage was set for another antiwar Democratic insurgency at the grassroots, now in large part the "netroots."[66] Howard Dean was its candidate, and as Dean exploded from the back of the pack to frontrunner status for the Democratic presidential nomination over the course of 2003, comparisons of him to McGovern became inevitable. The press and the Internet crackled with arguments as to how Dean was like or unlike McGovern—a radical or a moderate, unelectable or a magnet for the forces of change in American politics. Leaders of the DLC, aiming to squelch the Dean insurgency, had no doubt about the correct answers to such questions. In "The Real Soul of the Democratic Party," Al From and Bruce Reed wrote, "What activists like Dean call the Democratic wing of the Democratic Party is an aberration: the McGovern-Mondale wing, defined principally by weakness abroad and elitist, interest-group liberalism at home. That's the wing that lost 49 states in two elections, and transformed Democrats from a strong national party into a much weaker regional one."[67]

Dean's candidacy faded with the voting at the Iowa caucuses at the start of the 2004 campaign season, before his infamous "scream." That same contest thrust John Kerry to the fore as—it was presumed in a judgment that proved premature—the most electable Democratic candidate. Once more, a Massachusetts Democrat with a liberal record emerged with a fresh disguise to become the party's presidential nominee. "Reporting for duty" at the Democratic national convention, Kerry was rhetorically and visually defined in front of the television audience as a warrior Democrat for the post–September 11 world.[68] Like McGovern, Kerry had risen to national prominence as an impassioned spokesman for opposition to the Vietnam War. Contrary to McGovern, he tried to downplay his antiwar activities when he became a presidential candidate, highlighting instead his prior record of valor in combat.[69]

Kerry's carefully edited autobiographical campaign quickly went awry. Caught between his warrior image and initial support for Bush's invasion of Iraq, and his partisans' anger at that war and its deceptive origins, Kerry entangled himself in tortuous arguments. Much like the previous Massachusetts Democrat to run for president, the damage he inflicted on himself was magnified by unrelenting attacks from Republicans. In the newest edition of the text on attack politics, originally authored by Richard Nixon and updated by Lee Atwater, Karl Rove and his allies threw mud all over Kerry's war record and turned him into a suspect character on national security in an age of terrorism. The attack on Kerry again featured the text's preferred tactic of employing surrogates—in this case, the Swift Boat Veterans for Truth—to malign a Democrat while a Republican presidential candidate stands serenely aside. Yet another dysfunctional campaign and disliked candidate drove Democratic activists to despair by losing a presidential election that they were sure they should have won. Since 1972, Democrats had chosen a string of nominees whose identity and ideology were supposed to spare them the terrible defeat of the liberal McGovern in 1972. Kerry was the latest of these nominees whose alternative to straightforward liberalism did not usually produce much happier results.

Conclusion

George McGovern's unfortunate fate in the history of his party has been to serve as a negative reference point. After 1972 McGovern became, as his grassroots organizer Carl Wagner puts it, "a whipping-boy for everybody on the center-right of the Democratic Party."[70] From the Coalition for a Democratic Majority in the 1970s to the Democratic Leadership Council today, the name *McGovern* has conjured up the peril for the party of affirming a full-blown liberal vision in domestic and foreign affairs. But it is not only centrist or conservative Democrats who associate the McGovern campaign with disaster; some McGovernites who still consider themselves liberals share their view of its historical meaning. "I think," says McGovern aide Gordon Weil, "that the McGovern campaign was seen by liberals to have discredited liberalism."[71]

At the same time, Weil, like most McGovernites, believes that the 1972 campaign set "a standard of honesty and integrity," and that regardless of his blunders from the Democratic convention to Election Day, McGovern came out of the campaign as a "classy figure in American politics."[72] Weighing the consequences of adhering to such a standard, subsequent Democratic presidential nominees have looked elsewhere for their own codes of conduct. Fuzziness and evasiveness have been keynotes of almost every Democratic presidential campaign since 1972. Democratic partisans have been called upon to work their hearts out for candidates who ring nearly as inauthentic to them as to Republicans. The flight from liberal identity, tagged as a surefire loser, has not led to a more secure identity, but only to an ongoing identity crisis.

Democrats would have been less confused after 1972 had the party rejected McGovern's liberal values along with his liberal campaign identity. But the contrary was the case: the McGovern campaign summed up the sixties commitments to social justice and international cooperation that were seared into memory, above all, by the civil rights movement and the struggle against the Vietnam War, and these commitments would not be forgotten by most Democratic activists. If anything, they were elaborated for many in later years by a backlash from the right against social change and by new wars abroad. The social forces that entered the party through the McGovern campaign—the women's rights and gay rights causes—brought Democrats new electoral problems but also maintained their egalitarian compass. The peace forces that were incorporated in the party through the McGovern campaign were an even larger electoral problem but also kept alive its Vietnam-era ideal of a thoughtful and critical brand of patriotism.

The careers of many Democrats after 1972 reflected the conflicting tugs between liberal convictions and pragmatic politics. None handled this conflict so masterfully—yet ambiguously—as Bill Clinton. After eight years of Clinton in the presidency, the nature of his political identity remained just as elusive as when he was first elected. Was Clinton the author of a new Democratic synthesis, a "Third Way" beyond liberalism and conservatism—and beyond defeat? Or was his political identity closer to what both his right-wing and his left-wing critics suspected, devoid of core convictions altogether? The questions lingered over his successors, Al Gore and John Kerry, and remain relevant to his wife as well as she seeks the Democratic presidential nomination for 2008.

Bill Clinton's political odyssey since the McGovern campaign may be unique, but many of the youthful McGovernites who first made a mark in national politics in 1972 have engaged in their own struggles over political identity in the decades since. These struggles have taken several forms and had divergent outcomes, but all of them have been touched by the original experience of the McGovern insurgency. The stories of the McGovernites' careers after 1972 offer further insight into the identity crisis of the Democratic Party.

13

McGovernites

During the 1972 campaign, George McGovern asked Rick Stearns to stop off during a midwestern trip to see a wealthy businessman in Omaha who had endorsed the candidate's views on the war in Vietnam. As Stearns recalls, "I remember meeting this businessman, sitting around his kitchen table, and he seemed like a pretty smart guy." So Stearns, hoping to have a few thousand dollars in his bank account at the end of the campaign, asked the man for financial advice, and he replied: "I don't want to sound immodest, but I'm starting up a company and you could do worse than buy shares." Stearns reconsidered his initial impulse: "Wait a minute! I'm going to take financial advice from a guy who's supporting George McGovern? I don't think so!" It was another of the bad breaks—or bad decisions—that dogged the McGovernites. "Of course," Stearns laughs, "this was Warren Buffet, and the company he was talking about was Berkshire Hathaway. Had I [bought shares], I probably wouldn't be a judge today because I would be independently wealthy."[1]

McGovernites were not bound for either fortune or glory from the 1972 presidential campaign. Yet most have lived successful and prosperous lives since that year. Stearns is no exception. When the campaign ended he was twenty-eight, and while his political wizardry under the McGovern-Fraser rules had shaken the Democratic Party and roiled American politics in 1972, he was still a young man without a permanent career—so he enrolled in law school. With two breaks from his new career—to play major roles in the Udall primary campaign in 1976 and the Kennedy primary campaign in 1980—Stearns shifted his focus from politics to the law, becoming a prosecutor in Norfolk County, Massachusetts. In the early 1980s William Weld hired him as assistant U.S. attorney for the state, and Stearns "liked to brag that I was the highest-ranking Democrat in the Reagan administration." Governor Michael Dukakis later appointed him as a judge, and in 1993 President Bill Clinton, his old friend from their Oxford days, appointed him to a seat on the U.S. District Court in Boston.[2]

The roller-coaster ride of the McGovern campaign, from the astonishing heights in winning the nomination to the unstoppable plummet of the fall campaign, left the young McGovernites exhausted by Election Day 1972. Asked today about their experiences in the campaign, however, most emphasize the exhilaration. With a handful of exceptions, the McGovernites I've interviewed describe their experiences with phrases like "fabulous," "joyful," and "the best job I've ever had."[3] Rather than embarrassment at their massive defeat, they regard their affiliation with George McGovern as "a badge of honor."[4] Among high-level McGovernites, Harold Himmelman has moved the farthest distance ideologically—he is now a corporate lawyer whose political beliefs are summed up by his admiration for President George W. Bush—but Himmelman expresses the same pride in his participation in 1972 as any of his old colleagues.[5]

Perhaps because involvement in the McGovern campaign felt empowering rather than disillusioning in spite of the landslide defeat, the majority of the McGovernites to whom I have spoken have remained in public life. Tracing their post-1972 careers can sometimes feel like an exercise in "where are they now?" Yet in their later public lives, the McGovernites, a cadre of exceptionally talented activists, are a critical component in assessing the McGovern campaign's impact on American politics.

For the majority of McGovernites, who were under the age of thirty-five in 1972, the campaign was a formative political experience. How it informed the political futures of these young activists varied considerably, however. Two directions branching out from the McGovern campaign are especially discernible, and they explain a great deal about the dynamics of American politics after 1972 and the persisting identity crisis of the Democratic Party. For those who took the first, the McGovern campaign solidified the commitments that had brought the young activists into the insurgency; their subsequent lives, in or out of politics, have been a working out of these commitments. For those who took the second, the campaign was an eye-opening exposure to the vulnerabilities and weaknesses of liberal ideology and policy, and their lives since have featured a refashioning of their political creed. Both an enduring liberal idealism and its skeptical centrist challenger are legacies of the McGovern campaign.

Some of the McGovern workers of 1972 have become powerful political insiders, while others have followed careers that flowed organically out of their roles in an insurgency. Many have remained active in presidential politics. Indeed, it is useful to organize much of the story of the McGovernites' later lives around three presidential candidates: Ted Kennedy, Gary Hart, and Bill Clinton. Most of the characters that populate this chapter were young in 1972, and they are only now reaching their final years on the public stage. Yet one elder from 1972 remains essential to this tale, his own odyssey afterward a commentary on all of the rest: George McGovern himself.

Life after Insurgency

After the McGovern campaign was over, its young activists dispersed. Some became civil servants, others political consultants, still others journalists, and—reflecting a pattern evident on the McGovern campaign staff—a large number became practicing attorneys. For a campaign that prided itself on its grassroots character, a disproportionate number of McGovernites wound up working in Washington, D.C. Among them today are several, including Anne Wexler, Tony Podesta, and Gerry Cassidy, who founded firms whose websites proclaim that they are among the top lobbyists in the nation's capital. None of these three were volunteers for McGovern when he was a dark-horse insurgent: Wexler and Podesta made the pragmatic choice to back Muskie and only moved over to McGovern after their candidate flopped, while Cassidy was already working for McGovern on the Senate Select Committee on Nutrition and Human Needs.[6]

It is mainly among the original McGovernites (FMBNH—"for McGovern before New Hampshire") that one finds individuals whose subsequent careers most closely reflect the values of the McGovern insurgency. The liberal goals that they have pursued have varied, from empowering labor or opening relations with Cuba to women's rights and new gender relationships. Their careers are briefly cited here as reminders of the survival of McGovernite ideals in little-noticed places.

Scott Lilly joined the McGovern campaign in the summer of 1971 and became the regional "desk officer" for the central states. Shortly after the campaign ended, Lilly joined the staff of Congressman David Obey of Wisconsin, and he remained on Capitol Hill until 2004, when he became a senior fellow at the Center for American Progress (run by fellow McGovernite John Podesta). He served as staff director for the Joint Economic Committee and executive director of the Democratic Study Group when the Democrats controlled the House, and when I interviewed him in March 2003 he was the head of the minority staff for the House Appropriations Committee. At that time he was working on opposition to the impending war in Iraq, which he considered "as big a mistake as Vietnam was." Lilly, one of the few McGovernites in 1972 who had a feel for working-class politics, has dedicated himself to rectifying the McGovern campaign's mistakes in approaching blue-collar voters: "The first thing I did when I started working for [Congressman] Obey was working on labor issues and trying to rebuild the relationships between liberals and labor. That job's been done, but there are an awful lot of working people that aren't in the labor movement that we've lost, and that really needs to be a big part of our focus."[7]

Kirby Jones, a former Peace Corps volunteer, joined McGovern's campaign staff at about the same time as Lilly, motivated by McGovern's antiwar leadership and the presence of Frank Mankiewicz, Jones's "rabbi/mentor." Jones served for a time as McGovern's press secretary before being replaced by the more experienced Richard Dougherty. When the campaign ended, Jones was broke, and his McGovern credentials were not exactly valuable in landing him a job. With Mankiewicz, he formed a small firm to make educational videos, and through a complicated chain of events the two found themselves in Cuba, under contract to CBS News for the first American television interview with Fidel Castro. This journalistic coup shaped the rest of Jones's career: he began his own consulting firm in Washington on trade with Cuba and also established the U.S.-Cuba Trade Association. *Newsweek* has described Jones as possessing "better contacts in Cuba than any other American." Attacked by conservatives as an apologist for Castro, Jones has pursued a business career that reflects one of McGovern's longtime positions: from his maiden Senate speech in 1963 to his writings in recent years, McGovern has been an outspoken critic of the U.S. embargo against Cuba.[8]

Unlike Lilly or Jones, Marcia Greenberger began the 1972 campaign season as a volunteer for Senator Harold Hughes. When his campaign fizzled, she switched to McGovern, joining the campaign on a full-time basis in the spring. Selected to be the regional coordinator for the New England states after the Democratic convention, she "was working every waking hour" for the rest of the campaign and was too overwhelmed to give thought to larger issues, including the one that would dominate her subsequent career: women's rights. But after McGovern was defeated by a landslide, she came to two conclusions that set her apart from many of her colleagues: first, that the country had not repudiated McGovern's fundamental values and thus there was no need to move to the political center; and second, that her future lay not in political campaigns but in the world of nonprofit advocacy groups. "Feeling very empowered because of that campaign," Greenberger soon established the National Women's Law Center in Washington; she remains its co-president more than three decades later. Her organization became a preeminent legal advocate for women's rights in a wide range of areas. She views her work on women's issues today as continuous with her efforts in the early 1970s: "the core fights"—reproductive choice, job opportunities, equal pay, athletics—"remain the core fights."[9]

Whereas Greenberger's feminist vocation did not emerge until after the McGovern campaign ended, Amanda Smith learned her feminism while working for McGovern. Smith's practical education in gender relations through her role as the women's issues specialist on the McGovern campaign staff was described in Chapter 9. She put this education—"the McGovern campaign was my graduate school"—to effective use in her subsequent career. Relocating to North Carolina with her husband, Smith "started a project for the state's Department of Public Instruction . . . called New Pioneers, which was designed to remove sex stereotypes in vocational education—to put it in shorthand: girls in carpentry, boys in home ec." By 1978, Smith says, all of the states were mandated to have at least one person working on "vocational sex equity." Because these bureaucrats "didn't have a clue what to do, and I was literally the only person who had done [such a program] statewide," she became a freelance consultant and found great satisfaction in spreading her insights into how males and females might work together more cooperatively.[10]

Lilly, Jones, Greenberger, and Smith are representative of the McGovernites who have moved beyond presidential politics into vocations that still echo the concerns of the McGovern insurgency. An even larger number of the McGovernites I interviewed have retained a connection to presidential politics. The lessons they drew from McGovern's defeat, and the political orientations they took on after 1972, can be seen in the political networks and presidential ventures of Ted Kennedy, Gary Hart, and Bill Clinton.

The Kennedy Connection

McGovern's career in national politics was bound up with the Kennedys—with John Kennedy, who appointed him as director of Food for Peace; with Robert Kennedy, his ally in the Senate whose delegates he inherited at the 1968 Democratic convention; and with Ted Kennedy, who rebuffed his offer of the vice-presidential nomination but became his most enthusiastic and effective co-campaigner in the fall of 1972. It was this last, surviving Kennedy, the most prominent leader of the liberal cause after 1972, who held a similar importance for several alumni of the McGovern campaign. During Kennedy's failed challenge to President Carter for the 1980 Democratic nomination, three McGovernites reprised their major roles from 1972: Rick Stearns as the chief delegate hunter, Morris Dees as the principal fundraiser, and Bob Shrum as the top speechwriter. Carl Wagner, one of McGovern's earliest and best field organizers, now occupied the position of Kennedy's political director for the campaign. Even after Kennedy's defeat in his lone bid for the presidency, his Senate staff continued to draw veterans of the McGovern campaign: Jeff Smith, McGovern's aide-de-camp, became Kennedy's press secretary during the 1980s, while Greg Craig, a McGovern coordinator in Vermont, served during the same period as Kennedy's chief foreign-affairs aide.

Morris Dees devoted most of his time after 1972 to his Southern Poverty Law Center. Because his direct-mail fundraising for McGovern in 1972 was a bright spot of the campaign, however, he was much in demand afterward to work similar successes for other candidates. Dees had met Ted Kennedy during the McGovern campaign, liked him and his liberal positions on the issues, and urged him to run in 1976. When Kennedy demurred, Dees yielded to the request of Jimmy Carter, whom he had known for years, and became his fundraiser for the presidential primaries. Dees was again successful, but he didn't have the passion in 1976 that he had felt four years earlier. "It wasn't a labor of love," he says, "even though I liked Jimmy Carter." Disappointed by Carter's choices in the White House, Dees defected from Carter's reelection team late in 1979 and became the finance director for Kennedy's challenge to the president. Kennedy's failed bid was Dees's last hurrah in presidential politics.[11]

Bob Shrum, McGovern's most gifted speechwriter in 1972, found Carter's political convictions suspect in 1976 and resigned from his campaign staff as a matter of principle. Liberal champion Edward Kennedy was a much more comfortable fit for Shrum, who, after spending most of the 1970s working for McGovern on the Senate Select Committee on Nutrition and Human Needs, joined Kennedy's Senate staff as press secretary and speechwriter. It was Shrum who penned some of the most soaring rhetoric of contemporary liberal politics for Kennedy in 1980.[12] His classic was Kennedy's concession speech at the Democratic convention in New York that renominated President Carter. The words for this occasion that Shrum supplied to Kennedy—and that McGovern no doubt would have been pleased to utter as well—upheld the relevance of the liberal faith for conservative times: "The commitment I seek is not to outworn values but to old values that will never wear out. Programs may sometimes become obsolete, but the idea of fairness always endures. Circumstances may change, but the work of compassion must continue." Kennedy's closing lines brought the delegates in Madison Square Garden, contemplating a disheartening Carter-Reagan matchup ahead, to an emotional catharsis: "For me, a few hours ago, this campaign came to an end. For all those whose cares have been our concern, the work goes on, the cause endures, the hope still lives, and the dream shall never die."[13]

Ironically for someone associated with the most passionate liberal speeches since the 1960s—McGovern's "Come Home, America" and Kennedy's "The Dream Shall Never Die"—Shrum became a target for liberals as well as conservatives after leaving Kennedy's employ in 1984 to become a campaign consultant. As a professional consultant, Shrum was an undisputed heavyweight and had a string of successes helping Democratic candidates reach and remain in the Senate. But his critics increasingly portrayed him as a controlling figure who sold clients cookie-cutter populist strategies, and he was derided for a perfect losing record in presidential campaigns: 0–8 after John Kerry's defeat in 2004.[14] More recently, writers of clashing ideological perspectives have converged on Shrum as the symbol of what is wrong with the professionalization of American electoral politics. Journalist Joe Klein, an avowed centrist, lights into Shrum for spending "much of his adult life smoothing out the rhetoric of the politicians he works for, taking out the bumps and spontaneity, and in his later years as a professional consultant—long after he left Ted Kennedy's staff—eliminating the risky ideas . . . and, in the process, dulling the passion of politics."[15] Meanwhile, Jerome Armstrong and Markos Moulitsas Zúniga, avatars of the liberal blogosphere, flay Shrum as the "uber-consultant" who draws lavish commissions for outdated media campaigns that divert Democrats from the new possibilities of mass mobilization through the "netroots."[16]

Carl Wagner, Shrum's colleague in the 1980 Kennedy campaign, shares this antipathy toward professional consultants. With a background in both grassroots and progressive union politics, he went to work for Kennedy in 1978. After Kennedy's loss to Carter, Wagner says, he grew disillusioned with politics, feeling that the creative energy of the 1960s and 1970s was dissipating, and he shifted some of his focus to the communications industry, involving himself in cable television in the 1980s and the Internet in the 1990s. But he was episodically drawn back into politics during these years. In 1984 he helped his old boss from the McGovern campaign, Gary Hart, and three years later he was among a group of Bill Clinton's friends who flew to Little Rock to discuss Clinton's possible run for the presidency in 1988. Wagner is particularly proud of his role in managing Ron Brown's successful campaign in 1989 to become chair of the Democratic National Committee; Brown was the first African American ever to hold such a post in either party.[17]

Wagner laid out for me a sweeping critique of contemporary Democratic Party politics. In his forceful account of the intertwined organizational and ideological degradation of the party, the original McGovernite spirit remains unbowed. So contrary to the conventional wisdom, his perspective deserves a hearing.

In the 1960s and 1970s, Wagner says, "the winners and losers of politics were defined in terms of *policy*. The place to be at a Democratic convention was on the platform committee." With matters of peace, race, or sexual equality at stake, "policy was the point of participating in politics." A campaign politics that revolved around issues, the insurgencies of 1968 and 1972 demonstrated, engaged ordinary citizens in their home communities, and they became the "backbone of the political venture." But after Ted Kennedy's defeat in 1980, the reign of the professional consultants began in the Democratic Party, and its politics "veered . . . from issues to winning elections." The consultants proclaimed their superior expertise, but Wagner claims that they have not been all that effective with their personality-centered campaigns, and that even when their clients do win, they are handicapped in governing because they lack an organized base. It is the Republicans today, Wagner alleges, who understand the power of policy, who excel at grassroots organizing, and who—most of the time—win.[18]

Wagner disputes the Democratic Leadership Council's version of Democratic Party history since the 1960s. He denies the DLC's claim that the liberalism of McGovern and Kennedy was the unmaking of the party. Had the party shied away in the 1970s from its policy stands on equality, social justice, and peace, Democrats would have lost their "heart and soul" and their base along with them. Wagner is "immensely proud of the progressive agenda that came out of the Kennedy and McGovern politics . . . It's made the country a much better place," especially on civil rights and gender equality. In his alternative version of Democratic history, it is the centrism exemplified by the DLC and not liberalism that has hurt the party. During the two presidential terms of his old friend Bill Clinton, he points out, the Democrats sustained substantial losses at both the state and the congressional levels. "Moving to the middle," Wagner argues, has been "hazardous politics" for the Democrats.[19]

Still a firm believer in grassroots politics, Wagner argues that fundamental change in American politics comes from below and not from above, from the countryside and not the capital. Centrists in the Democratic Party, comfortably allied with professional campaign consultants, don't even try to mobilize the party's mass base; in reality, they fear that its passions will simply drive away moderate swing voters. But Democrats will only recover their lost energy and capacity for effective governance, Wagner submits, when they rediscover their grassroots through issue-based campaigning. "If we are not going to organize the progressive forces in the country," he concludes, "it doesn't matter who wins the elections . . . The debate will be dominated by institutional conservative forces."[20]

Gary Hart and the McGovern Legacy

Of all the veterans of the McGovern campaign, Gary Hart has had perhaps the most complicated relationship with its original political vision. Hart was the first McGovernite to shape a separate political identity after the campaign, thereby superseding—and implicitly criticizing—what McGovern had represented. When the media dubbed him the leading light of the "neoliberal" wing of the Democratic Party, Hart appeared to be casting aside McGovern's "New Politics" liberalism altogether. Yet the distance that McGovern's campaign manager ultimately moved from the leader who had brought him onto the national political stage was not as great as it seemed. In a way, what is most striking in the years since the McGovern campaign is Hart's fidelity to some of its fundamental ideals.

After McGovern's defeat Hart went home to Colorado and, in a burst of renewed energy, wrote a richly informative "chronicle" of the campaign, *Right from the Start*, in what he estimates was about ten weeks.[21] Toward the end of the book, Hart began to distinguish between the organizational side of the McGovern insurgency, which had been successful, and its issues side, which had not. The problem, as he diagnosed it, was that the liberal wing of the party, traditionally the "fount" of its creative ideas, "was running dry," and that "by 1972, American liberalism was near bankruptcy."[22] Hart soon took this then-startling critique of liberalism into Colorado politics, becoming the successful Democratic candidate for the Senate in 1974. His campaign stump speech was titled "The End of the New Deal," and when *Washington Post* reporter David Broder asked him about his new generation of Democrats (the so-called Watergate Babies), Hart famously replied, "We're not a bunch of little Hubert Humphreys."[23] The target of Hart's remark was McGovern's rival in 1972, not his own boss, but McGovern had always shared, despite Humphrey's accusations of radicalism, the same New Deal faith on domestic politics as his former mentor, and so Hart's repudiation touched him as well as Humphrey. At the same time, Hart was careful not to criticize publicly the man whom he had served devotedly for over two years. At the Colorado state party convention, he recalls, he received a standing ovation after "I simply said, 'It's been suggested that the price of getting [the Senate nomination] for me is to disavow my support of George McGovern, in which case the price is too high and I refuse to do so.'"[24]

Hart rejected the liberal label that McGovern has always worn, and in later years he was not much happier about the "neoliberal" label that the media attached to him. He considers ideological markers like "liberal" and "conservative" to be shallow categories, convenient boxes into which Washington political reporters dump leaders whose actual ideas they can't be bothered to understand. To Hart, the relevant political axis is not the conventional horizontal spectrum of left to right, but a vertical axis of past and future, on which both traditional liberals and traditional conservatives fall at the bottom.[25] He sees himself as resolutely committed to the future; the terms he prefers to describe his own political orientation are *progressive* and *reformer*.[26]

When Hart ran for president in 1984, his "new ideas" did not look much like the ideas at the center of the McGovern campaign twelve years earlier. For example, McGovern had pushed a redistributive economic program that featured higher taxes on the rich; Hart emphasized economic growth through a new "industrial strategy," vigorous global trade, and worker retraining. McGovern's key issues were moral, and his policy proposals were sometimes dangerously weak on details; Hart's programmatic reforms were extensively worked out in advance, but many tended to sound dry and technical.[27]

Although Hart was a different breed of insurgent than McGovern by 1984, nonetheless there were curious parallels between their presidential runs. The key face-off in 1984 was between McGovern's protégé, Hart, and Humphrey's protégé, Mondale. Like McGovern in 1972, Hart's insurgency erupted in New Hampshire, was opposed by the party regulars—especially the leadership of the AFL-CIO—and proved especially appealing to young and well-educated voters; Mondale, like Humphrey in 1972, drew his strongest support from the elderly, blue-collar voters, and minorities. This time, however, the regular prevailed: whereas Humphrey had failed to stop McGovern with the charge of radicalism, Mondale undercut Hart's momentum with a sarcastic question from a Wendy's hamburger commercial: "Where's the beef?" Lacking a cause, like ending the war in Vietnam, that might have lent his "new ideas" moral simplicity and power, Hart did not have an effective riposte.[28]

Yet Hart came close to capturing the Democratic presidential nomination in 1984, establishing himself as the party's frontrunner for 1988, and he was probably better off not having to have faced the popular Ronald Reagan. Continuing to develop his "new ideas," especially on foreign policy, he pulled far ahead of prospective Democratic rivals in the early polls for 1988. But in yet another parallel with McGovern, this one particularly painful, the better he did, the more the press pursued him. Once McGovern had emerged as a frontrunner, the press had played a significant role in remaking his image, presenting him first as a left-winger and then as a bungler. The press also gave Hart a difficult time: it portrayed his personality as chilly and hinted at his reputation as a womanizer. It was, of course, a press stakeout of Hart's apartment that led to the Donna Rice scandal, which, almost in a flash, destroyed his political career.[29]

Hart's political ideas, during and after his Senate career and presidential bids, both challenge and confirm the McGovern legacy. His trademark issue of "military reform" is an interesting case in point. McGovern touted an "alternative defensive budget" of large-scale cuts in 1972 that was savaged by both Humphrey and Nixon as antimilitary. Hart joined the Senate Armed Services Committee, took up the cause of military reform, and became a leading advocate of casting off hidebound strategies and modernizing the U.S. armed forces. Not for Hart was the damaging reputation of weakness on national security; his watchword in defense, the title of his co-authored book published before the second presidential run, was *America Can Win*.[30]

Look more closely at Hart's thinking on military matters in the 1980s, however, and certain affinities with McGovern's position begin to appear. Emphasizing better trained personnel and "maneuver warfare" and denouncing "giant new weapons systems for which there seemed no good purpose," Hart was propounding an astringent critique of the military-industrial complex not unlike McGovern's.[31] In a later work, *The Minuteman: An Army of the People* (1998), Hart's views even more closely resembled those of his old boss. Writing during the brief era between the collapse of the Soviet Union in 1991 and the terrorist attacks in 2001, Hart wondered why the giant military machine of the Cold War years remained largely intact. He proposed the replacement of an overly professionalized force structure with a smaller regular army, backed, in his central prescription, by large numbers of citizen-soldiers organized along the lines of the Revolutionary War militias. Hart's grassroots soldiers, much like bomber-pilot George McGovern in World War II, would be exemplars of civic duty, trained and ready to defend the nation's vital interests, but they would not be convenient tools for national leaders who wished to engage the United States in overseas adventures with a minimum of public discussion and debate.[32]

The image of the "minuteman" points to the philosophical and moral grounds upon which Hart and McGovern continue to agree: a faith in grassroots democracy and a common lodestar in its principal American theorist, Thomas Jefferson. However much the policy ideas of Hart's presidential campaigns diverged from McGovern's in 1972, the organizational style was unchanged. A number of old McGovernites assisted Hart's campaign. His campaign manager was Bill Dixon, Gene Pokorny's closest collaborator in pulling off McGovern's critical victory in the 1972 Wisconsin primary. Running against the party establishment, the model for Hart in 1984 was the insurgent one that he and McGovern had devised:

> Ours was not, needless to say, a highly-financed campaign . . . It was, as much as possible, a grassroots campaign. We did not have highly paid professional consultants—indeed, I don't think, any consultants. People that worked on the campaign were full-time. Probably more were salaried per capita than in the McGovern days twelve years earlier. But the style and basic approach was pretty much the same.[33]

Hart's admiration for Jefferson, apparent early in his political career, only grew more expansive over the years. He looked to Jefferson for philosophical guidance on decentralized government, political participation, and civic duty. Equally important to him were the Virginian's orientation toward the future and his radical notion that a stagnant political order must be periodically shaken up by a new generation that questions and then overturns the ruling assumptions of the past.[34] Shortly before McGovern published a slim volume to defend the "liberal tradition," which he traced back to Jefferson,[35] Hart elaborated a more radical tribute to Jeffersonian thought for his doctoral dissertation at Oxford University, published by that university's press in 2002 as *Restoration of the Republic: The Jeffersonian Ideal in 21st-Century America*. Ranging through the writings of many classic and contemporary political theorists in addition to Jefferson, Hart insisted that Jefferson's commitment to the small republic, regarded by most contemporary authorities as impractical for the complex modern world, is instead of great importance in view of the pathologies of today's "corrupt national state." If Hart's "new ideas" of the 1980s could verge on the technocratic, his embrace of old ideas from the most radical of the founders in the first decade of the twenty-first century was as idealistic as anything in the McGovern legacy.[36]

There is, in short, a great deal of the Gary Hart of 1972 still visible in the lawyer and scholar, a public man regardless of office, who continues to fire ideas at the American people. One final affinity between Hart and McGovern remains to be noted: both men are critics of the timidity of their party. On the eve of the war in Iraq, McGovern wrote, "Most of today's liberals are too intimidated for my taste."[37] As the American venture in Iraq descended toward disaster, Hart was no less disappointed in Democrats:

> "Waist deep in the Big Muddy and the big fool said to push on," warned an anti-Vietnam song those many years ago. The McGovern presidential campaign, in those days, which I know something about, is widely viewed as a cause for the decline of the Democratic Party, a gateway through which a new conservative era entered. Like the cat that jumped on a hot stove and thereafter wouldn't jump on any stove, hot or cold, today's Democratic

leaders didn't want to make that mistake again. Many supported the Iraq war resolution and—as the Big Muddy is rising yet again—now find themselves tongue-tied or trying to trump a war president by calling for deployment of more troops. Thus does good money follow bad and bad politics get even worse. History will deal with George W. Bush and the neoconservatives who misled a mighty nation into a flawed war . . . But what will history say about an opposition party that stands silent while all this goes on?[38]

The Clinton Network and the McGovern Legacy

In the summer of 1971, Anne Wexler assembled veterans of Joseph Duffey's losing New Politics campaign for Senate at her home in Westport, Connecticut, to discuss the upcoming presidential campaign. The consensus of the group was to work for Muskie as the most electable Democratic candidate with an acceptable position on the war in Vietnam. But Bill Clinton was a holdout.[39] Why did Clinton, already more of a moderate than most of his friends, opt for McGovern over Muskie? Ted Van Dyk has always suspected Clinton's motives, believing that he preferred the McGovern campaign because it offered a better opportunity to build a political network for his future ambitions.[40] But Clinton may have had another motive that, while no less personal, was less instrumental: one of his closest friends, Rick Stearns, was a top figure in the McGovern insurgency.[41]

What Clinton thought about his experiences as a McGovern organizer is not altogether clear either. The ten pages of his autobiography that describe his role in the McGovern campaign are not particularly forthcoming.[42] Certainly, they convey little of the warmth toward McGovern expressed by almost all of the roughly three dozen McGovernites I interviewed.[43] Jeff Smith, Clinton's superior during the McGovern campaign and his aide in the White House, relates an anecdote that offers insight into Clinton's relationship with his McGovernite past. The first time Smith spoke with Clinton after he was elected president, Smith said,

> "Mr. President, the last time I remember seeing you was in Texas . . . I remember when I shut the airplane door and then I looked out and I saw you on the tarmac there, alone, and I looked at McGovern and said, 'I didn't know which one of you looked the sadder.' I guess you both knew what was going to happen." And I expected Clinton to say, "Well, you know that's right, it's a tragic thing." Clinton didn't—I think he remembered it, but he wasn't about to acknowledge it . . . I think that Clinton had a special feeling in his heart for him, but he never let it show. Clinton and the DLC and Al From felt that everything that was wrong with the Democratic Party can be traced back to McGovern . . . I think he winced every time it was mentioned that he was a McGovern worker in '72.[44]

Never really a liberal of the McGovern stripe, Clinton soon became even more of a moderate than he was in 1972. During Clinton's first term in the White House, McGovern took the president's policies as an explicit repudiation of the liberal ideology he had represented in 1972. As he wrote in an op-ed piece late in 1994, "Although I have personal affection for Bill Clinton ever since he toiled in my unsuccessful 1972 campaign for the presidency, I am aware that he and his current team have been wary of any public association with 'McGovernism.'"[45]

Yet while Clinton distanced himself from the McGovern legacy, he could not be completely free of it. In military affairs he desired to dispel the stereotype that he was one of those squeamish Democrats in the McGovern mold who shied away from the use of force. Amid the post–Cold War climate of the 1990s, however, his military interventions abroad had to be justified mainly on humanitarian and democratic grounds; opposed by the majority of Republicans when he sent troops to Haiti, Bosnia, and Kosovo, he had the approval of McGovern.[46] In cultural politics, Clinton's positions on gay and lesbian rights were equivocal in the same way as McGovern's, and yet with the hostility of conservatives as backdrop, both men were seen as friendly by the gay and lesbian community. Clinton even had his own version in 1992 of the "three A's" problem that Republicans had dropped on McGovern during the 1972 campaign—acid (did Clinton smoke marijuana as a longhaired youth?), amnesty (did Clinton evade the draft to escape the war in Vietnam?), and abortion (was Clinton married to a militant feminist?). No matter how much Clinton modified his political identity after 1972, to the Republican right he remained what Newt Gingrich called him: "a countercultural McGovernik."[47]

For Clinton, the most important result of his time working for McGovern was the expansion of the personal network that would aid him in his political rise. Some of the connections in this network had already been established during Clinton's days as a Rhodes Scholar, an antiwar activist, and a Connecticut campaigner for Joe Duffey. But the McGovern campaign offered a larger stage, allowing Clinton to forge a national network among the talented political activists that had rallied to McGovern's cause. Betsy Wright, who first met Clinton when he was a McGovern coordinator for the fall campaign in Texas and who became his most important aide in Arkansas, says, "So few people probably remember that that's where it all went back to—the McGovern campaign . . . The core of people who took his candidacy and ran with it were people he had met during the McGovern campaign."[48]

When Gingrich dubbed Clinton a "countercultural McGovernik," he was trading on fading images from 1972—of longhaired youth, rebellious feminists, and dashiki-clad black militants—to tar Clinton's administration as extremist. This characterization of the president, his wife, and their associates was largely spurious—Clinton had long ago reached an accommodation with the conservative forces that dominated American politics after 1980—yet there remained a kernel of truth in it. The Clinton White House *was* stocked with McGovern campaign alumni, especially at its senior levels. Jeff Smith chaired a meeting in the Roosevelt Room of the West Wing on nominations for the Presidential Medal of Freedom. When someone brought up McGovern's name, Smith recalls, everybody said, "Oh, yeah, what a decent, what a first-rate guy." Looking around the table, he realized that more than half of the meeting's participants "had their lives connected with McGovern."[49]

Not every member of the Clinton network participated in the evolution toward centrism. Yet among McGovernites, it has been Clinton's people who represent the sharpest turn away from 1972. Two of those whose stories are bound up with Clinton's career and who share in his ideological journey are Sandy Berger and Eli Segal.

A member of McGovern's speechwriting team during the fall campaign in 1972, Samuel "Sandy" Berger became a central figure on the foreign-policy side of the Clinton presidency. Berger gained experience in the international arena by serving in the Carter State Department and was one of numerous Clinton friends urging him by 1988 to try for the White House. He eventually became the national security adviser to Clinton and an advocate for his post–Cold War perspective on the world. Berger sees the centrist foreign policy that he helped to shape during the Clinton presidency as an "evolution" beyond the positions of the McGovern campaign in 1972. McGovernites on the left, he argues, made the war in Vietnam into a metaphor for a misguided U.S. role in the world and developed the unfortunate mindset of "America at fault." By contrast, the alumni of the McGovern campaign who shifted toward the center with Clinton were "strong internationalists," believers in "a robust American role and even a robust use of American force." Liberals, he says, "stigmatized the Democratic Party as being an antimilitary party," but first Gary Hart and then Bill Clinton made important strides in overcoming this image and demonstrating that some Democrats were willing to use the armed forces in a confident and reasonable fashion.[50]

Before Berger became a McGovern speechwriter he was the deputy to Eli Segal, campaign manager for the California primary, and the two men remained close friends until Segal's death in 2006. Segal was in the top echelon of McGovern campaign strategists. Miles Rubin, the wealthy fundraiser, took a liking to him during the campaign and invited him to participate in Rubin's corporate conglomerate after the election. Highly successful in the business world over the next two decades, Segal was able to retire before the age of fifty in very comfortable circumstances. During his business career he kept his hand in the political careers of friends from the McGovern campaign: he was the chief of staff for the presidential campaigns of Gary Hart in 1984 and Bill Clinton in 1992. Clinton asked Segal to design and then head AmeriCorps, the chief symbol of his administration's New Democrat credo that citizen responsibilities must accompany citizen rights.[51]

Leaving the Clinton administration in 1996, Segal continued to serve his friend by forming a nonprofit Welfare-to-Work Partnership to implement the president's welfare program, a sore point among liberals. He was by this time a firm centrist, committed to Clinton's political project and skeptical of old-fashioned liberals who clung to the bureaucratic welfare approaches of the past. In 2000 he visited with McGovern in Rome and was struck by the fact that his old boss's thinking about poverty and welfare was little changed since the 1970s. McGovern's positions were idealistic, Segal told me. No one else he knew still talked about these issues the way that McGovern did.[52]

"The Original McGovernik"

George McGovern has never suffered from a political identity crisis. From the start of his political career to a remarkably active old age, he has always been an unreconstructed and unapologetic liberal. Whether one finds his current positions anachronistic, the expression of a liberalism long ago discredited, or courageous, the expression of a still-relevant liberalism that other Democrats are too scared to defend, the consistency of his political passions and moral concerns has been a defining mark of his public life.

Although scarred by his overwhelming defeat in 1972, McGovern has always been resilient, and he won reelection to the Senate in 1974. Six years later, however, he was ousted by South Dakota voters, a victim of a successful conservative crusade at the national level to target for defeat the leading liberals in the Senate. After departing from the Senate, McGovern remained active in liberal causes, forming a political organization (Americans for Common Sense), teaching at various universities, and serving as president from 1991–1997 of the Middle East Policy Council.[53] His name continued to be bandied about with abuse for 1972—by centrist Democrats seeking to reorient their party, and by conservative Republicans tarring the opposition as radical at home and soft abroad. But he took solace from the "love letters" that arrived long after the 1972 campaign. People still come up to him, McGovern relates, to say, "'You're the only Democrat that made me bleed and die for a cause'" or "'you're the last candidate I really believed in.'"[54]

McGovern takes pride in the large number of his former campaign workers who embarked upon careers in public life at all levels of government and in social activism.[55] Yet he experienced some distress when the two most prominent McGovernites in later years, Hart and Clinton, put ideological space between themselves and their one-time leader. During his brief campaign for the Democratic nomination in 1984 McGovern was asked if Hart, a strong contender for that nomination, had moved to the right since 1972. "Yes," McGovern answered, "and it has made me a little sad." McGovern interpreted Hart's political evolution after 1972 as a reflection of his Senate career from a conservative state—a situation with which he was personally familiar. Nonetheless, he was critical of Hart as "somewhat more fearful of taking strong progressive positions."[56] Clinton's centrist approach during his first term in the White House seemed to distress McGovern even more. After Clinton's party lost both the House and Senate in the 1994 elections, McGovern, borrowing from Gingrich's sarcastic gibe and calling himself "the original McGovernik," ascribed the voters' repudiation of the president to his political equivocations:

> Dramatic Democratic losses in the recent elections have prompted many commentators to assume that the Democratic leadership is too liberal for the majority of Americans . . . My conviction is that the Democratic Party has lost the confidence of the American people, not because it is too liberal, but because it has neither kept faith with the historic values of liberalism nor defended those values to the public.[57]

Any estrangement between McGovern and Clinton dissipated during Clinton's second term. In 1997 the president appointed McGovern to be the U.S. ambassador to the United Nations Food and Agriculture Organization in Rome. McGovern was grateful to Clinton for the chance to be an important actor once again in a field dear to his heart—and Clinton in turn soon appreciated McGovern's staunch support during the battle over his impeachment. Jeff Smith, a bridge between the two men, speculates on how the Republican effort to drive Clinton from office appeared to McGovern: "Here were these rabid right-wingers, with unlimited money and unlimited bile, going after [Clinton], and McGovern's going, 'hey, I've been there.'"[58]

Plunging enthusiastically into his new role as ambassador, McGovern developed a plan for a global school-lunch program, a natural extension of his work in Food for Peace and on the Senate Select Committee on Nutrition and Human Needs. In May 2000 he brought the plan to the Clinton White House, where, with the support of his former campaign aides John Podesta, the president's chief of staff, and Sandy Berger, the national security adviser, he secured the president's enthusiastic commitment of $300 million in initial funding. That August, McGovern was awarded the Presidential Medal of Freedom by Clinton in a White House ceremony. When I interviewed him a few days later, he was still aglow with the honor.[59]

After Clinton left the White House, McGovern continued his campaign to end hunger worldwide, but he also became a liberal gadfly for the Bush years. His commitment to do something on a grand scale to eradicate hunger was a testament to the decent ambition that had always fueled his politics. McGovern regarded the campaign against hunger as an American opportunity—and an American duty: "As an American, I have always thought that I live in the greatest country on earth. If we will now take the lead in ending world hunger, as only we can do, we will be an even greater country, and God's blessing and that of our fellow humans will be upon us."[60] Once President Bush proclaimed the doctrine of preemptive war and sent the military into Iraq, McGovern added to his case for ending world hunger the claim that the program would serve as a counter-symbol for American foreign policy. "Suppose," he wrote in 2004, "that instead of invading Iraq, the United States had persuaded the United Nations to join us in providing a good, nutritious school lunch every day to every schoolchild in Iraq . . . America will be safer in the feeding business than in the war business, and we will sleep better at night—the sleep of the just."[61]

As Bush drove post-Clinton politics back to the right, McGovern assumed a role that few others apparently wanted to play: defender of liberalism. In magazine articles and in a book, *The Essential America: Our Founders and the Liberal Tradition*, he argued that liberalism was not dead but merely in hiding. Too many liberals, he complained, "would just as soon keep their liberalism a secret." Rather than adopting a safer euphemism for liberalism, such as progressivism, McGovern argued in his book that the dreaded "L-word" named a great American tradition, as old and as indestructible as conservatism. It was a tradition that stretched back from John Kennedy and Lyndon Johnson to Franklin and Theodore Roosevelt, Woodrow Wilson, Abraham Lincoln, and Andrew Jackson, and that was ultimately rooted in the wisdom of the founders, especially Thomas Jefferson. American politics could not do without liberalism, McGovern claimed, without losing the creative source of its historical advances: "I challenge my conservative friends to name a single federal program now generally approved by both of our major parties that was not first pushed by liberals over the opposition of conservatives."[62]

With the onset of the war in Iraq, McGovern resumed an even more familiar role: antiwar critic. The United States, he feared, was making the same mistakes in Iraq against which he had warned forty years earlier. "We continue to place too much faith in reducing terrorism by military means," he wrote, "and pay not enough attention to other vital ingredients of security." The Bush administration was weakening and not enhancing U.S. security by defying world opinion and taking the nation into "a needless and hopeless war." As in the past, McGovern's words were tinged with grief toward the troops that paid a terrible price for an unwise military venture devised by armchair warriors: "the men and women of our occupying army are being picked off daily by Iraqi guerillas with no end in sight—shades of Vietnam."[63] Once again, he was unequivocal in advocating the withdrawal of U.S. forces from a military quagmire.[64] Nowhere was the essential continuity of his career as palpable as here: the most outspoken dove in the Senate during the war in Vietnam was now more outspoken than anyone in the Senate during the war in Iraq.

Conclusion

One of the most thoughtful answers to a standard question from my interviews of McGovernites—"what lessons did you take away from the 1972 campaign?"— came from Greg Craig, a Vermont coordinator for McGovern. He is now a Washington lawyer who has represented, among others, Bill Clinton, Alexander Solzhenitsyn, Kofi Annan, and the father of Elian Gonzalez, the shipwrecked Cuban boy whose return to his homeland may have cost Al Gore the electoral votes of Florida. Craig suggests that the McGovern campaign was hurt by its "romanticism." "The coalition that McGovern was trying to put together," he says, "which was essentially a coalition of people that felt left out and left behind, was never going to be the kind of coalition that could command a majority of the American people. You really had to move to the center on some important issues to be credible." He faults McGovern for failing "to reassure the vast majority of the American people that the country was in good shape [and] they were living good lives." But Craig also acknowledges that there was a cost to the Democratic Party when it moved to the center, especially as it came, under Clinton, to rely heavily on wealthy contributors: "What the Democratic Party has stood for on the fundamental issues—civil rights, women's rights, and economic opportunity—has been lost. You lose a little bit of the energy, excitement, and electricity of the history of the party that way. The Jacksonian, Rooseveltian tradition isn't alive, isn't real to people any more. And that's too bad!"[65]

There were many ways to read the lessons of the McGovern insurgency. Some McGovernites felt that the causes with which their campaign was identified were undimmed despite its landslide defeat, and they continued, outside or inside of politics, to serve these causes. Others, like Gary Hart, had a more complex relationship with the McGovern legacy, moving away from it on one political plane yet remaining anchored in it on another. It was those who linked their careers to Bill Clinton who traveled the greatest distance from the starting point of 1972, becoming New Democrats whose place in the political center was an ideological and strategic escape from the perils revealed in the insurgent Democratic politics of McGovern.

Save for the McGovernites who worked, most at junior levels, in the Carter administration, it was only the Clinton network that ever reached the heights of presidential power. In the eyes of the Clintonites, the experience of the McGovern campaign was a valuable initiation in politics, but they needed the subsequent process of political maturation before they were ready to exercise authority and shape policy. Sandy Berger suggests that the McGovern campaign was "an intellectual steppingstone for many people. A generation of people my age were inspired by John Kennedy as teenagers . . . to a sense of public service . . . George McGovern provided [some of] us the opportunity—at a very early age—to operate at a very high level, in trying to change the direction of the country, unsuccessfully. Many of us then wound up in the Clinton administration, actually governing."[66]

"Actually governing," for Berger, meant the politics of Clinton's Third Way, beyond and partly against the liberalism of McGovern. Yet Berger, like more liberal veterans of the McGovern campaign, recognizes that whatever the failures of the insurgency, in its passion to end the war in Vietnam it had been a special moment in modern American politics. "Even though this campaign was twenty points down," he remembers, "it was one of the most high morale campaigns I've ever been around. People knew why they were there. It was not about 'what kind of a job am I going to get if McGovern gets elected?'"[67] In the conventional wisdom of American politics, the McGovern campaign has continued to represent a negative reference point, but in the life story of the McGovernites, it has been, for all but a handful, a positive touchstone. Hart sums up its standing in their collective memory: "I think it was an honorable effort in the best tradition of American politics. There was no guile, there was no deception, there was no hidden agenda, in an era of hidden agendas. It was a true citizen movement."[68]

Epilogue

The story that this book has told does not offer comforting lessons for anyone. For liberal activists in the Democratic Party, it contains cautionary lessons about the difficulties of a campaign on the left, especially if it takes the form of an insurgency. For their centrist adversaries in the party, it suggests that the muffling of the liberal message brings a different set of problems, fostering timid and tepid candidates who fail to inspire anybody. Democrats of all stripes have been haunted by an identity crisis whose roots lie in the landslide defeat of 1972 and the fear of its recurrence. Republicans might take comfort from the Democrats' identity crisis—except that they confront one of their own, since the principles and policies of the Republican revolution have become increasingly stale and disconnected from the concerns of the majority of Americans.[1]

Many liberals would prefer to look back on the McGovern campaign with nostalgia rather than discomfort, as the last time they could feel passionate and honest as they rallied behind one of their own in a presidential election. Certainly, later insurgent liberals, who have never made it past the primaries, have not paid much heed to the electoral vulnerabilities of liberalism that the McGovern campaign made palpable. Yet any future campaign mounted by the liberal wing of the Democratic Party needs to grapple with these vulnerabilities. Several characteristics of the McGovern campaign that offered plump targets for the Republicans remain of great relevance today, and liberals cannot evade the problems that they pose if they want credibly to renew their claim to the party's leadership.

One vulnerable characteristic of contemporary liberalism laid bare during the McGovern campaign is the difficulty of criticizing flaws in American politics and society without coming across as negative about the United States itself. When Herman Talmadge remarked that McGovern sounded "mad at the country" in 1972, he put his finger on a dilemma that has troubled Democrats since the 1960s. The causes that have galvanized liberals—struggles against economic, social, and racial injustices; abuses against civil liberties; military misadventures abroad—are not easily couched in the sunny, optimistic tones that advantage a candidate in national elections. Liberalism's critical voice fits in a great American tradition—many of our most revered forebears were dissenters. But dissent is seldom popular in the moment, and when liberals point out the failings in American policy, their opponents are all too ready to brand their arguments unpatriotic.

A related vulnerability of contemporary liberalism is its reputation for weakness in defending the nation. The Democrats for Nixon ad depicting McGovern sweeping American forces off a game board while leaving Soviet forces untouched inaugurated a charge of which Republican campaign strategists would never tire. Republican citations of McGovern as the godfather of Democratic defeatism continue to be heard. Kenneth Mehlman, chairman of the Republican National Committee, told an interviewer in August 2006, "The history of the last generation is that when the Democrat Party becomes a doctrinaire, anti-use-of-American force party as it did in 1972, it didn't do well. A lot of Americans may have disagreed with a lot of aspects of the Vietnam War, but in 1972 they were not willing to support a candidate for president who said, 'Come home, America.'"[2] McGovern, a decorated war hero running against an opponent who had never seen combat, sought to reorient American foreign policy away from an excessive reliance on military force and toward a more cooperative brand of internationalism. Like liberals since, his argument that national security would be better served by this reorientation was met by the specious claim that a presidential candidate critical of the use of force in a particular case must be afraid of the use of force in all cases. Yet this claim was potent in 1972, and it was still effective in comparable circumstances thirty-two years later.

The McGovern campaign also opened an electoral era in which Republicans would successfully turn the historical tables and accuse the Democrats of being the party of "elitism." They would point to Democratic representation of the educated strata and cosmopolitan regions of the nation and the party's declining grip on the loyalties of blue-collar constituencies and heartland communities. Understandably, Democrats would protest that the most powerful elites in the nation—nestled in the corporations and all of the surrounding institutions that their concentrated wealth subsidized—were mainstays of the Republican Party. Nonetheless, the McGovern campaign was a genuine watershed in which college-educated issue activists took over the dominant position in the Democratic Party from its old labor/urban machine coalition. And the experience of that campaign revealed vexing problems in the ability of the new Democratic cadre to speak knowingly and sympathetically to the concerns and the values of working-class whites. More secular, intellectual, and middle class than the old liberalism, the New Politics liberalism that shaped the party from 1972 championed policies favorable to working-class interests but fell short, most of the time, in touching working-class hearts.

Compounding the difficulty for the Democratic Party in holding on to its old constituencies was the association with the identity politics that entered the party through the McGovern campaign. It was in 1972 that feminists first gained power in the party and pushed it toward a full-fledged commitment to women's rights. It was also in 1972 that the cause of gay and lesbian rights gained its first foothold in the party, linking Democrats to the most stigmatized minority in the

United States. Finding the touchstone of their political morality in the sixties struggle for civil rights for black Americans, liberal Democrats could hardly rebuff the later demands by other groups for their own equality. Yet McGovern's uncomfortable identification with the militant forces pushing for rapid and dramatic cultural change foreshadowed an enduring electoral problem. It was some comfort for liberal Democrats that survey data suggested growing tolerance among Americans for equal treatment of racial minorities, women, and even gays and lesbians. As with opposition to the war in Vietnam, however, a prophetic stance that history later upholds does not help much on Election Day.

Vulnerable in electoral contests on matters of patriotism, strength in defending the nation, connection to working-class constituencies, and identification with unsettling cultural change, liberal Democrats have been branded as surefire losers by their centrist adversaries in the party. Leaders of the Democratic Leadership Council thus continue, almost as often as Republicans, to bring up the McGovern campaign as a warning of the electoral debacle facing the Democratic Party if it lets liberals back into its command. Yet centrists should not be too quick to read the story of the McGovern campaign as a validation of their philosophy and strategy. The centrist record since 1972 is only marginally more impressive than that of the liberals. Counting Jimmy Carter and Bill Clinton as centrists, that wing of the party has only elected a presidential candidate under highly favorable circumstances—against weak opponents and when the economy and international events were strongly in its favor. Moreover, the Democratic Party as a whole can hardly be said to have thrived during the administrations of these centrist presidents. The McGovern campaign, derided for its failures, provides in its successes some clues to the continuing electoral (and governing) weakness of Democratic centrists—to vulnerabilities that centrists have evaded just as liberals have evaded their own.

One of the electoral vulnerabilities of centrist Democrats is that they engender a *conviction gap* with the Republicans. Intellectuals associated with the DLC have produced thoughtful manifestos staking out a centrist philosophy for American politics. Yet integral to the centrist approach has been a concern for the "inoculation" of their Democratic candidates on precisely those issues or themes upon which liberals, starting with McGovern, have been vulnerable. Shaping campaign positions out of a concern for "inoculation" invariably places centrist Democrats in a defensive crouch; centrists explain themselves by what they are not and out of a fear of what Republicans will say they are.[3] To make matters worse, defensiveness often bleeds over into pure expedience. The DLC's greatest success story, Bill Clinton, heralded a centrist Third Way, but when, under the guidance of an ideological cross-dresser like Dick Morris, he practiced "triangulation" in the White House, the Third Way between liberalism and conservatism looked like nothing so much as opportunism.[4]

Defensiveness and opportunism only exacerbate the identity crisis of the Democratic Party. In 2004 some voters who did not agree with President Bush or his policies nonetheless appeared to prefer his firm air of conviction to a Democratic challenger who seemed to have few convictions at all. Citing survey evidence, John Halpin and Ruy Teixeira write, "Despite difficult times for the GOP in early 2006, Republicans continue to hold double-digit advantages over Democrats on the key attribute of 'know what they stand for' and fewer than four in ten voters believe the Democratic Party has 'a clear set of policies for the country.'"[5] McGovern and his liberal heirs have had convictions whose electoral vulnerabilities at least might be faced and partially fixed; the historical record does not suggest that the centrist wing of the party can say the same.

The conviction gap between the centrists ascendant in the Democratic Party and the conservatives who dominate the Republican Party leads to a *passion gap* in presidential campaigns. Following the centrists' strategy, with its defensive crouch and constrained aspirations, Democratic presidential nominees such as Michael Dukakis, Al Gore, and John Kerry generate scant enthusiasm for their candidacies. Dispirited activists come to feel that their party has no fundamental purpose or message save opposition to the right wing. Democratic partisans may loathe the ideology of conservative Republicans, but some envy how their Republican counterparts at least have leaders in which to believe.

That McGovern still hears from numerous admirers that he was the last Democratic presidential nominee who touched their hearts is a solace for him but a sad comment on his party. The most successful feature of the McGovern campaign—and the one most relevant to the revival of the Democratic Party—was its grassroots army. It is doubtful that the centrist strategy can generate the passions that inspire that kind of army. Leaders of centrist organizations, from the Coalition for a Democratic Majority to the Democratic Leadership Council and the New Democrat Network, have insisted that they, and not the disproportionately liberal activists of the party, speak for rank-and-file Democrats. The claim is less impressive than it sounds, since activists in both parties have, for as long as political scientists have been studying the matter, been more ideological than the mass of generally moderate party followers.[6] It is also a claim that centrist organizations have not wanted to test, since they have remained small, elite organizations that do not even try to organize a mass following.

Perhaps the ultimate vulnerability for the centrist strategy of muffling the party's liberal values is that it fails the pragmatic test: it seldom works. The fate of Dukakis in 1988 has been paradigmatic for Democratic presidential candidates, with Clinton only a partial exception to the pattern. The centrist approach has been to seek the middle and deny all associations with the name and perspective of liberalism. But Republican attack artists have blasted through the centrist equivocations and pinned the liberal moniker on every Democratic presidential candidate, be they liberal or centrist. Democratic candidates, regularly put in the position of denying their party's most deeply held values, only deepen the impression that they are inauthentic as they awkwardly struggle to define what it is, other than liberalism, that they do in fact represent.

Twin evasions—by liberals shying away from a reckoning with their electoral vulnerabilities, by centrists glossing over the dispiriting effect of their defensive crouch—have left the Democrats wandering in a persistent identity crisis, even as their opponents grow increasingly divided and muddled themselves. Yet another round of Democratic soul-searching has been sparked by defeat in 2004 at the hands of a president whom Democrats despise more than any Republican since Nixon. Sophisticated and shrewd analyses since 2004 have laid bare the party's confused identity and generated some intriguing suggestions. Yet the analyses have, for the most part, fallen short in understanding the party's evolution since the 1960s and the paradox at the core of the identity crisis that it has produced.

Democrats are not likely to find guidance from the suggestion that they update the fighting faith of the original Cold War liberals from the Truman era for an age of international terrorism.[7] Regardless of its subtlety and moral modesty in theory, Cold War liberalism became militant interventionism in practice. It was discredited for most Democrats by its disastrous implementation in Vietnam. It has been the neoconservatives, the unreconstructed Cold War liberals and their heirs, who, in the Iraq debacle, have made this approach to the world twice cursed.

More promising is the recommendation that Democrats hark back to FDR and New Deal liberalism and establish their lost identity as the party of the common good.[8] For a party that has developed a reputation as a wrangling collection of self-regarding interest groups, indifferent to the concerns of the majority of ordinary Americans, a politics of the common good points toward ideological terrain upon which Democrats might reconnect with the constituencies that they have alienated. Yet the history underpinning this proposal is a bit skewed: a philosophy of the common good was present in the New Deal, but so was the interest-group liberalism that brought organized labor and senior citizens into the Democratic coalition. More important, the idea of a common good is probably too abstract and indistinct to serve as an identity for the Democratic Party. It is an idea that can be stretched to encompass almost any policy position and can be evoked by either party.

This is not the place—and I am not the person—to come up with a full-blown alternative that might help Democrats resolve their identity crisis. Yet the story of the McGovern campaign and its aftermath does hold some clues to a possible resolution. The McGovern campaign was a moment when Democrats had conviction and passion. It was also a moment when they went down to an overwhelming defeat. Examining the campaign with an eye to how to recapture the first without bringing on the second can serve as a therapeutic exercise for troubled Democrats.

Revisiting the McGovern campaign, we might learn that parties have strong messages not because they have labels or brands but because they articulate core convictions. It has not been the label of *conservative* that has been central to Republican electoral successes since 1980 but the core convictions that it expresses: small government, traditional values, a strong military. Democrats will not get far in addressing their own identity crisis if they fixate on a more appealing label for the party. Rather, they need to articulate and elaborate core convictions that can be counterpoised to those of the Republicans: economic justice, social equality, a more multilateral and multifaceted strategy for national security.

Centrists can readily object that these are precisely the values that have made liberals so vulnerable in national elections. Yet they *are* the animating values of most Democrats, and it is ultimately fruitless to hide them. Instead, Democrats, especially on the party's liberal wing, need to be working not to parade these values in defiance of the concerns of constituencies that have turned away from the party, but to reshape and refine them to take into account the beliefs and the interests of those constituencies. In this enterprise, unfortunately, George McGovern will not be a model: McGovern movingly articulated liberal convictions, but he did so in a fashion that pushed away many traditional Democrats. The best exemplar for this ideological feat remains the man who gave the Democratic Party its liberal identity in the first place: Franklin D. Roosevelt. FDR understood, better than any of his Democratic successors, how to blend the liberal vision of political transformation into the American political tradition, and how to make a new liberalism into the necessary next step in the progress of the ancestral American faith.

The question of what to call the Democrats' core convictions—progressive, liberal, or something else—is not the critical question. But it will inevitably come up, because Republicans can be counted on to label these convictions as *liberalism,* with all of the negative associations that they have attached to the word. When Democratic presidential candidates are assailed as liberal, they only heighten the confusion by further equivocating about what they are. They will be better served by acknowledging the label and giving an account of what it means in their own terms. They will come across as more authentic, as McGovern has recently argued, if they react with pride in the liberal tradition, with its heroes and its grand accomplishments, from social security to civil rights. The mounting failures of conservatism under George W. Bush suggest that its era of ascendancy might be coming to an end and that Americans might become open once again to its traditional alternative if it is convincingly defended.

An essential step in resolving the identity crisis of the Democratic Party is to recover what Democrats believe, their core—and liberal—convictions, and to refuse to conceal them any longer. Equally essential is the honesty to work through the traumas of liberal defeat, particularly 1972, and to learn from liberal failings. Battling against centrist Democrats and their circumspect strategies, liberal Democrats have had the luxury to revel in their ideological fortitude while neglecting its drawbacks. Ironically, a Democratic Party liberal wing that witnessed presidential candidates who stood by its core convictions might become less rigid and uncompromising about their applications. The twenty-year-old debate between liberals and centrists in the Democratic Party, now grown sterile and tiresome, might be superseded by a more fruitful discourse in which liberals and centrists unite around core convictions and struggle over the most pragmatic ways to get them across to the electorate.

I have suggested that the identity crisis of the Democratic Party has its origins in the McGovern insurgency of 1972, and that working through this critical piece of its history is part of the therapeutic process through which Democrats can regain their confidence that they know who they are. It is remarkable how fully the issues that troubled Democrats in 1972 remain vexing three and one-half decades later. Nonetheless, the brevity of the liberals' moment under McGovern does not presage inevitable frustration for liberalism in our own time. Several features of contemporary American politics suggest that the setting for a liberal presidential candidacy is more favorable than it was when McGovern ran. The Democratic Party is not as bitterly divided as it was in 1972, especially because so many of the intractable conservatives who fought McGovern to the end have shifted to the Republican side. The party's progressive groups, such as the feminists, are generally less militant and more pragmatic than they were in 1972, when they still had far to travel to reach their objectives. Even the Republicans' advantage in the area of national security—Nixon's hole card against McGovern—is not what it used to be after Bush's Iraq disaster.

Parties and ideologies do not dominate forever in American politics. New Deal liberalism remade American politics, but it eventually came apart amid racial conflict, a failed war in Vietnam, and an economic crisis. The Reagan alternative has had a powerful run for a generation, but its own contradictions have increasingly come to the fore in this decade. As the election results of 2006 indicate, American politics is opening once again to the Democrats. But they will muff their opportunity unless they figure out what they stand for. It will not be George McGovern's unreconstructed liberalism. It may well be a liberalism that speaks in his deeply American voice of honesty and humane values, even as it reaches out to meet the concerns of those Americans who rejected what they thought he was saying about their country.

Interviews

Between 2000 and 2006 I interviewed forty-seven participants on the events of 1972. I have listed them alphabetically. If no location is cited, the interview was conducted by phone.

Ronald Alheim, February 14, 2006, Niskayuna, New York
Samuel (Sandy) Berger, February 27, 2002, Washington, D.C.
Gerald Cassidy, July 14, 2005
Jack Chestnut, September 23, 2005
Gregory Craig, May 10, 2001, Washington, D.C.
Morris Dees, January 8, 2002
John Douglas, February 24, 2006
Sara Ehrman, May 10, 2001, Washington, D.C.
James K. Galbraith, June 5, 2002
Joseph Grandmaison, May 9, 2001, Washington, D.C.
Marcia Greenberger, May 11, 2001, Washington, D.C.
William Greider, September 27, 2005; October 27, 2005
Charles Guggenheim, April 12, 2002
Rob Gunnison, May 24, 2006
Gary Hart, June 12, 2002; June 18, 2002; June 26, 2002
Harold Himmelman, March 6, 2003, Washington, D.C.
Adam Hochschild, July 23, 2001
Barbara Holum, February 27, 2002, Washington, D.C.
John Holum, May 8, 2001, Washington, D.C.
Marcia Johnston, August 5, 2005
Kirby Jones, May 11, 2001, Washington, D.C.
Max Kampelman, September 19, 2005
Scott Lilly, March 3, 2003, Washington, D.C.
Frank Mankiewicz, February 28, 2002, Washington, D.C.
Ann Marcus, March 22, 2002
Yancey Martin, March 9, 2006
George McGovern, August 13, 2000, Stevensville, Montana; November 1, 2002;
    December 12, 2005
Doris Meissner, October 3, 2003
Marian Pearlman Nease, June 10, 2005
Jane Pierson, July 29, 2003

John Podesta, March 5, 2003, Washington, D.C.
Ted Pulliam, May 9, 2001, Washington, D.C.
Steve Robbins, April 25, 2005
Miles Rubin, February 27, 2002, Roslyn, Virginia
Eli Segal, October 26, 2001, Boston
Phyllis Segal, July 8, 2003
Robert Shrum, February 26, 2002, Washington, D.C.
Amanda Smith, May 2, 2001
Jeff Smith, March 5, 2003, Alexandria, Virginia
Richard Stearns, August 1, 2001, Boston
Robert Strauss, October 25, 2005
Ted Van Dyk, March 12, 2002
Carl Wagner, February 26, 2002, Washington, D.C.
Ben Wattenberg, February 18, 2006
Gordon Weil, February 12, 2002
Anne Wexler, May 8, 2001, Washington, D.C.
Betsy Wright, June 17, 2002

Notes

Abbreviations

GMMA   George Meany Memorial Archives, Silver Spring, Maryland

GMP   George S. McGovern Papers, Seeley G. Mudd Manuscript Library, Princeton University, Princeton, New Jersey

PFM   Papers of Frank Mankiewicz, McGovern Campaign, John F. Kennedy Library, Boston, Massachusetts

Introduction

1. David Brooks, "The Importance of Staying with Iraq," *New York Times*, November 20, 2005.

2. George McGovern, *Grassroots: The Autobiography of George McGovern* (New York: Random House, 1977), p. 102.

3. Arthur Schlesinger Jr., to George McGovern, June 16, 1972, GMP, Box 844.

4. Melina Mercouri to George McGovern, July 18, 1972, GMP, Box 837.

5. "Mild-Mannered McGovern Really an Extremist Who Would Disarm America, Open White House to Street Mobs," *First Monday*, May 1, 1972.

6. "McGovern People," *National Review*, March 17, 1972.

7. "McGovern Watch," *National Review*, April 28, 1972.

Chapter 1. "A Sixties Campaign in the Seventies"

1. Hunter S. Thompson, *Fear and Loathing: On the Campaign Trail '72* (New York: Popular Library, 1973), p. 478.

2. Ibid.

3. Quoted in Charles DeBenedetti, "A CIA Analysis of the Anti–Vietnam War Movement: October 1967," in Walter L. Hixson, ed., *The United States and the Vietnam War: Significant Scholarly Articles* (New York: Garland, 2000), p. 119.

4. Tom Wells, *The War Within: America's Battle over Vietnam* (Berkeley: University of California Press, 1994), pp. 107–8.

5. Ibid., pp. 172–74, 276–80, 366–70, 406–7.

6. Adam Garfinkle, "Aftermyths of the Antiwar Movement," in Hixson, *The United States and the Vietnam War*, pp. 184–88.

7. Charles DeBenedetti, *An American Ordeal: The Antiwar Movement of the Vietnam Era* (Syracuse, NY: Syracuse University Press, 1990), p. 263. On the Moratorium and Mobilization, see pp. 254–63, and Wells, *The War Within*, pp. 370–97.

8. Wells, *The War Within*, p. 425.

9. Terry H. Anderson, *The Movement and the Sixties: Protest in America from Greensboro to Wounded Knee* (New York: Oxford University Press, 1995), p. 380.

10. For a detailed history of Senate opposition to the war in Vietnam, see Robert Mann, *A Grand Delusion: America's Descent into Vietnam* (New York: Basic, 2001).

11. Ibid., pp. 491–98.

12. William H. Chafe, *Never Stop Running: Allard Lowenstein and the Struggle to Save American Liberalism* (New York: Basic, 1993), pp. 270–71; George McGovern, *Grassroots: The Autobiography of George McGovern* (New York: Random House, 1977), pp. 110–11; Robert Sam Anson, *McGovern: A Biography* (New York: Holt, Rinehart & Winston, 1972), pp. 2–11.

13. McCarthy quoted in Dominic Sandbrook, *Eugene McCarthy and the Rise and Fall of Postwar American Liberalism* (New York: Anchor, 2005), p. 170.

14. Richard T. Stout, *People* (New York: Harper & Row, 1970), pp. 7–34.

15. Mann, *A Grand Delusion*, p. 575.

16. George Rising, *Clean for Gene: Eugene McCarthy's 1968 Presidential Campaign* (Westport, CT: Praeger, 1997), p. 68.

17. For an admiring account, see Evan Thomas, *Robert Kennedy: His Life* (New York: Simon & Schuster, 2000), pp. 351–61; for a critical account, see Ronald Steel, *In Love with Night: The American Romance with Robert Kennedy* (New York: Simon & Schuster, 2000), pp. 140–46.

18. Mann, *A Grand Delusion*, pp. 597–602.

19. Lewis L. Gould, *1968: The Election That Changed America* (Chicago: Ivan R. Dee, 1993), p. 83.

20. McGovern, *Grassroots*, pp. 117–23.

21. Gloria Steinem, *Outrageous Acts and Everyday Rebellions*, 2nd ed. (New York: Henry Holt, 1995), p. 93; Sandbrook, *Eugene McCarthy*, p. 208.

22. Lewis Chester, Godfrey Hodgson, and Bruce Page, *An American Melodrama: The Presidential Campaign of 1968* (New York: Dell, 1969), pp. 625–27.

23. McGovern, *Grassroots*, p. 123.

24. Sandbrook, *Eugene McCarthy*, pp. 189, 191, 206–7; Stout, *People*, pp. 114–15, 131–32, 167, 243–46.

25. Jack Chestnut telephone interview, September 23, 2005; Blair Clark to Senator McGovern, Re: Gene McCarthy, May 12, 1972, GMP, Box 835; Jack Anderson, "McGovern Still Looks to Kennedy," *Washington Post*, July 11, 1972.

26. Wexler interview, May 8, 2001, Washington, D.C.

27. Jules Witcover, *85 Days: The Last Campaign of Robert Kennedy* (New York: G. P. Putnam's Sons, 1969), pp. 116–17.

28. Ibid., pp. 130, 137, 216.

29. Stout, *People*, pp. 121–25.

30. Wexler interview.

31. Kennedy quoted in Theodore H. White, *The Making of the President 1972* (New York: Atheneum, 1973), p. 23.

32. Hart telephone interview, June 12, 2002.

33. Commission on Party Structure and Delegate Selection, quoted in Austin Ranney, *Curing the Mischiefs of Faction: Party Reform in America* (Berkeley: University of California Press, 1975), p. 102.

34. McGovern, *Grassroots*, p. 130.

35. Byron Shafer, *Quiet Revolution: The Struggle for the Democratic Party and the Shaping of Post-Reform Politics* (New York: Russell Sage Foundation, 1983), pp. 32–38.

36. McGovern, *Grassroots*, p. 136.

37. Shafer, *Quiet Revolution*, pp. 195–96. Shafer's massive book provides a richly detailed account of the McGovern-Fraser Commission's history.

38. Eli Segal interview, October 26, 2001, Boston.

39. *Mandate for Reform,* quoted in McGovern, *Grassroots*, p. 151.

40. "Summary of the Official Guidelines of the Commission on Party Structure and Delegate Selection," in Shafer, *Quiet Revolution*, pp. 541–45.

41. Denis G. Sullivan et al., *The Politics of Representation: The Democratic Convention 1972* (New York: St. Martin's Press, 1974), p. 23.

42. Shafer, *Quiet Revolution*, pp. 163–73, 541; Ranney, *Curing the Mischiefs of Faction*, pp. 188–91; McGovern, *Grassroots*, pp. 143–49.

43. Shafer, *Quiet Revolution*, pp. 460–91.

44. Penn Kemble and Josh Muravchik, "The New Politics and the Democrats," *Commentary*, December 1972, pp. 78–83.

45. Austin Ranney, a member of the reform commission, mentions this allegation but scoffs at it. Ranney, *Curing the Mischiefs of Faction*, pp. 208–9.

46. Segal interview; Wexler interview.

47. Lanny J. Davis, *The Emerging Democratic Majority: Lessons and Legacies from the New Politics* (New York: Stein & Day, 1974).

48. Kemble and Muravchik, "The New Politics and the Democrats," pp. 82, 83. For a less polemical and more scholarly version of this argument, see Shafer, *Quiet Revolution*, especially pp. 523–39.

Chapter 2. Decent Ambition

1. William Greider, "Candidate McGovern: Quite Self-Contained," *Washington Post*, July 14, 1972.

2. Frank Mankiewicz to Senator McGovern, October 25, 1971, PFM, Box 20.

3. McGovern interview, August 13, 2000, Stevensville, Montana.

4. On the Humphrey-Johnson relationship, see Robert A. Caro, *Master of the Senate: The Years of Lyndon Johnson* (New York: Alfred A. Knopf, 2002), pp. 450–59; and Robert Mann, *A Grand Delusion: America's Descent into Vietnam* (New York: Basic, 2001), pp. 499–503.

5. Hart telephone interview, June 12, 2002.

6. The principal biographical sources for McGovern are Robert Sam Anson, *McGovern: A Biography* (New York: Holt, Rinehart & Winston, 1972); George McGovern, *Grassroots: The Autobiography of George McGovern* (New York: Random House, 1977); and Thomas J. Knock, "'Come Home, America': The Story of George McGovern," in Randall B. Woods, ed., *Vietnam and the American Political Tradition: The Politics of Dissent* (New York: Cambridge University Press, 2003), pp. 82–120.

7. McGovern, *Grassroots*, p. 13.

8. Richard Meryman, "'I Have Earned the Nomination,'" *Life*, July 7, 1972.

9. Anson, *McGovern*, p. 23.

10. Ibid., pp. 279–80; Richard Dougherty, *Goodbye, Mr. Christian: A Personal Account of McGovern's Rise and Fall* (Garden City, NY: Doubleday, 1973), pp. 49–50.

11. McGovern, *Grassroots*, p. 34.

12. Ibid., pp. 38–39.

13. Anson, *McGovern*, pp. 15–19.

14. Ibid., p. 25.

15. McGovern, *Grassroots*, p. 10; Knock, "'Come Home, America,'" p. 86.

16. McGovern, *Grassroots*, pp. 10–11; Anson, *McGovern*, pp. 50, 56.

17. Roosevelt quoted in Frances Perkins, *The Roosevelt I Knew* (New York: Harper & Row, 1964), p. 330.

18. McGovern, *Grassroots*, pp. 18–30; Anson, *McGovern*, pp. 34–48; Knock, "'Come Home, America,'" pp. 87–88.

19. Stephen E. Ambrose, *The Wild Blue: The Men and Boys Who Flew the B-24s over Germany, 1944–45* (New York: Simon & Schuster, 2001), pp. 173–208, 225–45.

20. Roy P. Basler, ed., *The Collected Works of Abraham Lincoln*, Vol. 1 (New Brunswick, NJ: Rutgers University Press, 1953), p. 439.

21. Shrum interview, February 26, 2002, Washington, D.C.

22. Jeff Smith interview, March 5, 2003, Alexandria, Virginia.

23. McGovern, *Grassroots*, p. 31.

24. Anson, *McGovern*, pp. 51–53, 156; Knock, "'Come Home, America,'" pp. 88, 110.

25. McGovern, *Grassroots*, p. 25.

26. Author's conversation with McGovern, August 13, 2000, Stevensville, Montana.

27. In 1970 McGovern told his fellow senators: "'I'm fed up to the ears with old men dreaming up wars for young men to die in,'" and he called, sarcastically, for the congressional backers of the war in Southeast Asia to go fight it themselves. Anson, *McGovern*, pp. 179–80. In 2002, in a speech at the State University of New York at Albany, I heard him say much the same thing as war with Iraq loomed.

28. McGovern, *Grassroots*, pp. 12, 39–49; Anson, *McGovern*, pp. 27–30, 55–63.

29. Knock, "'Come Home, America,'" pp. 89–90; McGovern, *Grassroots*, pp. 47–49.

30. McGovern, *Grassroots*, p. 40.

31. Ibid., pp. 40–43. On Lattimore, see Robert P. Newman, *Owen Lattimore and the "Loss" of China* (Berkeley: University of California Press, 1992).

32. Anson, *McGovern*, pp. 58–61.

33. McGovern interview.

34. Anson, *McGovern*, pp. 63–66.

35. McGovern, *Grassroots*, pp. 49–51.

36. Anson, *McGovern*, p. 70.

37. McGovern, *Grassroots*, p. 57.

38. Ibid., pp. 53–66; Anson, *McGovern*, pp. 68–75.

39. Dougherty, *Goodbye, Mr. Christian*, p. 140.

40. Anson, *McGovern*, p. 79.

41. McGovern, *Grassroots*, p. 68.

42. Anson, *McGovern*, pp. 81–84.

43. Knock, "'Come Home, America,'" pp. 93–95; Anson, *McGovern*, pp. 86–93.

44. McGovern, *Grassroots*, pp. 81–83.

45. Thomas J. Knock, "Feeding the World and Thwarting the Communists: George McGovern and Food for Peace," in David F. Schmitz and T. Christopher Jespersen, eds., *Architects of the American Century: Individuals and Institutions in Twentieth-Century U.S. Foreign Policymaking* (Chicago: Imprint, 1999), pp. 98–120.

46. McGovern, *Grassroots*, pp. 88–91.

47. David S. Broder, "Sen. McGovern Is Nominated for Presidency on First Ballot," *Washington Post*, July 13, 1972.

48. Anson, *McGovern*, pp. 134–37.

49. Gordon L. Weil, *The Long Shot: George McGovern Runs for President* (New York: W. W. Norton, 1973), p. 129.

50. George McGovern, *The Third Freedom: Ending Hunger in Our Time* (New York: Simon & Schuster, 2001), pp. 69–78.

51. McGovern quoted in Knock, "'Come Home, America,'" p. 83.

52. Anson, *McGovern*, pp. 130–34.

53. McGovern, *Grassroots*, p. 93.

54. Ibid., pp. 276–86; George McGovern, *The Essential America: Our Founders and the Liberal Tradition* (New York: Simon & Schuster, 2004), pp. 73–74.

55. McGovern, *Grassroots*, p. 97.

56. Mann, *A Grand Delusion*, pp. 361–68.

57. McGovern quoted in ibid., p. 420.

58. McGovern, *Grassroots*, p. 107.

59. Johnson quoted in Mann, *A Grand Delusion*, p. 442.

60. Mann, *A Grand Delusion*, pp. 659–70.

61. McGovern quoted in Mann, *A Grand Delusion*, p. 669.

62. Grandmaison interview, May 9, 2001, Washington, D.C.

63. John Holum interview, May 8, 2001, Washington, D.C.

64. Theodore H. White, *The Making of the President 1972* (New York: Atheneum, 1973), p. 215.

Chapter 3. The Left-Center Strategy

1. The fullest accounts of the Cedar Point meeting are Gary Warren Hart, *Right from the Start: A Chronicle of the McGovern Campaign* (New York: Quadrangle, 1973), pp. 16–19; and Theodore H. White, *The Making of the President 1972* (New York: Atheneum, 1973), pp. 42–44.

2. George McGovern, *Grassroots: The Autobiography of George McGovern* (New York: Random House, 1977), p. 155.

3. Douglas telephone interview, February 24, 2006.

4. Hart, *Right from the Start*, p. 5. McGovern and Hart had first discussed this strategy three months earlier.

5. Ibid., p. 18.

6. Magruder quoted in Ernest R. May and Janet Fraser, eds., *Campaign '72: The Managers Speak* (Cambridge, MA: Harvard University Press, 1973), pp. 51–52.

7. Mankiewicz interview, February 28, 2002, Washington, D.C.

8. McGovern, *Grassroots*, p. 157.

9. Robert Sam Anson, *McGovern: A Biography* (New York: Holt, Rinehart & Winston, 1972), pp. 245–47.

10. Jeff Smith interview, March 5, 2003, Alexandria, Virginia.

11. McGovern, *Grassroots*, p. 159.

12. Ibid., pp. 169–71; Hart, *Right from the Start*, pp. 3–15. McGovern had hired several Senate staffers in 1969—David Beale, John Stacks, and Richard Leone—whose role was to prepare for his presidential bid, but all three had left his employ by early 1970. See Anson, *McGovern*, pp. 243–45, 261–63.

13. For biographical details on Hart, I have drawn from Randall Rothenberg, *The Neoliberals: Creating the New American Politics* (New York: Simon & Schuster, 1984), pp. 128–30; and Mark Karlin, "Gary Hart on Gods and Caesars," http//:www.alternet.org, January 2, 2006.

14. Hart telephone interview, June 12, 2002.

15. Stearns interview, August 1, 2001, Boston.

16. Ibid.

17. George McGovern, *An American Journey: The Presidential Campaign Speeches of George McGovern* (New York: Random House, 1974), pp. 4–5.

18. Hart, *Right from the Start*, pp. 51–78.

19. Johnston telephone interview, August 5, 2005.

20. Jones interview, May 11, 2001, Washington, D.C.

21. Amanda Smith telephone interview, May 2, 2001.

22. For biographical details on Mankiewicz, I have drawn from White, *Making of the President 1972*, pp. 102–04; Jeremy Brosowsky, "Frankly Speaking," *Business Forward*, March 2001; and my interview with Mankiewicz.

23. Van Dyk telephone interview, March 12, 2002.

24. Ted Van Dyk to George McGovern, November 30, 1971, GMP, Box 848.

25. Hart, *Right from the Start*, pp. 93–94, 112–13. On the Muskie endorsements strategy, see White, *Making of the President 1972*, pp. 78–80.

26. McGovern interview, August 13, 2000, Stevensville, Montana.

27. Gallup Opinion Index, March 1972, Report No. 81 (Gallup Opinion Index, Princeton, NJ).

28. James M. Naughton, "McGovern Vows to Press Nixon on War and National Priorities," *New York Times,* November 14, 1972; McGovern, *Grassroots,* pp. 233–34.

29. H. R. Haldeman, *The Haldeman Diaries: Inside the Nixon White House* (New York: Berkley, 1995), p. 575.

30. Dan T. Carter, *The Politics of Rage: George Wallace, the Origins of the New Conservatism, and the Transformation of American Politics* (New York: Simon & Schuster, 1995), pp. 412–14, 448–50.

31. David S. Broder, "The Political Scramble," *Washington Post,* April 4, 1972.

32. "A Message of Discontent from Wisconsin," *Time,* April 17, 1972.

33. Rowland Evans and Robert Novak, "Rank and File Defy Leaders," *Washington Post,* April 3, 1972.

34. McGovern interview.

35. David G. Lawrence, *The Collapse of the Democratic Presidential Majority: Realignment, Dealignment, and Electoral Change from Franklin Roosevelt to Bill Clinton* (Boulder, CO: Westview, 1996), pp. 47–51.

36. Ibid., p. 23.

37. Hart, *Right from the Start,* pp. 111–15.

38. Wagner interview, February 26, 2002, Washington, D.C.

39. Ibid.

40. Quoted in Hart, *Right from the Start,* p. 115.

41. Hart, *Right from the Start,* pp. 107–9.

42. McGovern, *Grassroots,* pp. 179–81.

43. Grandmaison interview, May 9, 2001, Washington, D.C.

44. Hart, *Right from the Start,* pp. 120–21.

45. Ibid., p. 121.

46. "Ed Muskie's Underwhelming Victory," *Newsweek,* March 20, 1972.

47. Rubin interview, February 27, 2002, Roslyn, Virginia.

48. Anthony Summers, *The Arrogance of Power: The Secret World of Richard Nixon* (New York: Penguin, 2001), pp. 381–82.

49. Quoted in "Ed Muskie's Underwhelming Victory," *Newsweek,* March 20, 1972.

50. Grandmaison interview.

51. "From New Hampshire to Florida," *Time,* March 20, 1972.

52. Frank Mankiewicz to Senator McGovern, November 1971, PFM, Box 20.

53. Ted Van Dyk to Senator McGovern, Re: Florida, January 12, 1972, GMP, Box 868.

54. Hart, *Right from the Start,* pp. 130–32; Yancey Martin telephone interview, March 9, 2006.

55. Gordon Weil, *The Long Shot: George McGovern Runs for President* (New York: W. W. Norton, 1973), pp. 62–63.

56. Dominic Sandbrook, *Eugene McCarthy and the Rise and Fall of Postwar American Liberalism* (New York: Anchor, 2005), pp. 251–53.

57. Hart, *Right from the Start,* pp. 20–21, 65–67, 137–40; White, *Making of the President 1972,* pp. 98–100; "Success at Last for George," *Time,* April 17, 1972.

58. Hart, *Right from the Start,* p. 139.

59. Weil, *The Long Shot,* p. 65.

60. Wagner interview.

61. "A Message of Discontent from Wisconsin," *Time,* April 17, 1972.

62. Ibid.

63. Helen Dewar, "Win Is Predicted for McGovern Today," *Washington Post,* April 4, 1972.

64. "A Message of Discontent from Wisconsin," *Time*, April 17, 1972.

65. David S. Broder, "McGovern Sees HHH as Candidate to Beat," *Washington Post*, April 6, 1972.

66. McGovern quoted in David S. Broder, "McGovern Wins; Lindsay Quits," *Washington Post*, April 5, 1972.

67. Weil, *The Long Shot*, p. 65.

68. Louis H. Bean, "Looking for Clues in Wisconsin: Effects of the Crossover," *Washington Post*, April 7, 1972; Jack Chestnut quoted in May and Fraser, *Campaign '72*, p. 118.

69. Rowland Evans and Robert Novak, "Anybody but McGovern," *Washington Post*, April 6, 1972.

70. G. L. Weil, "Thoughts after Wisconsin," n.d., GMP, Box 850.

71. Hart, *Right from the Start*, pp. 152–53, 156–59; David S. Broder, "Warming Up to McGovern," *Washington Post*, April 23, 1978.

72. Hart, *Right from the Start*, pp. 159, 162.

73. "Now, It's a New Democratic Race," *Newsweek*, May 8, 1972.

74. Hart, *Right from the Start*, pp. 147–52, 163–67; Himmelman interview, March 6, 2003, Washington, D.C.

75. Haynes Johnson, "McGovern Cut into HHH 'Vital Center,'" *Washington Post*, May 4, 1972.

76. Hart, *Right from the Start*, p. 167.

77. Himmelman interview.

78. Hunter S. Thompson, *Fear and Loathing: On the Campaign Trail '72* (New York: Popular Library, 1973), p. 189.

79. Tom Braden, "'Going after Hubert' Has Begun," *Washington Post*, May 2, 1972.

80. Weil, *The Long Shot*, p. 95; Mary Russell, "McGovern Seeks to Lure Wallace Voters," *Washington Post*, May 1, 1972.

81. Stearns interview.

82. Jonathan Cottin, "McGovern Swept Convention States on Work of Silent Majorities," *National Journal*, July 1, 1972.

83. "The McGovern Phenomenon," *Newsweek*, May 8, 1972.

84. Mary Russell, "McGovern's 'Radical Views' Attacked," *Washington Post*, May 6, 1972.

85. Don Oberdorfer, "Humphrey Gains in Nebraska Race," *Washington Post*, May 9, 1972; Weil, *The Long Shot*, pp. 96–98; Hart, *Right from the Start*, pp. 169–70.

86. McGovern, *Grassroots*, p. 162.

87. Hart quoted in William Chapman, "California Crucial," *Washington Post*, May 11, 1972.

88. Don Oberdorfer, "McGovern, HHH Win Primaries: Nebraska," *Washington Post*, May 10, 1972. Humphrey won the West Virginia primary over Wallace on the same day that McGovern won Nebraska.

89. Leroy F. Aarons, "McGovern Begins Buildup for Campaign in California," *Washington Post*, April 8, 1972.

90. Jack Chestnut telephone interview, September 23, 2005.

91. Rubin interview.

92. Eli Segal and Sandy Berger to Gary Hart and Frank Mankiewicz, Re: Report on California Primary, June 18, 1972, GMP, Box 845; Hart, *Right from the Start*, pp. 181–82.

93. Rubin interview; David S. Broder, "McGovern Canvassing Tactic Tested," *Washington Post*, May 29, 1972.

94. Hart, *Right from the Start*, pp. 182–84.

95. Segal and Berger to Hart and Mankiewicz, June 18, 1972, GMP, Box 845.

96. Rubin interview.

97. David S. Broder, "McGovern Gets Chavez Support," *Washington Post*, May 20, 1972.

98. Sally Quinn, "When Stars Have Political Stripes," *Washington Post*, June 4, 1972.

99. See Carl Solberg, *Hubert Humphrey: A Biography* (New York: W. W. Norton, 1984), pp. 432–35.

100. George Lardner Jr. and Lou Cannon, "HHH Says McGovern Plan Perils U.S.," *Washington Post*, May 25, 1972; Steven V. Roberts, "Now the Big One: It May Be Winner Take All," *New York Times*, June 4, 1972.

101. Don Oberdorfer, "California Poll Gives McGovern 46-to-26 Pct. Lead over HHH," *Washington Post*, June 2, 1972; Caddell in May and Fraser, *Campaign '72*, p. 136.

102. David S. Broder, "HHH at End of Trail," *Washington Post*, June 6, 1972.

103. Haynes Johnson, "McGovern's 'Victory Special' on a Fast Track in California," *Washington Post*, June 4, 1972.

104. Miles Rubin to Senator George McGovern, June 15, 1972, GMP, Box 843; Leroy F. Aarons, "McGovern Calif. Edge: 44 to 39%," *Washington Post*, June 8, 1972.

105. Aarons, "McGovern Calif. Edge."

106. Haynes Johnson, "McGovern: New Constituency," *Washington Post*, June 8, 1972.

107. Gallup Opinion Index, Report No. 84, June 1972 (Gallup Opinion Index, Princeton, NJ).

108. Harris data cited in Lanny J. Davis, *The Emerging Democratic Majority: Lessons and Legacies from the New Politics* (New York: Stein & Day, 1974), p. 201.

109. Magruder quoted in May and Fraser, *Campaign '72*, pp. 136–37.

110. Fred Dutton, "Some Notes on the National Campaign as of Mid-May," GMP, Box 853.

111. William Greider, "McGovern No Coward, Crew of Bomber Says," *Washington Post*, June 17, 1972; "McGovern Produces War Record," *Washington Post*, June 18, 1972.

112. Davis, *The Emerging Democratic Majority*, pp. 189–203.

Chapter 4. A Downward Arc

1. Quoted in "Can McGovern Put It All Together?" *Newsweek*, June 19, 1972.

2. "Can McGovern Put It All Together?" *Newsweek*, June 19, 1972; Gary Warren Hart, *Right from the Start: A Chronicle of the McGovern Campaign* (New York: Quadrangle, 1973), pp. 195–99; David S. Broder, "Trounced, HHH Vows Effort at Convention," *Washington Post*, June 8, 1972; Don Oberdorfer, "Muskie Balks at Yielding to McGovern," *Washington Post*, June 10, 1972.

3. Lilly interview, March 3, 2003, Washington, D.C.

4. Mankiewicz interview, February 28, 2002, Washington, D.C.

5. McGovern telephone interview, November 1, 2002.

6. Joseph Kraft, "Stopping McGovern," *Washington Post*, June 11, 1972; "'Anybody but McGovern,'" *Newsweek*, July 17, 1972.

7. Lou Cannon, "Aerobatics and Party Politics," *Washington Post*, July 2, 1972.

8. Mary Russell and Stephen Isaacs, "Humphrey Jubilant at Ruling," *Washington Post*, July 8, 1972.

9. "'Anybody but McGovern,'" *Newsweek,* July 17, 1972.

10. Wattenberg telephone interview, February 18, 2006.

11. Lou Cannon, "HHH Men Trying to Curb McGovern," *Washington Post*, June 17, 1972; Lou Cannon, "Why Winner-Take-All," *Washington Post*, June 25, 1972.

12. Byron E. Shafer, *Quiet Revolution: The Struggle for the Democratic Party and the Shaping of Post-Reform Politics* (New York: Russell Sage Foundation, 1983), p. 143; Cannon, "Why Winner-Take-All," *Washington Post*, June 25, 1972.

13. Humphrey quoted in Lou Cannon, "Aerobatics and Party Politics," *Washington Post*, July 2, 1972.

14. McGovern campaign press release, June 20, 1972, GMP, Box 830.

15. Richard Meryman, "'I Have Earned the Nomination': An Interview with George McGovern," *Life*, July 7, 1972.

16. Gordon L. Weil, *The Long Shot: George McGovern Runs for President* (New York: W. W. Norton, 1973), p. 137.

17. Stearns interview, August 1, 2001, Boston.

18. Cannon, "Aerobatics and Party Politics," *Washington Post*, July 2, 1972.

19. McGovern quoted in William Chapman, "Winner-Take-All Void," *Washington Post*, June 30, 1972.

20. Theodore H. White, *The Making of the President 1972* (New York: Atheneum, 1973), pp. 164–66.

21. Jim Mann, "McGovern Loses in High Court," *Washington Post*, July 8, 1972.

22. Van Dyk telephone interview, March 12, 2002.

23. Richard L. Lyons, "Platform Draft Displeases Wallace, McGovern Backers," *Washington Post*, June 26, 1972; Richard L. Lyons, "Democratic Platform Gets Praise, Scorn," *Washington Post*, June 28, 1972; Joseph Kraft, "McGovern Makes Room," *Washington Post*, June 29, 1972.

24. Jackson quoted in Leroy F. Aarons, "Rivals Attack McGovern as Liability," *Washington Post*, July 10, 1972.

25. Hart, *Right from the Start*, p. 217.

26. David S. Broder, "Key Ruling Puts McGovern on Verge of Victory," *Washington Post*, July 10, 1972.

27. Kampelman quoted in Jack Anderson, "O'Brien Ruling Won for McGovern," *Washington Post*, July 15, 1972.

28. Kampelman telephone interview, September 19, 2005.

29. White, *The Making of the President 1972*, pp. 172–74.

30. Hart, *Right from the Start*, p. 225.

31. Ibid., pp. 210–12, 220–21, 223–24.

32. Jeane Kirkpatrick, *The New Presidential Elite: Men and Women in National Politics* (New York: Russell Sage Foundation, 1976), p. 6.

33. Hart, *Right from the Start*, pp. 225–26; Hunter S. Thompson, *Fear and Loathing: On the Campaign Trail '72* (New York: Popular Library, 1973), pp. 285–310.

34. Hart, *Right from the Start*, pp. 226–27.

35. Mankiewicz interview.

36. "Speech by Willie L. Brown, Jr. to the Democratic National Convention, Miami Beach, Florida, July 10, 1972," appendix in James Richardson, *Willie Brown: A Biography* (Berkeley: University of California Press, 1996), pp. 411–12.

37. Richardson, *Willie Brown*, pp. 208–10.

38. Hart telephone interviews, June 12, 2002, and June 18, 2002.

39. "How McGovern Brought It Off," *Newsweek*, July 24, 1972.

40. Eli Segal interview, October 26, 2001, Boston.

41. Jack Chestnut telephone interview, September 23, 2005.

42. Wattenberg interview.

43. Rowland Evans and Robert Novak, "The Other Democrats," *Washington Post*, July 14, 1972.

44. "Introducing . . . the McGovern Machine," *Time*, July 24, 1972.

45. Weil, *The Long Shot*, p. 125.

46. Ibid., p. 127.

47. Rowland Evans and Robert Novak, "How the Tax Plank Lost," *Washington Post*, July 16, 1972.

48. Van Dyk interview.

49. O'Hara quoted in Ernest R. May and Janet Fraser, eds., *Campaign '72: The Managers Speak* (Cambridge, MA: Harvard University Press, 1973), p. 186.

50. Hart, *Right from the Start*, pp. 233–34.

51. Hart telephone interview, June 18, 2002.

52. www.cures-not-wars.org/ibogaine/chap04.html.

53. Testimony of E. Howard Hunt, September 24, 1973, www.watergate.info/judiciary/BKIISOF.PDF.

54. William Greider, "McGovern Offers Party His Legions," *Washington Post*, July 15, 1972.

55. Hart, *Right from the Start*, p. 243.

56. I was able to locate only one preconvention memo on prospective running mates in the McGovern Papers at Princeton: Ted Van Dyk to Senator McGovern, Re: The Vice Presidency, June 7, 1972, GMP, Box 868.

57. George McGovern, *Grassroots: The Autobiography of George McGovern* (New York: Random House, 1977), pp. 193–94.

58. On Humphrey and Muskie, see Carl Solberg, *Hubert Humphrey: A Biography* (New York: W. W. Norton, 1984), pp. 366–67. On Nixon and Agnew, see Lewis Chester, Godfrey Hodgson, and Bruce Page, *An American Melodrama: The Presidential Campaign of 1968* (New York: Dell, 1969), pp. 541–48.

59. Jules Witcover, *Marathon: The Pursuit of the Presidency, 1972–1976* (New York: Viking, 1977), pp. 359–68.

60. Hart, *Right from the Start*, pp. 238–41; Weil, *The Long Shot*, pp. 161–66.

61. Hart, *Right from the Start*, pp. 241–42; Weil, *The Long Shot*, pp. 166–67; McGovern, *Grassroots*, pp. 197–98.

62. Mankiewicz interview; Transcript, Lawrence F. O'Brien Oral History Interview XXX, November 4, 1987, by Michael L. Gillette, Internet Copy, LBJ Library.

63. Weil, *The Long Shot*, pp. 164–65; Weil telephone interview, February 12, 2002.

64. McGovern, *Grassroots*, pp. 198–99.

65. "Eagleton's Own Odyssey," *Time*, August 7, 1972.

66. Mankiewicz interview.

67. "How McGovern Brought It Off," *Newsweek*, July 24, 1972; "Introducing . . . the McGovern Machine," *Time*, July 24, 1972.

68. Shrum interview, February 26, 2002, Washington, D.C.

69. George McGovern, *An American Journey: The Presidential Campaign Speeches of George McGovern* (New York: Random House, 1974), pp. 17–24. I have omitted the lyrics from an American anthem (written by a genuine radical) that McGovern quoted in his peroration: "This Land Is Your Land."

70. White, *The Making of the President 1972*, pp. 184–86.

71. McGovern interview, August 13, 2000, Stevensville, Montana.

72. Joseph Alsop, "A Bloody Convention?" *Washington Post*, June 5, 1972.

73. "Introducing . . . the McGovern Machine," *Time*, July 24, 1972.

74. Hart telephone interview, June 12, 2002.

75. David S. Broder, "Some Leftover Notes," *Washington Post*, July 18, 1972.

76. Arthur H. Miller et al., *A Majority Party in Disarray: Policy Polarization in the 1972 Election* (Ann Arbor: University of Michigan Institute for Social Research, 1973), p. 44.

77. Johnston telephone interview, August 5, 2005.

78. McGovern, *Grassroots*, p. 220.

79. Transcript of the *Dick Cavett Show,* December 12, 1972, in GMP, Box 826.

80. Weil, *The Long Shot*, p. 171.

81. Quoted in Hart, *Right from the Start*, p. 251.

82. Hart, *Right from the Start*, pp. 252–53.

83. Ibid., p. 252; Mankiewicz interview.

84. Mankiewicz interview.

85. Hart, *Right from the Start*, pp. 253–54.

86. McGovern, *Grassroots*, p. 203.

87. Hart, *Right from the Start*, pp. 255–56.

88. William Greider, "Vacation Ordeal," *Washington Post*, July 29, 1972.

89. McGovern, *Grassroots*, pp. 204–6.

90. McGovern quoted in Richard Dougherty, *Goodbye, Mr. Christian: A Personal Account of McGovern's Rise and Fall* (Garden City, NY: Doubleday & Company, 1973), pp. 184–85.

91. McGovern, *Grassroots*, p. 207.

92. Ibid., pp. 206–7.

93. George McGovern, *Terry: My Daughter's Life-and-Death Struggle with Alcoholism* (New York: Villard, 1996), p. 96.

94. Mankiewicz interview.

95. "McGovern's First Crisis: The Eagleton Affair," *Time*, August 7, 1972.

96. Rick Greg to Frank Mankiewicz, n.d., PFM, Box 17.

97. McGovern, *Grassroots*, pp. 208–9.

98. Dougherty, *Goodbye, Mr. Christian*, pp. 190–92.

99. "A Crisis Named Eagleton," *Newsweek*, August 7, 1972.

100. Memo quoted in Weil, *The Long Shot*, p. 174. Also see Dougherty, *Goodbye, Mr. Christian*, p. 176.

101. Mankiewicz interview. Hunter Thompson heard during the campaign that Eagleton's pills were in his wife's name, and after the election McGovern confirmed the story to him. Thompson, *Fear and Loathing*, pp. 476–77.

102. Mankiewicz interview.

103. McGovern, *Grassroots*, p. 210.

104. William Greider and Laurence Stern, "McGovern Hints Eagleton May Go," *Washington Post*, July 29, 1972.

105. Mankiewicz interview.

106. Eagleton quoted in George Lardner Jr., "Eagleton Insists He'll Stay in Race," *Washington Post*, July 30, 1972.

107. McGovern, *Grassroots*, pp. 214–15.

108. "McGovern, Eagleton Statements and News Parley," *New York Times*, August 1, 1972.

109. McGovern, *Grassroots*, pp. 214–15.

110. McGovern telephone interview, November 1, 2002.

111. "'Self, It Won't Be Easy,'" *Newsweek*, August 7, 1972; "Eagleton's Own Odyssey," *Time*, August 7, 1972.

112. Caddell quoted in May and Fraser, *Campaign '72*, p. 211.

113. "McGovern's First Crisis," *Time*, August 7, 1972.

114. McGovern, *Grassroots*, p. 192.

115. Mankiewicz interview.

116. Shrum interview.

117. Dougherty, *Goodbye, Mr. Christian*, p. 213.

118. Jones interview, May 11, 2001, Washington, D.C.

119. "It's McGovern and . . . uh . . . Shriver," *Newsweek*, August 14, 1972.

120. McGovern, *Grassroots*, p. 222.

121. Hart, *Right from the Start*, p. 264.

Chapter 5. "A Long, Slow Crawl"

1. "'Human Beings Fused Together,'" *Time*, October 23, 1972.

2. "The Hard-Luck Crusade," *Time*, November 6, 1972; "The Look of a Landslide," *Newsweek*, November 6, 1972.

3. Greider telephone interview, September 27, 2005.

4. McGovern interview, August 13, 2000, Stevensville, Montana.

5. Gary Warren Hart, *Right from the Start: A Chronicle of the McGovern Campaign* (New York: Quadrangle, 1973), pp. 202–3; Ernest R. May and Janet Fraser, eds., *Campaign '72: The Managers Speak* (Cambridge, MA: Harvard University Press, 1973), pp. 189–91.

6. Theodore H. White, *The Making of the President 1972* (New York: Atheneum, 1973), pp. 318–20.

7. Mankiewicz interview, February 28, 2002, Washington, D.C.

8. Himmelman interview, March 6, 2003, Washington, D.C.

9. Berger interview, February 27, 2002, Washington, D.C.

10. George McGovern, *Grassroots: The Autobiography of George McGovern* (New York: Random House, 1977), p. 236.

11. Ted Van Dyk to Senator McGovern, Re: Themes on this trip, August 31, 1972, GMP, Box 868.

12. "A Lot of Beginning Anew," *Newsweek*, August 21, 1972.

13. "Making Up," *Time*, September 4, 1972; McGovern, *Grassroots*, pp. 227–30; McGovern interview. While Johnson had nice things to say about McGovern in the privacy of their conversation at the ranch, he took a much more unfavorable tone toward the antiwar candidate in private communications with President Nixon and John Connally. See Richard Nixon, *RN: The Memoirs of Richard Nixon, Vol. 2* (New York: Warner, 1979), pp. 167–68; and H. R. Haldeman, *The Haldeman Diaries: Inside the Nixon White House* (New York: Berkley, 1995), pp. 590, 602, 604–5.

14. McGovern interview.

15. William Greider, "McGovern Plans Touring in Tandem with Party Stars," *Washington Post*, September 7, 1972; William Greider, "Kennedy Gets Crowds for McGovern in PA," *Washington Post*, September 14, 1972.

16. "The Beginning of the Beginning?" *Newsweek*, September 11, 1972; Haynes Johnson, "Nixon Best on Image," *Washington Post*, October 22, 1972.

17. George Lardner Jr., "2 Top Aides of McGovern Are Quitting," *Washington Post*, September 8, 1972; "The Democrats Try to Get Organized," *Time*, September 11, 1972.

18. Hart, *Right from the Start*, pp. 282–83; Transcript, Lawrence F. O'Brien Oral History Interview XXX, November 4, 1987, by Michael L. Gillette, Internet Copy, LBJ Library.

19. "The Clockwork Convention," *Newsweek*, September 4, 1972.

20. Richard Dougherty, *Goodbye, Mr. Christian: A Personal Account of McGovern's Rise and Fall* (Garden City, NY: Doubleday, 1973), pp. 220–21.

21. McGovern, *Grassroots*, p. 235.

22. Seymour Melman to Senator George McGovern, September 11, 1972, GMP, Box 837.

23. Hart, *Right from the Start*, p. 289.

24. Gallup Opinion Index, October, 1972, Report No. 88 (Gallup Opinion Index, Princeton, NJ).

25. Hart, *Right from the Start*, p. 277.

26. George Gallup, "Volunteers for McGovern Abound," *Washington Post*, September 14, 1972.

27. Pulliam interview, May 9, 2001, Washington, D.C.

28. Galbraith telephone interview, June 5, 2002.

29. Hochschild telephone interview, July 23, 2001; Craig interview, May 10, 2001, Washington, D.C.

30. Stearns interview, August 1, 2001, Boston.

31. Gordon L. Weil, *The Long Shot: George McGovern Runs for President* (New York: W.W. Norton, 1973), p. 225.

32. McGovern interview.

33. Lawrence Feinberg, "Shriver Assails 'Nameless' Campaign," *Washington Post*, September 14, 1972.

34. William Greider, "McGovern Issues Debate Challenge; Nixon Aide Says No," *Washington Post*, July 23, 1972.

35. George Lardner Jr., "The 'Whole' Man," *Washington Post*, September 23, 1972.

36. "The Issue of McGovern," *Time*, October 16, 1972.

37. McGovern interview.

38. Philip Roth to Ted Van Dyk, September 8, 1972, GMP, Box 843.

39. McGovern, *Grassroots*, p. 241.

40. "Vietnam Television Speech," October 10, 1972, Guggenheim Productions, Washington, D.C.

41. George McGovern, *An American Journey: The Presidential Campaign Speeches of George McGovern* (New York: Random House, 1974), p. 110.

42. Ibid., pp. 111–12.

43. McGovern, *Grassroots*, p. 242.

44. William Greider, "McGovern Keeps His Faith," *Washington Post*, October 17, 1972.

45. McGovern, *An American Journey*, pp. 155, 158.

46. Ibid., p. 52.

47. Mankiewicz interview.

48. McGovern, *An American Journey*, p. 81.

49. Hart, *Right from the Start*, p. 306.

50. McGovern handwritten note, n.d., GMP, Box 852.

51. Hart, *Right from the Start*, p. 314.

52. McGovern interview.

53. Timothy Crouse, *The Boys on the Bus* (New York: Ballantine, 1973), p. 371.

54. William Greider, "McGovern Keeps His Faith," *Washington Post*, October 17, 1972.

55. "The Look of a Landslide," *Newsweek*, November 6, 1972; McGovern, *Grassroots*, pp. 244–46.

56. McGovern, *An American Journey*, pp. 129–30.

57. Ibid., pp. 135–36.

58. William Greider, "McGovern Lured by Faithful Crowd," *Washington Post*, November 6, 1972.

59. Hart, *Right from the Start*, pp. 309–11.

60. McGovern, *Grassroots*, p. 246.

61. Ibid.; McGovern interview.

62. Peter Goldman and Richard Stout, "McGovern's Politics of Righteousness," *Newsweek*, November 6, 1972.

63. Crouse, *Boys on the Bus*, p. 380.

64. "Tommy Smothers in Chicago," October 31, 1972, Reigner—Reel No. 7, GMP, Box 846.

65. Jeff Smith interview, March 5, 2003, Alexandria, Virginia.

66. Mary McGrory, "Can He Do It?" *America*, November 4, 1972.

67. Jeff Smith interview.

68. John Holum interview, May 8, 2001, Washington, D.C.

69. McGovern, *Grassroots*, p. 247.

Chapter 6. "Radical"?

1. "Radical," archives of Guggenheim Productions, Inc., Washington, D.C.
2. William Greider, "McGovern TV Ads: Picture of a Moderate," *Washington Post*, October 1, 1972.
3. "Radical."
4. "How Radical Is McGovern?" *Newsweek*, June 19, 1972.
5. McGovern quoted in ibid.
6. John Holum interview, May 8, 2001, Washington, D.C.
7. Scott quoted in George McGovern, *Grassroots: The Autobiography of George McGovern* (New York: Random House, 1977), p. 162.
8. Gordon Weil, *The Long Shot: George McGovern Runs for President* (New York: W. W. Norton, 1973), pp. 95–98; Gary Warren Hart, *Right from the Start: A Chronicle of the McGovern Campaign* (New York: Quadrangle, 1973), pp. 169–70; Mary Russell, "McGovern's 'Radical Views' Attacked," *Washington Post*, May 6, 1972.
9. On Evans and Novak, see Timothy Crouse, *The Boys on the Bus* (New York: Ballantine, 1974), pp. 117–29.
10. Rowland Evans and Robert Novak, "Anybody but McGovern," *Washington Post*, April 6, 1972.
11. Rowland Evans and Robert Novak, "Behind Humphrey's Surge," *Washington Post*, April 27, 1972.
12. Rowland Evans and Robert Novak, "McGovern on the Defensive," *Washington Post*, May 28, 1972.
13. Rex Weiner, "Counterculture Choices," reprinted in *Buffalo Courier*, August 24, 1972, clipping in GMP, Box 854.
14. In my interviews with McGovernites who were under age thirty-five at the time of the campaign, slightly more than half were either lawyers or attending law school.
15. Hochschild telephone interview, July 23, 2001.
16. McGovern interview, August 13, 2000, Stevensville, Montana; McGovern telephone interview, December 12, 2005; author's conversation with McGovern, Stevensville, Montana, August 13, 2000.
17. Robert Sam Anson, *McGovern: A Biography* (New York: Holt, Rinehart & Winston, 1972), pp. 58–61.
18. McGovern, *Grassroots*, p. 45.
19. William Safire, *Before the Fall: An Inside View of the Pre-Watergate White House* (New York: Belmont Tower, 1975), p. 645.
20. See Alan Brinkley, *The End of Reform: New Deal Liberalism in Recession and War* (New York: Vintage, 1996).
21. Godfrey Hodgson, *America in Our Time: From World War II to Nixon—What Happened and Why* (New York: Vintage, 1976), p. 76.
22. Wilson quoted in Lawrence W. Levine, *Defender of the Faith—William Jennings Bryan: The Last Decade, 1915–1925* (Cambridge, MA: Harvard University Press, 1987), p. 48.
23. Amanda Smith telephone interview, May 2, 2001.
24. Greider telephone interview, September 27, 2005.
25. McGovern interview, August 13, 2000, Stevensville, Montana.
26. Ibid.
27. Berger interview, February 27, 2002, Washington, D.C.
28. Ibid.
29. Shrum interview, February 26, 2002; John Holum interview; Berger interview.
30. McGovern, *Grassroots*, p. 249.

31. George McGovern, *An American Journey: The Presidential Campaign Speeches of George McGovern* (New York: Random House, 1974), p. 203.

32. Ibid., pp. 191–95.

33. Ibid., pp. 75–83.

34. Ibid., p. 161.

35. Ibid., pp. 121–25.

36. Garry Wills, "McGovern and the Politics of Conscience: A Motiveless Benignity," *New York*, October 23, 1972.

37. On the jeremiad as an American rhetorical form, see Sacvan Bercovitch, *The American Jeremiad* (Madison: University of Wisconsin Press, 1978).

38. See Bruce Miroff, *Icons of Democracy: American Leaders as Heroes, Aristocrats, Dissenters, and Democrats* (Lawrence: University Press of Kansas, 2000), pp. 102–4.

39. Hunter S. Thompson, *Fear and Loathing: On the Campaign Trail '72* (New York: Popular Library, 1973), p. 84.

40. Weil, *The Long Shot*, pp. 69–70.

41. Galbraith telephone interview, June 5, 2002.

42. Van Dyk telephone interview, March 12, 2002; Galbraith interview.

43. John Holum interview.

44. McGovern, *An American Journey*, pp. 207–8.

45. McGovern quoted in Stanley Karnow, "McGovern: Curb Military, Broaden Social Development," *Washington Post*, July 5, 1972.

46. McGovern, *An American Journey*, p. 112.

47. Ibid., pp. 109–15.

48. Ibid., pp. 115–18.

49. William Greider, "McGovern Calls for Idealism, Would Abandon Power Politics in World Affairs," *Washington Post*, October 6, 1972.

50. McGovern, *An American Journey*, pp. 85–96.

51. George C. Wilson, "McGovern on Defense: A Disciple of Eisenhower," *Washington Post*, June 25, 1972.

52. McGovern, *An American Journey*, p. 107.

53. Ibid., p. 108.

54. Tobin quoted in "The Debate over Income Redistribution," *Business Week*, June 17, 1972.

55. Weil, *The Long Shot*, pp. 72–76.

56. Ibid., pp. 75–78.

57. "Taking His Chances with Businessmen," *Business Week*, July 15, 1972.

58. Eli Sagan to Frank Mankiewicz, July 20, 1972, PFM, Box 28.

59. Weil telephone interview, February 12, 2002.

60. Galbraith interview.

61. Ken Schlossberg to Senator McGovern, Re: Political Implications of the tax reform/income redistribution program, June 6, 1972, GMP, Box 868; John Kenneth Galbraith to Senator George McGovern, June 8, 1972, GMP, Box 829; Weil, *The Long Shot*, pp. 84–87.

62. Shrum interview.

63. McGovern, *An American Journey*, pp. 137–52.

64. Weil interview.

65. "The McGovernomics Men," *Time*, July 17, 1972.

66. Weil interview; Shrum interview.

67. Jeff Smith interview, March 5, 2003, Alexandria, Virginia.

68. Theodore H. White, *The Making of the President 1972* (New York: Atheneum, 1973), pp. 218–19.

69. McGovern, *Grassroots*, pp. 161–62; Weil, *The Long Shot*, pp. 98–99; McGovern-Shriver Issues/Research, radio script on amnesty, Papers of Abram Chayes, John F. Kennedy Library, Box 5.

70. Shirley MacLaine, *You Can Get There from Here* (New York: W. W. Norton, 1975), p. 80.

71. McGovern, *Grassroots*, pp. 160–61; radio script on abortion, Chayes Papers, Box 5.

72. Weil, *The Long Shot*, pp. 99–101; radio script on marijuana, Chayes Papers, Box 5.

73. Shrum interview.

74. James M. Wall to George McGovern, November 29, 1972; James M. Wall, "Politics and Morality: An Exclusive Interview with George McGovern," typescript with editing by McGovern, both in GMP, Box 849.

75. McGovern interview, August 13, 2000, Stevensville, Montana; McGovern, *Grassroots*, pp. 262–63.

76. E. J. Dionne observes that the New Right learned from Nixon's campaign against McGovern how to exploit social and cultural issues: "'Acid, amnesty, and abortion' became a symbolic battle cry that was, in one form or another, to dominate Republican politics for many years." E. J. Dionne Jr., *Why Americans Hate Politics* (New York: Simon & Schuster, 1991), p. 228.

Chapter 7. A Grassroots Army

1. This account of Greg Craig in Vermont is drawn from his campaign reports in GMP, Box 824, and from my interview with Craig, May 10, 2001, Washington, D.C.

2. Gary Warren Hart, *Right from the Start: A Chronicle of the McGovern Campaign* (New York: Quadrangle, 1973), p. v.

3. Wagner interview, February 26, 2002, Washington, D.C.

4. Grandmaison interview, May 9, 2001, Washington, D.C.; Hart, *Right from the Start*, pp. 62–64.

5. Pokorny quoted in Hugh Sidey, "A Boy Who Wants to Prove It Works," *Life*, April 28, 1972.

6. Mary McGrory, "Young 'Pro' Wins for McGovern," GMP, Box 767; Hart, *Right from the Start*, pp. 20–21.

7. Grandmaison interview.

8. Wagner interview.

9. Himmelman interview, March 6, 2003, Washington, D.C.

10. Hart, *Right from the Start*, p. 120.

11. Podesta interview, March 5, 2003, Washington, D.C.

12. Hart, *Right from the Start*, pp. 181–82. Reporting for the *Washington Post* two days before the California primary, Haynes Johnson put the number of McGovern campaign workers at 35,000 while pointing out that "Humphrey essentially has only himself." Haynes Johnson, "McGovern's 'Victory Special' on a Fast Track in California," *Washington Post*, June 4, 1972.

13. David S. Broder, "California or Bust," *Washington Post*, May 23, 1972.

14. Steven V. Roberts, "Now the Big One. It May Be Winner Take All," *New York Times*, June 4, 1972.

15. Johnston telephone interview, August 5, 2005; Barbara Holum interview, February 7, 2002, Washington, D.C.

16. Ehrman interview, May 10, 2001, Washington, D.C.

17. Gallup Opinion Index, January 1972.

18. Ed O'Donnell, James Galbraith, and Tom Southwick to Students for McGovern Coordinators, n.d., personal files of James K. Galbraith. I am grateful to Galbraith for sending me copies of numerous memos and manuals sent out by National Students and Youth for McGovern.

19. Galbraith telephone interview, June 5, 2002.

20. Jeff Gralnick to Ed O'Donnell, October 20, 1971, PFM, Box 28.

21. Robbins telephone interview, April 25, 2005.

22. Anonymous to Frank Mankiewicz, October 3, 1972, PFM, Box 14.

23. Hart telephone interview, June 12, 2002.

24. Jeff Smith interview, March 5, 2003, Alexandria, Virginia.

25. Edwin Selby to Senator George McGovern, forwarded to the campaign by James W. Symington, July 17, 1972, GMP, Box 845.

26. "What Is Wrong with the Southern California Campaign?" n.d., GMP, Box 848.

27. Saul Reider et al. to Senator George S. McGovern, September 17, 1972, PFM, Box 15.

28. Marin County McGovern Finance Committee to Fred Dutton, Gary Hart, and Frank Mankiewicz, September 29, 1972, PFM, Box 15.

29. Ed O'Donnell to Gary Hart et al., September 8, 1972, PFM, Box 28.

30. Hart, *Right from the Start*, p. 30.

31. Jeff Smith interview.

32. Lilly interview, March 3, 2003, Washington, D.C.

33. Johnston interview.

34. Hart, *Right from the Start*, pp. 133–36.

35. Hart interview.

36. Podesta interview.

37. Gunnison telephone interview, May 24, 2006.

38. Jones interview, May 11, 2001, Washington, D.C.

39. Gordon L. Weil, *The Long Shot: George McGovern Runs for President* (New York: W. W. Norton, 1973), pp. 195–221; Ted Van Dyk to Senator McGovern, September 1, 1972, PFM, Box 28; Jean Westwood to Senator McGovern, n.d., GMP, Box 852.

40. Weil, *The Long Shot*, p. 209.

41. George Cunningham to Senator McGovern, Re: The Campaign Operation, August 11, 1972, GMP, Box 868.

42. Mankiewicz interview, February 28, 2002, Washington, D.C.

43. Dees quoted in Ernest R. May and Janet Fraser, eds., *Campaign '72: The Managers Speak* (Cambridge, MA: Harvard University Press, 1973), p. 226.

44. Weil telephone interview, February 12, 2002.

45. Hart, *Right from the Start*, p. 295; Hart interview; John Holum interview, May 8, 2001, Washington, D.C.

46. Richard Dougherty, *Goodbye, Mr. Christian: A Personal Account of McGovern's Rise and Fall* (Garden City, NY: Doubleday, 1973), pp. 140–42.

47. McGovern telephone interview, November 1, 2002.

48. Jeff Gralnick to Ted Van Dyk, October 19, 1971, PFM, Box 28.

49. Hart, *Right from the Start*, p. 98.

50. Rubin interview, February 27, 2002, Roslyn, Virginia; Hart, *Right from the Start*, p. 126.

51. Nease telephone interview, June 10, 2005.

52. George McGovern, *An American Journey: The Campaign Speeches of George McGovern* (New York: Random House, 1974), p. 19.

53. Estimates on the total of small donations and number of small contributors come from Dees telephone interview, January 8, 2002, and Jeff Smith interview.

54. Dees interview; Morris Dees with Steve Fiffer, *A Lawyer's Journey: The Morris Dees Story* (Chicago: American Bar Association, 2001).

55. Dees interview; Dees, *A Lawyer's Journey*, pp. 134–37.

56. Dees interview; Hart, *Right from the Start*, pp. 118–19; Gary Hart to Dear . . . , August 1972, personal files of Morris Dees. Dees sent me copies of the direct-mail letters.

57. Miles Rubin, Memorandum, May 31, 1972, PFM, Box 27.

58. Rowland Evans and Robert Novak, "McGovern and the Fat Cats," *Washington Post*, July 19, 1972.

59. Rubin interview.

60. George McGovern, *Grassroots: The Autobiography of George McGovern*, pp. 172–73; Rubin interview; Sally Quinn, "McGovern's Beatty," *Washington Post*, June 5, 1972; Sally Quinn, "Getting It Together for McGovern," *Washington Post*, June 15, 1972.

61. William Greider, "Money Pours In," *Washington Post*, October 20, 1972.

62. Transcript, Lawrence F. O'Brien Oral History Interview XXX, November 4, 1987, by Michael L. Gillette, Internet Copy, LBJ Library.

63. Guggenheim telephone interview, April 12, 2002.

64. Hunter S. Thompson, *Fear and Loathing: On the Campaign Trail '72* (New York: Popular Library, 1973), p. 273.

65. "George McGovern," archives of Guggenheim Productions, Inc., Washington, D.C.

66. Guggenheim interview.

67. Hart, *Right from the Start*, p. 292; Grandmaison interview.

68. Guggenheim interview.

69. "Nixon" and "The Dollar," both produced by Tony Schwartz, archives of Guggenheim Productions, Inc., Washington, D.C.

70. Guggenheim interview.

71. McGovern, *An American Journey*, p. 237.

72. Edgar Berman, *Hubert: The Triumph and Tragedy of the Humphrey I Knew* (New York: G. P. Putnam's Sons, 1979), p. 148.

73. Jones interview.

74. Ibid.

75. Greider telephone interview, September 27, 2005.

76. Ibid. David Broder commented after the election that "the only things we were able to report about the President's campaign were those things which he selected to make available for reporting." Broder quoted in May and Fraser, *Campaign '72*, p. 261.

77. Mackin quoted in Timothy Crouse, *The Boys on the Bus* (New York: Ballantine, 1974), p. 280.

78. Crouse, *Boys on the Bus*, p. 281.

79. McGovern quoted in David S. Broder, "McGovern Hits Nixon Letting 'Lackeys' Do His 'Dirty Work,'" *Washington Post*, September 26, 1972.

80. Crouse, *Boys on the Bus*, p. 337.

81. Hart, *Right from the Start*, p. 295.

82. Galbraith interview.

83. Robbins interview.

Chapter 8. Democratic Insurgency

1. Van Dyk telephone interview, March 12, 2002.

2. McGovern telephone interview, November 1, 2002.

3. Transcript of *Face the Nation,* May 28, 1972, in GMP, Box 830.

4. Hart quoted in Ernest R. May and Janet Fraser, eds., *Campaign '72: The Managers Speak* (Cambridge, MA: Harvard University Press, 1973), p. 134.

5. Gordon Weil, "Briefing Papers for First California Debate," n.d., GMP, Box 850; John Holum to Senator McGovern, "Re: Tuesday Debate," n.d., GMP, Box 830.

6. Eli Segal interview, October 26, 2001, Boston.

7. McGovern telephone interview, November 1, 2002.

8. Rowland Evans and Robert Novak, "Off Go Humphrey's Gloves," *Washington Post*, May 15, 1972.

9. Humphrey quoted in George Lardner Jr. and Lou Cannon, "HHH Says McGovern Plan Perils U.S.," *Washington Post*, May 25, 1972.

10. Adam Walinsky to Senator McGovern, n.d., GMP, Box 849.

11. Eli Segal interview.

12. Max M. Kampelman to Frank Mankiewicz, March 7, 1972, PFM, Box 19.

13. Kampelman telephone interview, September 19, 2005.

14. Hart telephone interview, June 12, 2002.

15. Mankiewicz interview, February 28, 2002, Washington, D.C.

16. Gary Warren Hart, *Right from the Start: A Chronicle of the McGovern Campaign* (New York: Quadrangle, 1973), p. 69.

17. Jeff Smith interview, March 5, 2003, Alexandria, Virginia.

18. George McGovern, *Grassroots: The Autobiography of George McGovern* (New York: Random House, 1977), pp. 49–51.

19. E. J. Dionne Jr., *Why Americans Hate Politics* (New York: Simon & Schuster, 1992), p. 45.

20. Stephen Isaacs, "The Kiddies' Crusade—and Its Aging Leader," *Washington Post*, June 18, 1972.

21. Grandmaison interview, May 9, 2001, Washington, D.C.

22. Jeane Kirkpatrick, *The New Presidential Elite: Men and Women in National Politics* (New York: Russell Sage Foundation, 1976), p. 68.

23. Everett Carll Ladd Jr. with Charles D. Hadley, *Transformations of the American Party System: Political Coalitions from the New Deal to the 1970s*, 2nd ed. (New York: W. W. Norton, 1978), p. 229.

24. Ibid., p. 198.

25. On the decline in labor union membership, see ibid., p. 192. On the decline in the vote contribution of the urban machines, see Richard L. Rubin, *Party Dynamics: The Democratic Coalition and the Politics of Change* (New York: Oxford University Press, 1976), p. 93. On the increasing liberalism and Democratic Party identification of the college-educated, see Ladd, *Transformations of the American Party System*, p. 241.

26. See Byron E. Shafer, *The Two Majorities and the Puzzle of Modern American Politics* (Lawrence: University Press of Kansas, 2003), pp. 161–62.

27. McGovern interview, August 13, 2000, Stevensville, Montana.

28. Van Dyk interview; Amanda Smith telephone interview, May 2, 2001; Jones interview, May 11, 2001, Washington, D.C.; Hart interview.

29. Bill Clinton, *My Life* (New York: Alfred A. Knopf, 2004), p. 151.

30. Biographical details on Stearns are drawn from Stearns interview, August 1, 2001, Boston; and David Maraniss, *First in His Class: A Biography of Bill Clinton* (New York: Simon & Schuster, 1995), pp. 159–60.

31. Gordon L. Weil, *The Long Shot: George McGovern Runs for President* (New York: W. W. Norton, 1973), p. 67.

32. Hart interview.

33. McGovern quoted in David S. Broder, "McGovern to Woo Party's Old Guard," *Washington Post*, April 28, 1972.

34. Lilly interview, March 3, 2003, Washington, D.C.

35. Minutes of the Executive Council, AFL-CIO, July 19, 1972, GMMA, Box RG4–007 (Minutes).

36. On the Meany-Nixon relationship, see Archie Robinson, *George Meany and His Times: A Biography* (New York: Simon & Schuster, 1981), pp. 304–20; and Allen J. Matusow, *Nixon's Economy: Booms, Busts, Dollars, and Votes* (Lawrence: University Press of Kansas, 1998), pp. 158–63, 196–97, 211–12.

37. Weil, *The Long Shot*, pp. 130–31.

38. On the 14B incident, see Theodore H. White, *The Making of the President 1972* (New York: Atheneum, 1973), pp. 212–13; and Robert Sam Anson, *McGovern: A Biography* (New York: Holt, Rinehart & Winston, 1972), pp. 142–43. According to columnist Jack Anderson, at the heart of the incident was a misunderstanding: McGovern had actually won the agreement of AFL-CIO lobbyists to switching his vote because it was not needed, but they subsequently failed to communicate this fact to the union hierarchy. Jack Anderson, "Meany's Feud with Sen. McGovern," *Washington Post*, July 8, 1972.

39. See Taylor E. Dark, *The Unions and the Democrats: An Enduring Alliance* (Ithaca, NY: Cornell University Press, 1999), pp. 80–83.

40. Ibid., pp. 83–91.

41. Transcript of *Face the Nation*, September 3, 1972, in GMP, Box 731.

42. AFL-CIO Department of Legislation, GMMA, Box 77.

43. Quoted in Peter Milius and David S. Broder, "AFL-CIO Ponders McGovern," *Washington Post*, June 19, 1972.

44. Barkan quoted in *John Herling's Labor Letter*, August 19 and 26, 1972, p. 4. Herling was a labor journalist critical of Meany. His newsletter, a rich source of information on organized labor's political activities, can be found in the Meany Archives.

45. George Meany, Address before the 16th Constitutional Convention of the United Steelworkers of America, Las Vegas, Nevada, September 18, 1972, in George Meany Files, GMMA, Box 83.

46. Taylor E. Dark III, "From Resistance to Adaptation: Organized Labor Reacts to a Changing Nominating Process," in William G. Mayer, ed., *The Making of the Presidential Candidates 2004* (Lanham, MD: Rowman & Littlefield, 2004), pp. 173–74.

47. George McGovern to George Meany, April 10, 1972, Meany Files, GMMA, Box 44.

48. William Greider, "McGovern Is Defiant," *Washington Post*, July 20, 1972.

49. McGovern's scribbled note is in GMP, Box 852.

50. Howard D. Samuel, "The Year the AFL-CIO Didn't Endorse a President," unpublished manuscript. Samuel, executive director of the pro-McGovern labor coalition, died on the day that our phone interview was scheduled. I am grateful to his family for sending me a copy of his article.

51. Glover quoted in *John Herling's Labor Letter*, August 19 and 26, 1972, p. 4.

52. Dark, "From Resistance to Adaptation," pp. 176–77.

53. Wagner interview, February 26, 2002, Washington, D.C.

54. The photograph appears in Nelson Lichtenstein, *State of the Union: A Century of American Labor* (Princeton, NJ: Princeton University Press, 2002), p. 169.

55. Transcript of *The Today Show*, October 24, 1972, in Meany Files, GMMA, Box 130.

56. George Meany, Address before the 34th Convention of the International Association of Bridge, Structural, and Ornamental Iron Workers, August 30, 1972, in Meany Files, GMMA, Box 83.

57. Rubin, *Party Dynamics*, p. 56.

58. Robbins telephone interview, April 25, 2005.

59. David S. Broder, "McGovern Sees HHH as Candidate to Beat," *Washington Post*, April 6, 1972.

60. Wagner interview.

61. Robbins interview.

62. McGovern interview, August 13, 2000, Stevensville, Montana.

63. Cassidy telephone interview, July 14, 2005; Wagner interview.

64. Lilly interview.

65. Eli Segal to Joel Swerdlow, Re: Suggested literature for working class, farm areas, n.d., GMP, Box 845.

66. Richard Krickus, *Pursuing the American Dream: White Ethnics and the New Populism* (New York: Anchor, 1976), p. 241.

67. Royko quoted in White, *Making of the President 1972*, p. 165.

68. Ken [Schlossberg] and Gerry [Cassidy] to Senator McGovern, Re: Catholic-Ethnic Strategy, n.d., GMP, Box 844.

69. Cassidy interview.

70. Shirley MacLaine, *You Can Get There from Here* (New York: W. W. Norton, 1975), p. 79.

71. Cassidy interview.

72. Lilly interview.

73. Frank Mankiewicz to Raymond Pace Alexander, October 20, 1972, PFM, Box 11.

74. Weil, *The Long Shot*, pp. 102–6.

75. Stearns interview; McGovern telephone interview, December 12, 2005.

76. Weil, *The Long Shot*, p. 222.

77. McGovern telephone interview, December 12, 2005.

78. "Wooing the Jewish Vote," *Newsweek*, August 21, 1972; "The Jewish Swing to Nixon," *Time*, August 21, 1972.

79. "McGovern on Quotas," McGovern-Shriver '72 press release (drafted by Richard Cohen), n.d., PFM, Box 20.

80. White, *Making of the President 1972*, p. 346.

81. Jeff Smith interview.

82. Pulliam interview, May 9, 2001, Washington, D.C.

83. Jonathan Cottin, "McGovern Swept Convention States on Work of Silent Majorities," *National Journal*, July 1, 1972.

84. Patrick H. Caddell to Senator George McGovern, Re: The South in 1972, June 21, 1972, GMP, Box 823.

85. Julian Bond to George McGovern et al., Re: The Wallace Vote, October 17, 1972, GMP, Box 822.

86. Frank Mankiewicz to Eli Segal, August 15, 1972, GMP, Box 836.

87. William Greider, "Southern Democrats Fearful of McGovern Heading Ticket," *Washington Post*, June 2, 1972.

88. Weil, *The Long Shot*, p. 132; Rowland Evans and Robert Novak, "Governors Grill McGovern," *Washington Post*, June 9, 1972; Eli Segal to Gary Hart, Memorandum, October 1, 1972, GMP, Box 845.

89. Ladd, *Transformations of the American Party System*, p. 158.

90. McGovern, *Grassroots*, p. 232.

91. Ted Pulliam to Jeff Smith, "Trip Book—Revised, Northern New Jersey," for September 20, 1972. I am grateful to Ted Pulliam for supplying me with a copy of this briefing paper from his personal files.

92. Hart, *Right from the Start*, pp. 276–78.

93. Lilly interview.

94. Rubin interview, February 27, 2002, Roslyn, Virginia.

95. Himmelman interview, March 6, 2003, Washington, D.C.

96. Hart, *Right from the Start*, p. ix.

97. Ronald Radosh, *Divided They Fell: The Demise of the Democratic Party, 1964–1996* (New York: Free Press, 1996), pp. 133–82.

98. Herbert S. Parmet, *The Democrats: The Years after FDR* (New York: Oxford University Press, 1976), p. 286.

99. On the decay of the Democratic Party in the 1950s and 1960s, see Alan Ware, *The Breakdown of Democratic Party Organization, 1940–1980* (Oxford, UK: Oxford University Press, 1985);

and David G. Lawrence, *The Collapse of the Democratic Presidential Majority: Realignment, Dealignment, and Electoral Change from Franklin Roosevelt to Bill Clinton* (Boulder, CO: Westview, 1996).

100. David Plotke, *Building a Democratic Political Order: Reshaping American Liberalism in the 1930s and 1940s* (New York: Cambridge University Press, 1996), p. 144.

101. Steven M. Gillon, *The Democrats' Dilemma: Walter F. Mondale and the Liberal Legacy* (New York: Columbia University Press, 1992), p. xxvi.

102. To observe this identity crisis in recent Democratic candidates, compare the statements of Al Gore in 2000 with the speeches he made in 2002 and afterward or the positions of John Kerry in 2004 versus 2005–2007.

Chapter 9. Mass Movements and McGovernites

1. Details on McGovern at the women's caucus meeting are drawn from Myra MacPherson, "Women Boo as McGovern Skirts Their Issues," *Washington Post,* July 11, 1972; and Susan and Martin Tolchin, *Clout: Womanpower and Politics* (New York: Coward, McCann & Geoghegan, 1974), pp. 46–47.

2. Bella Abzug with Mim Kelber, *Gender Gap: Bella Abzug's Guide to Political Power for American Women* (Boston: Houghton Mifflin, 1984), p. 34.

3. Mankiewicz interview, February 28, 2002, Washington, D.C.

4. Hart telephone interview, June 18, 2002.

5. On the changes in representation and platform planks from 1968 to 1972, see Jeane Kirkpatrick, *The New Presidential Elite: Men and Women in National Politics* (New York: Russell Sage Foundation, 1976), p. 84.

6. See Ruth Rosen, *The World Split Open: How the Modern Women's Movement Changed America* (New York: Penguin, 2001), pp. 143–260.

7. Pierson telephone interview, July 29, 2003.

8. Byron Shafer, *Quiet Revolution: The Struggle for the Democratic Party and the Shaping of Post-Reform Politics* (New York: Russell Sage Foundation, 1983), pp. 460–91.

9. Shirley MacLaine to Senator George McGovern et al., July 25, 1972, GMP, Box 836.

10. Amanda Smith telephone interview, May 2, 2001.

11. Pierson interview.

12. Gloria Steinem, *Outrageous Acts and Everyday Rebellions*, 2nd ed. (New York: Henry Holt, 1995), p. 114.

13. Amanda Smith to McGovern Organizers, Re: National Women's Political Caucus (NWPC), December 1971, PFM, Box 28.

14. Lilly interview, March 3, 2003, Washington, D.C.

15. George McGovern to L. B. Maytag Jr., February 28, 1972, GMP, Box 885.

16. Colette Nijhof to Senator McGovern, March 3, 1972, GMP, Box 885.

17. Shirley MacLaine, *You Can Get There from Here* (New York: W. W. Norton, 1975), pp. 79–80; Tolchins, *Clout,* pp. 47–48.

18. "McGovern Stand Irks Caucus," *Washington Post,* June 27, 1972.

19. Pierson interview; Phyllis Segal telephone interview, July 8, 2003.

20. Gary Warren Hart, *Right from the Start: A Chronicle of the McGovern Campaign* (New York: Quadrangle, 1973), pp. 225–27; Stearns interview, August 1, 2001, Boston.

21. Phyllis Segal interview.

22. Hart interview.

23. "The Outsiders on the Inside," *Newsweek,* July 24, 1972; "Eve's Operatives," *Time,* July 24, 1972.

24. Steinem quoted in "The Outsiders on the Inside," *Newsweek*, July 24, 1972.

25. Abzug and MacLaine quoted in "Eve's Operatives," *Time*, July 24, 1972.

26. Steinem, *Outrageous Acts*, p. 120.

27. Stearns interview.

28. Phyllis Segal interview. On the importance of Segal's research paper on women's under-representation, see Shafer, *Quiet Revolution*, p. 470.

29. Pierson interview.

30. Meissner telephone interview, October 3, 2003.

31. Tolchins, *Clout*, p. 49.

32. Ehrman interview, May 10, 2001, Washington, D.C.

33. Hart interview.

34. Germaine Greer, "McGovern, the Big Tease," *Harper's Magazine*, October 1972.

35. Meissner interview.

36. Phyllis Segal interview.

37. Pierson interview.

38. Amanda Smith, "Women in the McGovern Campaign," n.d., PFM, Box 28.

39. George McGovern to Gloria Steinem, November 20, 1971, GMP, Box 885.

40. Amanda Smith interview.

41. Ibid.

42. Ibid.

43. Ehrman interview.

44. Amanda Smith interview.

45. Greenberger interview, May 11, 2001, Washington, D.C.

46. Amanda Smith interview.

47. Ibid.

48. Barbara Holum interview, February 27, 2002, Washington, D.C.

49. Wright telephone interview, June 17, 2002.

50. Ehrman interview.

51. Amanda Smith interview.

52. Guy Charles to Kirby Jones, January 1, 1972, PFM, Box 19.

53. Shrum interview, February 26, 2002, Washington, D.C.

54. George McGovern to Dr. Bruce Voeller, March 15, 1972, with attached statement, PFM, Box 19.

55. Alheim interview, February 14, 2006, Niskayuna, New York.

56. Marcus telephone interview, March 22, 2002.

57. Norman Mailer, *St. George and the Godfather* (New York: New American Library, 1972), p. 53.

58. Minority plank on "Sexual Orientation," in PFM, Box 19.

59. Denis G. Sullivan et al., *The Politics of Representation: The Democratic Convention 1972* (New York: St. Martin's, 1974), p. 100. Supporters of the gay-rights plank rounded up enough signatures at the Platform Committee meeting to get their position heard on the floor in Miami Beach by agreeing to back other minority planks, including some from the Wallace campaign. Alheim interview.

60. Lilly interview.

61. Barbara Holum interview.

62. Ehrman interview.

63. James Foster and Dr. Frank E. Kameny to Senator George McGovern, October 18, 1972, PFM, Box 19.

64. Mankiewicz interview.

65. Alheim interview.

66. Shirley MacLaine, ed., *McGovern: The Man and His Beliefs* (New York: Artists and Writers for McGovern, 1972), p. 57.

67. "Voting Black?" *Newsweek*, June 12, 1972; Shola Lynch, "Chisholm '72: Unbought and Unbossed," Realside Productions, 2005.

68. Hart, *Right from the Start*, pp. 14–15; Martin telephone interview, March 9, 2006.

69. Laird Harris to Scott Lilly, Joe Grandmaison, and Steve Robbins, Re: Michigan Primary, n.d., GMP, Box 868.

70. R. W. Apple Jr., "McGovern Continues to Lag in Bid for Black Votes," *New York Times*, May 19, 1972.

71. Hart interview.

72. Jackson quoted in "McGovern Works for the People," brochure for the black community, n.d., personal files of Ted Pulliam.

73. Charles Guggenheim to Gary Hart et al., May 9, 1972, PFM, Box 15.

74. Eli Segal and Sandy Berger to Gary Hart and Frank Mankiewicz, Re: Report on California Primary, June 18, 1972, GMP, Box 845.

75. Kampelman telephone interview, September 19, 2005.

76. Haynes Johnson, "McGovern: New Constituency," *Washington Post*, June 8, 1972.

77. Segal and Berger to Hart and Mankiewicz, June 18, 1972, GMP, Box 845.

78. Austin Scott, "Fauntroy Says He Has Pledges to Assure McGovern Victory," *Washington Post*, June 26, 1972.

79. Marie Brookter with Jean Curtis, *Here I Am—Take My Hand* (New York: Harper & Row, 1974), pp. 135–37; Lynch, "Chisholm '72"; Sullivan et al., *The Politics of Representation*, pp. 44–51.

80. Mankiewicz interview. For conflicting perspectives on the black rebellion at the DNC meeting, see George McGovern, *Grassroots: The Autobiography of George McGovern* (New York: Random House, 1977), pp. 218–20; and Theodore H. White, *The Making of the President 1972* (New York: Atheneum, 1973), pp. 190–91.

81. Martin interview; Yancey Martin to Senator McGovern, August 20, 1972, GMP, Box 836.

82. Brookter, *Here I Am*, p. 82.

83. E-mail communication from Steve Robbins, February 10, 2006; Hart, *Right from the Start*, pp. 287–89; Joel Swerdlow to Steve Robbins, August 27, 1972, GMP, Box 847.

84. Transcript of Willie Brown, Reigner—Reel No. 2 (in Willie Brown file), GMP, Box 822.

85. George Gallup, "Black Voters Favor McGovern by Ratio of More Than 4 to 1," *Washington Post*, September 23, 1972.

86. Arthur H. Miller et al., *A Majority Party in Disarray: Policy Polarization in the 1972 Election* (Ann Arbor: University of Michigan Institute for Social Research, 1973), pp. 77, 84.

87. "The Landslide: How and Why," *Newsweek*, November 13, 1972; Lanny J. Davis, *The Emerging Democratic Majority: Lessons and Legacies from the New Politics* (New York: Stein & Day, 1974), p. 192.

88. Wagner interview, February 26, 2002, Washington, D.C.

89. For radical illusions about youth, see John and Margaret Rowntree, "Youth as a Class," in Massimo Teodori, ed., *The New Left: A Documentary History* (Indianapolis: Bobbs-Merrill, 1969), pp. 385–91; and Herbert Marcuse, *An Essay on Liberation* (Boston: Beacon, 1971).

90. A best-selling work in this vein was Charles A. Reich, *The Greening of America: How the Youth Revolution Is Trying to Make America Livable* (New York: Random House, 1970).

91. Frederick G. Dutton, *Changing Sources of Power: American Politics in the 1970s* (New York: McGraw-Hill, 1971), pp. 16, 19. Dutton did observe that among youth there was still a depoliticized "philistine majority" (p. 52).

92. Sullivan et al., *The Politics of Representation*, pp. 54–57.

93. Anne Wexler to Field Organizers, n.d., GMP, Box 850; Wexler interview, May 8, 2001, Washington, D.C.

94. "The Young: Turning Out—or Off?" *Time*, September 25, 1972.

95. Richard Krickus, *Pursuing the American Dream: White Ethnics and the New Populism* (Garden City, NY: Anchor, 1976), p. 228.

96. Miller et al., *A Majority Party in Disarray*, p. 85.

97. Stearns interview.

98. Hart, *Right from the Start*, p. 222.

Chapter 10. A Textbook for Attack Politics: The Master vs. McGovern

1. McGovern interview, August 13, 2000, Stevensville, Montana.

2. "How Mr. Nixon Woos the Democrats," *Newsweek*, October 2, 1972.

3. Clayton Fritchey, "Democrats (?) for Nixon Group," *Washington Post*, August 26, 1972.

4. Stephen E. Ambrose, *Nixon: The Triumph of a Politician, 1962–1972* (New York: Simon & Schuster, 1989), p. 552.

5. Nixon quoted in Stanley I. Kutler, *The Wars of Watergate: The Last Crisis of Richard Nixon* (New York: Alfred A. Knopf, 1990), p. 239.

6. John Holum interview, May 8, 2001, Washington, D.C.

7. George McGovern, *Grassroots: The Autobiography of George McGovern* (New York: Random House, 1977), p. 47.

8. Mankiewicz interview, February 28, 2002, Washington, D.C.

9. McGovern, *Grassroots*, p. 158.

10. Mankiewicz interview.

11. Gallup Opinion Index, June 1972, Report No. 84 (Gallup Opinion Index, Princeton, NJ).

12. Nixon quoted in Stanley I. Kutler, ed., *Abuse of Power: The New Nixon Tapes* (New York: Free Press, 1997), p. 137.

13. Nixon quoted in Ambrose, *Nixon: The Triumph of a Politician*, pp. 637–38.

14. Richard Nixon, *RN: The Memoirs of Richard Nixon*, Vol. 2 (New York: Warner, 1979), p. 107.

15. Ibid., p. 7.

16. Keith W. Olson, *Watergate: The Presidential Scandal That Shook America* (Lawrence: University Press of Kansas, 2003), p. 33.

17. John Ehrlichman, *Witness to Power: The Nixon Years* (New York: Pocket, 1982), pp. 298–99.

18. Nixon, *RN*, p. 144.

19. Nixon quoted in Kutler, *Abuse of Power*, p. 114.

20. Nixon quoted in Ambrose, *Nixon: The Triumph of a Politician*, p. 647.

21. Dan T. Carter, *The Politics of Rage: George Wallace, the Origins of the New Conservatism, and the Transformation of American Politics* (New York: Simon & Schuster, 1995), pp. 439–43.

22. Nixon and Haldeman quoted in Kutler, *Abuse of Power*, p. 66.

23. Haldeman quoted in ibid., p. 73.

24. William Safire, *Before the Fall: An Inside View of the Pre-Watergate White House* (New York: Belmont Tower, 1975), pp. 639–55.

25. For a critical account of the "Nixon as liberal" thesis, see David Greenberg, *Nixon's Shadow: The History of an Image* (New York: W. W. Norton, 2003), pp. 319–37.

26. Joan Hoff, *Nixon Reconsidered* (New York: Basic, 1994), p. 144. Also see Melvin Small, *The Presidency of Richard Nixon* (Lawrence: University Press of Kansas, 1999), pp. 185–214, 309.

27. Jonathan Schell, *The Time of Illusion* (New York: Vintage, 1976), p. 175.

28. J. Brooks Flippen, *Nixon and the Environment* (Albuquerque: University of New Mexico Press, 2000), p. 28.

29. Ibid., p. 49.

30. Ibid., pp. 158–88.

31. See Allen J. Matusow, *Nixon's Economy: Booms, Busts, Dollars, and Votes* (Lawrence: University Press of Kansas, 1998), pp. 80–83, 149–81, 192–98, 219–22.

32. Ibid., pp. 184–92, 219–20.

33. Edward R. Tufte, *Political Control of the Economy* (Princeton, NJ: Princeton University Press, 1978), p. 52.

34. On Nixon's risking of a summit cancellation, see Ambrose, *Nixon: The Triumph of a Politician*, pp. 535–41.

35. At the same time that the Nixon administration was accusing McGovern of advocating "surrender" in South Vietnam, Henry Kissinger was quietly assuring the Chinese that the United States was prepared to accept a Communist takeover in Saigon so long as enough time had passed after the withdrawal of U.S. forces to save American face. "Kissinger Papers: U.S. OK with Takeover," *New York Times*, May 27, 2006.

36. Gallup Opinion Index, October 1972, Report No. 88 (Gallup Opinion Index, Princeton, NJ).

37. See Robert Mason, *Richard Nixon and the Quest for a New Majority* (Chapel Hill: University of North Carolina Press, 2004), pp. 161–91.

38. Thomas Byrne Edsall with Mary D. Edsall, *Chain Reaction: The Impact of Race, Rights, and Taxes on American Politics* (New York: W. W. Norton, 1992), pp. 74–98.

39. See Ambrose, *Nixon: The Triumph of a Politician*, pp. 520–22, 523–24, 542, 553, 555–56, 587, 623.

40. Nixon quoted in Richard Krickus, *Pursuing the American Dream: White Ethnics and the New Populism* (Garden City, NY: Anchor, 1976), pp. 253, 255.

41. "Politicking with Fat Cats and Ethnics," *Time*, October 9, 1972; H. R. Haldeman, *The Haldeman Diaries: Inside the Nixon White House* (New York: Berkley, 1995), p. 619.

42. Safire, *Before the Fall*, pp. 553–63; Krickus, *Pursuing the American Dream*, pp. 253–61.

43. Safire, *Before the Fall*, pp. 579–83, 646.

44. Nixon quoted in Ambrose, *Nixon: The Triumph of a Politician*, p. 542.

45. Nixon, *RN*, p. 163.

46. Anthony Summers, *The Arrogance of Power: The Secret World of Richard Nixon* (New York: Penguin, 2001), pp. 398–99.

47. Haldeman, *The Haldeman Diaries*, p. 573.

48. Charles Colson to George Meany, September 4, 1972, Meany Files, GMMA, Box 130.

49. George C. Wilson, "Laird Assails McGovern Cuts," *Washington Post*, July 7, 1972.

50. Carroll Kilpatrick, "Secretary Rogers Calls McGovern's War Plan Unsound," *Washington Post*, July 16, 1972.

51. William Greider, "McGovern Scored on Welfare," *Washington Post*, August 31, 1972.

52. Haynes Johnson, "Agnew Lashes Out at McGovern as Radical Candidate," *Washington Post*, July 1, 1972.

53. Quoted in "Dole: Partisan Statements," Sept. 15, 1972, C.R.E.P., GMP, Box 828.

54. Nixon quoted in Kutler, *Abuse of Power*, pp. 112–13. The White House later supplied the IRS with a list of about 500 McGovern contributors, but IRS Commissioner Johnnie Walters refused to take action against them. John A. Andrew III, *Power to Destroy: The Political Uses of the IRS from Kennedy to Nixon* (Chicago: Ivan R. Dee, 2002), p. 220.

55. Kutler, *Abuse of Power*, pp. 127–28.

56. "Dole Questions McGovern Credentials to Lecture Nation on Morality in Government," Republican National Committee press release, October 25, 1972, GMP, Box 825.

57. Harold Himmelman to Frank Mankiewicz, May 29, 1973, PFM, Box 25.

58. Kutler, *Abuse of Power*, p. 250; Fred Emery, *Watergate: The Corruption of American Politics and the Fall of Richard Nixon* (New York: Simon & Schuster, 1995), pp. 117–18.

59. Kutler, *Abuse of Power*, p. 199.

60. Jeffrey Toobin, *A Vast Conspiracy: The Real Story of the Sex Scandal That Nearly Brought Down a President* (New York: Random House, 1999), pp. 100–104, 146–49.

61. "Possible Acts of Political Sabotage," October 11, 1972, PFM, Box 25.

62. Tony Podesta to Frank Mankiewicz, July 1, 1973, PFM, Box 25.

63. J. William Heckman Jr. to Frank Mankiewicz, July 16, 1973, PFM, Box 25.

64. "California Primary Campaign Incidents," Papers of Kirby Jones, John F. Kennedy Library, Box 11.

65. McGovern interview.

66. Theodore H. White, *The Making of the President 1972* (New York: Atheneum, 1973), p. 17.

67. Safire, *Before the Fall*, p. 639.

Chapter 11. Excavating the Landslide

1. George McGovern, *Grassroots: The Autobiography of George McGovern* (New York: Random House, 1977), p. 248; Jeff Smith interview, March 5, 2003, Alexandria, Virginia.

2. George McGovern, *An American Journey: The Presidential Campaign Speeches of George McGovern* (New York: Random House, 1974), pp. 41–42.

3. Gunnison telephone interview, May 24, 2006.

4. Galbraith telephone interview. June 5, 2002.

5. Jeff Smith interview.

6. Barbara Holum interview, February 27, 2002, Washington, D.C.

7. Nease telephone interview, June 10, 2005.

8. John Holum interview, May 8, 2001, Washington, D.C.

9. McGovern interview, August 13, 2000, Stevensville, Montana.

10. "Comparing Landslides," *Time*, November 20, 1972.

11. Theodore H. White, *The Making of the President 1972* (New York: Atheneum, 1973), pp. 342–45.

12. Chalmers M. Roberts, "The Clearest Choice That Wasn't," *Washington Post*, November 9, 1972.

13. "Look Back in Anger," *Time*, November 27, 1972.

14. "The Defeat," *New York Times*, November 9, 1972.

15. Aram Bakshian Jr., "McGovernism: R.I.P.," *New York Times*, November 17, 1972.

16. David S. Broder, "McGovern's Rejection," *Washington Post*, November 14, 1972.

17. Wattenberg quoted in Ernest R. May and Janet Fraser, eds., *Campaign '72: The Managers Speak* (Cambridge, MA: Harvard University Press, 1973), p. 233.

18. James M. Naughton, "McGovern Vows to Press Nixon on War and National Priorities," *New York Times*, November 14, 1972.

19. McGovern quoted in "McGovern Vacationing in Caribbean," *Washington Post*, November 10, 1972.

20. McGovern quoted in Hunter S. Thompson, *Fear and Loathing: On the Campaign Trail '72* (New York: Popular Library, 1973), p. 469.

21. Mankiewicz interview with Frank McGee, TV Caps, Reel No. 337, November 10, 1972, GMP, Box 836.

22. Thompson, *Fear and Loathing*, p. 482.

23. Hart quoted in May and Fraser, *Campaign '72*, p. 231.

24. Thompson, *Fear and Loathing*, pp. 484–86.

25. Gordon L. Weil, *The Long Shot: George McGovern Runs for President* (New York: W. W. Norton, 1973), p. 233.

26. Weil telephone interview, February 12, 2002.

27. Arthur H. Miller et al., *A Majority Party in Disarray: Policy Polarization in the 1972 Election* (Ann Arbor: University of Michigan Institute for Social Research, 1973).

28. Ibid., p. 75.

29. Ibid., pp. 27–29; David G. Lawrence, *The Collapse of the Democratic Presidential Majority: Realignment, Dealignment, and Electoral Change from Franklin Roosevelt to Bill Clinton* (Boulder, CO: Westview, 1996), p. 99.

30. Lawrence, *The Collapse of the Democratic Presidential Majority*, p. 174.

31. Ibid., pp. 72–73.

32. Ibid., pp. 96–99.

33. Miller et al., *A Majority Party in Disarray*, pp. 44, 72, 42, 56.

34. Ibid., pp. 56–58.

35. "The Landslide: How and Why," *Newsweek*, November 13, 1972.

36. Richard L. Rubin, *Party Dynamics: The Democratic Coalition and the Politics of Change* (New York: Oxford University Press, 1976), p. 4.

37. White, *The Making of the President 1972*, p. 343.

38. Bill Clinton, *My Life* (New York: Alfred A. Knopf, 2004), p. 194.

39. Harris Poll cited in Richard Krickus, *Pursuing the American Dream: White Ethnics and the New Populism* (Garden City, NY: Anchor, 1976), p. 262.

40. John B. Judis and Ruy Teixeira, *The Emerging Democratic Majority* (New York: Scribner, 2002), pp. 37–39.

41. John H. Kessel, *Presidential Campaign Politics*, 4th ed. (Pacific Grove, CA: Brooks/Cole, 1992), pp. 270–71; Lawrence, *The Collapse of the Democratic Presidential Majority*, pp. 97–99.

42. Kessel, *Presidential Campaign Politics*, pp. 270–71; Lawrence, *The Collapse of the Democratic Presidential Majority*, pp. 97–99.

43. Miller et al., *A Majority Party in Disarray*, pp. 60–62.

44. Shrum interview, February 26, 2002, Washington, D.C.

45. McGovern, *An American Journey*, pp. 232–46.

46. McGovern, *Grassroots*, p. 255.

47. Mankiewicz interview, February 28, 2002, Washington, D.C.

Chapter 12. The Legacy of the McGovern Campaign

1. Galbraith telephone interview, June 5, 2002.

2. Shrum interview, February 26, 2002, Washington, D.C.

3. Rowland Evans and Robert Novak, "The Other Democrats," *Washington Post*, July 14, 1972; "Democrats: Strauss Triumphant," *Newsweek*, December 18, 1972.

4. Strauss telephone interview, October 25, 2005.

5. Ibid.

6. "A Blow for Moderation," *Time*, December 18, 1972.

7. "Democrats: Strauss Triumphant," *Newsweek*, December 18, 1972.

8. Strauss interview.

9. McGovern telephone interview, December 12, 2005.

10. George Lardner Jr., "McGovern's List Quite a Gold Mine," *Washington Post*, November 14, 1972.

11. Jeff Smith interview, March 5, 2003, Alexandria, Virginia.

12. Strauss interview.

13. McGovern interview.

14. Jeff Smith interview.

15. Lilly interview, March 3, 2003, Washington, D.C.; Galbraith interview.

16. Rowland Evans and Robert Novak, "Anti–New Politics Liberals," *Washington Post*, November 12, 1972.

17. Wattenberg telephone interview, February 18, 2006; Kampelman telephone interview, September 19, 2005; Max M. Kampelman, *Entering New Worlds: The Memoirs of a Private Man in Public Life* (New York: Harper Collins, 1991), pp. 232–33; Herbert S. Parmet, *The Democrats: The Years after FDR* (New York: Oxford University Press, 1976), p. 305; and Sidney Blumenthal, *The Rise of the Counter-Establishment: From Conservative Ideology to Political Power* (New York: Times, 1986), pp. 126–27.

18. Wattenberg interview.

19. Jerry W. Sanders, *Peddlers of Crisis: The Committee on the Present Danger and the Politics of Containment* (Boston: South End, 1983), p. 150.

20. Hart telephone interview, June 26, 2002.

21. Sanders, *Peddlers of Crisis*, pp. 149–233; Blumenthal, *The Rise of the Counter-Establishment*, pp. 128–32, 134, 140–42.

22. Peter G. Bourne, *Jimmy Carter: A Comprehensive Biography from Plains to Postpresidency* (New York: Scribner, 1997), pp. 223–31.

23. Shrum quoted in Jules Witcover, *Marathon: The Pursuit of the Presidency, 1972–1976* (New York: Viking, 1977), p. 320.

24. Henry A. Plotkin, "Issues in the 1976 Presidential Campaign," in Gerald M. Pomper et al., *The Election of 1976: Reports and Interpretations* (New York: David McKay, 1977), p. 42.

25. Adam Clymer, *Edward M. Kennedy: A Biography* (New York: Harper Collins, 2000), pp. 269–70.

26. Burton I. Kaufman, *The Presidency of James Earl Carter Jr.* (Lawrence: University Press of Kansas, 1993), pp. 37–50.

27. Carter quoted in David Skidmore, *Reversing Course: Carter's Foreign Policy, Domestic Politics, and the Failure of Reform* (Nashville, TN: Vanderbilt University Press, 1996), p. 41.

28. Sanders, *Peddlers of Crisis*, pp. 235–76; Kaufman, *The Presidency of James Earl Carter Jr.*, pp. 151–66; and Skidmore, *Reversing Course*, pp. 26–148.

29. Stearns interview, August 1, 2001, Boston.

30. Charles Peters, "A Neoliberal's Manifesto," in Charles Peters and Phillip Keisling, eds., *A New Road for America: The Neoliberal Movement* (Lanham, MD: Madison, 1985), p. 189.

31. See Randall Rothenberg, *The Neoliberals: Creating the New American Politics* (New York: Simon & Schuster, 1984).

32. Charles Peters, "Introduction," in Peters and Keisling, eds., *A New Road for America*, p. 7.

33. Dan Balz, "Party Chairman Puts Democrats behind a Freeze," *Washington Post*, September 21, 1983.

34. O'Neill quoted in Margot Hornblower, "Alternate A-Freeze Plan Passes: House Approves Reagan-Backed Bill, 204–202," *Washington Post*, August 6, 1982.

35. *Congressional Record—House*, May 4, 1983, pp. 11052–53.

36. Ibid., December 8, 1982, p. 29461.

37. Ibid., p. 29464.

38. Steven M. Gillon, *The Democrats' Dilemma: Walter F. Mondale and the Liberal Legacy* (New York: Columbia University Press, 1992), p. 136.

39. Ibid., pp. 317–32; Gerald M. Pomper, "The Nominations," in Gerald M. Pomper et al., *The Election of 1984: Reports and Interpretations* (Chatham, NJ: Chatham House, 1985), pp. 16–17.

40. Hart quoted in Gillon, *The Democrats' Dilemma*, p. 333.

41. Richard Michael Marano, *Vote Your Conscience: The Last Campaign of George McGovern* (Westport, CT: Praeger, 2003).

42. Ibid., pp. 151–83.

43. Hedrick Smith, "Democrats' Foreign Policies Veer away from Past Line," *New York Times*, August 4, 1984.

44. Kenneth S. Baer, *Reinventing Democrats: The Politics of Liberalism from Reagan to Clinton* (Lawrence: University Press of Kansas, 2000), pp. 64–75.

45. Ibid., pp. 40–44.

46. Ibid., p. 58.

47. Thomas Ferguson and Joel Rogers, *Right Turn: The Decline of the Democrats and the Future of American Politics* (New York: Hill & Wang, 1986), pp. 27–28.

48. Baer, *Reinventing Democrats*, p. 97.

49. Hart interview.

50. Marjorie Randon Hershey, "The Campaign and the Media," in Gerald M. Pomper et al., *The Election of 1988: Reports and Interpretations* (Chatham, NJ: Chatham House, 1989), pp. 77–78.

51. Dukakis aide quoted in Sidney Blumenthal, *Pledging Allegiance: The Last Campaign of the Cold War* (New York: Harper Collins, 1990), p. 234.

52. Dukakis quoted in Blumenthal, *Pledging Allegiance*, p. 244.

53. Blumenthal, *Pledging Allegiance*, p. 245.

54. Ibid., pp. 300–301, 310.

55. Ibid., pp. 257–66.

56. Hershey, "The Campaign and the Media," p. 95.

57. Baer, *Reinventing Democrats*, pp. 120–42.

58. Ibid., pp. 159–65.

59. Ibid., pp. 163–92.

60. Stephen Skowronek, "The Setting: Change and Continuity in the Politics of Leadership," in Michael Nelson, ed., *The Elections of 2000* (Washington, DC: Congressional Quarterly), p. 16.

61. Baer, *Reinventing Democrats*, pp. 193–228.

62. Ibid., pp. 230–54.

63. Paul J. Quirk and William Cunion, "Clinton's Domestic Policy: The Lessons of a 'New Democrat,'" in Colin Campbell and Bert A. Rockman, eds., *The Clinton Legacy* (New York: Chatham House, 2000), pp. 200–25.

64. Bruce Miroff, "Courting the Public: Bill Clinton's Postmodern Education," in Steven E. Schier, ed., *The Postmodern Presidency: Bill Clinton's Legacy in U.S. Politics* (Pittsburgh: University of Pittsburgh Press, 2000), pp. 106–23.

65. Wilson Carey McWilliams, "The Meaning of the Election," in Gerald M. Pomper et al., *The Election of 2000* (New York: Chatham House, 2001), pp. 179–80.

66. Joe Trippi, *The Revolution Will Not Be Televised: Democracy, the Internet, and the Overthrow of Everything* (New York: Harper Collins, 2004).

67. Al From and Bruce Reed, "The Real Soul of the Democratic Party," May 15, 2003, http://www.dlc.org.

68. Kerry quoted in James W. Ceaser and Andrew E. Busch, *Red over Blue: The 2004 Elections and American Politics* (Lanham, MD: Rowman & Littlefield, 2005), p. 117.

69. Sharleen Leahey, "Johnny We Hardly Knew You—John Kerry: War Hero or Warrior for Peace?" http://www.commondreams.org.

70. Wagner interview, February 26, 2002, Washington, D.C.

71. Weil telephone interview, February 12, 2002.

72. Ibid.

Chapter 13. McGovernites

1. Stearns interview, August 1, 2001, Boston.

2. Ibid.

3. Lilly interview, March 3, 2003, Washington, D.C.; Shrum interview, February 26, 2002, Washington, D.C.; Pulliam interview, May 9, 2001, Washington, D.C.

4. Jeff Smith interview, March 5, 2003, Alexandria, Virginia.

5. Himmelman interview, March 6, 2003, Washington, D.C.

6. Carl Wagner pointed out to me the characteristic difference in career paths between the original McGovernites and those who joined the campaign at later stages. Wagner interview, February 26, 2002, Washington, D.C.

7. Lilly interview.

8. Jones interview, May 11, 2001, Washington, D.C.; *Newsweek* quoted in http://www .alamarcuba.com.

9. Greenberger interview, May 11, 2001, Washington, D.C.

10. Amanda Smith telephone interview, May 2, 2001.

11. Dees telephone interview, January 8, 2002; Morris Dees with Steve Fiffer, *A Lawyer's Life: The Morris Dees Story* (Chicago: American Bar Association, 2001), pp. 195–99.

12. http://www.democracycorps.com/meet/shrum.

13. Kennedy quoted in Adam Clymer, *Edward M. Kennedy: A Biography* (New York: HarperCollins, 2000), pp. 316, 318.

14. Shrum interview; David M. Halbfinger, "In Middle of the Kerry Storm, a Man Known to Whirlwinds," *New York Times*, November 12, 2003; "Fits and Starts," *Newsweek*, November 15, 2004.

15. Joe Klein, *Politics Lost: How American Democracy Was Trivialized by People Who Think You're Stupid* (New York: Doubleday, 2006), pp. 23–24.

16. Jerome Armstrong and Markos Moulitsas Zúniga, *Crashing the Gate: Netroots, Grassroots, and the Rise of People-Powered Politics* (White River Junction, VT: Chelsea Green, 2006), pp. 156, 79–82, 101–03.

17. Wagner interview; David Maraniss, *First in His Class: A Biography of Bill Clinton* (New York: Simon & Schuster, 1995), pp. 441–43.

18. Wagner interview.

19. Ibid.

20. Ibid.

21. Hart telephone interview, June 26, 2002.

22. Gary Warren Hart, *Right from the Start: A Chronicle of the McGovern Campaign* (New York: Quadrangle, 1973), p. 328.

23. Sidney Blumenthal, *Pledging Allegiance: The Last Campaign of the Cold War* (New York: Harper Collins, 1990), p. 116.

24. Hart interview.

25. Ibid.

26. See Gary Hart, *The Good Fight: The Education of an American Reformer* (New York: Random House, 1993).

27. Gary Hart, *A New Democracy: A Democratic Vision for the 1980s and Beyond* (New York: William Morrow, 1983), pp. 27–117.

28. Gerald M. Pomper, "The Nominations," in Gerald M. Pomper et al., *The Election of 1984: Reports and Interpretations* (Chatham, NJ: Chatham House, 1985), pp. 1–34; Hart, *The Good Fight*, pp. 206–15.

29. Richard Ben Cramer, *What It Takes: The Way to the White House* (New York: Vintage, 1993), pp. 375–93, 431–75.

30. Gary Hart with William S. Lind, *America Can Win: The Case for Military Reform* (Bethesda, MD: Adler & Adler, 1986).

31. Hart, *The Good Fight*, pp. 113–14, 162–78.

32. Gary Hart, *The Minuteman: Restoring an Army of the People* (New York: Free Press, 1998).

33. Hart interview.

34. Hart, *The Good Fight*, pp. 38–53.

35. George McGovern, *The Essential America: Our Founders and the Liberal Tradition* (New York: Simon & Schuster, 2004), pp. 79–91.

36. Gary Hart, *Restoration of the Republic: The Jeffersonian Ideal in 21st-Century America* (New York: Oxford University Press, 2002). Hart's Jeffersonian themes turned up in some unlikely places. Writing under the pen name of John Blackthorn, Hart published a novel, *I, Che Guevara*, in 2000. In his plot, an aging Fidel Castro finally permits free elections in Cuba. Cuban Communists and anti-Castro exiles from the United States, left versus right but similarly stuck in the past, line up to fight bitterly for the fruits of power. But out of the mountains comes a mysterious leader, an aged Che Guevara who survived the CIA killers in Bolivia three decades earlier, to organize a third—and winning—alternative for the election. No longer a Marxist guerrilla who advocates armed struggle, Hart's Che has been resurrected as a champion of the grassroots, a Latin American Jefferson whose insurgent movement is "one of radical democracy" and whose rallying cry is "the true republic." John Blackthorn [Gary Hart], *I, Che Guevara: A Novel* (New York: William Morrow, 2000), pp. 38–53, 204.

37. George McGovern, "The Case for Liberalism: A Defense of the Future against the Past," *Harper's Magazine*, December 2002.

38. Gary Hart, "Who Will Say 'No More'?" *Washington Post*, August 24, 2005.

39. Wexler interview, May 8, 2001, Washington, D.C.; Maraniss, *First in His Class*, p. 266.

40. Van Dyk telephone interview, March 12, 2002.

41. Stearns interview; Maraniss, *First in His Class*, p. 266.

42. Bill Clinton, *My Life* (New York: Alfred A. Knopf, 2004), pp. 189–98.

43. My requests for an interview with the former president were turned down by a staff member on the grounds that Clinton's schedule was already too crowded.

44. Jeff Smith interview.

45. George McGovern, "A Word from the Original McGovernik," *Washington Post*, December 25, 1994.

46. Author's conversation with McGovern, August 13, 2000, Stevensville, Montana.

47. Gingrich quoted in John F. Stacks, "The Election Stampede," *Time*, November 21, 1994.

48. Wright telephone interview, June 17, 2002.

49. Jeff Smith interview.

50. Berger interview, February 27, 2002, Washington, D.C.

51. Eli Segal interview, October 26, 2001, Boston; Rubin interview, February 27, 2002, Roslyn, Virginia; Steven Waldman, *The Bill: How the Adventures of Clinton's National Service Bill Reveal What Is Corrupt, Comic, Cynical—and Noble—about Washington* (New York: Viking, 1995), pp. 33–50; Bryan Marquard, "Eli Segal [Dead], at 63; Clinton Aide Helped Design AmeriCorps, Welfare Plan," *Boston Globe*, February 21, 2006.

52. Eli Segal interview.

53. Richard Michael Marano, *Vote Your Conscience: The Last Campaign of George McGovern* (Westport, CT: Praeger, 2003), pp. 21–43; Russell E. Willis, "Ambassador McGovern, Elder Statesman," in Robert P. Watson, ed., *George McGovern: A Political Life, a Political Legacy* (Pierre: South Dakota State Historical Society Press, 2004), pp. 143–47.

54. McGovern interview, August 13, 2000, Stevensville, Montana.

55. Ibid.

56. McGovern quoted in Marano, *Vote Your Conscience*, p. 152.

57. McGovern, "A Word from the Original McGovernik."

58. Jeff Smith interview.

59. George McGovern, *The Third Freedom: Ending Hunger in Our Time* (New York: Simon & Schuster, 2001), pp. 24–28; Willis, "Ambassador McGovern, Elder Statesman," pp. 147–54; McGovern interview.

60. McGovern, *The Third Freedom*, p. 15.

61. McGovern, *The Essential America*, pp. 118–19.

62. Ibid., pp. 64, 79–97, 57.

63. Ibid., pp. 100, 15.

64. George McGovern and William R. Polk, *Out of Iraq: A Practical Plan for Withdrawal Now* (New York: Simon & Schuster, 2006).

65. Craig interview, May 10, 2001, Washington, D.C.

66. Berger interview.

67. Ibid.

68. Hart interview.

Epilogue

1. Robert Borosage, "Rejecting the Right," *American Prospect*, January/February 2007.

2. Mehlman quoted in Peter Wallsten, "GOP Leaders Are Hoping to Turn the War into a Winner," *Los Angeles Times*, August 8, 2006.

3. See John Halpin and Ruy Teixeira, "The Politics of Definition, Part III," http://www.prospect.org, April 26, 2006.

4. Gary Hart offers one of the most stinging critiques of centrist Democrats' lack of convictions. See his *The Courage of Our Convictions: A Manifesto for Democrats* (New York: Times, 2006), pp. 40–41, 44, 63–66.

5. John Halpin and Ruy Teixeira, "The Politics of Definition, Part I," http://www.prospect.org, April 20, 2006.

6. Herbert McCloskey, Paul J. Hoffman, and Rosemary O'Hara, "Issue Conflict and Consensus among Party Leaders and Followers," *American Political Science Review*, June 1960.

7. Peter Beinart, *The Good Fight: Why Liberals—and Only Liberals—Can Win the War on Terror and Make America Great Again* (New York: Harper Collins, 2006).

8. Michael Tomasky, "Party in Search of a Notion," *American Prospect*, May 2006; John Halpin and Ruy Teixeira, "The Politics of Definition, Part IV," http://www.prospect.org, April 27, 2006.

Index

National Airlines, 206
National Broadcasting Company (NBC), 174
National Governorsí Conference, 68, 197
National Labor Committee for McGovern-
Shriver, 188
National Review, 5–6
National Students and Youth for McGovern,
159–160
National Womenís Advisory Council for
McGovern, 209
National Womenís Law Center, 213, 282
National Womenís Political Caucus (NWPC),
205–211, 214
NBC (National Broadcasting Company),
174
Nebraska, 157
1972 primary in, 63–64, 69
Nelson, Gaylord, 86
neoconservatives, 200, 262, 264–265
neoliberalism, 268, 271, 272, 287
Neustadt, Richard E., 77
New Democrat Network, 302
New Democrats, 292, 296, 302
New Hampshire, 16, 39, 69, 123, 270, 287
1972 primary in, 45, 48, 49, 53–55, 56, 57,
58, 60, 63, 65, 106, 156, 157, 158, 160, 168,
181, 190
New Jersey, 69, 199
Newman, Paul, 170
New Politics liberals, 3, 4, 7, 20, 23–24, 59,
71, 80, 81, 82, 121–122, 164, 182, 183, 188,
194, 267, 286, 300
echoes in 1980s of, 267–271, 272, 273
in 1960s, 6, 12
Newsweek, 54, 72, 96, 97, 100, 101, 103, 114,
120, 228, 255, 263, 282
New York, 101, 115, 170, 195, 237
1972 primary in, 75, 181–182, 206, 216, 220
New York Society of Security Analysts speech
(McGovern), 102, 135–136
New York Times, 2, 93, 159, 220, 250
Nguyen Van Thieu, 131
Nicaragua, 268–269
Nichols, Mike, 170
Nicholson, Jack, 170
Nitze, Paul, 13
Nixon presidential campaign of 1972,
attack ads of, 106, 172, 228
"clockwork convention" of, 103

Committee to Re-Elect the President
(CREEP) in, 103, 229
dirty tricks by, 55, 83–84, 241–243
surrogate speakers in, 70, 106, 121, 174–175,
230, 233, 239–240, 244
as textbook for later Republican
campaigns, 171, 229–230, 232, 244,
273, 276
Nixon, Richard
captures mood of 1972 in campaign, 11, 51,
243, 250–252
and Catholics, 237–238, 255–256
constructs personal majority in 1972,
236–239
economic policies of (*see under* economic
policy)
electoral assets in 1972 of, 232–233, 243, 254
environmental policies of, 234
and ethnics, 192, 237–238
foreign policy of, 69, 131, 172, 186, 235–236,
243–244
and Jews, 237, 238
as "liberal," 233–234
as master strategist, 228–230, 232, 235–
236, 243–244
"northern strategy" of, 236–237
orchestrates attacks on McGovern, 231–232
policies as reelection tools for, 233–236
popularity of in 1972, 49–50, 254–255
and the press, 103–104, 107, 110, 173, 174–
175, 239–240, 258
"southern strategy" of, 236
views on McGovern of, 230, 231–232
and workers, 234, 238–239, 255–256
nonprimary states, 21, 62–63, 225–226
Norris, George, 136
North American Free Trade Agreement, 274
North Carolina, 282
Northwestern University, 26, 27, 30–32, 123,
136
Novak, Robert, 50–51, 170, 178, 264
shapes radical image of McGovern, 51, 59,
62, 64, 121
"nuclear freeze" issue, 268–269, 271

Obey, David, 281
OíBrien, Lawrence, 78, 79, 103, 165, 171, 205,
222, 242
OíHara, James G., 78, 83